*The Black Presence
in the Era of the
American Revolution*

BICKERSTAFF's
BOSTON
ALMANACK,

For the Year of our REDEMPTION, 1782.

Being the Second after Leap-Year ; and the Sixth Year of INDE-
PENDENCY. Fitted for the Meridian of BOSTON, N. E.
Lat. 42° 25° N. Long. from London 69° 27° W.
Wherein may be found all Things necessary for this WORK.
To which is added, A SCALE of DEPRECIATION,
and a great Variety of other entertaining Matter.

TIME is the Effect of Motion, born a Twin,
    And with the World did equally begin ;
Time like a Stream that hastens from the Shore,
Flies to an Ocean where 'tis known no more.
All must be swallow'd in this endless Deep,
And Motion rest in everlasting Sleep.   DRYD. OVID.

BOSTON : Printed by E. RUSSELL, at his Printing-Office in
Essex-street, near Liberty-stump, South-end. (Pr. 7d. single

The Black Presence in the Era of the American Revolution

Revised Edition

Sidney Kaplan
and
Emma Nogrady Kaplan

The University of Massachusetts Press

Amherst

This book is published with the support of the
William Monroe Trotter Institute,
University of Massachusetts
at Boston.

Frontispiece: This woodcut portrait of Phillis
Wheatley appeared on the cover of a popular al-
manac eight years after the publication of her
Poems in 1773.

Library of Congress Cataloging-in-Publication Data

Kaplan, Sidney, 1913–
    The black presence in the era of the American
Revolution — Rev. ed. / Sidney Kaplan and
Emma Nogrady Kaplan.
        p. cm.
    Bibliography: p.
    Includes index.
    ISBN 0–87023–663–6 (pbk. : alk. paper)
    1. United States—History—Revolution, 1775–
1783—Afro-Americans—Exhibitions. 2. Afro-
Americans—Portraits—Exhibitions. 3. Afro-
Americans—History—To 1863—Exhibitions.
I. Kaplan, Emma Nogrady, 1911–   . II. Title.
E269.N3K36   1989
973′.0496073—dc19   88–22111
                                              CIP

British Library Cataloguing in Publication data are
available.

Contents

Foreword

This book had its genesis in 1973 during the bicentennial celebration of the Declaration of Independence, as the catalog of an exhibition at the National Portrait Gallery of the Smithsonian Institution in Washington, D.C. Revised and enlarged in text, document, and picture, the present volume appears at a time when Massachusetts is memorializing "The 350th Anniversary of the First Landing of Africans" on its soil in 1638. To make this possible, The William Monroe Trotter Institute at the University of Massachusetts, Harbor Campus, Boston, has given liberal support, for which thanks are due to its director, Dr. Wornie L. Reed, and to Charles F. Desmond, Vice Chancellor for Student Affairs.

The authors are beholden to a large number of individuals and institutions—too many to list—for their knowledge and generosity. This is made clear, we hope, in the footnotes, the Sources, and the captions of the illustrations. We would like to mention a few whose expertise lightened our burdens: the reference librarians at the University of Massachusetts, Amherst; Billie R. Bozone, Librarian, Smith College Library, as well as Elaine N. Miller, Reference Librarian, Mary Courtney, Circulation Librarian, and, especially, John G. Graiff, Interlibrary Loans; Elise Bernier-Feeley, Reference Librarian, Forbes Library, Northampton; William Milhomme, Reference Supervisor, Massachusetts Archives, Boston; Phil Lapsansky, Curator, Afro-Americana Collection, Library Company of Philadelphia.

We would like to reiterate our thanks to Beverly J. Cox, Curator of Exhibitions, and to Richard K. Doud, Keeper, Catalog of American Portraits, at the National Portrait Gallery.

Pam Wilkinson, managing editor of the University of Massachusetts Press, has improved our work by her careful guidance.

SIDNEY and EMMA NOGRADY KAPLAN
Northampton, Massachusetts
June, 1988

The Black Presence
in the Era of the
American Revolution

I

Homage to Liberty

The recent celebration of the bicentennial of the American Revolution—a revolution that promised liberty and justice for all—provides an opportune moment for a fresh view of one feature of the event that for two centuries has been absent from the official rhetoric of the Fourth of July. It is the aim of these pages to help restore to the national memory a historic fact that has been long suppressed or forgotten—the living presence of black men and women during the thirty years that stretched from the martyrdom of Crispus Attucks in the Boston Massacre of 1770 to the conspiracy of Gabriel Prosser in Virginia at the turn of the century.

In 1855, when William C. Nell, the pioneer black historian and abolitionist, published his *Colored Patriots of the American Revolution*,* it was his friend Harriet

Beecher Stowe who wrote the introduction to the volume. In evaluating the services of the black soldiers and sailors who had fought for the independence of the new nation, she observed, we should reflect upon them as unusually "magnanimous," for they served "a nation which did not acknowledge them as citizens and equals, and in whose interests and prosperity they had less at stake. It was not for their own land they fought, nor even for a land which had adopted them, but for a land which had enslaved them, and whose laws, even in freedom, oftener oppressed than protected. Bravery, under such circumstances, has a peculiar beauty and merit."

Not all were patriots. As Benjamin Quarles points out in his study *The Negro in the American Revolution,* the role of the black soldier or sailor in the Revolutionary War "can best be understood by realizing that his major loyalty was not to a place nor a people, but to a principle. Insofar as he had freedom of choice, he was likely to join the side that made him the quickest and best of-

---

*Eight years later, George Livermore wrote that Nell's popular book was already out of print, but that "a new edition, considerably enlarged," would soon be published. It never appeared (*An Historical Research* . . . [Boston, 1863], 162).

fer in terms of those 'unalienable rights' of which Mr. Jefferson had spoken. Whoever invoked the image of liberty, be he American or British, could count on a ready response from the blacks." It was loyalty "to a principle" that the Pennsylvania artist Samuel Jennings was inspired to delineate in his symbol-laden, antislavery painting of 1792, *Liberty Displaying the Arts and Sciences,* which still hangs on a wall of Benjamin Franklin's Library Company of Philadelphia. A family of slaves "pays homage," as Jennings wrote, to the goddess of liberty, at whose feet lies a broken chain, "an Emblem of her aversion to slavery," while in the background a black man strums a banjo as his brothers and sisters sing and dance around a liberty pole crowned with laurel [fig. 1].

Nell tells an apt story to illustrate this loyalty to principle: "Seymour Burr was a slave in Connecticut. . . . Though treated with much favor by his master, his heart yearned for liberty, and he seized an occasion to induce several of his fellow slaves to escape in a boat, intending to join the British, that they might become freemen; but being pursued by their owners, armed with the instruments of death, they were compelled to surrender." Burr's master "asked what inducement he could have for leaving him." Burr replied, *that he wanted his liberty.* His owner finally proposed, that if he would give him the bounty money, he might join the American army, and at the end of the war be his own man. Burr, willing to make any sacrifice for his liberty, consented, and served faithfully during the campaign, attached to the Seventh Regiment. . . . He was present at the siege of Fort Catskill, and endured much suffering from starvation and cold."

For slaves, especially in the south, the choice was clear. The moral logic and natural right of linking two ideas—freedom for whites and freedom for blacks—was in the

air in South Carolina as early as the Stamp Act agitation of the 1760s. In Charleston, as the white Sons of Liberty unfurled a British flag in the streets with the revolutionary word emblazoned across it, and the crowds cried "Liberty Liberty and stamp'd paper," the wealthy merchant and former slave trader Henry Laurens recorded that a "Peculiar incident, revealing in what dread the citizens lived among the black savages . . . was furnish'd . . . by some negroes who, apparently in thoughtless imitation, began to cry 'Liberty.' " Thus Thomas Peters, a slave in Virginia, accepted Lord Dunmore's promise of freedom, joined the British army, sailed with the king's fleet to Nova Scotia at the end of the war, and ultimately returned to Africa to play a part as a founding father of Sierra Leone.

That for blacks the revolution was incomplete would be clear enough at an early stage. "Haven't I heard your Fourth-of-July speeches?" asks George Harris in *Uncle Tom's Cabin.* "Don't you tell us all once a year, that governments derive their just power from the consent of the governed? Can't a fellow *think,* that hears such things?" It was the same point that Frederick Douglass made to a white audience in Rochester nine years before the outbreak of the Civil War: "This Fourth of July is *yours,* not *mine.*"

For some readers long nourished—or starved—on a stale textbook version of a revolution that pictured a few million whites split into patriots and Tories while half a million slaves toiled quietly and loyally in the fields, the sheer existence of a black revolutionary generation, on and off the field of battle, may come as news from a buried past. Since that fateful day in the summer of 1619 when twenty kidnapped Africans dragged their feet onto American soil, the nation's slaves had never rested in their chains. Emerging now from the forced anonymity of a century and a half of bond-

1. Samuel Jennings, *Liberty Displaying the Arts and Sciences*, oil, 1792.
The Library Company of Philadelphia.

age—moved no doubt by the slogans of liberty that filled the air—an advance guard of blacks, distinguished by the "peculiar beauty and merit" of their struggle for freedom and dignity, endowed with a variety of gifts and powers, forced an entrance onto the stage of American history as movers and shapers. Here are a few of their portraits and deeds in picture and word—as soldier and sailor, founder of the black church, fighter for equality, organizer of school, lodge, and society; as scientist, writer, poet, artist, captain, physician, frontiersman, and rebel.

II

Preludes to the Declaration

Crispus Attucks and the Boston Massacre

During the fall of 1750, a quarter of a century before the Declaration of Independence, a Massachusetts slave by the name of Crispus struck a revolutionary blow for his own liberty. The *Boston Gazette* on October 2 told the story: "Ran away from his Master *William Brown from Framingham* . . . a Molatto Fellow, about 27 Years of age, named *Crispas*, 6 Feet two Inches high, short curl'd Hair, his Knees nearer together than common: had on a light colour'd Bearskin Coat. . . ." Deacon Brown offered ten pounds as a reward, but Crispus was never taken. He next appears in the record, twenty years later, as Crispus Attucks, a man who strikes a revolutionary blow for American liberty—the first martyr of the American Revolution [fig. 2].

The tale of the Boston Massacre, depicted by Paul Revere in his famous broadside, has often been told [fig. 3]. For a year and a half the king had quartered his trucu-

RAN-away from his Master *William Brown* of *Framingham*, on the 30th of *Sept.* last, a Molatto Fellow, about 27 Years of Age, named *Crispas*, 6 Feet two Inches high, short curl'd Hair, his Knees nearer together than common; had on a light colour'd Bearskin Coat, plain brown Fustian Jacket, or brown all-Wool one, new Buckskin Breeches, blue Yarn Stockings, and a check'd woollen Shirt. Whoever shall take up said Run-away, and convey him to his abovesaid Master, shall have *ten Pounds*, old Tenor Reward, and all necessary Charges paid. And all Masters of Vessels and others, are hereby caution'd against concealing or carrying off said Servant on Penalty of the Law. *Boston. October* 2. 1750.

2. *Boston Gazette,* October 2, 1750.
Massachusetts Historical Society.

lent redcoats upon the outraged citizens of Boston to enforce by cutlass and bayonet obnoxious laws passed in London without the people's consent. On March 5, 1770, grievances, long simmering, came to a boil. A week later the *Massachusetts Gazette* reported the affair: "Monday Evening . . . Several Soldiers of the 29th Regiment were abusive

The BLOODY MASSACRE perpetrated in King—t—Street BOSTON on March 5th 1770 by a party of the 29th REGt

BUTCHER'S HALL

Engrav'd Printed & Sold by PAUL REVERE BOSTON

Unhappy Boston! see thy Sons deplore,
Thy hallow'd Walks besmear'd with guiltless Gore.
While faithless P—n and his savage Bands.
With murd'rous Rancour stretch their bloody Hands;
Like fierce Barbarians grinning o'er their Prey,
Approve the Carnage, and enjoy the Day.

If scalding drops from Rage from Anguish Wrung
If speechless Sorrows lab'ring for a Tongue.
Or if a weeping World can ought appease
The plaintive Ghosts of Victims such as these;
The Patriot's copious Tears for each are shed,
A glorious Tribute which embalms the Dead.

But know, Fate summons to that awful Goal.
Where Justice strips the Murd'rer of his Soul:
Should venal C—ts the scandal of the Land.
Snatch the relentless Villain from her Hand.
Keen Execrations on this Plate inscrib'd,
Shall reach a Judge who never can be brib'd.

The unhappy Sufferers were Messrs. Saml Gray, Saml Maverick, Jams Caldwell, Crispus Attucks & Patk Carr
Killed. Six wounded; two of them (Christr Monk & John Clark) Mortally

3. Paul Revere, *The Bloody Massacre perpetrated in King Street Boston on March 5th* 1770, engraving, 1770. National Gallery of Art, Rosenwald Collection.

in the Street, with their Cutlasses, striking a Number of Persons: About 9 o'Clock some young Lads . . . met three Soldiers, two of them with drawn Cutlasses . . . who stop'd the Lads, and made a stroke at them, which they returned, having Sticks in their Hands; one of the Lads was wounded in the Arm;

presently 10 or 12 Soldiers came from the Barracks with their Cutlasses drawn . . . a Scuffle ensued, some seeing the naked Swords flourishing ran and set the Bells a ringing: This collected the People, who at length made the Soldiers retire to their Barracks. . . ." Some of "the People" then walked to the Custom House on King Street, where they chided the lone sentinel, charging him with mauling a boy with the butt of his gun. Snowballs and pieces of ice flew through the air. With the sentinel crying for help, Captain Thomas Preston and a squad of eight ran to his aid, "formed in an half Circle," and "loaded and pointed their Guns breast-high to the People. . . ."

It was then that another group of citizens, apparently led by a tall robust man with a dark face, appeared on the scene. There "came down a number from Jackson's corner," testified Andrew, a slave, at the subsequent trial, "huzzaing and crying, Damn them, they dare not fire, we are not afraid of them; one of these people, a stout man with a long cordwood stick, threw himself in, and made a blow at the officer . . . cried kill the dogs, knock them over; this was the general cry. . . ." Pressed to identify the "stout man," Andrew replied that it was "the Molatto who was shot." Five martyrs fell that night: Samuel Gray, ropemaker; James Caldwell, mate; Samuel Maverick, apprentice joiner; Patrick Carr, an Irish leather worker; and the "stout man," the first to die, "named Attucks, who was born in Framingham, but lately belonging to New-Providence [Bahamas], and was here in order to go for North-Carolina, killed on the Spot, two Balls entering his Breast." On Thursday, the corpse of Attucks was taken from Faneuil Hall, "all the Bells tolled a solemn Peal," and the five were interred "in one Vault in the middle buryingground . . ." [fig. 4].

THUS, Crispus Attucks passed into history. Little is known of his personal life. In local lore his father was an African, his mother an Indian, probably a descendant of John Attucks, a converted Christian who was executed for treason in 1676 because he sided with his own people during King Philip's War. The word "attuck" in the language of the Natick Indians means "deer." As a slave in Framingham, Crispus was known as a good judge of cattle, buying and selling on his own. He probably also worked as a seaman on coastal vessels. It is possible that he had arrived in Boston on a Nantucket whale ship.

At the trial of the king's officers, the fallen Attucks seemed very much alive. The evidence given in court, the newspaper reports, the earliest tradition, all single him out, in praise or blame, as the shaper of the event [fig. 5]. For John Adams, one of the lawyers for the crown and later to be the second president of the newly formed nation, it was all blame: Attucks was one of "a mob"—"a motley rabble of saucy boys, negroes and molattoes, Irish teagues and outlandish jack tarrs." Here is Adams in his final plea:

this Attucks . . . appears to have undertaken to be the hero of the night; and to lead this army with banners, to form them in the first place in *Dock square,* and march them up to *King street* with their clubs . . . this man with his party cried, do not be afraid of them . . . to have his reinforcement coming down under the command of a stout Molatto fellow, whose very looks was enough to terrify any person, what had not the soldiers then to fear? He had hardiness enough to fall in upon them, and with one hand took hold of a bayonet, and with the other knocked the man down: this was the behaviour of Attucks . . . a Carr from *Ireland,* and an *Attucks* from Framingham, happening to be here, shall sally out upon their thoughtless enterprizes, at the head of such a rabble of Negroes, &c. as they can collect together. . . .

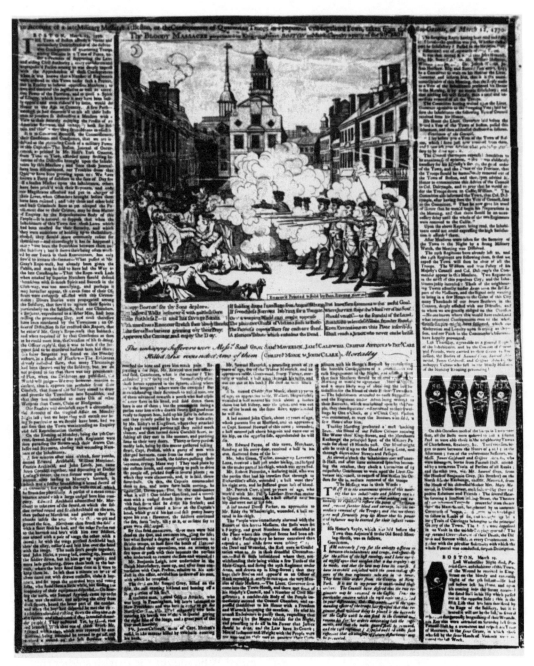

4. Paul Revere, *An account of a late Military Massacre at Boston . . . taken from the* Boston Gazette, *March 12, 1770,* broadside engraving. Courtesy of the New-York Historical Society.

Curiously enough, it is possible that some three years later Adams had second thoughts on the matter. In an entry in his diary on a Monday in July 1773, he copied a letter by an unknown writer, perhaps a black, to Governor Thomas Hutchinson [fig. 6]:

> You will hear from Us with Astonishment. —You ought to hear

5. From *The Trial of William Weems, James Hartegan . . . for the murder of Crispus Attucks* (Boston 1770). Mount Holyoke College Library.

6. Diary of John Adams, July 1773. Massachusetts Historical Society.

from Us with Horror. You are chargeable before God and Man, with our Blood—The Soldiers were but passive Instruments, were Machines, neither moral nor voluntary Agents in our Destruction more than the leaden Pelletts, with which we were wounded.—You was a free Agent— You acted, cooly, deliberately, with all that premeditated Malice, not against Us in Particular but against the People in general, which in the Sight of the Law is an ingredient in the Composition of Murder. You will hear further from Us hereafter.

The signature is "Crispus Attucks."

On March 5, 1858, black abolitionists in Boston, including William C. Nell and Lewis Hayden, inaugurated a Crispus Attucks Day. A "festival" was held in Faneuil Hall. As Wendell Phillips approached the rostrum, he noticed an exhibit of revolutionary relics including a cup owned by Attucks, an engraving of Emanuel Leutze's *Washington Crossing the Delaware* with black Prince Whipple at the stroke oar, and the silk flag that John Hancock had presented to Boston's black company, the Bucks of America. "Emerson said the first gun heard round the world was that of Lexington," declared Phillips: "Who set the example of guns? Who taught the British soldier that he might be defeated? Who first dared look into his eyes? Those five men! The 5th of March was the baptism of blood. . . . I place, therefore, this Crispus Attucks in the foremost rank of the men that dared. When we talk of courage, he rises, with his dark face, in the clothes of the laborer, his head uncovered, his arm raised above him defying bayonets . . . when the proper symbols are placed around the base of the statue of Washington, one corner will be filled by the colored man defying the British muskets."*

Aftermath of Attucks: Portraits in Petitions

The blood of Attucks nourished the tree of liberty, in Jefferson's phrase, in two ways. Five years after the massacre, when protest gave way to arms, the name of the man who first had "dared" was still green in the memory of the minutemen—black and white—who took their stand at Lexington and Bunker Hill. More immediately, the spirit of Attucks doubtless spurred New England blacks openly to question the anomaly of human bondage in a nation about to be born and fighting for its independence under the slogan of "Liberty or Death!" Such a questioner was Caesar Sarter of Newburyport, who in midsummer 1774 wrote the remarkable essay for the *Essex Journal* of Salem that appears here [fig. 7]. At the same moment, black protest was mounting to a higher stage—the resolution to organize and peti-

---

*Thirty years later, during the fall of 1888, a monument commemorating the Boston Massacre (to be known as the Crispus Attucks Monument) would be unveiled on Boston Common. The project was promoted by fifty prominent citizens headed by black and white abolitionists, among them Lewis Hayden, Archibald H. Grimké, William H. Dupree, A. E. Pillsbury, and ex-Governor John F. Andrew. The whole enterprise was assailed by members of the Massachusetts Historical Society and the New England Historic Genealogical Society who reviled Attucks in the manner of John Adams and were rebutted in the historian John Fiske's keynote address. Frederick Douglass had been invited to deliver the dedicatory oration in Faneuil Hall; he was unable to attend but sent an eloquent letter. Here and there the petty war against the reputation of Crispus Attucks still continues.

tion the government. Five petitions of the years 1773 and 1774 echo the patriot James Otis's cry for the rights of man with a new intensity and deserve to be enshrined among the treasures of our literature. The mood is one of exasperation, even anger, although the phraseology is sometimes cautious. Freedom is their impassioned theme.

On January 6, 1773, to Governor Hutchinson and the General Court came "the humble Petition of many Slaves, living in the Town of Boston, and other Towns in the Province . . . who have had every Day of their Lives imbittered with this most intollerable Reflection, That, let their Behaviour be what it will, nor their Children to all Generations, shall ever be able to do, or to possess and enjoy any Thing, no not even *Life itself,* but in a Manner as the *Beasts that perish.* We have no Property! We have no Wives! No Children! We have no City! No Country! . . ." The signature, ironically, is "Felix." This "humble Petition" of Boston slaves describing their "intollerable" condition was in fact the first public protest to a legislature made by blacks in New England. Quickly published as a pamphlet, the urgency of Felix's argument was buttressed with two letters by "A Lover of True Liberty" and "The Sons of Africa" [fig. 8].

Three months later, on April 20, a printed leaflet in the form of a letter to the delegates of the towns in the House of Representatives was circulated by four slaves—Peter Bestes, Sambo Freeman, Chester Joie, and Felix Holbrook (the same Felix?)—"in behalf of our fellow slaves in this province. and by order of their Committee" [fig. 9]. The letter begins with a taunt: "We expect great things from men who have made such a noble stand against the designs of their *fellow-men* to enslave them" and continues with a suggestion: now, at least, allow the "*Africans* . . . one day in a week to work for themselves, to enable them to earn money,"

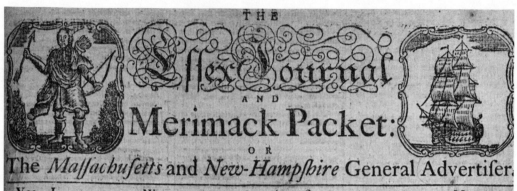

7. Caesar Sarter to the *Essex Journal and Merimack Packet,* Salem, Massachusetts, August 17, 1774. Courtesy, American Antiquarian Society.

in order that they may buy their freedom. Even so, they saw no future in America: "[we will] leave the province . . . as soon as we can, from our joynt labours procure money to transport ourselves to some part of the coast of *Africa,* where we propose a settlement." (Long before Sierra Leone and Liberia, Martin Delany and Marcus Garvey.) The House tabled the petition. When the four slaves appealed to the governor, he said that he could not assist them.*

In June another petition was sent to Hutchinson and the General Court "in behalf [of] all those who by divine Permission are held in a state of slavery, within the bowels of a free Country." The fragment that survives has the flavor of the Declaration of Independence: "Your Petitioners apprehend they have in comon with other men a naturel right to be free and without molestation to injoy such property as they may acquire by their industry, or by any other means not detrimental to their fellow men. . . ."

---

*This printed leaflet of April 20, 1773, has an interesting history. Its black authors sent it to the press, but it was turned down. Later the same year it was printed in Boston at the end of John Allen's *Oration*

Upon the Beauties of Liberty, where it is stated that the letter was "offered to one of the Publishers of a Newspaper, but was refused a place; but as the printer is determined, even at the hazard of his life, to maintain

Province of the MASSACHUSETTS-BAY.
To his Excellency
THOMAS HUTCHINSON, Esq;
GOVERNOR ;
To the Honorable
His Majesty's COUNCIL, and

To the Honorable House of REPRESENTATIVES
in General Court assembled at Boston, the
6th Day of *January*, 1773.

The humble PETITION of many SLAVES,
living in the Town of BOSTON, and other
Towns in the Province is this, namely,

THAT your EXCELLENCY and Honors, and
the Honorable the Representatives would
be pleased to take their unhappy State and Condition under your wise and just Consideration.

WE desire to bless GOD, who loves Mankind, who sent his Son to die for their Salvation,
and who is no Respecter of Persons ; that he hath
lately put it into the Hearts of Multitudes on both
Sides of the Water, to bear our Burthens, some
of whom are Men of great Note and Influence ;
who have pleaded our Cause with Arguments
which we hope will have their weight with this
Honorable Court.

WE presume not to dictate to your EXCEL-
LENCY and Honors, being willing to rest our
Cause on your Humanity and Justice ; yet would
beg Leave to say a Word or two on the Subject.

ALTHOUGH some of the Negroes are vicious,
(who doubtless may be punished and restrained
by the same Laws which are in Force against
other of the King's Subjects) there are many
others of a quite different Character, and who,
B   if

8. Petition of slaves living in Boston and other towns to the House of Representatives, January 6, 1773, signed "Felix," from *The Appendix . . .* (Boston, 1773). Courtesy of the Library of Congress.

A year later, on May 25, 1774, there came still another petition to the new governor, Thomas Gage, and the General Court from "a Grate Number of Blackes of the Province . . . held in a state of Slavery within a free and christian Country." This document cannot be greatly shortened without damage; here is most of it verbatim:

> Your Petitioners apprehind we have in common with all other men a naturel right to our freedoms without Being depriv'd of them by our fellow men as we are a freeborn Pepel and have never forfeited this Blessing by aney compact or agreement whatever. But we were unjustly dragged by the cruel hand of power from our dearest frinds and sum of us stolen from the bosoms of our tender Parents and from a Populous Pleasant and plentiful country and Brought hither to be made slaves for Life in a Christian land. Thus we are deprived of every thing that hath a tendency to make life even tolerable, the endearing ties of husband and wife we are strangers to. . . . Our children are also taken from us by force and sent maney miles from us. . . . Thus our Lives are imbittered. . . . There is a great number of us sencear . . . members of the Church of Christ how can the master and the slave be said to fulfil that command Live in love let Brotherly Love contuner and abound Beare yea onenothers Bordenes. How can the master be said to Beare my Borden when he Beares me down with the . . . chanes of slavery. . . . Nither can we reap an equal benefet from the laws of the Land which doth

inviolable that inestimable Priviledge of mankind, Liberty of the press, which can never be wanted more than at this time, when near one-sixth part of the inhabitants of *America* are held in *Real Slavery*, under the different pretences of interest and religion . . . for the reasons above, [he] shall comply with the request of an Advocate for a multitude of these distressed People. . . ." In his well-known study of the ideological origins of the revolution, Bernard Baylin has surveyed the literature of the time in which a few white writers exposed the hypocrisy in patriots' complaints that they were enslaved by king and Parliament, while at the same time they remained silent about their own slaves. Yet Baylin omits any mention of the exposure by blacks of this hypocrisy in their public utterance, individual and collective.

BOSTON, April 20th, 1773.

SIR,

THE efforts made by the legiſlative of this province in their laſt ſeſſions to free themſelves from ſlavery, gave us, who are in that deplorable ſtate, a high degree of ſatisfaction. We expect great things from men who have made ſuch a noble ſtand againſt the deſigns of their *fellow-men* to enſlave them. We cannot but wiſh and hope Sir, that you will have the ſame grand object, we mean civil and religious liberty, in view in your next ſeſſion. The divine ſpirit of *freedom*, ſeems to fire every humane breaſt on this continent, except ſuch as are bribed to aſſiſt in executing the execrable plan.

WE are very ſenſible that it would be highly detrimental to our preſent maſters, if we were allowed to demand all that of *right* belongs to us for paſt ſervices ; this we diſclaim. Even the *Spaniards*, who have not thoſe ſublime ideas of freedom that Engliſh men have, are conſcious that they have no right to all the ſervices of their fellow-men, we mean the *Africans*, whom they have purchaſed with their money ; therefore they allow them one day in a week to work for themſelve, to enable them to earn money to purchaſe the reſidue of their time, which they have a right to demand in ſuch portions as they are able to pay for (a due appraizment of their ſervices being firſt made, which always ſtands at the purchaſe money.) We do not pretend to dictate to you Sir, or to the honorable Aſſembly, of which you are a member : We acknowledge our obligations to you for what you have already done, but as the people of this province ſeem to be actuated by the principles of equity and juſtice, we cannot but expect your houſe will again take our deplorable caſe into ſerious conſideration, and give us that ample relief which, *as men*, we have a natural right to.

BUT ſince the wiſe and righteous governor of the univerſe, has permitted our fellow men to make us ſlaves, we bow in ſubmiſſion to him, and determine to behave in ſuch a manner, as that we may have reaſon to expect the divine approbation of, and aſſiſtance in, our peaceable and lawful attempts to gain our freedom.

WE are willing to ſubmit to ſuch regulations and laws, as may be made relative to us, until we leave the province, which we determine to do as ſoon as we can from our joynt labours procure money to transport ourſelves to ſome part of the coaſt of *Africa*, where we propoſe a ſettlement. We are very deſirous that you ſhould have inſtructions relative to us, from your town, therefore we pray you to communicate this letter to them, and aſk this favor for us.

In behalf of our fellow ſlaves in this province,
And by order of their Committee.

PETER BESTES,
SAMBO FREEMAN,
FELIX HOLBROOK,
CHESTER JOIE.

For the REPRESENTATIVE of the town of *Thompson*

9. Circular letter of Peter Bestes, Sambo Freeman, Felix Holbrook, Chester Joie, Boston, April 20, 1773. Courtesy of The New-York Historical Society.

not justifi but condemns Slavery or if there had bin aney Law to hold us in Bondage . . . ther never was aney to inslave our children for life when Born in a free Countrey. We therefore Bage your Excellency and Honours will . . . cause an act of the legislative to be pessed that we may obtain our Natural right our freedoms and our children to be set at lebety at the yeare of twenty one. . . .

Finally, in June, the same petition was submitted once more, this time with a significant addition: "give and grant to us some part of the unimproved land, belonging to the province, for a settlement, that each of us may there quietly sit down under his own fig tree" and enjoy "the fruits of his labour." Once more, the General Court voted to let the question "subside."

It is clear that the petitioners' indignation did not subside. At the end of that summer Abigail Adams wrote to her husband, John: "There has been in town a conspiracy of the negroes. At present it is kept pretty private, and was discovered by one who endeavored to dissuade them from it. . . . They conducted in this way . . . to draw up a petition to the Governor, telling him they would fight for him provided he would arm them, and engage to liberate them if he conquered" [fig. 10]. Had she read the earlier petitions? "I wish most sincerely," she concluded, "there was not a slave in the province; it always appeared a most iniquitous scheme to me to fight ourselves for what we are daily robbing and plundering from those who have as good a right to freedom as we have."

The "conspiracy" did not confine itself to Boston. In April 1775 it was reported in the press that in Bristol County, among the "traitors" of a Tory gang called "Col. Gilbert's banditti," which had received its

10. Abigail Adams to John Adams, Boston, September 22, 1774. Massachusetts Historical Society.

arms from a British man-of-war in the harbor at Newport, Rhode Island, there were "several [armed] Negroes." All thirty-five, white and black, were lodged in the Taunton jail. That same spring, a few weeks before the skirmish at Lexington, "the Negroes in the counties of Bristol and Worcester . . . petitioned the Committees of Correspondence . . . convened in Worcester" to assist them in obtaining their "freedom." Was there an implied threat to seek their freedom elsewhere if their petition was denied? Perhaps; at any rate, a few months later a patriot county convention replied with a resolution: "we abhor the enslaving of any of the human race, and particularly of the NEGROES in this country . . ." [fig. 11].

. Americans !---Liberty or Death !---Join or Die .

Massachusetts Spy

Or, American ORACLE of Liberty

WHEREAS the NEGROES in the counties of Briftol and Worcefter, the 24th of March laft, petitioned the Committees of Correfpondence for the county of Worcefter (then convened in Worcefter) to affift them in obtaining their freedom. THEREFORE,

In County Convention, June 14th, 1775.

RESOLVED, That we abhor the enflaving of any of the human race, and particularly of the NEGROES in this country. And that whenever there fhall be a door opened, or opportunity prefent, for any thing to be done toward the emancipating the NEGROES; we will ufe our Influence and endeavour that fuch a thing may be effected; *Atteft.* WILLIAM HENSHAW, Clerk.

11. *Massachusetts Spy* (Worcester), June 21, 1775. Courtesy, American Antiquarian Society.

The Shot Heard Round the World: Lexington and Concord, Bunker Hill, and Great Bridge

The alarm that Mrs. Adams expressed to her husband mirrored the anger of Boston's slaves at the hypocrisy of white legislators who gave lip service to liberty where blacks were concerned. True enough, following the lead of James Otis in the 1760s, a few bold spokesmen like the Reverend Isaac Skillman, who appealed for the rights of man in his oration of 1772 "upon the Beauties of Liberty," included the black man in their cries for justice. A week before Bunker Hill, slaves in the counties of Worcester and Bristol petitioned the Committee of Correspondence "to assist them in obtaining their freedom." Shortly thereafter, white delegates to a county convention in Worcester declared that they abhorred "the enslaving of any of the human race" and stated that whenever a "door opened they would strive for the emancipation of the negroes." But the indifference of assemblies and governors to the repeated appeals of the slave petitioners rankled deeply. Speculating on how the British might exploit black exasperation, in June 1775 General Thomas Gage considered raising a regiment of freed slaves, five months before Lord Dunmore had formulated a similar plan in Virginia: "Things are now come to that Crisis, that we must avail ourselves of every resource, even to raise the Negroes, in our cause."

It is clear that the blacks of Boston and its environs, newly awakened to a sense of their own unity and stirred by the promise of a dawn of liberty for all, found themselves at a fork in the road. Which way to freedom? When the embattled farmers fired the shot heard round the world, it is probable that in New England most blacks saw their destiny, if only dimly, in the triumph of a democratic revolution that might somehow, in the shakeup of things, give substance to its slogans. Thus, even though at the start they were barred from the ranks by legislators and generals, black slaves and freemen insisted on taking part in the struggle.

TOWARD the close of February 1775 General Gage sent two British officers from Boston to map the roads in the counties of Suffolk and Worcester. Posing as countrymen, "they had no trouble until they arrived in Watertown." Ensign D'Berniere reported that: "a little out of this town we went into a tavern, a *Mr. Brewer's,* a whig, we called for dinner, which was brought in by a black woman, at first she was very civil, but afterwards began to eye us very attentively; she then went out and a little after returned, when we observed to her that it was a very fine country, upon which she answered so it is, and we have brave fellows to defend it, and if you go up any higher you will find it is so . . . we resolved not to sleep there that night . . .*John,* our servant . . . told us that she knew Capt. *Brown* very well, that she had seen him five years before at *Boston* . . . that she knew our

errant was to take a plan of the country; that she had seen the river and road through *Charlestown* on the paper; she also advised him to tell us not to go any higher, for if we did we should meet with very bad usage. . . ."

A month or so later, in early April, Gage again sent out two spies—Tory John Howe and a Colonel Smith—to map the countryside around Worcester. At a tavern in the town where he waited for breakfast, Howe wrote in his journal: "there came in a negro woman to wait on the table; Col. Smith asked her where we two could find employment; she looked Col. Smith in the face, and said, Smith you will find employment enough for you and all Gen. Gage's men in a few months." Smith "appeared to be thunderstruck" and complained to the landlord, "you have a saucy wench here." The landlord replied that "she had been living in Boston, and had got acquainted with a great many British officers and soldiers there. . . ." Smith said later to Howe, "if he came out with his regiment [by] that road, he would kill that wench," whereupon he scampered back to Boston. A little later, near a huge butterwood tree, Howe met "a negro man setting traps" who told him that "the people were going to cut it down to stop the regulars from crossing with their cannon." Asked about the taverns in the neighborhood, the black trapper informed him that one was kept by "a good liberty man," the other by "a wicked tory."

WHEN patriots in arms gathered at Lexington and Concord on April 19, 1775, to confront the redcoats from Boston, black minutemen with flintlocks were among them [fig. 12]. Early on the ground was the Lexington slave "Prince Easterbrooks, (a Negro man)," as he is described in the report of the wounded, who had enlisted in Captain John Parker's company, the first to

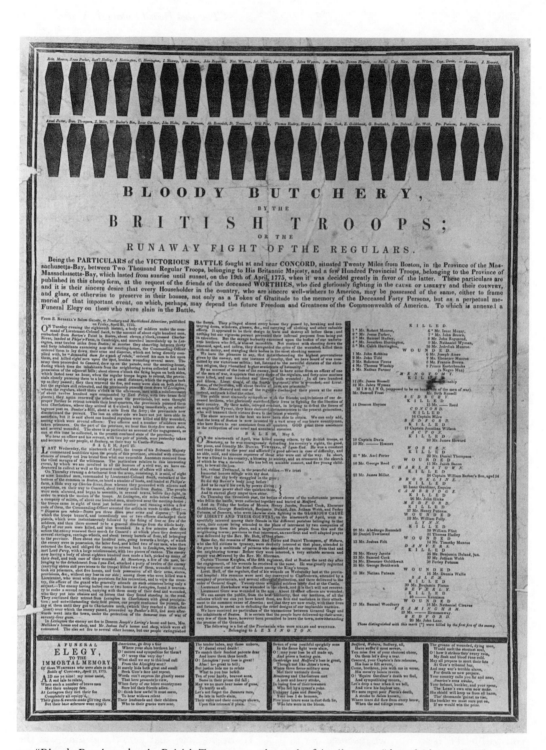

12. "Bloody Butchery, by the British Troops . . . the 19th of April, 1775," broadside, undated. Massachusetts Historical Society.

get into the fight. He would serve in almost every major campaign of the war [fig. 13]. From Framingham—the town that Crispus Attucks had fled—came another slave, Peter Salem, private in Captain Simon Edgel's company; from Braintree, Pompy, a private in Captain Seth Turner's company; from Brookline, Prince, slave of Joshua Boylston, in Captain Thomas White's company; and from parts unknown, one Pomp Blackman, later in the Continental Line. Cato Stedman and Cato Boardman had joined Captain Samuel Thatcher's company in Cambridge. Young Cuff Whitemore of Cambridge and Job Potama and Isaiah Bayoman of Stoneham, all in Captain Benjamin Lock's company of Arlington, had signed on "as soldiers in the *Massachusetts Service* for the promotion of American Liberty" [fig. 14], and smelled their first powder as they harassed the British at Lincoln. On the last lap of the British retreat back into Boston, Lieutenant Mackenzie of the Royal Welsh Fusileers observed that a Negro "was wounded near the houses close to the Neck, out of which the Rebels fired to the last."

Addressing the Ladies' Soldiers' Aid Society of West Cambridge in 1864, Samuel Abbot Smith related that even the "exempts," twelve old men on the alarm list, turned out and "chose for their leader David Lamson, a mulatto, who had served in the [French and Indian] war, a man of undoubted bravery and determination. They took their position . . . behind a bank wall of earth and stones. . . . The [redcoat] convoy soon made its appearance . . . Lamson ordered his men to rise and aim directly at the horses, and called out to them to surrender. No reply was made, but the drivers whipped up their teams. Lamson's men then fired, killing several of the horses and two of the men and wounding others. . . . The frightened drivers leaped from their places, and with the guards, ran directly to the

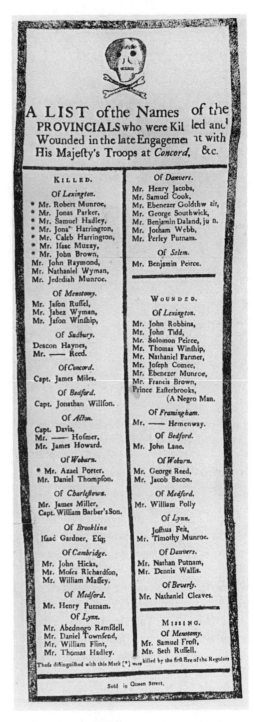

13. "A List of the Names of the Provincials who were Killed and Wounded . . . at Concord," broadside, undated. Massachusetts Historical Society.

14. "Return of Cap.ᵗ Benj.ⁿ Lock's Company in the 37th Reg. of Foot in the Continental Army, . . . Oct. 6, 1777" (detail). Massachusetts Archives, Revolutionary Rolls, 56:250.

shore of Spy Pond, into which they threw their guns . . . near Spring Valley, they met an old woman, named mother Batherick, digging dandelions, to whom they surrendered themselves, asking her protection . . . saying to her prisoners, as she gave them up, 'If you ever live to get back, you tell King George that an old woman took six of his grenadiers prisoners.' " David Lamson went on to serve as a private in the taking of Dorchester Heights in March 1776, and the next year in Colonel Josiah Whitney's regiment in Rhode Island.

Two months later at the bloody Battle of Bunker Hill, among the score or so of black soldiers who held their fire until they could

see the whites of the enemy's eyes were Cuff Whitemore and Peter Salem, again in the thick of the fray. According to Samuel Swett, the earliest chronicler of the battle, Whitemore "fought bravely in the redoubt. He had a ball through his hat . . . fought to the last, and when compelled to retreat, though wounded . . . he seized the sword [of a British officer] slain in the redoubt . . . which in a few days he unromantically sold. He served faithfully through the war, with many hair-breadth 'scapes from sword and pestilence."

Peter Salem, although not the only black hero of Bunker Hill, is the best known, probably because of a mistaken reading of John Trumbull's dramatic reconstruction, *The Battle of Bunker Hill.** Trumbull witnessed the fireworks from Roxbury across the harbor and possibly met Salem after the fight, but in his picture, done in London eleven years later, he chose to show the presence of black patriot soldiers in the fray by depicting prominently a white officer from Connecticut with his black servant holding a musket. There is indeed another black soldier, unidentified, to be discerned under the flags at the top of the picture, who may be

---

*Trumbull's *Battle of Bunker Hill,* sometimes cited with Gericault's *Raft of the Medusa* as a seminal work in the genesis of realistic history-painting, won early applause. Sir Joshua Reynolds commended its "vigorous coloring" and Benjamin West thought it *"the best picture* of a modern battle that has been painted." When Abigail Adams viewed the canvas in 1786, she wrote to a friend: "my whole frame contracted, my blood shivered . . . [Trumbull] is the first painter who had undertaken to immortalize . . . those great actions, that gave birth to our nation." Goethe saw the painting in 1797 while it was being copied in an engraving by J. G. von Müller in Stuttgart. He praised it highly in a letter to Schiller: "His talent shows itself particularly in the character portraits brought out in bold strokes." Madame de Brehan, a friend of Thomas Jefferson and Maria Cosway, commissioned Trumbull to repeat the figures of the lieutenant and his musket bearer in a small painting.

15. J. G. Müller, *The Battle of Bunker's Hill,* engraving after John Trumbull, 1798. Courtesy of the Library of Congress.

Peter Salem, whose famous musket is preserved at the Bunker Hill Monument [figs. 15 and 16].

That Peter Salem had a good eye is clearly attested in the early commentary. In 1787 the New England historian Dr. Jeremy Belknap recorded in his diary that someone who was present at the battle had told him that "A negro man belonging to Groton, took aim at Major Pitcairne, as he was rallying the dispersed British Troops, & shot him thro' the head. . . ." Swett's chronicle is the first published account of the dramatic moment when the king's soldiers charged the patriot works for the third time: "Among the foremost of the leaders was the gallant Maj. Pitcairn, who exultingly cried 'the day is ours,' when Salem, a black soldier, and a number of others, shot him through and he fell. . . ." Minuteman

Salem had already faced Pitcairn at Lexington, where the British officer "had caused the first effusion of blood." Swett concluded that "a contribution was made in the army for Salem and he was presented to Washington as having slain Pitcairn." Some thirty years later, in 1855, William C. Nell noted that in the older engravings of the battle, based on Trumbull, Peter Salem "occupies a prominent position; but in more recent editions, his figure is *non est inventus*. A significant but inglorius omission." No summer soldier, Salem was present with his famous gun at Saratoga and Stony Point. After the war he returned to Massachusetts, built a cabin near Leicester, and wove cane for a living. In 1816, he died at the poorhouse in Framingham.

Also at Bunker Hill that June day in 1775 were Barzillai Lew of Chelmsford and

16. John Trumbull, *Lt. Grosvenor and his Negro Servant,* oil, 1786. Yale University Art Gallery, The Mabel Brady Garvan Collection.

Salem Poor of Andover. Lew, a veteran of the French and Indian War, thirty-two years old, six feet high, enlisted in Captain John Ford's company of the Twenty-seventh Massachusetts Regiment. He marched to Ticonderoga and served in the army a full seven years as front-line soldier, fifer, and drummer. A legend has come down that he "organized for guerilla warfare at a later period of the struggle a band of Negro men, all in one family, known as Lew's men." But where is there a depiction of "The Spirit of '76" that shows a black fifer or drummer?

Most celebrated of the black soldiers who fought at Bunker Hill was twenty-eight-year-old Salem Poor, freeman and church member, who left his wife behind to enlist in the militia company captained by Benjamin Ames. For his valor and intrepidity—he was perhaps responsible for picking off another important redcoat, Lieutenant Colonel James Abercrombie—fourteen officers who had been on the field that day (including Colonel William Prescott) submitted a petition six months later to the General Court, suggesting that the Conti-

17. Recommendation of Salem Poor for his bravery "in the late Battle of Charlestown," December 5, 1775. Massachusetts Archives, 180: 241.

nental Congress itself bestow "The Reward due to so great and Distinguished a Caracter":

> The Subscribers begg leave to Report to your Honorable House, (which Wee do in justice to the Caracter of so Brave a Man) that under Our Own observation, We declare that A Negro Man Called Salem Poor of Col. Frye's Regiment—Capt. Ames. Company—in the late Battle at Charles-town, behaved like an Experienced officer, as Well as an Excellent Soldier, to Set forth Particulars of his Conduct Would be Tedious. Wee Would Only begg leave to Say in the Person of this said Negro Centers a Brave & gallant Soldier [fig. 17].

There is no record that a "Reward" was ever given to Salem Poor, who went on to serve at Valley Forge and White Plains.

AT Lexington, Concord, and Bunker Hill, a year before the Declaration of Independence, black soldiers and white fired the first shots of the revolution in the north. Not long after, black soldiers and white—on both sides—would fire the first shots in the south. At the Battle of the Great Bridge near Norfolk, Virginia, during the winter of 1775, a detachment of Lord Dunmore's army, including black soldiers of his Ethiopian Regiment, sallied out of their island fort, crossed a bridge over the Elizabeth River, drove back the patriot guards with heavy fire, and attacked Colonel William Woodford's Second Virginia Regiment waiting in the breastworks. Woodford, who had employed a black spy to dupe the redcoats into thinking that his defense was weak, was ready for the assault. The fight was short and furious—the British retreated into their fort.

Among the stubborn guards at the bridge was a black freeman from Portsmouth by the name of William Flora. Captain Thomas Nash, who was wounded during the engagement, later wrote down his memory of the day: "Flora, a colored man, was the last sentinel that came into the breast work . . . he did not leave his post until he had fired several times. Billy had to cross a plank to get to the breast work, and had fairly passed over it when he was seen to turn back, and deliberately take up the plank after him, amidst a shower of musket balls. He . . . fired eight times." Thirty years later, in 1806, when William Flora—by this time a prosperous businessman and property owner who had bought the freedom of his slave wife and children—applied for a land grant, his old commander testified that he had served "in the Continental line untill the siege of York . . . and was held in high esteem as a soldier." Virginia granted the black veteran one hundred acres in gratitude for his revolutionary service [fig. 18].

A local historian who knew Flora well in his later years recalled that the old man had "volunteered to act as a marine under Commodore Decatur" in the second war against England: "He was true patriot to the last. I recollect that when the troops of Norfolk and Portsmouth were under arms . . . in consequence of the cowardly attack on the frigate *Chesapeake* by the British ship *Leopard,* Billy Flora made his appearance with his gun on his shoulder . . . observing that he had brought with him the same musket which he had fought with at the Great Bridge."

The Declaration of Independence

"We hold these truths to be self-evident, that all men are created equal, that they are endowed by their Creator with certain unalienable Rights, that among these are Life, Liberty, and the pursuit of Happiness." When on July 4, 1776, "the Representatives of the united States of America, in General Congress," proclaimed this revolutionary doctrine to the world, what might have been the reactions of the black people of the new nation—of Salem Poor and William Flora, for example?

On the eve of the Declaration, blacks had already engaged in a struggle for their own independence—not only in their petitions to colonial governments in New England, but also in a variety of covert and overt modes of resistance from New Jersey to Georgia.* If the historical record so far has

---

*Herbert Aptheker, in chapter 8 of his groundbreaking *American Negro Slave Revolts* (New York, 1943), has recorded more than a few conspiracies and revolts during the twenty years from 1755 to 1775. These have been supplemented by Gerald W. Mullin's *Flight and Rebellion: Slave Resistance in Eighteenth-Cen-*

18. Office of the Governor. Bounty Warrants. Certification of William Flora's service in the 15th Virginia Regiment, July 16, 1806. Archives Branch, Virginia State Library and Archives, Richmond.

revealed only a few dozen instances of sporadic conspiracy and revolt, it should be recalled that in 1774 James Madison had cautioned that it was "prudent such attempts should be concealed as well as suppressed."

In April 1775, eight months before Lord Dunmore's proclamation of freedom to those slaves who would flee their patriot masters and join the British, the governor of Maryland ordered four hundred stands of arms to put down possible uprisings in four counties. Later, in the fall, the Committee of Inspection in Dorchester County wrote a worried report: "The insolence of the Negroes in this county is come to such a height, that we are under the necessity of disarming them. . . . We took about

tury Virginia (New York, 1972) and by Peter H. Wood, " 'Taking Care of Business' in Revolutionary South Carolina: Republicanism and the Slave Society," in *The Southern Experience in the American Revolution*, ed. Jeffrey T. Crow and Larry E. Tise (Chapel Hill, 1978), 268–93.

eighty guns, some bayonets, swords, etc. The malicious and imprudent speeches of some among the lower classes of whites have induced them to believe that their freedom depends on the success of the king's troops." As for the situation farther south, there is a revealing entry in John Adams's diary for September 24, 1775: "In the evening . . . two gentlemen from Georgia, came into our room. . . . These gentlemen gave a melancholy account of the State of Georgia and South Carolina. They say that if one thousand regular troops should land in Georgia, and their commander be provided with arms and clothes enough, and proclaim freedom to all the negroes who would join his camp, twenty thousand negroes would join it from the two Provinces in a fortnight. The negroes have a wonderful art of communicating intelligence among themselves; it will run several hundreds of miles in a week or fortnight. They say their only security is this; that all the king's friends, and tools of government, have large plantations and property in negroes; so that the slaves of the Tories would be lost, as well as those of the Whigs."

Did "all men" referred to in the Declaration of Independence include African Americans? Where in this manifesto of equality was the word "slave" to be found? (Jefferson had been forced by the slavocrats of Georgia and South Carolina to delete his attack on the slave trade in his first draft of the Declaration, and only an ambiguous phrase would remain in the final document on the question of bondage.) Searching every line for an acknowledgment of the tyranny of white racism in the colonies, all that Salem Poor and William Flora might discover was an indictment of George III: "He has excited domestic insurrections amongst us," a reference to the British generals who had offered liberty, with a gun, to the slaves of patriots, "and has endeavoured to bring on the inhabitants of our frontiers, the merciless Indian savages" [fig. 19]. Was the Tory ex-governor, Thomas Hutchinson, correct when he pointed out the clash between a theory of equality for "all men" and the reality of depriving "more than a hundred thousand Africans of their rights to liberty"? And if Poor and Flora knew that the Congress in fact had repudiated Jefferson's denunciation of the slave trade—the clause that John Adams called the "vehement phillipic against Negro slavery"—would this knowledge have transformed the Declaration into something they could in good conscience defend? Yet, examine the problem from another angle. Conceding that the Declaration had in fact not abolished slavery in the year 1776, might not its noble phrases hold at least the promise of a future society with liberty for all? And shouldn't blacks fight for that promise?

There is little doubt that such questions troubled the minds of slaves and freemen as they tried to figure their stake in the new

nation. Enlisting in the patriot cause on land and sea, they would continue to affix their names and marks to agonized petitions that echo and reecho the language of the Declaration, which seemed to demand "Life, Liberty, and the pursuit of Happiness" for black Americans as well as white.

Thus, in Massachusetts six months after the Declaration, the petition of "A Great Number of Negroes who are detained in a State of slavery in the Bowels of a free & Christian Country" once again asserted their "Natural & unalienable right to that freedom, which the great Parent of the Universe hath bestowed equally on all mankind," and admonished the General Court:

> [Following] the laudable example of the good People of these States, your Petitioners have long & patiently waited the event of Petition after Petition. . . . they can not but express their astonishment that it has never bin considered that every principle from which America has acted in the course of her unhappy difficulties with Great-Britain pleads stronger than an thousand arguments . . . [that] they may be restored to the enjoyment of that freedom which is the naturel right of all Men. . . .

Eight Boston blacks, most of them freemen, signed this petition, four with their marks: Prince Hall (organizer of the African Lodge of Freemasons), Lancaster Hill, Peter Bess, Brister Slenser, Jack Pierpont, Nero Funelo, Newport Sumner, and Job Look [fig. 20]. The General Court responded by passing the buck; a cautious letter to Congress in Philadelphia asking for advice was drafted but never sent. Thus the petition of the eight blacks in 1777 was killed in committee and Massachusetts, which would never pass a law abolishing slavery, had to wait

19. From Thomas Jefferson's copy of his rough draft of the Declaration, made for James Madison in the spring of 1783. Courtesy of the Library of Congress, *Declaration of Independence,* (Washington, 1943), pl. 8.

until 1782 when Elizabeth Freeman abolished it in court.

In Connecticut during the spring of 1779 a freedom-seeking petition of "the Negroes in the Towns of Stratford and Fairfield," signed by Prime and Prince, queried the Hartford meeting of the General Assembly as to "whether it is consistent with the present Claims of the united States, to hold so many Thousand, of the Race of Adam, our Common Father, in perpetual Slavery." Is it not a "flagrant Injustice" that those "nobly contending, in the Cause of Liberty" deny that "Reason & Revelation join to declare, that we are the creatures of that God, who made of one Blood, and Kindred, all the Nations of the Earth?" [fig. 21].

More personal petitions by Connecticut blacks who had become state property after their Tory owners had fled are not rare at this time. The "memorial of Great Prince, Little Prince, Luke, Caesar, and Prue and her three children—all friends to America, but *slaves*" (dated "Lyme, Election day, 1779")—explains that "their late master was a Tory, and fled from his native country to *his* master, King George. . . . That your memorialists, though they have flat noses,

20. Petition of "a great number of Negroes" to the Massachusetts General Court, January 13, 1777. Massachusetts Archives, 212: 132, 132a.

crooked shins, and other queerness of make, peculiar to Africans, are yet of the human race, free-born in our own country, taken from thence by man-stealers, and sold in this country as cattle in the market, without the least act of our own to forfeit liberty; but we hope our good mistress, *the free State of Connecticut,* engaged in a war with tyranny, will not sell good honest Whigs and friends of the freedom and independence of America, as we are, to raise cash to support the war; because the Whigs ought to be *free;* and the *Tories* should be sold." The memorial's eloquence was lost on the General Assembly.

Elsewhere in Connecticut the story re-peated itself. During the fall of 1779 Pomp, a "slave of absconded" Norwalk Loyalists—he was "about Thirty Years of Age and of firm and healthy Constitution and able to well-provide for himself and a {free} Wife and Child"—likewise petitioned the Assembly for his freedom. From Farmington in May 1780 came the plea of the black soldier Joseph Mun, slave of a Waterbury Tory. Mun describes himself as "a poor African," who, "while but a Child was snatched by the hand of Fraud and violence from his Native Land and all his dear Connexions. . . ." He asks: "Have not the Great Parents of the Universe . . . made of one blood all Nations of men for to dwell on the face of the

21. Petition of Prime, Prince, and others, to the Connecticut General Assembly, May 4, 1779, final page. Connecticut Archives, Revolutionary War, 1st Series, 30: 232a–d.

earth . . . ?" Was he not "in Common with others entitled to Freedom and the unalienable rights of Humanity . . . ?" In 1776, he had demanded the consent of his old master to join the army; he had served since the start of the war "in the defense of the Rights & Liberties of this Country and in hope to lay foundations for organizing his own Freedom and is now enlisted in the Continental Army. . . ." His master had fled to the enemy, but just before taking off he had sold the "unfortunate Petitioner" in order "to elude the law."

In Portsmouth, New Hampshire, during the fall of 1779, twenty "Natives of Af-rica . . . born free," including Prince Whipple, who in 1776 had crossed the Delaware in General Washington's boat, implored the House and Council sitting in Exeter to restore their freedom "for the sake of justice, humanity and the rights of mankind." They argued that "the God of Nature gave them Life and Freedom, upon the Terms of the most perfect Equality with other men, That Freedom is an inherent right of the human Species, not to be surrendered, but by Consent, for the Sake of social Life; that private or public Tyranny and Slavery, are alike detestable to Minds conscious of the equal Dignity of human

THE
NEW-HAMPSHIRE GAZETTE;
OR,
STATE JOURNAL, and GENERAL ADVERTISER.

[Vol. XXIV.]   SATURDAY, JULY 15, 1780.   [No. 1238.]

The following is a copy of the petition of a number of the Negroes now detained in slavery at Portsmouth, &c. lately presented the General Assembly of this State, who accordingly granted them a hearing; but, we hear, the further consideration thereof is postponed... the amusement of our readers.

THE petition of *Nero Brewster*, and others, natives of Africa, now forcibly detained in slavery, in said state, most humbly sheweth, That the God of Nature gave them life and freedom, upon terms of the most perfect equality with other men; that freedom is an inherent right of the human species, not to be surrendered, but by consent, for the sake of social life; that private or public tyranny and slavery, are alike detestable to minds conscious of the equal dignity of human nature; that in power and authority of individuals, derived solely from a principle of coercion, against the wills of individuals, and to dispose of their persons and properties, consists the completest idea of private and political slavery; that all men being amenable to the Deity for the ill improvement of the blessings of his providence, they hold themselves in duty bound, strenuously to exert every faculty of their minds, to obtain that blessing of freedom which they are justly entitled to from that beneficent Creator; that thro' ignorance & brutish violence of their native countrymen, and by sinister designs of others, (who ought to have taught them better)& by the avarice of both, they, while but children, and incapable of self-defence, whose infancy might have prompted protection, were seized, imprisoned, and transported from their native country, where, (tho' ignorance and inchristianity prevailed) they were born free to a country, where (tho' knowledge, christianity and freedom, are their boast) they are compelled, and their unhappy posterity, to drag on their lives in miserable servitude.—Thus, often is the parent's cheek wet for the loss of a child, torn by the cruel hand of violence from her aking bosom! Thus, often, and in... in, is the infant's sigh, for the nurturing care of it's bereaved parent! and thus, do the ties of nature and blood, become victims, to cherish the vanity and luxury of a fellow-mortal! Can this be right? Forbid it gracious Heaven!

Permit again your humble slaves to lay before this honorable Assembly, some of those grievances which they daily experience and feel; tho' fortune hath dealt out our portions with rugged hand, yet hath she failed in the disposal of our persons to those who claim us as their property; of them, as masters, we do not complain: but, from what authority they assume the power to dispose of our lives, freedom and property, we would wish to know.—Is it from the sacred volumes of christianity? There we believe it is not to be found! But here hath the cruel hand of slavery made us incompetent judges; but those, we are told, are founded in reason and justice; it cannot be found there! Is it from the volumns of nature? No, here we can read with others! Of this knowledge, slavery cannot wholly deprive us; here, we know we ought to be free agents! here, we feel the dignity of human nature! here, we feel the passions and desires of men, tho' check'd by the rod of slavery! here, we feel a just equality! here, we know that the God of Nature made us free! Is their authority assumed from custom? if so, let that custom be abolished, which is not founded in... reason not religion. Should the humanity and benevolence of this honorable Assembly restore us to that state of liberty of, which we have been so long deprived, we conceive that those, who are our present masters, will not be sufferers by our liberation, as we have most of us spent our whole strength and the prime of our lives in their service; and as freedom inspires a noble confidence, and gives the mind an emulation to vie in the noblest efforts of enterprize, and as justice and humanity are the result of your deliberations, we fondly hope that the eye of pity and the heart of justice may commiserate our situation and put us upon the equality of freemen, and give us an opportunity of evincing to the world our love of freedom, by exerting ourselves in her cause, in opposing the efforts of tyranny and oppression over the country in which we ourselves have been so injuriously enslaved.

Therefore, your humble slaves most devoutly pray, for the sake of injured liberty, for the sake of justice, humanity, and the rights of mankind; for the honor of religion, and by all that is dear, that your honors would graciously interpose in our behalf, and enact such laws and regulations as in your... may regain our liberty and be rank'd in the class of free agents, and that the name of SLAVE may no more be heard in a land gloriously contending for the sweets of freedom; and your humble slaves as in duty bound will ever pray.

Portsmouth, Nov. 12. 1779.

22. "The petition of *Nero Brewster,* and others, natives of Africa," Portsmouth, New Hampshire, November 12, 1779, *New-Hampshire Gazette,* July 15, 1780. New Hampshire Historical Society.

Nature. . . ." It was not until the spring of 1780 that House and Council deigned to notice the petition of the twenty, and then only to table it. In the meantime, the petitioners were ordered by the legislature to publish their plea in the pages of the *New-Hampshire Gazette,* where it was printed in mid-July, signed by only one of the petitioners, Nero Brewster [fig. 22].

Black petitioners were not confined to New England. In March 1780 Pennsylvania enacted a law for the gradual abolition of slavery. When, more than a year later, diehard conservatives connived to annul this law and thereby thrust blacks newly freed by it back into bondage, a group of the aggrieved petitioned the legislature to hold fast: "We fear we are too bold, but our all is at stake. The grand question of slavery or liberty is too important for us to be silent—it is the momentous passion of our lives; if we are silent this day, we may be silent for ever; returned to slavery, we are deprived of even the right of petitioning." This petition

The Freeman's Journal, Sept. 21.

23. Letter from Cato and Petition to the Pennsylvania Assembly, *Freeman's Journal: or, the North-American Intelligencer* (Philadelphia), September 19, 1781, "Postscript . . . Sept. 21." The Historical Society of Pennsylvania.

appeared on the front page of the Philadelphia *Freeman's Journal* for September 21, 1781. Next to it on the same page was the letter of one Cato, who echoed the outrage of the petitioners: "I am a poor negro who with my self and children have had the good fortune to get my freedom. . . . I am told the assembly are going to pass a law to send us all back to our masters . . . this would be the cruellest act. . . . To make a law to hang us all would be merciful . . . for many of our masters would treat us with unheard of barbarity . . ." [fig. 23].

A Declaration of Independence—for whom? The arguments of these black petitioners reverberate through the era of the revolution, and beyond.

III

Bearers of Arms: Patriot and Tory

On the eve of the revolution, there were two and one half million Americans in the rebellious colonies. Of these, half a million were black—a few free, the rest slaves. It has been estimated that during the years of war some five thousand blacks served on the patriot side. The black soldier or sailor was, in fact, eager to fight on two fronts—for his own freedom and for the freedom of his country. Therefore, when white governors or generals running short of manpower in the army and navy, or white masters chary of risking their necks on the battlefield, promised a slave his freedom if he joined the ranks, he was more than willing to shoulder a musket.

The struggle for liberty by black people was not an innovation of 1776. Their attempts to shatter their chains had begun on the slave ships during the earliest years of the African diaspora, when some of the kidnapped and tortured were able to rise in revolt on the voyages across the Atlantic. Painful memories—some old, some fresh—of the middle passage, experienced at first

or second hand, were still vivid in the minds of blacks, slave and free, who joined the patriot and Tory forces. A slip of a girl from Senegal whose African name is lost to history, destined to be the poet Wheatley, traveling as cargo in 1761 on a Boston schooner named *Phillis,* may have witnessed the tensions leading to insurrection. In his letter of instruction to the slaver's captain, the ship's owner cautioned him to be careful: "be Constantly Upon your Gard Night & Day & Keep good Watch that you may Not be Cutt of[f] by Your Own Slaves Neavour So Fiew on Board Or that you Are Not Taken by Sirprise. . . ."

The insurrections on the ocean did not cease during the time of the revolution, as a few entries in the logs of the slavers of a single state make clear. Calculating their profits, two ship owners of Newport, Rhode Island, wrote to their brokers during the summer of 1774: "Pray get Insurance on the Brigt. *Othello,* George Sweet Mast'r, at and from hence to the Coast of Africa. . . . We have never made enquirty, if an Insurrection

REPRESENTATION of an INSURRECTION on board A SLAVE-SHIP.

Shewing how the crew fire upon the unhappy Slaves from behind the BARRICADO, *erected on board all Slave ships, as a security whenever such commotions may happen.*

See the privy councils report part I. Art: SLAVES.
Minutes of evidence before the House of Commons.
Wadstrom's Essay on Colonization §. 471.

24. From C. B. Wadstrom, *An Essay on Colonization . . .* , Part Second (London, 1795), 85–87. Library of the Boston Athenaeum.

of the Slaves shou'd happen, and a Loss arise thereon, more or less, if your Underwriters pay in the Case. . . ." The Newport slave traders knew the risks of their business. During the fall of 1776 a worried report from the Rhode Island slaver *Thames,* anchored off the African coast near Accra, described in detail an event of Friday, November 8: "we had the misfortune to lose 36 of the best slaves we had by an Insurrection. . . . We had 160 Slaves on board [who] were that day lett out of the Deck Chaines in order to wash, about 2 OClock. They began by siesing upon the Boatswain. . . . They continued to threw Staves, billets of wood etc. and in endeavoring to get down the Barricado, or over it for

upwards of 40 Minutes, when finding they could not effect it, all the Fantee and most of the Accra Men Slaves jumped over board, in my opinion to get up abaft. . . ." There were other revolts aboard Rhode Island slavers in 1785 and 1796 as well as on two Massachusetts slavers, the *Felicity* in 1789 and the *Nancy* in 1793, another on a New London, Connecticut, ship in 1791 [fig. 24].

Once landed on the soil of the colonies, the slaves from New York to Georgia continued their resistance in various modes of masquerade, sabotage, flight, conspiracy, and revolt. The documentation by historians of their freedom-seeking restlessness has grown year after year.

It was not easy for slave owners to arm their chattels, and two southern states resisted the idea to the end. Nor was the anxiety confined to the south. In Bucks County, Pennsylvania, during the summer of 1776, Henry Wynkoop wrote to the patriot Committee of Safety: "The people in my Neighborhood have been somewhat alarmed with fears about Negroes & disaffected people injuring their families when they are out in the Service. . . ." To quiet fears, he suggested that additional powder be sent to his neighbors.

As Lorenzo J. Greene once pointed out, the black population might have been assessed by both patriots and Tories as crucial in the balance of military power. But in July 1775, when Washington arrived in New England to take command, one of his earliest orders barred "Negroes" and "Vagabonds" from the army. Many months passed before the general and the Congress saw the light. Thereafter recruitment of black soldiers went on apace. During the winter of 1777 a German officer traveling through western Massachusetts was struck by the fact that a slave could "take the field in his master's place; hence you never see a regiment in which there are not negroes, and there are well-built, strong, husky fellows among them." In early spring of 1778 a Moravian farmer in Bethlehem, Pennsylvania, wrote in his diary: "From New England there arrived a company of soldiers, composed of whites, blacks and a few Stockbridge Indians, who were lodged over night." After the Battle of Monmouth, Adjutant General Alexander Scammell could report the names of over 750 black soldiers in fourteen brigades of the Continental Army. On the roll of Captain David Humphreys's black Connecticut company in 1781–83, among the forty-eight surnames, ten are Freedom, Freeman, or Liberty. On

July 4, 1781, Baron Ludwig von Closen, an aide-de-camp to General Rochambeau, viewing the army at White Plains, noted in his journal: "A quarter of them were negroes, merry, confident, and sturdy."* Soon after the Siege of Yorktown, a young French sublieutenant sketched in watercolors in his notebook four foot-soldiers of the patriot army—one of whom is a black light infantryman of the First Rhode Island Regiment [fig. 25].

There were, of course, many blacks who fought with the Tories. The British, always short of men in spite of the large contingent of German mercenaries, saw clearly from the start the role that black power might play in the struggle ahead. When slaves abandoned their patriot masters in response to the blandishments of Lord Dunmore and Sir Henry Clinton, the decision to join the British was for them, as for their brothers on the opposite side, a blow struck against American slavery and for their own independence [fig. 26]. It is possible that tens of thousands of slaves in South Carolina and Georgia went over to the British. Some blacks fled into the swamps and the forests or conspired to fight their own battle for freedom. By the war's end, fourteen thou-

---

*Von Closen has other first-hand observations of blacks in his journal. In 1782 he records a meeting with "a slave ship, under an Austrian flag, coming from the Guinea coast and bound for the Cape. . . . The commerce . . . in negroes is an abominable and cruel thing, in my opinion. On board these ships they are treated worse than beasts; men are on one side, and women on the other, in the forepart of the ship. There is an iron chain which crosses from one side to the other, to which they are all attached, 2 by two, except for the few who are necessary for assistance in the maneuvers. All these unfortunate beings are naked, and at the least movement that does not suit the Captain, they are beaten to a pulp. . . . the loss of a fifth of them, from sickness or despair during a voyage of 2 or 3 months, is expected."

25. Jean-Baptiste-Antoine DeVerger, *American Foot Soldiers, Yorktown Campaign,* watercolor, 1781. Anne S. K. Brown Military Collection, Brown University Library.

sand black men, women, and children, some still bound to fleeing Tory masters, some now free and ready to begin new lives in new places, had been evacuated by the British from Savannah, Charleston, and New York, and transported to Florida, Nova Scotia, Jamaica, and, later, Africa.

The black soldier and sailor of the revolution, whether he fought for Congress or king, served in a variety of ways—as infantryman, artilleryman, scout, guide, spy, pilot, guard, courier, wagoner, orderly, cook, waiter, able seaman, privateersman, and military laborer of all sorts. In a few cases, blacks formed their own units.

How many were killed or wounded, we can only guess. Some were heroes. Not long after they had fallen, most of them were forgotten. The white memory of things recorded in print and paint usually left them out.

A Trio with the Generals: William Lee, James Armistead Lafayette, Agrippa Hull

In 1768 George Washington bought a slave named William from Mary Lee. Seven years later, when Washington took command of the Continental Army, William Lee journeyed with him to Massachusetts and continued at the general's side as servant and orderly through thick and thin to the close

26. The Black Pioneers to Sir Henry Clinton, New York, January 1, 1781. William L. Clements Library, The University of Michigan.

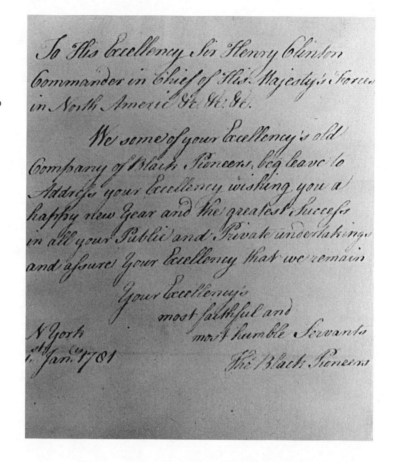

of the war. In John Trumbull's portrait of Washington at West Point, painted in London in 1780, the artist shows young William, in a turban, holding the bridle of the general's horse [fig. 27]. The fighting over, William returned to Virginia with Washington to serve the Mount Vernon household for the next twenty years. It is as a factotum of the Washington family—George and Martha with their grandchildren—that Edward Savage portrayed the black veteran in 1796 [fig. 28]. The genre of both these paintings, white master and black servant—a traditional one for the white artist—perhaps conceals the deep feeling that Washington had for his revolutionary comrade. When William in 1784 asked the general if he could bring to

Mount Vernon his wife, Margaret Thomas, a free woman of Philadelphia, Washington reluctantly agreed: "I cannot refuse his request . . . as he has lived with me so long and followed my fortunes through the War with fidility."

Washington's soul-searching about the rightness of slavery is well known. There was "not a man living," he wrote to two friends in 1786, who wished more sincerely than he "to see some plan adopted by which slavery may be abolished by law." When he died in 1799, his will provided that upon Martha's death all his slaves should be liberated, but "to my *Mulatto* man William (calling himself William Lee) I give immediate freedom. . . . I allow him an annuity of thirty dollars during his natural life . . .

27. John Trumbull, *George Washington,* oil, 1780. Metropolitan Museum of Art (accession no. 24.109.88).

and this I give him as a testimony of my sense of his attachment to me, and for his faithful services during the Revolutionary War" [fig. 29].

In June 1804 on a visit to Mount Vernon, the artist Charles Willson Peale, who would later paint a vivid portrait of the black Muslim Yarrow Mamout, sought out the aged William Lee, whom he found in an outbuilding, crippled, cobbling shoes. The two sat down together and talked about old times and how to live a long, healthy life.

In March 1781 Washington rushed General Lafayette to Virginia in an effort to stop Cornwallis. Shortly thereafter, a slave by the name of James, in New Kent County, asked his master, William Armistead, for permission to enlist under the French major general. That spring and summer, Lafayette felt a crucial necessity to recruit black troops. He called for four hundred laborers and wagoners, and wrote frantically to Washington: "Nothing but a treaty of alliance with the Negroes can find us dragoon

28. Edward Savage, *The Washington Family,* oil, 1796. Courtesy, The Henry Francis du Pont Winterthur Museum.

29. Excerpt from the will of George Washington pertaining to William Lee, 1799. Fairfax County Courthouse, Virginia.

30. Jean-Baptiste Le Paon,
Lafayette at Yorktown, oil,
1783. Art Collection,
Lafayette College. Gift of
Mrs. John Hubbard.

Horses . . . it is by this means the enemy have so formidable a Cavalry." As a master spy, James gave yeoman service. After the surrender at Yorktown, when Cornwallis visited Lafayette's headquarters, he was amazed to see there the black man he had believed to be *his* spy [fig. 30].

The war over, in November 1784 James met Lafayette in Richmond. In his own hand the Frenchman wrote a testimonial which he handed to James, certifying that the ex-spy had rendered "services to me while I had the honour to command in this state. His intelligence from the enemy's camp were industriously collected and more faithfully delivered. He perfectly acquitted himself with some important commissions I gave him and appears to me entitled to every reward his situation can admit of" [fig. 31]. It is barely possible that James, whose "situation" was still that of a slave, by his very presence played a certain part in clarifying the thinking of the marquis about race and slavery. It was about this time that Lafayette began to develop the outlook that would move him in 1783 to propose to

31. Lafayette's certificate, November 21, 1784, commending James Armistead Lafayette, with engraving after portrait by John B. Martin. Courtesy of Virginia Historical Society.

Washington a plan "which might greatly benefit the black part of mankind. Let us unite in purchasing a small estate where we may try the experiment to free the Negroes and use them only as tenants." Five years later in Paris, Lafayette would be a fervent sponsor of the Society of the Friends of the Blacks.

During the autumn of 1786 the General Assembly of Virginia, echoing Lafayette's words—"at the peril of his life found means to frequent the British camp, and thereby faithfully executed important commissions entrusted to him by the marquis"—emancipated James, ordering that his master be compensated at the going auction-block figure. When thirty-odd years later the free-man, "now poor and unable to help himself," petitioned for relief, the state gave him sixty dollars and finally placed him on the regular pension list.

In 1824 Lafayette, on a triumphal return visit to America, came to Richmond. The black veteran, who for a long time had called himself James Lafayette, and the French nobleman who had survived *his* revolution, greeted each other. The scene can be imagined the more vividly because it was probably during this year that the artist John B. Martin, whose portrait of Chief Justice John Marshall hangs in the Supreme Court, painted the aging James Lafayette in a military coat {fig. 32}.

During the summer of 1844 Francis Parkman spent a few days in Stockbridge, a town in western Massachusetts. On July 7 he recorded in his journal: "The old Negro . . . had been a soldier in W's army. He had four children in the churchyard, he said with a solemn countenance, but 'these are my children' he added, stretching his cane over a host of little boys. 'Ah, how much we are consarned to fetch them up well and virtuous' etc. He was very philosophical and every remark carried the old patriarch into lengthy orations on virtue and temperance. He looked on himself as father to all Stockbridge" {fig. 33}. The old patriarch was Agrippa Hull, a black veteran who, sixty years before his conversation with the noted historian, had served as orderly to the noble Pole, General Tadeusz Kósciuszko, who, the story goes, wanted to take him to Poland after the revolution. To this day, Hull is a legendary figure in the Berkshire town where his portrait, complete with cane, in the historical room of the library broods over memorabilia of the past.

Agrippa Hull was born free in Northampton in 1759. At age six—so the story goes—a black man by the name of Joab,

32. John B. Martin, *James Armistead Lafayette,* oil, ca. 1824.
Valentine Museum, Richmond, Virginia.

33. Unknown artist, *Agrippa Hull,* oil, 1848 (after daguerreotype by Anson Clark, 1844). Stockbridge Public Library, Stockbridge, Massachusetts.

former servant to Jonathan Edwards, brought him to Stockbridge. On May 1, 1777, the eighteen-year-old youth—"5 ft. 7 in.; complexion, black; hair wool"—en-

listed for the duration as a private in the brigade of General John Paterson of the Massachusetts Line. For two years he served as an orderly for Paterson, and then for another four years and two months for Paterson's friend, the Polish patriot, in spheres of action ranging from Saratoga to Eutaw Springs. In South Carolina, assigned to assist the surgeons, Hull always remembered with horror the bloody amputations. In July 1783 at West Point he received his discharge, signed by George Washington.

Back home in Stockbridge he farmed a small plot, did odd jobs, acted as butler for the local gentry and as major domo at weddings, and adopted as his daughter the child of a runaway slave from New York, one Mary Gunn, whose posterity still lives in Stockbridge. The town historian, who knew him well, recorded his marriages: "Not long after the case of Mum Bett [Elizabeth Freeman] had been decided, Jane Darby, the slave of Mr. Ingersoll of Lenox . . . left her master and took refuge in Stockbridge. She and Agrippa soon agreed to tread life's path in company; but her master endeavored to seize her. Agrippa applied to Judge [Theodore] Sedgwick for aid, and obtained her discharge. She was a woman of excellent character, and made a profession of her faith in Christ. Some years after her death, Agrippa married Margaret Timbroke, who still lives respected among us." He became the village seer. In 1797, when Kósciuszko visited the United States, Hull traveled to New York. There was an affectionate reunion; no doubt both smiled as they recalled the time the general surprised the orderly dressed in his commander's uniform in the midst of a party Agrippa had thrown for his black friends. It was on this visit in 1797 that Kósciuszko, a lover of liberty, was awarded a gift of land in Ohio, which he directed be sold to found a school for blacks.

In 1828, when Hull was seeking to have his soldier's pension mailed directly to his home, his friend Charles Sedgwick wrote to the official in charge: "I enclose his dis-

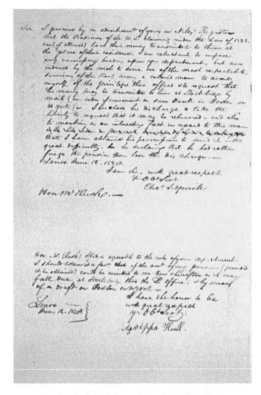

34. Charles Sedgwick and Agrippa Hull to Acting Secretary of State Richard Rush, June 12, 1828. National Archives, Washington, D.C.

charge & take the liberty to request that it may be returned—and also to mention as an interesting fact in regard to this man that I have obtained his permission to send it with great difficulty, he declaring that he had rather forego the pension than lose the discharge" [fig. 34]. Ten years later, after a long illness, he died.

Agrippa Hull "had a fund of humor and mother-wit," recalled the novelist Catharine Maria Sedgwick, "and was a sort of Sancho Panza in the village, always trimming other men's follies with a keen perception, and the biting wit of wisdom." After his death he was remembered as having "no cringing servility" in his makeup, always feeling "himself every whit a man." He would argue: "It is not the *cover* of the book, but what the book *contains*. . . . Many a good book has dark covers," or, "Which is the worst, the white black man, or the black white man? to be black outside, or to be black inside?" He was once overheard "in his public prayers" giving "thanks for the kind notice of his 'white neighbors to a poor black nigger.' " (The eavesdropper was unaware of the ploy of irony.) Another anecdote gives the measure of his character: "Once, when servant to a man who was haughty and overbearing, both Agrippa and his master attended the same church, to listen to a discourse from a distinguished mulatto preacher [Lemuel Haynes?] . . . the gentleman said to Agrippa, 'Well, how do you like nigger preaching?' 'Sir,' he promptly retorted, 'he was half black and half white; I like *my* half, how did you like *yours?*' "

A Muster of Brave Soldiers and Sailors

After the fireworks were over on July 4, 1847, John Greenleaf Whittier, poet laureate of antislavery, was moved to right a historic wrong. The result was a lead editorial in the *National Era* entitled "The Black Men of the Revolution of 1776 and the War of 1812." "The return of the Festival of our National Independence," Whittier began, "has called our attention to a matter which has been very carefully kept out of sight by orators and toast-drinkers. We allude to the participation of colored men in the great struggle for Freedom." As a pacifist Quaker, he had no desire "to eulogize the shedders of blood, even in a cause of acknowledged justice," but

> when we see a whole nation doing honor to the memories of one class of its defenders, to the total neglect of another class, who had the misfortune to be of darker complexion, we can-

not forego the satisfaction of inviting notice to certain historical facts, which for the last half century have been quietly elbowed aside. . . . Of the services and sufferings of the colored soldiers of the Revolution, no attempt has, to our knowledge been made to preserve a record. They have had no historian. With here and there an exception, they all passed away, and only some faint tradition of their campaigns under Washington, and Greene, and Lafayette, and of their cruisings under Decatur and Barry, lingers among their descendants. Yet enough is known to show that the free colored men of the United States bore their full proportion of the sacrifices and trials of the Revolutionary war.

THE faces of William Lee, Agrippa Hull, and James Lafayette have come down to us in paint because they were closely and valuably linked with famous generals. Such portraits are rare. The thousands of black rank and file who fought on the patriot side—who marched, sailed, spied, piloted, scouted—remain almost invisible, often nameless, except as we can feebly try to reconstruct their reality from a few, sometimes grudging, words scattered here and there in the meager (where black is concerned) records of the time. As Benjamin Quarles puts it, "The typical Negro soldier was a private, consigned as if by caste, to the rank and file. Even more than other privates, he tended to lack identity. Often he bore no specific name. . . ."

On board the Connecticut warship *General Putnam* were at least five black crewmen: Joseph Colly, Cato Jones, Cesar Landon, Cesar Sabens, and Cuff, the cook. When, in March 1781, Maryland needed ships, a tidewater patriot replied to the plea of the Council that he would send "his

35. Unknown artist, *Revolutionary War Sailor,* oil, ca. 1780. Collection of Alexander A. McBurney, Kingston, Rhode Island.

schooner Cheerfully," but with "a Negro Skipper, as no white man would go." We would like to know more about this fearless black skipper even as we understand more clearly why General Washington, two years earlier, had written to Major Henry Lee: "I have granted a Warrant for the 1000 Dolls. promised the Negro pilots. . . ." The vigorous portraits of two nameless seamen have survived to attest to the reality of the black presence in the revolutionary navy [figs. 35 and 36].

36. Unknown artist, *Portrait of a Black Sailor,* oil, ca. 1790. Privately owned.

In John Marshall's *Life of George Wash-ington* there is a description of an episode in which General Daniel Morgan, outnum-bered, routed the British dragoons under Tarleton. Lieutenant Colonel William

Washington, leader of the patriot cavalry and a relative of General Washington, was about to be cut down by a British sword "when a waiter, too small to wield a sword, saved him by wounding the officer with a

37. William Ranney, *The Battle of Cowpens*, oil, 1845. Frederick Donhauser, Stony River, Alaska.

ball from a pistol." In 1845 William Ranney painted the scene, perhaps out of Marshall, perhaps from tradition, with the youth as a bugler [fig. 37]. The Continental Congress awarded General Morgan a gold plaque for his triumph at Cowpens, but we do not even know the name of the brave black lad rendered so vigorously by the imagination of the artist.

Sometimes the record has the laconic eloquence of an epitaph: "Zechery Prince now ded, Recd his freedom"—so reads a brief line on a payroll of Simsbury, Connecticut, troops in the spring of 1779 [fig. 38]. In the log of the ship-of-war *Ranger,* at anchor in Charleston harbor on February 25, 1780, there is this entry: "at 10 this Night a Negro Called Cesar Hodgsdon died." But who *was* Zechery Prince [fig. 39]? And who *was* Cesar Hodgsdon? We grope for the man

and have to be content with a phrase. Here is a cluster of vignettes, short and long, randomly assembled, which, read together as a collective profile, furnish a sketchy portrait of a sizable group of black soldiers and seamen of the revolution.

Garshom Prince

The biblical name Gershom refers to the son of Moses and his wife Zipporah, daughter of Jethro, who tradition records was black. The revolutionary soldier Garshom Prince was born around 1733 in Rhode Island or Connecticut, slave or servant of Captain Robert Durkee, with whom he fought in the French and Indian War and in the revolution. At Quebec he made himself a powder horn. Later, in the Battle of Wyoming, Pennsylvania, in 1778, he lost his life. The horn was taken from his lifeless

38. Excerpt from payroll of Simsbury, Connecticut, soldiers in the Continental Army, April 10, 1779. Connecticut State Library.

39. Logbook of U.S. ship of war *Ranger,* February 25, 1780. National Archives, Washington, D.C.

body on the field. Carved with sketches of houses and ships, it bore the inscriptions: "GARSHOM PRINCE his horn made at Crown Point Septm. ye 3rd day 1761" and "PRINCE NEGRO HIS HORNM" [fig. 40].

Harry, Cupid, Aberdeen

The armed schooner *Liberty* in the navy of Virginia, commanded by Captain James Barron (later to be Commodore Barron, senior officer of the United States Navy), fought twenty sharp actions during the war. When in his old age the commodore put down his memories of the *Liberty,* he wrote of the "courageous patriots who had served on board of her during the war. Amongst these, I take pleasure in stating there were several coloured men, who, I think, in justice to their merits should not be forgotten. Harry (a slave, belonging to Captain John Cooper) was distinguished for his zeal and

daring; Cupid (a slave of Mr. William Ballard) stood forth on all occasions as the champion of liberty, and discharged all his duties with a fidelity that made him a favorite of all the officers. It is well known, indeed, in Virginia, that many of the African race were zealous and faithful soldiers in the cause of freedom, and one of them, in particular, named Aberdeen, distinguished himself so much as to attract the notice of many of our first officers and citizens, and among them, of Patrick Henry, who befriended him as long as he lived." In 1783, in its "Act directing the Emancipation of certain Slaves who have served as Soldiers," the Virginia General Assembly freed Aberdeen, who had "labored a number of years in the public service at the lead mines. . . ."

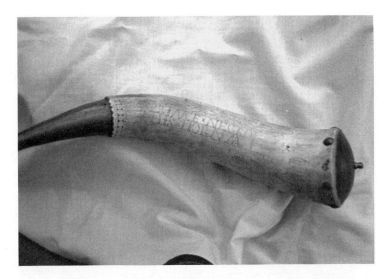

40. Garshom Prince, powder horn, 1761. Wyoming Historical and Geological Society, Wilkes-Barre, Pennsylvania.

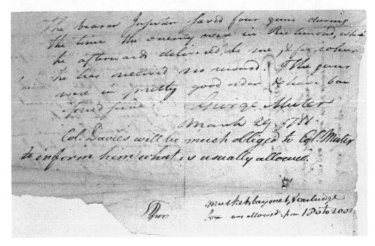

41. Office of the Governor. Letters Received by the Executive Colonel George Mutter to Governor Thomas Jefferson, March 29, 1781. Archives Branch, Virginia State Library and Archives, Richmond.

Jupiter

On a fading scrap of paper, miraculously preserved, a Virginia colonel by the name of George Muter certifies on March 29, 1781, that "Jupiter (negro) saved four guns during the time the enemy were in Richmond, which he afterwards delivered to me & for which he has received no reward" [fig. 41].

Antigua

In March 1783 a slave by this name was lauded by the General Assembly of South Carolina for his skill in "procuring information of the enemy's movements and de-

signs." He "always executed the commissions with which he was entrusted with diligence and fidelity, and obtained very considerable and important information, from within the enemy's lines, frequently at the risk of his life." To reward him, the assembly liberated his "wife named Hagar, and her child" [fig. 42]. Presumably Antigua remained a slave.

Prince Whipple

There are two well-known paintings that depict the crossing of the Delaware on that wintry Christmas Eve in 1776. The earlier

AN ORDINANCE for enfranchising a Negro Woman and her No. 1168. Child, late the property of Mr. John Smyth.

WHEREAS, a negro man named Antigua, a slave, lately belonging to Mr. John Harleston, deceased, was employed for the purposes of procuring information of the enemy's movements and designs, by John Rutledge, Esq. late Governor of this State; and whereas, the said negro man, Antigua, always executed the commissions with which he was entrusted with diligence and fidelity, and obtained very considerable and important information, from within the enemy's lines, frequently at the risk of his life; and whereas, it is but just and reasonable that the said negro man, Antigua, should receive some reward for the services which he has performed for the State; Preamble.

I. *Be it therefore ordained*, by the honorable the Senate and House of Representatives, in General Assembly met, and by the authority of the same, That the said Antigua's wife, named Hagar, and her child, both lately belonging to Mr. John Smyth, shall, forever hereafter, be deemed and taken as free persons; and they shall be, and are hereby, enfranchised and forever delivered and discharged from the yoke of slavery, to all intents and purposes whatsoever; any law, usage or custom to the contrary thereof in any wise notwithstanding. Ordained that Hagar and her child be forever enfranchised.

II. *And be it further ordained* by the authority aforesaid, That this ordinance shall be deemed a public ordinance, and all courts in this State are to take notice of the same, without special pleading. This a public ordinance.

In the Senate House, the twelfth day of March, in the year of our Lord one thousand seven hundred and eighty-three, and in the seventh year of the independence of the United States of America.

JOHN LLOYD, *President of the Senate.*
HUGH RUTLEDGE, *Speaker of the House of Representatives.*

42. Thomas Cooper, ed., *The Statutes at Large of South Carolina* (Columbia, 1838), 4:545. Courtesy of the Library of Congress.

of the two, a huge canvas, was painted by Thomas Sully in 1819 for the state of South Carolina. It shows Washington astride a mettlesome white horse on a snowy riverbank attended by four mounted men, three of them white officers, the fourth a young black soldier [fig. 43]. The other, more familiar, picture, painted by Emanuel Gottlieb Leutze in 1851, shows the general standing in a rowboat moving through the ice. One of the oarsmen is black. According to a tradition there seems no reason to question (and first put into print by Nell in 1851) the black trooper who crossed the river with Washington and who is thus depicted by Sully and Leutze is Prince Whipple, "body-guard to Gen. Whipple, of New Hampshire, who was Aid to General Washington" [fig. 44].

Nell recounts something of Whipple's life: "Prince Whipple was born at Amabou, Africa, of comparatively wealthy parents. When about ten years of age, he was sent by them, in company with a cousin, to America, to be educated. An elder brother had returned four years before, and his parents

were anxious that their child should receive the same benefits. The captain who brought the two boys over proved a treacherous villain, and carried them to Baltimore, where he exposed them for sale, and they were both purchased by Portsmouth men, Prince falling to Gen. Whipple. He was emancipated during the war, was much esteemed, and was once entrusted by the General with a large sum of money to carry from Salem to Portsmouth. He was attacked on the road, near Newburyport, by two ruffians; one he struck with a loaded whip, the other he shot. . . . Prince was beloved by all who knew him. He was the 'Caleb Quotem' of Portsmouth, where he died at the age of thirty-two, leaving a widow and children."

James Forten

Friend of Richard Allen, Absalom Jones, Paul Cuffe, and William Lloyd Garrison, this founding father of abolitionism [fig. 45] was born free in 1766 in Philadelphia, where he briefly attended the school of the antislavery Quaker Anthony Benezet. When he was fifteen he enlisted as

43. J. N. Gimi, *Washington Crossing the Delaware,* engraving, after painting by Thomas Sully, 1819. Courtesy of the Library of Congress.

a powder boy on the *Royal Louis,* a privateer commanded by Stephen Decatur, Sr., with a crew of two hundred, twenty of whom were black. Its first action was a bloody affair for both sides, but the English brig-of-war struck its colors. On the next cruise, the heavily armed English frigate *Amphyon,* supported by two other warships, forced Decatur to surrender. It was a bad moment for young Forten. Black prisoners were rarely exchanged; usually the British sold them in the West Indies.

But Forten was lucky. On board the *Amphyon* the captain's son, a lad of the same age, took a fancy to him, was astounded at his skill at marbles, and persuaded his father to offer Forten the life of an aristocrat in England. "No, No!" Forten said he replied, "I am here a prisoner for the liberties of my country; I never, never, shall prove a traitor to her interests!" Instead of the West Indies, he was shipped off to the prison ship *Jersey,* anchored off Long Island. "Thus," he later observed, "did a game of marbles save me from a life of West Indian servitude."

Aboard the *Jersey,* he sometimes doubted his luck as the days slowly passed. A thousand prisoners crowded her foul hold; ten thousand died miserably during the war in the rotten old hulk. Nell records a noble deed, later attested by its beneficiary: "An officer . . . was about to be exchanged for a British prisoner, when the thoughtful mind of Forten conceived the idea of an easy escape for himself in the officer's chest; but . . . a fellow-prisoner, a youth, his junior in years . . . was thought of. . . . the offer was accepted, and Forten had the

44. Paul Girardet, *Washington Crossing the Delaware,* engraving after Emanuel Leutze's painting, 1851. Miriam and D. Wallach Division of Art, Prints and Photographs, New York Public Library, Astor, Lenox and Tilden Foundations.

satisfaction of assisting in taking down the 'chest of old clothes' . . . from the side of the prison ship." The rescued youth grew up to become a captain in the navy.

After seven months in the floating hell, he was released in a general exchange of prisoners and walked home to Philadelphia.

James Forten would go on to a long and distinguished career. During the next half century, he would make his mark on the times as inventor, manufacturer, philanthropist, and organizer of protest. He was always fond of recalling his youth. In 1833, nearing sixty, he said: "My great grandfather was brought to this country as a slave from Africa. My grandfather obtained his own freedom. My father never wore the yoke. He rendered valuable service to his country in the war of our Revolution; and I, though then a boy, was a drummer in that war. I was taken prisoner, and was made to suffer not a little on board the *Jersey* prison-ship."

Oliver Cromwell

When this black veteran reached his hundredth year during the spring of 1852, the *Burlington* [New Jersey] *Gazette* carried the following story:

The attention of many of our citizens has, doubtless, been arrested by the appearance of an old colored man, who might have been seen, sitting in front of his residence, in East Union Street, respectfully raising his hat to those who might be passing by. His attenuated frame, his silvered head, his feeble movements, combine to prove that he was very aged; and yet, comparatively few are aware that he is among the survivors of the gallant army who fought for the liberties of our country "in the days which tried men's souls."

On Monday last, we stopped to speak to him, and asked him how old

45. Unknown artist, *James Forten* [?], watercolor. The Historical Society of Pennsylvania.

he was. He asked the day of the month, and . . . replied with trembling lips, "I am very old—I am a hundred years old today."

His name is Oliver Cromwell. . . . He enlisted in a company commanded by Capt. Lowery, attached to the Second New Jersey Regiment, under the command of Col. Israel Shreve. He was at the battles of Trenton, Princeton, Brandywine, Monmouth, and Yorktown, at which latter place, he told us, he saw the last man killed. Although his faculties are failing, yet he relates many interesting reminiscences of the Revolution. He was with the army at the retreat of the Delaware, on the memorable crossing of the 25th of December, 1776, and relates the story of the battles of the succeeding days with enthusiasm. He gives the details of the march from Trenton to Princeton, and told us, with much humor, that they "knocked the British about lively" at the latter place. . . .

Cromwell, who had been "brought up a farmer," joined up in his early twenties and served for six years and nine months under the immediate command of Washington. His discharge, said Dr. James McCune Smith, the eminent New York abolitionist, "at the close of the war, was in Washington's own hand-writing, of which he was very proud, often speaking of it" [fig. 46]. When Cromwell died in January 1853, he had seen his grandchildren to the third generation.

George Latchom

In 1781 the British landed at Henry's Point in Virginia where they were met by the militia under Colonel John Cropper. In this engagement, George Latchom, still a

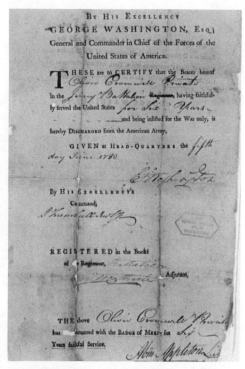

46. Honorable discharge with Badge of Merit of Oliver Cromwell, private, June 5, 1783. National Archives, Washington, D.C.

slave, played a heroic role. The colonel's biographer has preserved the details:

During the fight the militia retreated, leaving Cropper and a negro named George Latchom, who were in advance of the rest, engaged actively with the invaders. These two kept up the firing, until the foe were within a few rods of them, when they were compelled to fall back. Cropper had to retreat through a sunken, boggy marsh, in which he stuck fast up to the waist in soft mud, the enemy at the time being so close as to prepare to bayonet him.

At this critical juncture the faithful colored man fired and killed the foremost man, and seized hold of Cropper and dragged him by main strength out of the mud, and taking him on his back, carried him safely to dry land. This required great strength upon his part, Cropper weighing in the neighborhood of two hundred pounds.

Cropper thereupon bought Latchom from his owner, set him free, and "befriended him in every way he could, as an evidence of his gratitude, till Latchom's death."

Black Samson

In the folklore of Delaware there is preserved the figure of a black patriot, unlisted on any muster role, who fought well at the Battle of Brandywine in September 1777. As the story is told, he had witnessed near Chadds Ford the brutal murder by British troops of a white man who had befriended him, and in "the fight at Brandywine next day, Black Samson, a giant Negro, armed with a scythe, swept his way through the red ranks like a sable figure of Time." His schoolmaster friend "had taught him; his daughter had given him food. It is to avenge them that he is fighting." Over a century later, the black poet Paul Laurence Dunbar would be moved by the legend to put it into verse:

> Straight through the human harvest,
>   Cutting a bloody swath,
> Woe to you, soldier of Briton!
>   Death is abroad in his path.
> Flee from the scythe of the reaper,
>   Flee while the moment is thine,
> None may with safety withstand him,
>   Black Samson of Brandywine.

Edward Hector

Another black hero of the Battle of Brandywine was an artilleryman, Edward Hector, thirty-three years old, a private in Captain Hercules Courtney's company, Third Pennsylvania Artillery of the Continental Line. He died in 1834, a no-

nagenarian. The *Free Press* of Norristown carried his obituary:

> Edward Hector, a colored man and a veteran of the Revolution. Obscurity in life and oblivion in death, is too often the lot of the worthy—they pass away, and no "storied stone" perpetuates the remembrance of their noble actions. . . . During the war of the revolution, his conduct, on one memorable occasion, exhibited an example of patriotism and bravery which deserves to be recorded. At the battle of Brandywine he had charge of an ammunition wagon, attached to Col. Proctor's regiment, and when the American army was obliged to retreat, an order was given . . . to abandon them to the enemy. . . . The heroic reply of the deceased was uttered in the true spirit of the revolution: "The enemy shall not have my team; I will save my horses, or perish myself!" He instantly started on his way, and as he proceeded, amid the confusion of the surrounding scene, he calmly gathered up . . . a few stands of arms which had been left on the field by retreating soldiers, and safely retired with wagon, team and all, in the face of the victorious foe. Some years ago a few benevolent individuals endeavored to procure him a pension, but without success. The Legislature of Pennsylvania, however, at the last session, granted him a donation of $40.00, which was all the gratuity he ever received for his Revolutionary services. . . .

Enough to bury Edward Hector.

Lambert Latham and Jordan Freeman

On Groton Heights, across the Thames from New London, the state of Connecticut in 1830 erected a granite shaft "in memory of the brave patriots who fell in the massacre at Fort Griswold near this spot on the 6th of September, A.D. 1781, when the British under the command of the traitor Benedict Arnold, burnt the towns of New London & Groton." On that shaft, inscribed on a marble tablet, are the names of the eighty-four patriots slain that day; at the top is the name of Lieutenant Colonel William Ledyard, their commander; at the bottom, segregated by the label "Colored men," are the names of Sambo Latham and Jordan Freeman. On the day the shaft was dedicated a black man in the crowd, William Anderson of New London, recollecting what "two veterans who were present at the battle" had told him of the event, reflected somewhat bitterly on the inscription: "One of these men was the brother of my grandmother, by the name of Lambert, but called Lambo,—since chiselled on the marble monument by the American classic appellation of 'Sambo'" [fig. 47].*

Lambert worked for a farmer named Latham and when the alarm came the two men were out in a field taking care of the cattle. The assault by the British was a deadly one: "Finally, the little garrison was overcome, and, on the entrance of the enemy, the British officer inquired, 'Who commands this fort?' The gallant Ledyard replied, 'I once did; you do now,'—at the

same time handing his sword, which was immediately run through his body to the hilt. . . . Lambert, being near Col. Ledyard when he was slain, retaliated upon the officer by thrusting his bayonet through his body. Lambert, in return, received from the enemy *thirty-three bayonet* wounds, and thus fell, nobly avenging the death of his commander." According to a tradition in the Latham family, "Lambo fought manfully by his master's side up to the time he was slain. In the hottest of the conflict he stood near his master, loading and discharging his musket with great rapidity, even after he had been severely wounded in one of his hands."

On that same day, an eyewitness recalled, the British commander of the assault, Major Montgomery, as he scaled a wall of the fort, "was killed by spears in the hands of Captain Shapley and a black man named Jordan Freeman," who was Colonel Ledyard's orderly.

Jack Sisson

Reports of the derring-do capture of British Major General Richard Prescott at his headquarters near Newport, Rhode Island, in July 1777 by a patriot team of commandos soon got into song and ballad. In the annals of the time, the black volunteer who played an important part in this caper goes by several names—Jack or Tack Sisson, and Prince. (He would later enlist for the duration as a private in Colonel Christopher Greene's First Rhode Island battalion.) Lieutenant Colonel Barton, states one of the earliest newspaper reports of the event, "selected and engaged about forty men to go with him on a secret expedition, by water in five batteaus . . . he told them his design, acknowledged it was hazardous. . . . If any of them were unwilling to engage in the enterprize, they were then at full liberty to decline it. . . . On putting the matter to their

---

*Parker Pillsbury, the New Hampshire abolitionist, wrote to Nell in 1855 about "the two brave men of color" who fell with Ledyard: "All the names of the slain, at that time, are inscribed on a marble tablet, wrought into the monument—*the names of the colored soldiers last,*—and not only last, but a blank space is left between them and the whites; in genuine keeping with the "Negro Pew" distinction—setting them not only below others, but by themselves, even after that. And it is difficult to say why. They were not the last in the fight. . . . And the name of Jordan Freeman stands away down, last on the list of heroes—perhaps the greatest hero of them all."

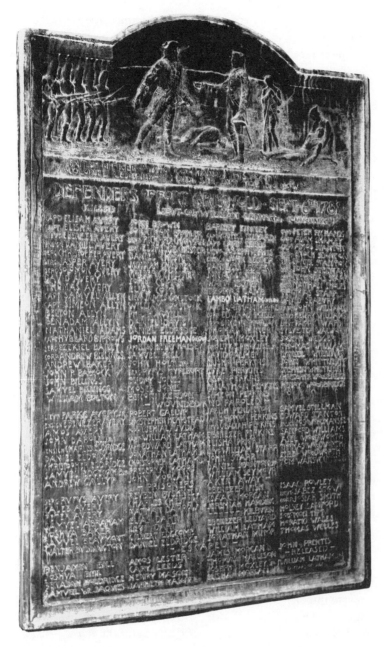

47. Tablet at Old Fort Griswold, Groton, Connecticut. Fort Griswold State Park.

choice, they unanimously resolved to go with him, and told him to lead them on to honor. They then set off with muffled oars on a dark night. . . ." With Sisson as one of the boat steerers, they "passed the enemy's forts," slipped through his "ships of war," and landed near Prescott's headquarters. "The col. went foremost, with a stout active Negro, close behind him, and another at a small distance. . . ." Barton and Sisson made short work of the single sentinel at the door. With "the rest of the men surrounding the house, the Negro, with his head, at the second stroke, forced a passage into it, and then into the general's chamber . . . the colonel calling the general by name, told him he was a prisoner, he replied he knew it, and rising from his bed desired time to put on his clothes. The colonel told him to put on his breeches. . . ."

Legend has it that not long after Prescott's exchange for the American general Charles Lee, he was dining aboard the British admiral's ship off Newport and called for a song by a Yankee lad, a prisoner, thirteen years old. The ballad he sang was allegedly composed by a Newport sailor.

> A tawney son of Afric's race
>   Them through the ravine led,
> And entering then the Overing
>   house,
>   They found him in his bed.
>
> But to get in they had no means
>   Except poor Cuffee's head,
> Who beat the door down, then
>   rushed in,
>   And seized him in his bed.
>
> Stop, let me put my breeches on,
>   The general then did pray.
> Your breeches, massa, I will take,
>   For dress we cannot stay.

Catherine Williams, the biographer of Colonel Barton, wrote down a dozen years after Sisson's death her memory of him in his last years. Through her genteel racism one can glimpse the old veteran: "A black servant of the Colonel . . . a faithful attendant and shrewd fellow, and one who, in his own opinion at least, formed a very important personage in the expedition . . . he continued to regret to the day of his death, that his name had never appeared in any account of the transaction. After the capture of Prescott, [Jack] was made a drummer. . . . He was remarkably small. . . . On all public days he usually made his appearance on the parade ground, dressed in complete uniform, and his appearance was a perfect holiday to all the little urchins about

street, who would immediately crowd around, to listen to his stories, and hear him in his cracked voice sing the old Ballad, beginning 'Brave Barton.' "

The *Providence Gazette* of November 3, 1821, published his obituary: "In Plymouth (Mass.) . . . a negro man, aged about 78 years. He was one of the forty brave volunteers. . . ."

Quaco

During the British occupation of Newport, Quaco's Tory master sold him to a colonel in the king's army. Quaco fled to the patriot line with valuable information. In January 1782 the General Assembly of Rhode Island, in recognition that "the information he then gave, render[ed] great and essential service to this state and the public in general," declared him "a freeman."

Pompey Lamb

The brilliance of "Mad" Anthony Wayne in his assault at Stony Point on the Hudson in 1779 is well known. The legend of Pompey, slave of Captain Lamb, who guided Wayne's troops and made the assault possible has faded away—even though Washington Irving in his *Life of George Washington* singled out Pompey Lamb for praise:

> About eight in the evening, they arrived within a mile and a half of the forts, without being discovered. Not a dog barked to give the alarm—all the dogs in the neighborhood had been privately destroyed beforehand. About half-past eleven, the whole moved forward, guided by a negro of the neighborhood who had frequently carried fruit to the garrison, and served the Americans as a spy. He led the way, accompanied by two stout

men disguised as farmers. The countersign was given to the first sentinel. . . . While the negro talked with him, the men seized and gagged him. . . .

Saul Matthews

As spy and guide, this slave proved himself of inestimable value. In 1781 Josiah Parker, colonel of the Virginia militia, said that he "deserved the applause of his country." Luther P. Jackson, historian of the black soldier in revolutionary Virginia, has sketched Saul's career at the front:

This slave of Thomas Matthews "shouldered his musket" and went over to the American side in the early months of the war . . . in 1781 during the campaign of the British in the vicinity of Portsmouth, Saul, at the risk of his life, was sent into the British garrison. . . . He brought back military secrets of such value to Colonel Parker that on the same night, serving as a guide, he led a party of Americans to the British garrison. . . . On another occasion in 1781, when Saul's master and many other Virginians had fled into the adjoining state of North Carolina, he was sent by them to Norfolk to secure similar intelligence concerning the movement and plans of the British troops. For his services as a spy and a soldier such distinguished army officers as Baron von Steuben, Lafayette, Peter Muhlenburg, and General Nathaniel Greene praised him to the highest.

After the war Saul's master changed, but he continued to labor as a slave. In 1792 he petitioned the Virginia legislature for his freedom and in November of that year, "in consideration of many very essential services rendered to this Commonwealth during the late war," he was granted his "full liberty and freedom . . . as if he had been born free."

Austin Dabney

Patriots in Georgia were wary of arming their slaves. Only a few instances have turned up of the emancipation of black veterans for their service in the war. David Monday was one emancipated soldier; Georgia paid his owner 100 guineas and freed him.

Another was Austin Dabney. In the Battle of Kettle Creek early in 1779, "the hardest ever fought in Georgia," Dabney, an artilleryman who had been given his freedom in order to serve in his master's place, fought in Colonel Elijah Clark's corps. "No soldier under Clark," wrote a former governor of Georgia in 1855, "was braver, or did better service during the revolutionary struggle." Shot in the thigh, Dabney was rescued and nursed back to health by a white soldier named Harris. In gratitude, Dabney worked for the Harris family; out of his own pocket he sent his rescuer's eldest son through college and then arranged for his legal training.

Although Dabney was a pensioner, because he was black he was denied a chance in the lottery for land open to revolutionary veterans in 1819. When the legislature finally granted him 112 acres for his "bravery and fortitude" in "several engagements and actions," a group of whites in Madison County protested the award, claiming "it was an indignity to white men, for a mulatto to be put upon an equality with them in the distribution of the public land" [fig. 48].

Austin Dabney existed gingerly, a friend of a few upper-class white veterans of the

48. Land grant to Austin Dabney. *Acts of the General Assembly of the State of Georgia* (Milledgeville, Georgia, 1821).

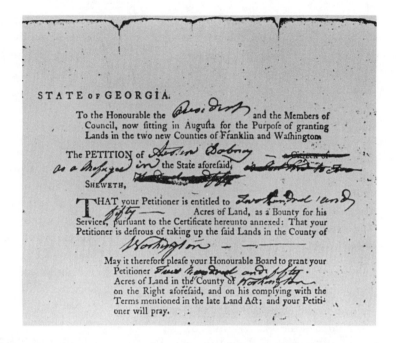

revolution. "He owned fine horses, attended the racecourse, entered the list for the stake. . . ." In his old age, in "the evening after the adjournment of the court in Danielsville, he usually went into the room occupied by the judges and the lawyers, where, taking a low seat, he listened to what was said, or himself told of the struggles between the Whigs and the Tories in upper Georgia and South Carolina. His memory was retentive, his understanding good, and he described what he knew well."

Caesar Tarrant

For four years, Caesar, a slave in the Tarrant family of Hampton, Virginia, served in the state's navy as a pilot on the armed *Patriot,* steering the vessel in its most important engagement south of the Virginia capes. Throughout the action, he "behaved gallantly." Other black seamen on the *Patriot* were David Baker, Jack Knight, Mark Starlins, Pluto, and Cuffee. The last, a pilot, died from injuries received in service. Tarrant was aboard the *Patriot* when she cap-

tured the *Fanny* on its way to Boston with supplies for the British.

In 1789 the Virginia legislature set Caesar Tarrant free, because he had "entered very early into the service of his country, and continued to pilot the armed vessels of this state during the late war." During the next half dozen years, the ex-slave and veteran bought several pieces of property in Hampton, and in 1796, when he died, willed houses and lots to his "loving wife." Thirty-five years later, the government granted to his daughter Nancy, 2,666 acres of land in Ohio in recognition of her father's crucial part in the operations of the Virginia navy.

Jude Hall

Nell tells the story of a black who enlisted for the war as a private in the Second Battalion of New Hampshire troops, commanded by Colonel Nathan Hale: "Jude Hall was born at Exeter. . . . He served faithfully eight years, and fought in most all the battles, beginning at Bunker Hill. He was called a great soldier, and was known in New Hampshire to the day of his death by the name of 'Old Rock.' " Nell goes on to relate the history of Jude Hall's family: "Singular to relate, three of his sons have been kidnapped at different times, and reduced to slavery. James was put on board a New Orleans vessel; Aaron was stolen from Providence, in 1807; William went to sea in the bark *Hannibal,* from Newburyport, and was sold in the West Indies, from whence he escaped after ten years of slavery, and sailed as captain of a collier from Newcastle to London."

Titus

Not exactly a brave soldier, but an interesting person. Hundreds of black seamen served on patriot privateers. Titus, of Salem, Massachusetts, served as a business agent for the privateers and he did well in his job according to the entry of August 13, 1781, in the diary of William Pynchon: "Fair and cool. News that Mrs. Fairfield's son died in the prison ship at New York. Three more privateers are taken. . . . Mrs. Cabot makes her will; in it gives Titus, her negro, £40 and his freedom in case he shall continue in her service henceforth till her death. Titus cares not, as he gets money apace, being one of the agents for some of the privateersmen, and wears cloth shoes, ruffled shirts, silk breeches and stockings, and dances minuets at Commencement; it is said he has made more profits as agent than Mr. Ansil Alcock. . . ."

Minny

The short and simple annals of the brave—and black. Scene: Convention of Delegates of Virginia, Saturday, June 15, 1776. Business: "A petition of Lucretia Pritchett . . . setting forth that in a late attack on a piratical [British] tender in Rappahannock river, Minny, a negro man . . .

voluntarily entered himself on board a vessel commanded by Mr. Hugh Walker, and being used to the water, and a good pilot, bravely and successfully exerted himself against the enemy, until he was unfortunately killed, whereby the estate of the said Joseph Pritchett was deprived of a valuable slave . . . since the said slave was lost by means of a meritorious act, in defence of the country, she [asks to be reimbursed] the value thereof." Two weeks later, the Virginia delegates awarded Lucretia Pritchett one hundred dollars for the death of her slave Minny.

"Captain" Mark Starlins

Another reminiscence of Commodore James Barron in his old age is all there is to furnish a glimpse into the life of the black Virginia pilot, Mark Starlins, who called himself "Captain." The commodore remembered "a very singular and meritorious character in the person of an African, who had been brought over to this country when he was young, and soon evinced a remarkable attachment to it; he was brought up as a pilot, and proved a skilful one, and a devoted patriot," who sometimes "allowed his patriotism to get the better of his judgment." The "noble African," wrote Barron, "lived and died a slave soon after the peace, and just before a law was passed that gave freedom to all those devoted men of colour who had so zealously volunteered their services in the patriotic cause." Starlins was held in high estimation "by all worthy citizens, and, more particularly, by all the navy officers of the State."

John Peterson

As he begins his tale of the capture of the British spy Major André, Nell relates that Peterson (like James Forten) was a prisoner in the "notorious Prison Ship" at New York, until one dark night he tied a bundle of clothes on his head, crept down the anchor chains, and slipped into the water. But Nell's main concern is the way in which the black private has been omitted in the usual accounts of the André affair, and he reprints from the Westchester *Herald* the long obituary, which, he suggests, is "worthy of republication a hundred times. . . ." Here is the obituary, somewhat reduced:

John Peterson, a colored man (mulatto) departed this life October 2d, at his late residence in the village of Peekskill, aged 103 years. Peterson was brought up in the family of . . . Isaac Sherwood [who] had entered the Continental army, as a first lieutenant, and Peterson . . . begged the privilege of accompanying him into the service. . . .

This regiment was in the memorable battle of Stillwater, in Saratoga county, at the time Gen. Burgoyne surrendered his whole army. . . . Lieut. Sherwood, who always sought the post of danger, received in the action a mortal wound. Peterson watched over this brave officer with untiring perseverance, night and day, until he expired, and after his death, followed his remains to the public burying-ground in the city of Albany. . . . The devoted attachment of Peterson to the gallant and much-lamented lieutenant was observed by Col. Van Cortlandt, who, without solicitation, gave him his discharge from the service, to enable him to return home with the effects which belonged to the lieutenant. . . .

On the morning of the 21st of September, 1780, Moses Sherwood and Peterson were engaged in making cider, at Barrett's farm, in Cortlandt. . . . they had taken their arms with them. . . . It was on that day that the Vulture sloop-of-war came to anchor . . . having brought up André for the purpose of holding an interview with the traitor Arnold. . . . [Moses Sherwood] saw a barge filled with armed men from the Vulture, in company with a gun-boat, approaching the shore . . . whereupon they seized their guns and . . . concealed themselves behind some rocks, and as the barge came sweeping along towards the place where they were lying, Peterson fired. His aim had been well directed, for an oar was seen to drop from the hands of one of the men on board, and much confusion was observed among them. A second shot from Sherwood compelled them to return to the Vulture, which they did under cover of canister and grapeshot from the gun-boat. . . . Many [armed townsmen] now hastened to the end of Teller's Point with a field-piece. . . . They erected a small redoubt, and opened a well-directed fire on the Vulture, and she fired in return several broadsides directed towards the redoubt.

André . . . saw from his window the Vulture slip her cable and make sail for New York. This circumstance prevented him from returning to the city by water . . . which led to his capture at Tarrytown. But for the firing of Peterson and Sherwood upon the barge, it is more than probable he would have returned to the Vulture in safety.

Peterson received a pension from the United States for his military services, and General Philip Van Cortlandt gave him a house and lot in Cortlandt town, where he lived until he moved to Peekskill. "He retained through a long life" his obituary concludes, "the character of an honest man and a faithful soldier, and was much esteemed by all who knew him."

Jehu Grant

In 1832, when he was almost eighty, a black veteran living in Connecticut wrote to the War Department claiming a federal pension. His name was Jehu Grant. His initial letter of application and a second letter buttressing his claim reveal not only his life in the army as a wagoner and waiter but also his frustration when he was refused a pension—for an incredible reason:

> he was a slave to Elihu Champlen who resided at Narragansett, Rhode Island. At the time he left him, his master was called a Tory and in a secret manner furnished the enemy when shipping lay nearby with sheep, cattle, cheese, etc., and received goods from them. And this applicant being afraid his master would send him to the British ships, ran away sometime in August 1777 . . . he went right to Danbury and enlisted . . . was put to teaming with a team of horses and wagon, drawing provisions and various other loading for the army for three or four months until winter set in, then was taken as a servant to John Skidmore, wagon master general, and served with him until spring, when the troops went to the Highlands . . . on the Hudson River, a little above the British lines . . . sometime in June, when his master either sent or came, this applicant was given up to his master again, and he returned. . . .

In 1834, two years later, proslavery bureaucrats in the Pension Office in Wash-

ington rejected Jehu Grant's claim. Their reason? During his time of service in the patriot army he had in fact been a fugitive slave! It took old Grant another two years to recover from the rebuff. In 1836, in an angry, ironic reply signed with his mark, he wrote to the Commissioner of Pensions:

> In April 1834 I received a writing from Your Honor, informing me that my "services while a fugitive from my master's service was not embraced in the Pension Act of June 1832," and that my "papers were placed on file." . . . I now pray that I may be permitted to express my feelings more fully. . . .
>
> I was then grown to manhood, in the full vigor and strength of life. . . . when I saw liberty poles and the people all engaged for the support of freedom, I could not but like and be pleased with such thing (God forgive me if I sinned in so feeling). And living on the borders of Rhode Island, where whole companies of colored people enlisted, it added to my fears and dread of being sold to the British. These considerations induced me to enlist into the American army, where I served faithful about ten months, when my master found and took me home. Had I been taught to read or understand the precepts of the Gospel, "Servants, obey your masters," I might have done otherwise, notwithstanding the songs of liberty that saluted my ear, thrilled through my heart. But feeling conscious that I have since compensated my master for the injury he sustained by my enlisting, and that God has forgiven me for so doing, and that I served my country faithfully, and that they having enjoyed

the benefits of my service . . . I cannot but feel it becoming me to pray
Your Honor to review my declaration. . . .

 . . . I must be upward of eighty
years of age and have been blind for
many years, and, notwithstanding
the aid I received from the honest industry of my children, we are still
very needy and in part are supported
from the benevolence of our
friends. . . . I humbly set my claim
upon the well-known liberality of
government.

Perhaps Jehu Grant died soon after he sent
off this letter. Whether he ever got his pension is not known.

Three Black Units

There were two all-black units in the Continental Army; a third unit voyaged from
Haiti with the French. Colonel Christopher
Greene's First Rhode Island Regiment distinguished itself for efficiency and gallantry
throughout the war—perhaps the war
would have ended sooner if its example had
been heeded. Little is known about the
Bucks of America, a Massachusetts company, except that John Hancock chose it for
special honor. The Black Brigade of Saint
Domingue, Haiti, in this day of Pan-African aspiration, needs to be better known.*

THE Black Regiment of Rhode Island came
into being because that state was not able to
supply its quota of white troops to the Continental Line—and because blacks wanted
to fight for their own freedom. The ra-
tionale of the decision to create this unit is
of some interest. Since history had supplied
"frequent precedents of the wisest, the
freest, and bravest nations having liberated
their slaves, and enlisted them as soldiers to
fight in defence of their country," and since
the British had "taken possession of the capital, and of a greater part" of the state, it
was simply "impossible . . . to furnish re-
cruits. . . ." Therefore Rhode Island's legislature in February 1778 voted that any slave
volunteering for the new battalions would
be declared "absolutely free" and entitled to
the wages and bounties of a regular soldier
[fig. 49].

 Colonel Christopher Greene, with Washington's blessing, hurried north from Valley
Forge and before the spring was over he had
begun to train the black soldiers who made
up this extraordinary unit. The test of fire
for the Black Regiment came all too soon in
the Battle of Rhode Island, which General
Lafayette called "the best fought action of
the war." General John Sullivan, with six
brigades, confronted a powerful force of
British and Hessian troops. The Black Regiment—with its core of ninety-five ex-slaves
and thirty freedmen, most of them raw re-
cruits—assigned to what turned out to be
one of the hottest sectors of the American
right wing, was the special target of repeated Hessian charges. But here the Ger-
mans "experienced a more obstinate
resistance than they had expected," noted an

---

*In Louisiana, a colony of Spain during the revo-
lution, two black companies of militiamen fought
against the British. "Assigned the mission of driving
the British from the Gulf Coast and the banks of the
Mississippi, Bernardo Gálvez [governor of Louisiana]
mobilized a task force of 670 men of all nations and
colors of whom eighty were free blacks. . . . These
troops, a company of Pardos (or mulattoes) and Mor-
enos (or Negroes) [helped] to capture Baton Rouge in
1779, Mobile in 1780, and Pensacola in 1781. . . .
Gálvez specifically cited the blacks. 'No less deserving
of eulogy are the companies of Negro and Free Mulat-

toes' who 'conducted themselves with as much valor
and generosity as the white.' " (Roland C. McConnell,
"Louisiana's Black Military History, 1729–1865," in
Louisiana's Black Heritage, ed. Robert R. Macdonald,
John R. Kemp, Edward F. Haas [New Orleans,
1979], 34–35)

49. "Return of Freemen Inlisted during the War in 1st Rhode Island Battalion." Rhode Island Historical Society.

on-the-spot observer. "They found large bodies of troops behind the work and at its sides, chiefly wild looking men in their shirt sleeves, and among them many negroes." "It was in repelling these furious onsets," wrote a Rhode Island historian in 1860, "that the newly raised black regiment, under Col. Greene, distinguished itself by deeds of desperate valor. Posted behind a thicket in the valley, they three times drove back the Hessians who charged repeatedly down the hill to dislodge them." The day after the battle, the Hessian colonel "applied to exchange his command and go to New York, because he dared not lead his regiment again to battle, lest his men shoot him for having caused so much loss." On the day after the battle, General Sullivan announced that "by the best Information the Commander-in-Chief thinks that the Regiment will be intituled to a proper share of the Honours of the day."

This was the Black Regiment's first action—but not its last. One of the few American units that enlisted for the entire war, it proved itself again at Red Bank, Points Bridge, and Yorktown. "In the at-

tack made upon the American lines, near Croton river, on the 13th of May, 1781," wrote Nell, "Colonel Greene, the commander of the regiment, was cut down and mortally wounded: but the sabres of the enemy only reached him through the bodies of his faithful guard of blacks, who hovered over him to protect him, *and every one of whom was killed.*"

Traveling in Connecticut in 1781, the Marquis de Chastellux noted in his journal on January 5: "At the ferry-crossing I met with a detachment of the Rhode Island regiment. . . . The majority of the enlisted men are Negroes or mulattoes; but they are strong, robust men, and those I saw made a very good appearance." When the victorious American army passed in review at Yorktown during the following July, Baron von Closen observed that "three-quarters of the Rhode Island regiment consists of Negroes, and that regiment is the most neatly dressed, the best under arms, and the most precise in its maneuvres."

ABOUT all that is now known of Boston's all-black unit was recorded by Nell in 1855:

At the close of the Revolutionary War, John Hancock presented the colored company, called the "Bucks of America," with an appropriate banner, bearing his initials, as a tribute to their courage and devotion throughout the struggle [fig. 50]. The "Bucks," under the command of Colonel Middleton, were invited to a collation in a neighboring town, and, *en route* were requested to halt in front of the Hancock Mansion, in Beacon street, where the Governor and his son united in the above presentation.

Three years after Nell gave his account, there took place in Boston an exhibition of "interesting relics and mementoes of the olden time," including the banner of the black company as well as "a flag presented to an association of colored men, called the 'Protectors,' who guarded the property of Boston merchants" during the revolution. Sitting in the audience was "Mrs. Kay, daughter of the Ensign who received the banner" from Hancock. During the Civil War, Nell, who had purchased the banner from Mrs. Kay, presented it to the Massachusetts Historical Society, whose proceedings for 1862 describe it as "a silk flag, bearing the device of a Pine-tree and a Buck, with the initials 'J. H.' and 'G. W.' over a scroll, on which appear the words, 'The Bucks of America.'" And there was also a silver badge with the initials of the soldier, to be pinned on his coat, with the same pine tree, buck, and thirteen stars stamped on one side of it—on the other, a shield with the French fleur-de-lis, perhaps a salute to Lafayette [fig. 51].*

The role of the Bucks of America and of its black colonel during the revolution is somewhat elusive; military records have not so far revealed documentary evidence for such a unit. Perhaps the Bucks were simply another name for the Protectors, to which Wendell Phillips alluded as an "association of colored men . . . who guarded the property of Boston merchants." Nor does Colonel Middleton (or any other black officer) appear in the army or militia records, although it has been said that Middleton witnessed the Battle of Groton Heights in Connecticut in 1781. It may have been that the rank of colonel was bestowed on Middleton by Governor Hancock himself to identify him as the commander of a volunteer black posse comitatus to patrol Boston during the war and protect the city from Tory sabotage.

But whatever the military obscurity of *Colonel* Middleton during the war years, the *man* George Middleton did exist, and after the fighting was over he lived a long, full life as a solid citizen engaged in the struggle for civil rights in the Boston community.

George Middleton's name, apart from a record of his marriage in 1778, first appears in 1779 as a leading member of Prince Hall's African Lodge of Freemasons, and from then on, as a close coworker of Hall's in the activities of the African Lodge.* The census of 1790 lists Middleton as head of a family of three. When black Masons in Philadelphia organized themselves into a lodge with Absalom Jones as Master, the vote to approve their warrant was taken at a gathering in George Middleton's house on Pinckney Street. In 1796, with Hall and forty-two other black men, Middleton organized a Boston African Benevolent Society and was licensed by the city as a teacher for the Society. In 1800, when sixty-seven

---

*In 1781 Isaiah Thomas's *Massachusetts Spy* (Worcester) adopted a new device for its masthead which embodied in part a chain of thirteen links, a star in each link, and the fleur-de-lis of the French alliance. (Joseph T. Buckingham, *Specimens of Newspaper Literature* . . . [Boston, 1852], 1:240)

---

*See "Prince Hall: Organizer," below, 202.

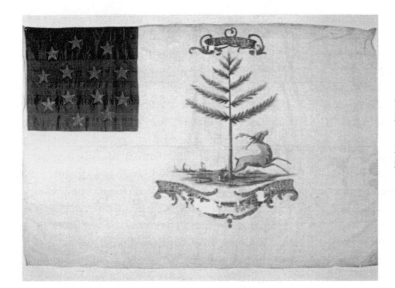

50. The Bucks of America, silk flag, 40″ × 62″, 1776–1780. Massachusetts Historical Society.

blacks signed a plea for the establishment of an African school for their children, it was Middleton who submitted the petition to the Boston town meeting. After the death of Prince Hall and his successor Nero Prince, George Middleton would be elected to the office of third Grand Master of the African Lodge of Freemasons in Boston.

Lydia Maria Child has left us a sketch of George Middleton, whom she knew well in his hale old age when he played the violin and still retained his skill as a "horse-breaker." She tells a story in which he displays his youthful revolutionary fire in "subduing" some "mettlesome colts." The occasion was the celebration of an anniversary of the abolition of the slave trade, held annually by the blacks of Boston:

> It became a frolic with the white boys to deride them on this day, and finally . . . to drive them . . . from the Common. The colored people became greatly incensed by this mockery of their festival, and rumor reached us . . . that they were determined to resist the whites, and were going armed with this intention. . . . Soon, terrified children

51. Badge of Bucks of America, Medallion, 1776–1780. Massachusetts Historical Society.

and women ran down Belknap street, pursued by white boys, who enjoyed their fright. The sounds of battle approached; clubs and brickbats were flying in [all] directions. At this crisis, Col. Middleton opened his door, armed with a loaded musket, and, in a loud voice, shrieked death to the first white who should approach. Hundreds of human beings, white and black, were pouring down the street. . . . Col. Middleton's voice could be heard above every other, urging his party to turn and resist to the last. His appearance was terrific, his musket was levelled, ready to sacrifice the first white man that came within its range. The colored party, shamed by his reproaches, and fired by his example, rallied. . . .

The names of the Bucks of America (with one exception), their visages, their exploits of "courage and devotion" are so far lost to history. What remains is the bright banner and badge.

THE Volunteer Chasseurs, another black outfit, from far-off Haiti—a brigade of the seaborne French expedition that supported General Lincoln in Georgia during the autumn of 1779—fought first in the American Revolution and then went on to join the struggle for nationhood in their own country, the second to achieve independence from Europe in the New World.

The aim of the Franco-American army was to evict the British from Savannah. In early September, a French fleet of thirty-three sail, under the command of the comte d'Estaing, anchored off the Georgia coast and debarked its troops. As reported in the *Paris Gazette,* there were 2,979 "Europeans" and 545 "Colored: Volunteer Chasseurs, Mulattoes, and Negroes, newly raised at St.

Domingo," the latter called the Fontages Legion after its French commander.

Among the colored volunteers in the patriot cause were young men destined to become famous in the Haitian revolution— among them were Andre Rigaud and Louis Jacques Beauvais, noncoms at Savannah; Martial Besse, a general under the Versailles Convention; Jean-Baptiste Mars Belley, deputy to the convention [fig. 52]; and Henri Christophe, future king. Many tales are told of twelve-year-old Christophe at Savannah—that he volunteered as a freeborn infantryman, that he was orderly to a French naval officer, and that he had been a slave and earned his freedom by his service in the Black Brigade [fig. 53].

To dislodge the well-entrenched enemy, Lincoln and d'Estaing decided to attack. But the British fought well, aided, it must be said, by hundreds of "armed blacks"— gathered from the countryside to build redoubts, mount cannon, and serve as guides and spies. "Having fallen in with a Negro named Quamino Dolly," wrote a participant in the siege, "Colonel Campbell induced him, by a small Reward, to conduct the Troops, by a private Path through the Swamp, upon the Right of the Americans."* Georgian patriots, however, fearful of slave revolt, always refused to give their bondsmen guns in exchange for liberty. As

---

*These black allies of the British suffered terribly in the aftermath. A French officer in Savannah, after its later evacuation by the British, recorded in his journal: "The large number of negroes they had requisitioned as laborers spread the plague in town. These miserable creatures could be found in every corner, either dead or dying. No one took the trouble to bury them, so you can imagine the infection this must have engendered. Still, a large number of them survived. Most were reclaimed by the inhabitants. Negroes without masters found new ones among the French, and we garnered a veritable harvest of domestics. Those among us who had no servant were happy to find one so cheap."

52. Anne Louis Girodet de Roucy-Trioson, *Jean-Baptiste Mars Belley,* oil, 1797. Musée National du Château de Versailles.

the French and Americans, raked by heavy fire, pulled back in retreat, the British, determined to wipe them out, charged. It was now that the Black Brigade, stationed as a reserve in the rear guard, showed its mettle by preventing the annihilation of the allied force. Count Casimir Pulaski, at the head of the cavalry, fell in this action. Martial Besse and Henri Christophe returned to Saint Domingue with slight wounds [fig. 54].

There is an ironic sequel. Eighteen years later when General Besse visited the United States on official business, he disembarked at Charleston, "dressed in the uniform of his grade," and was forced by the authorities to put up a bond as required by the law of South Carolina for all incoming blacks. It was only after the French consul in Charleston protested that General Besse was a representative of his government, and that, moreover, he had been wounded at the siege of Savannah, that the bond was remitted.

53. Richard Evans, *Henri Christophe,* oil, ca. 1818. Formerly in the collection of the late Sir Bruce S. Ingram, London. Present whereabouts unknown.

In the Service of the King

During the time of the revolution, white patriots, north and south, had to confront the hard fact that black people were doing some deep thinking about which side, if any, they should join. In one of his "Landscapes" of New York life near his homestead in Orange County, St. John Crévecour, the "American farmer," has the chairwoman of the local patriot committee lecture the slave of a Loyalist: "Well, Nero. . . . They say you are a good fellow, only a little Torified like most of your colour." And there is the well-known anecdote of the slave of General Sullivan of New Hampshire, related by Nell in 1855: "When his master told him that they were on the point of starting for the army, to fight for liberty, he shrewdly suggested, that it would be a great satisfaction to know that he was indeed going to fight for *his* liberty. Struck with the reasonableness and justice of this suggestion, Gen. S. at once gave him his freedom." The general

CHARLESTOWN, October 20.

The following are some of the reasons that have been assigned, why the assault on Savannah did not succeed, viz.

1st. The enemy having a much more numerous garrison than had been represented; being said to consist of about 1700 effective regulars, and a great number of sailors, marines, militia, armed blacks, &c.

2d. Their having the advantage of the presence, skill and activity of so able and indefatigable an officer as the Hon. Col. Maitland; who, while our army were obliged to wait for the bringing up proper cannon and mortars from the fleet, (which took up many days, and was attended with inconceivable difficulties, on account of the distance of the shipping, and a series of tempestuous weather) was night and day incessantly engaged in adding to the strength and number of the works, upon which, it is said, he employed upwards of 2000 negroes.

3dly. The enemy having, by some means or other, discovered the approach of our columns, a full hour before it was possible for them to reach their respective stations; by which they had an opportunity of pouring upon their assailants, such a heavy and incessant front, flank and cross fire, as no troops whatever could have sustained, without being disordered, and occasioned the order for discontinuing the assault even while the brave French troops had gained one of the enemy's works, and our, as brave troops, another.

Several frigates having been since dispatched from the Count D'Estaing's fleet, on different routes, and several other very striking circumstances, have given rise to a conjecture, that a strong combined squadron will soon appear in a quarter where least expected.— One of the frigates, it is said, has been met steering for Havanna, and another going into Chesapeak Bay.

Nov. 3. Last Sunday his most Christian Majesty's frigate, Iphigenie, commanded by M. de Kersaint, sailed upon a cruize. 'Tis remarkable that during the time this ship was in port, though there were near 1000 foreign sailors here at once, not the smallest riot happened.

54. "An account of the Battle of Savannah . . . , October 20, 1779," *New Jersey Gazette*, December 8, 1779. Courtesy of the Library of Congress.

was an unusual person, but the anecdote suggests why some two hundred slaves volunteered to join Greene's First Rhode Island Regiment in the cause of American independence, while four times that number in Virginia fled their patriot masters to join Dunmore's Ethiopian Regiment in the king's cause.

For slaves, the idea of freedom of body and soul was more important than tea and taxes. In a war between white patriot and white Tory, both upholders of the abominable institution, the question for Africans, enslaved in America for a century and a half, was clear enough: In which camp was there a better future for black freedom? The question was a simple one; the answer, always framed in terms of freedom, was often complex and perilous, dependent on place, time, and opportunity; one had to size up promises made by whites, Whig and Tory, desperately in need of black manpower for their own purposes. All blacks, slave or free, did not make the same choice, and there were some who sought their own path in flight or revolt.

Among the black Whitecuffs, a free family in New York, there was (as Herman Melville would say later in a Civil War poem) a "conflict of convictions." The story emerges from the evidence in hearings held in 1784 by a parliamentary commission to look into the claims of Loyalists—among them one "Benjamin Whitecuff (a Black)," a twenty-year-old New Yorker: "He says he was born at Hempstead in King's County . . . his Father was a Freeman and he was born a Freeman.—At the beginning of the Troubles he was a Farmer,—and worked with his Father on his Farm—His Father took the American side and was a Sergeant in their Service. He would have persuaded him to go too but he refused. His older Brother went with him [the father] . . . he was employed for 2 years as a Spy by Sir Henry Clinton and Sir William Ayscough. . . . He says he was hung up by the Rebels at Cranbury in the Jerseys . . . for three minutes but was saved by Detachment of the 5th light Company. . . . He has heard his Father was killed at Chestnut Hill. His Brother was killed at German Town. . . . He can't read—his Memorial was drawn out by a Lawyer."

Of course, black resistance to oppression was not a new phenomenon in the south. At Christmastide 1769, a few months before the Boston Massacre, in Hanover County, Virginia, an outraged slave, whipped by an overseer, slashed at him with an ax.

Gerald W. Mullin, citing the news story in the *Virginia Gazette,* has sketched the outcome: "He missed, but a group of slaves jumped on the white and administered such a severe beating that the 'ringleader' [the whipped slave] intervened and saved his life. The overseer ran off in search of reinforcements; and instead of fleeing or arming themselves, the slaves tied up two other whites and 'whipped [them] till they were raw from neck to waistband.' Twelve armed whites arrived, and the slaves retreated into a barn where they were soon joined by a large body of slaves, 'some say forty, some fifty.' The whites 'tried to prevail by persuasion,' but the slaves, 'deaf to all, rushed upon them with desperate fury, armed wholely with clubs and staves.' Two slaves were shot and killed, five others were wounded, and the remainder fled." Such possibilities were perceived fearfully by slave owners on the eve of the revolution, as a letter written by the chairman of the Safety Committee in Chatham, North Carolina, on July 15, 1775, makes clear. From Beaufort County word had arrived of "an intended insurrection of the negroes against the whole people. . . . We immediately sent off an Express to Tarborough to alarm the inhabitants there . . . and appointed upwards of one hundred men as patrolers. . . . By night we had in custody and in gaol near forty under proper guard." The Safety Committee found the affair "a deep laid Horrid Tragick Plan for destroying the inhabitants of this province without respect of persons, age or sex . . . five negroes were whipt this day by order." The next day the Committee "ordered several to be severely whipt and sentenced several to receive 80 lashes each, to have both Ears crapd which was executed in the presence of the Committee and a great number of spectators." Reports came in of "negroes being in arms on the line of Craven and Pitt

[county] and prayed assistance of men and ammunition which we readily granted. We posted guards upon the roads, for several miles that night."

The anxious writers see a plot of the Tories to seduce the slaves of patriots, to line them up on the British side in the looming struggle. "We keep taking up, examining and scourging more or less every day; from whichever part of the County they come they all confess nearly the same thing, Vizt that they were one and all on the night of the 8th inst to fall on and destroy the family where they lived, then to proceed from House to House (Burning as they went) until they arrived in the Back Country where they were to be received with open arms by a number of Persons there appointed and armed by Government for their Protection, and as a further award they were to be settled in a free Government of their own." There is a P.S. at the end: "In disarming the negroes we found considerable ammunition."

Three years before the ex-bondsmen of the Ethiopian Regiment donned their British uniforms, Dunmore had explored the critical question of slave loyalty as a matter of military-political strategy. What jogged his thinking was probably Lord Mansfield's opinion in the Somerset case which, in effect, freed all slaves entering England, reports of which had reached the colonies by the summer of 1772. The news was in the *Virginia Gazette.* In 1773 an advertisement for a runaway couple claimed they were on their way to Britain, "where they imagine they will be free (a Notion now too prevalent among the Negroes, greatly to the vexation and Prejudice of their Masters)." A year later, a similar notice complains that a fugitive Bacchus has fled his master in frontier Georgia and would attempt "to board a vessel for Great Britain . . . from the knowledge he has of the late Determination of Somerset's Case." Responding in 1772 to the colonial secretary, Dunmore remarked that some American slave owners, "with great reason, trembled at the facility that our enemy would find in Such a body of men, attached by no tye to their Master nor to the Country. . . . It was natural to Suppose that their Condition must inspire them with an aversion to both, and therefore are ready to join the first that would encourage them to revenge themselves, by which means a Conquest of this Country would inevitably be effected in a very short time. . . ."

In late April 1775, as Salem Poor was making his way to Bunker Hill, a group of Virginia blacks, presented with a new possibility of winning freedom without fleeing across the Atlantic, sought out the royal governor and offered to fight for the crown. In June General Thomas Gage sounded the alarm to Lord Barrington, the colonial secretary in London: "Things are now come to that crisis, that we must avail ourselves of every resource, even to raise the Negros, in our cause." Lord Dunmore was not yet ready, although for six months he had pondered the idea, feeling that "all the Slaves" were "on the side of the Government."* In

---

*Dunmore's strategy had a tradition in British military history. Captain Woodes Rogers, preparing for a battle in the summer of 1709, wrote in his journal for August 16: "This Day I muster'd our Negroes [slaves] aboard the *Duke,* being about 35 lusty Fellows; I told them, That if we met the *Spaniards* or *French,* and they would fight, those that behav'd themselves well should be free Men; 32 of 'em immediately promis'd to stand to it, as long as the best *Englishman,* and desired they might be improv'd in the Use of Arms, which some of them already understood; and that if I would allow 'em Arms and Powder, these would teach the rest. Upon this I made *Michael Kendall,* the *Jamaica* free Negro, who deserted from the *Spaniards* to us at *Gorgona,* their Leader . . . and to confirm our Contract made them drink a Dram all round to our good Success; at the same time I gave 'em Bays for Clothes, and told them they must now

mid-November a detachment of Dunmore's troops with black privates among them whipped the colonial militia at Kemp's Landing and slaves captured one of the patriot colonels. The time and place were right—on November 7 at the scene of the victory, Dunmore proclaimed "all indented Servants, Negroes, or others, (appertaining to Rebels) free, that are able and willing to bear Arms" in the king's cause [fig. 55]. That the proclamation accelerated the flight of slaves to the British is reflected a week later in an advertisement in the *Virginia Gazette* for the return of "Charles, who is a very shrewd, sensible fellow, and can both read and write," who ran away from his master because of a "determined resolution to get liberty, as he conceived by flying to lord Dunmore" [fig. 56].

The phrase "appertaining to rebels" is crucial—only the slaves of patriots are offered their freedom. The fugitive slaves of Tories will remain on their plantations or be sent back to their owners. As John Adams noted in his diary after a conversation with two southerners, the British had a problem: "These gentlemen gave a melancholy account of the State of Georgia and South Carolina. They say that if one thousand regular troops should land in Georgia, and their commander is provided with arms and clothes enough, and proclaim to all the negroes, who would join his camp, twenty thousand negroes would join it from the two Provinces in a fortnight. The negroes have a wonderful art of communicating intelligence among themselves; it will run several hundreds of miles in a week or fortnight. They say, their only security is this; that all the king's friends, and tools of government, have large plantations, and prop-

---

look upon themselves as *Englishmen,* and no more as Negro Slaves to the *Spaniards,* at which they express'd themselves highly pleas'd. . . ."

55. "Proclamation of
Earl of Dunmore,"
broadside, November 7,
1775. Tracy W.
McGregor Library, Uni-
versity of Virginia.

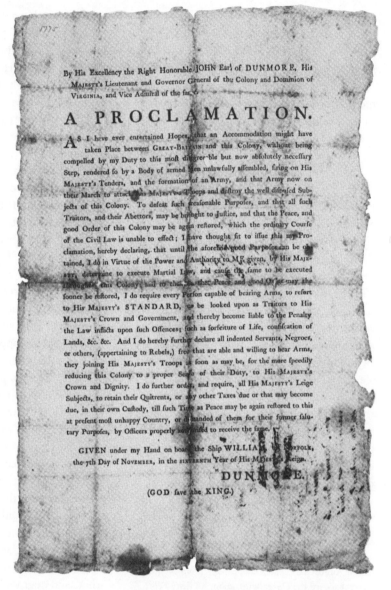

By His Excellency the Right Honorable JOHN Earl of DUNMORE, His Majesty's Lieutenant and Governor General of the Colony and Dominion of VIRGINIA, and Vice Admiral of the same.

A PROCLAMATION.

AS I have ever entertained Hopes, that an Accommodation might have taken Place between GREAT-BRITAIN and this Colony, without being compelled by my Duty to this most disagreeable but now absolutely necessary Step, rendered so by a Body of armed Men unlawfully assembled, firing on His Majesty's Tenders, and the formation of an Army, and that Army now on their March to attack His Majesty's Troops and destroy the well disposed Subjects of this Colony. To defeat such treasonable Purposes, and that all such Traitors, and their Abettors, may be brought to Justice, and that the Peace, and good Order of this Colony may be again restored, which the ordinary Course of the Civil Law is unable to effect; I have thought fit to issue this my Proclamation, hereby declaring, that until the aforesaid good Purposes can be obtained, I do in Virtue of the Power and Authority to ME given, by His Majesty, determine to execute Martial Law, and cause the same to be executed throughout this Colony; and to the end that Peace and good Order may the sooner be restored, I do require every Person capable of bearing Arms, to resort to His Majesty's STANDARD, or be looked upon as Traitors to His Majesty's Crown and Government, and thereby become liable to the Penalty the Law inflicts upon such Offences; such as forfeiture of Life, confiscation of Lands, &c. &c. And I do hereby further declare all indented Servants, Negroes, or others, (appertaining to Rebels,) free that are able and willing to bear Arms, they joining His Majesty's Troops as soon as may be, for the more speedily reducing this Colony to a proper Sense of their Duty, to His Majesty's Crown and Dignity. I do further order, and require, all His Majesty's Leige Subjects, to retain their Quitrents, or any other Taxes due or that may become due, in their own Custody, till such Time as Peace may be again restored to this at present most unhappy Country, or demanded of them for their former salutary Purposes, by Officers properly authorised to receive the same.

GIVEN under my Hand on board the Ship WILLIAM off Norfolk, the 7th Day of NOVEMBER, in the sixteenth Year of His Majesty's Reign.

DUNMORE.

(GOD save the KING.)

erty in negroes; so that the slaves of the Tories would be lost, as well as those of the Whigs."*

As the *Virginia Gazette* appealed to the slaves with frantic arguments to cling to their kind masters—"Be not then, ye negroes, tempted by his proclamation to ruin your selves"—Patrick Henry assailed the proclamation as "fatal to the publick Safety" and counseled "early and unremitting Attention to the Government of the Slaves." A broadside to the plantations strongly advised that "Constant, and well directed Patrols" were "indispensably necessary" to prevent the runaways from flocking to the royal standard [fig. 57]. Meanwhile, blacks piloted Dunmore's amphibian guer-

---

*As Silas Deane wrote to John Jay on December 3, 1776, the Americans could use the same ploy: "*Omnia tentanda* is my motto, therefore I hint the playing of their own game on them, by spiriting up the *Caribs* in *St. Vincent's,* and the negroes in Jamaica, to revolt."

AQUIA, STAFFORD county, *November* 8, 1775.

RAN off laſt night from the ſubſcriber, a negro man named CHARLES, who is a very ſhrewd, ſenſible fellow, and can both read and write; and as he always has waited upon me, he muſt be well known through moſt parts of *Virginia* and *Maryland*. He is very black, has a large noſe, and is about 5 feet 8 or 10 inches high. He took a variety of clothes, which I cannot well particularize, ſtole ſeveral of my ſhirts, a pair of new ſaddle bags, and two mares, one a darkiſh, the other a light bay, with a blaze and white feet, and about 3 years old. From many circumſtances, there is reaſon to believe he intends an attempt to get to lord Dunmore; and as I have reaſon to believe his deſign of going off was long premeditated, and that he has gone off with ſome accomplice, I am apprehenſive he may prove daring and reſolute, if endeavoured to be taken. His elopement was from no cauſe of complaint, or dread of a whipping (for he has always been remarkably indulged, indeed too much ſo) but from a determined reſolution to get liberty, as he conceived, by flying to lord Dunmore. I will give FIVE POUNDS to any perſon who ſecures him, and the mares, ſo that I get them again. ROBERT BRENT.

56. *Virginia Gazette,* November 16, 1775. Courtesy of the Library of Congress.

SIR,

AS the Committee of Safety is not ſitting, I take the Liberty to encloſe you a Copy of the Proclamation iſſued by Lord Dunmore; the Deſign and Tendency of which, you will obſerve, is fatal to the publick Safety. An early and unremitting Attention to the Government of the SLAVES may, I hope, counteract this dangerous Attempt. Conſtant, and well directed Patrols, ſeem indiſpenſably neceſſary. I doubt not of every poſſible Exertion, in your Power, for the publick Good; and have the Honour to be, Sir,

Your moſt obedient and very humble Servant,

P. HENRY.

HEAD QUARTERS, WILLIAMSBURG,
November 20, 1775.

57. Patrick Henry, Circular Letter of November 20, 1775, broadside. Courtesy of the Library of Congress.

58. News item, "Liberty to slaves," *Maryland Gazette,* December 14, 1775. Maryland Historical Society, Baltimore.

WILLIAMSBURG, *December 2.*

Since lord Dunmore's proclamation made its appearance here, it is said he has recruited his army, in the counties of Princess Anne and Norfolk, to the amount of about 2000 men, including his black regiment, which is thought to be a considerable part, with this inscription on their breasts :---" Liberty to slaves."---However, as the rivers will henceforth be strictly watched, and every possible precaution taken, it is hoped others will be effectually prevented from joining those his lordship has already collected.

The army that went down last week, under command of col. Woodford, to obstruct Dunmore's progress of inlisting men in the lower counties, fell in with a party of twelve or thirteen of Dunmore's friends, and made them all prisoners. Lieut. col. Scott, with the advanced guard, upon his arrival at the Great Bridge, found the enemy intrenched there, and it is said a smart firing began by some of the riflemen, which was returned, and continued a considerable time on both sides, but to what effect we know not. It is also said, that Thursday last was fixed upon by our troops to begin a general attack ; they were healthy, in good spirits, and had great prospect of success.

Some accounts from Norfolk are, that Dunmore's party has demolished several houses back of the town, and fortified themselves ; also, that col. Hutchings, and some other gentlemen, their prisoners, had been removed to the ships on account of the gaol having been set on fire.

A copy of the Oath extorted from the people of Norfolk and Princess Anne by Lord Dunmore.

rilla forays, helped man his crews, and foraged widely to keep him in food. Within a week, five hundred bondsmen had answered his call. He gave them guns "as fast as they came in." By the first of December nearly three hundred blacks in uniform, with the words "Liberty to Slaves" inscribed across their breasts, were members of "Lord Dunmore's Ethiopian Regiment" [fig. 58].

For the patriotic slave masters of Virginia and points south, the Ethiopian Regiment was a terrifying version of the old nightmare of black revolt. In mid-December the Virginia Convention published its answering proclamation: pardon to runaways who returned to their masters; a warning to the "seduced" that the penalty for slave insurrection was death without benefit of clergy [fig. 59]. It should be noted that four months earlier the royal governor of South Carolina had reported to Lord Dartmouth the execution of Thomas Jeremiah, a black pilot and fisherman of Charleston: "under colour of Law, they hanged & burned, an unfortunate wretch, a Free Negroe of considerable property, one of the most valuable & useful men in his way in the Province, on suspicion of instigating an Insurrection. . . ." Henry Laurens, patriot president of the Provincial Congress, was of the

VIRGINIA, Dec. 14, 1775.

By the REPRESENTATIVES *of the* PEOPLE *of the Colony and Dominion of* VIRGINIA, *affembled in* GENERAL CONVENTION.

A DECLARATION.

WHEREAS lord Dunmore, by his pro-clamation, dated on board the fhip William, off Norfolk, the 7th day of No-vember 1775, hath offered freedom to fuch able-bodied flaves as are willing to join him, and take up arms, againft the good people of this colony, giving thereby encouragement to a general infurrection, which may induce a neceffity of inflicting the feveceft punifhments upon thofe un-happy people, already deluded by his bafe and infidious arts; and whereas, by an act of the General Affembly now in force in this colony, it is enacted, that all negro or other flaves, confpiring to rebel or make infurrection, fhall fuffer death, and be excluded all benefit of clergy: We think it proper to declare, that all flaves who have been, or fhall be feduced, by his lordfhip's proclamation, or other arts, to defert their mafters' fervice, and take up arms againft the inhabitants of this colony, fhall be liable to fuch punifhment as fhall hereafter be directed by the General Con-vention. And to the end that all fuch, who have taken this unlawful and wicked ftep, may return in fafety to their duty, and efcape the punifhment due to their crimes, we hereby promife pardon to them, they furrendering themfelves to col. Wil-liam Woodford, or any other commander of our troops, and not appearing in arms after the publication hereof. And we do farther earneftly recommend it to all hu-mane and benevolent perfons in this colony to explain and make known this our offer of mercy to thofe unfortunate people. EDMUND PENDLETON, prefident.

59. "Declaration of General Assembly of Virginia," broadside, December 15, 1775. Courtesy of John Carter Brown Library at Brown University.

opinion that Jerry *had* conspired to foment an insurrection, as was testified by one Sambo, another harbor worker: "there is a great war coming soon," said Jeremiah; "what shall we poor Negroes do in a schooner?" asked Sambo—to which Jeremiah replied: "set the Schooner on fire, jump on shore and join the soldiers . . . the war was come to help the poor Negroes." Even more damaging had been the testi-mony of Jemmy, a slave Jeremiah first de-nied knowing but who was shown to be his wife's brother, for Jemmy had sworn that Jeremiah was to have "the Chief Command of the said Negroes, that . . . he had Powder enough already, but that he wanted more arms. . . ." The Virginia Convention also decreed that slaves taken in arms would be sold in the West Indies—this from pa-triots who indicted his majesty for support-ing the slave trade. But the fugitives, perhaps a thousand strong, all too willing to strike a blow for their own freedom, were not to be bribed or frightened.

Yet the Tory operation "Liberty to Slaves" was only a partial success. Blacks could understand the hollowness of Dun-more's libertarian pretenses—he offered freedom only to the "able and willing" slaves of rebels and helped Tory masters re-trieve their runaways—and knew that he had blocked the colony's effort to halt the slave trade. On December 9 at the Battle of Great Bridge—the Lexington of the south—the British force of six hundred, nearly half of which was black, was thrown back by Woodford's Second Virginia Regi-ment. Dunmore then retreated to his ships with his troops and there continued to train black soldiers in the use of small arms. But in March Dunmore had to advise the secre-tary of state that although recruitment of blacks was going on "very well, a fever crept in amongst them which carried off a great many Very fine fellows." In July it was re-ported to the Maryland Council of Safety that some black deserters from the British had smallpox. "The shores are full of dead bodies, chiefly negroes." By spring's end only "150 effective Negro men" were left. Had not the fever killed off "an incredible number of our people, especially blacks," Dunmore reported in June, the Ethiopian Regiment might have grown to two thou-

sand. In August the harassed British fleet
was forced to abandon the Virginia coast.
Seven ships sailing northward had aboard
some three hundred black soldiers who
would fight on other fields.

But Dunmore's defeat did not alter basic
British policy. In fact, southern slaves were
everywhere joining the British. At Savannah a patriot colonel wrote to Washington:
"The men-of-war at Tybee . . . [are] encouraging our slaves to desert to them, pilfering our sea island for provisions." Almost
two hundred slaves from various plantations
had answered the call to desert. When the
news, via "a negro hired to ride post in the
Continental Service," reached Henry Laurens in Charleston, it ruffled his humanitarian soul. Although it was "an awful
business . . . to put even fugitive & Rebellious Slaves to death," he advised the
Council of Safety in Georgia "to seize & if
nothing else will do to destroy all those Rebellious Negroes upon Tybee Island or
wherever they may be found." Two years
later, in June 1778, Pennsylvania Tory
Joseph Galloway, formulating grand strategy for the earl of Dartmouth in a report on
the "Strength of America in Respect to Her
Number of fighting Men," reiterated the
Virginia governor's early appraisal:

> The Negroes are truly intestine En-
> emies, and must in proportion to
> their Numbers subtract from the
> Strength of the Colony where they
> are, because they are Slaves, and de-
> sirous of recovering their freedom,
> and are ever ready to embrace an op-
> portunity of doing it, and therefore it
> is but just, in determining on the
> strength of America, to deduct their
> Number of fighting Men, which is
> 150,000. . . . And let it be further
> added, that in the Class of fighting
> Men among the Negroes, there are no

> men of property, none whose Attach-
> ments would render them averse to
> the bearing of Arms against the Re-
> bellion—and that more fighting Men
> might be raised among them, upon
> proper Encouragement, than among
> the whites, though they amount to
> three times their Number.

Mrs. Galloway, like Abigail Adams, also
worried. In her diary for December 9,
1778, she wrote: "She talked to me about
keeping slaves, but I oppos'd her. I am not
convinced it is right . . . dream'd of our
Negroes & cou'd not get them out of My
Mind . . . am Uneasy about them . . . ye
slaves runs in my mind . . . took an
Anodine but had no good rest."

The judgment of Dunmore and Galloway was reaffirmed a year later when Sir
Henry Clinton, commander-in-chief of the
king's forces, proclaimed from his Westchester, New York, headquarters that he
would guarantee to any slave coming over to
the British his full freedom and choice of
military assignment [fig. 60]. "Their property [slaves] we need not seek," echoed John
André, the ill-fated English spy, "it flies to
us and famine follows." One of these items
of property, "Duncan a Negro belonging to
Mr. Dill a Carpenter in Charlestown," André told Sir Henry, "run away from thence
last night by going up Cooper River . . .
whence he got a Canoe" and brought crucial
intelligence of the situation inside the be-
sieged city [fig. 61].

Anguished patriots agreed with André: a
pseudonymous Antibiastes in a broadside of
1777 urged the Americans to liberate their
black servicemen: "Our non-emancipated
soldiers are almost irresistibly tempted to
desert to our foes, who never fail to employ
them against us." In his journal for September 20, 1777, Henry Melchior Muhlenberg, a Lutheran pastor, set down a

60. Sir Henry Clinton's "Philipsburg Proclamation," June 30, 1779. The William L. Clements Library, The University of Michigan.

conversation with two blacks, servants of an English family leaving Philadelphia: "They secretly wished that the British army might win, for then all Negro slaves will gain their freedom. It is said that this sentiment is almost universal among the Negroes in America." Certainly this sentiment was pervasive among blacks south of the Potomac. In May 1776, in North Carolina, a committee to prevent the desertion of blacks recommended to the provincial congress that all masters "on the south side of *Cape-Fear River* . . . remove such male slaves as are capable of bearing arms, or otherwise assisting the enemy, into the country, remote from the sea. . . ." A few months later, in Georgia, slave owners publicly worried about "the vast number of Negroes we have,

perhaps of themselves sufficient to subdue us." Writing to the president of Congress in February 1777, General Robert Howe recommended that seven to eight thousand regulars be retained in South Carolina at all times to control the "numerous black domestics who would undoubtedly flock in multitudes to the Banners of the enemy whenever an opportunity arrived." (In 1770 Lieutenant Governor William Bull of South Carolina had stated that in time of "great danger the militia is to be reenforced with a number of Trusty Negroes, and we have many such, not exceeding one-third of the corps they are to join." Apparently seven years later, these "Trusty Negroes" had diminished in number.) In 1778 the Georgia Assembly, afraid that "grave danger might

26
Duncan a Negro belonging to Mr Bell a
Carpenter in Charlestown runaway from
thence last night by going up Cooper River
landing at the Quarter House & comming across
to Creightons landing from whence he got a
Canoe to Rose's back Landing. —
They are still at Work at the Bay and
making a Redoubt at the Right of the
Lines on Cooper River.
They are also hard at Work in
getting the Guns from the Shipping in
Cooper River the Notre Dame was sunk
Yesterday Afternoon in Marsh Channel.
The Queen of France is to be sunk &

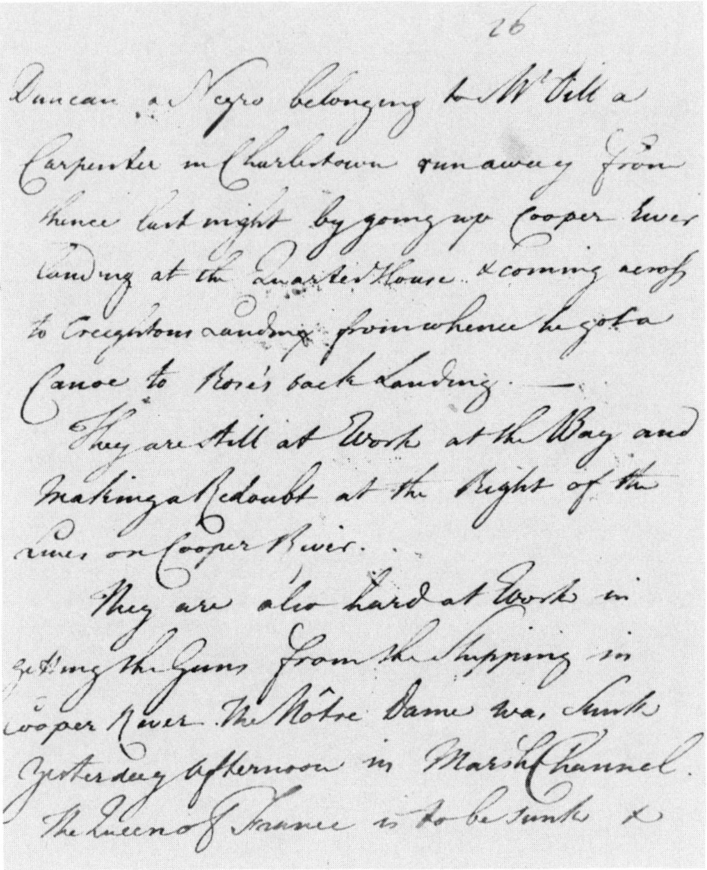

61. John André's report of intelligence, ca. May 12, 1780, excerpt. The William L. Clements Library, The University of Michigan.

arise from insurrections," ordered one-third of each county's troops to serve as a permanent local patrol.

In spite of the desperate ingenuity of the colonial governments—even New York had its "Commission for Detecting and Defeating Conspiracies"—the runaways bolted. An American prisoner on board the British ship *Roebuck* in Delaware Bay on May 26, 1776, wrote out an eyewitness report of the operation:

> On that night there came three negro men from the shore in a canoe, who were shaked hands with, and kindly received and entertained. . . . [an officer] afterwards asked them if there would come more of their people on board; that if they did they would be well used. The negroes said there would. He then asked them if there were any shirtmen or forces lying near; they told him there were none nearer than six miles. He then asked them if there were any cattle near the shore on the main; they said there was plenty. He then asked them if they thought there was any danger in landing to get them; they said there was no danger. He then asked them if they could get some fowls that night for the officers . . . they said they could get fowls and sheep. He then told them they should be well paid; and, besides, should be free when this disturbance was over, which he expected would be very soon, and then each of them should have a plantation

of Rebels' land. After which one of the negroes went and brought some fowls and geese, which this deponent heard making a noise coming up the side of the ship; and also brought his wife and two children, and another negro man. . . .

Sometimes the black fugitives were caught, as a South Carolina trial record makes clear. In early spring of 1776, two whites asleep in the forecastle of their schooner tied to a wharf on the Potomac were surprised about midnight by four slaves from four nearby plantations. The slaves demanded that the boat be sailed to the Coon River and that "they should have the Guns to go on shore with . . . promising no hurt should be done. . . ." But "the negroes, not being able to Manage the Vessell," their white prisoners "stered to Maryland," where three of the slaves were captured. Charles and Kitt were sentenced to hang and Harry to receive thirty lashes on his bare back. Five springs later, in 1781, John Tayloe's slave Billy, accused of waging war against Virginia "in an armed vessel," was found guilty of high treason by a patriot court. He was sentenced "to be hanged by the neck until dead and his head to be severed from his body and stuck up at some public cross road on a pole." Two of the six judges dissented: "a slave in our opinion Cannot Commit treason against the State, not being Admitted to the Privileges of a Citizen [a slave] owes the State No Allegiance. . . ." Governor Thomas Jefferson apparently concurred, reprieving Billy until the legislature decreed that a slave could not be found guilty of treason.

More often, probably, the fugitives got through. In December 1777, a Baltimore newspaper described a spectacular escape from a Potomac plantation. Twenty-one blacks—fifteen men, two women, and four children—broke into a barn in which the master kept his boat and used the vessel to sail to the British. Three news items in patriot papers of 1780 related the exploits of a black guerrilla leader, a veteran of Virginia's Ethiopian Regiment, operating in Monmouth County, New Jersey. During the first week of June, "Ty with his party of about 20 blacks and whites, last Friday afternoon took and carried prisoners Capt. Barns Smock and Gilbert Vanmater," spiked the four pounder, and ran off with the artillery horses [fig. 62]. A fortnight later, "Ty with 30 blacks, 36 Queen's Rangers, and 30 refugee tories, landed at Conascung . . . got in between our scouts" undiscovered, and "carried off" several whites and blacks as well as "a great deal of stock." There were casualties on both sides. In September, "72 men, composed of New-Levies, Refugees and Negroes . . . about an hour before day, attacked the house of Captain Joshua Huddy." The *"brave Negro Tye* [one of Lord Dunmore's crew]" was among the wounded, and news of his guerrilla strikes no longer appears in the press, yet even after the surrender of Cornwallis, black Loyalists continue their forays: "We hear from Monmouth," reported the *New Jersey Gazette* on June 5, 1782, that "a refugee landed with about 40 whites and 40 blacks, at Forked-River, and burnt Samuel Brown's salt-works, and plundered him; they then proceeded Southward towards Barnegat, for the purpose of burning the salt-works along shore between those places."

Thus, tens of thousands of slaves chose *their* way of striking for freedom. Most of them served the British—always short of men—as an indispensable labor force, in some cases armed with shovels and muskets. Many served as orderlies, mechanics, and artisans—and as cooks, carpenters, sawyers, teamsters, wagoners, turnwheelers, and blacksmiths. Some served as spies, guides,

62. Extract of a letter
from Monmouth County,
New Jersey, June 12,
1780, *Pennsylvania Gazette
and Weekly Advertiser,*
June 21, 1780. Courtesy
of the Library of Congress.

Extract of a letter from Monmouth county, June 12.
"Ty, with his party of about 20 blacks and whites,
last Friday afternoon took and carried off prisoners, Capt.
Barns Smock and Gilbert Vanmater; at the same time
spiked up the iron four pounder at Capt. Smock's house,
but took no ammunition: Two of the artillery horses,
and two of Capt. Smock's horses, were likewise taken off."
The above-mentioned Ty is a Negroe, who bears the
title of Colonel, and commands a motly crew at Sandy-
Hook.

man-of-war men, and pilots. So rare are
their names in the annals of the time, that
two at random must suffice to hint at the
host. In July 1776 Christopher Gadsden, in
reporting a victory in southern waters over
an enemy squadron, appended a postscript:
"As soon as the action began, the *Commodore*
[a British ship] ordered to be put into a
place of safety, negro Sampson, a black pilot." Six months later, north of New York, a
patriot colonel complained to his general
that "a scouting party . . . brought in a
stout negro fellow, the property of a Tory
(one Peck), who is now with the enemy; and
the negro has been employed as a spy to
bring them accounts of our motions"
[fig. 63]. Sampson and Peck were not at all
unique.

Many, drilled in the manual of arms, saw
action in the field. In April 1782 General
Nathanael Greene informed Washington
that the British had armed and put in uniform at least seven hundred blacks. The
Ethiopian Regiment was not the only black
unit. That same spring two members of a
black cavalry troop, about a hundred
strong, were killed in a skirmish at Dorchester, South Carolina. Evacuating Boston,
the royal army sailed to Halifax with a
"Company of Negroes." Philadelphia had a

"Company of Black Pioneers." A Brunswick
contingent under Baron von Riedesel, supporting Burgoyne, took back to Germany
its corps of Afro-American drummers
[fig. 64]. And just as blacks had fought
with the British in the first skirmishes of
the war, so they also fought in the last—
and for the same reasons. In 1781 the General Assembly of British East Florida had offered to liberate any slave who showed
courage in battle and to outfit him with a
red coat and silver badge. Nine days after
the signing of the Treaty of Peace in April
1783, a Tory colonel, Andrew Deveux of
South Carolina, with a task force of 220
men sailed out of St. Augustine in five privateers to recapture the Bahamas from
Spain. The troops that debarked near
Nassau and demanded the surrender of the
Spanish fortress were both black and white.

It seems probable that most of the blacks
serving with the British left the country of
their own will. (When Isaac and Kitt, in
New York, were urged by their Virginia
master to return to the plantation—he
promised to forget that they had run
away—they both spurned the idea; Isaac
said he had heard that slaves who went back
were "treated with great severity.") When
the king's armies departed from the United

COLONEL MALCOM TO GENERAL HEATH.

Niack, December 7th, 1776.

SIR: I had the honour to receive your most obliging letter of the 4th instant yesterday, and am exceeding happy that the conduct of the regiment under my command hath merited the approbation which your Honour very politely expresses.

A scouting party, which went down to hover on the verge of the enemy's quarters about *English Neighbourhood*, brought in a stout negro fellow, the property of a Tory, (one *Peck*,) who is now with the enemy; and the negro has been employed as a spy to bring them accounts of our motions. I beg to know how I must dispose of him.

I request your Honour will inform me if the Treasury is moved. I expect my abstracts from Head-Quarters to-day, and would be glad to get the cash here.

I have the honour to be, with due respect, sir, your most obedient and very humble servant,

W. MALCOM.

To Major-General *Heath*, at *Peekskill*.

I have forty men just going out again.

63. Colonel W. Malcolm to Major General William Heath, December 7, 1776. Massachusetts Historical Society.

States at the war's end, there went with them at least fourteen thousand blacks—six thousand from Charleston and four thousand each from Savannah and New York. Some were still the slaves of Tories; most were ex-slaves whose possible path to freedom, in their eyes, had led to the losing camp of Dunmore, Clinton, and Cornwallis. They sailed to Halifax, Jamaica, St. Lucia, Nassau, and England, grimly hopeful of the chance to begin a new life. "If anything," Quarles adds, "these figures are a bit low, and they do not, of course, include those who went off with the French, nor the thousands—perhaps around five thousand—whom the British carried away prior to the surrender of Yorktown." There were also some forty-five hundred black refugees who had fled South Carolina and Georgia and made their way to East Florida.

Some of the royal army's black soldiers and laborers—victims of callous treatment by redcoat officers—did not leave in the British ships. A sequence of events jotted down in his journal by the Hessian captain Johann Ewald, campaigning in Virginia in 1781, might be seen as a pattern of betrayal, sad enough to touch even a mercenary's heart:

[April 17] Because I lacked some cavalry . . . twelve Negroes were mounted and armed. I trained them as well as possible and they gave me thoroughly good service, for I sought to win them by good treatment, to which they were not accustomed.

[June 21] . . . Lord Cornwallis had permitted each subaltern to keep two horses and one Negro, each captain, four horses and two Negroes, and so on, according to rank. . . . this order was not strictly carried out. . . . Every officer had four to six horses and three or four Negroes, as well as one or two Negresses for cook

Drittes Regiment Garde.
Chef. Se. Hochfürstliche Durchlaucht der Landgraf

64. *Hessian Third Guard Regiment,* engraved by J. C. Müller after drawing by J. H. Carl, ca. 1784. Anne S. K. Brown Military Collection, Brown University Library.

and maid . . . I can testify that every soldier had his Negro, who carried his provisions and bundles. This multitude always hunted [foraged] at a gallop, and behind the baggage followed well over four thousand Negroes of both sexes and all ages. . . . They had plundered the wardrobes of their masters and mistresses, divided the loot. . . . a completely naked Negro wore a pair of silk breeches, another a finely colored coat, a third a silk vest without sleeves, a fourth an elegant shirt, a fifth a fine churchman's hat, and a sixth a wig.— . . . one Negress wore a silk skirt, another a lounging robe with a long train. . . .

If one imagines all these variegated creatures on thousands of horses, then one has the complete picture. . . .

[October 14] I would just as soon forget to record a cruel happening. On the same day of the enemy assault, we drove back to the enemy all of our black friends, whom we had taken along to despoil the countryside. We had used them to good advantage and set them free, and now, with fear and trembling, they had to face the reward of their cruel masters. Last night, I came across a great number of these unfortunates. In their hunger, these unhappy people would have soon devoured what I had . . . we should have thought more about their deliverance at this time.

There were other black soldiers and laborers who, after the war was over, were either abandoned by the British or chose to continue their fight for freedom at home. A Georgia historian recorded in 1859 the known facts about a "corps" of some three hundred "runaway negroes, the leaders of which, having been trained to arms by the British during the siege of Savannah, still called themselves the 'King of England's Soldiers,' and ravaged both sides of the Savannah River, plundering and murdering, to the great alarm of the people; who also feared that the presence of this body of freebooters would lead to a general and bloody insurrection of the slaves in that vicinity." On May 6, 1786, a detachment of Georgia and South Carolina militia, guided by a few Catawba Indians, stormed the maroons in their improvised fortress, which consisted of a rectangular breastwork of logs and cane about a hundred yards wide and half a mile long. Many of the King of England's Soldiers were killed or captured; some escaped into the tangled brakes.

This was not the end of the resistance. In November, the *Massachusetts Gazette* printed a report from Georgia:

> October 19. A number of runaway negroes (supposed to be upwards of 100) having sheltered themselves on Bellisle Island, about 17 or 18 miles up Savannah river, and for some time past committed robberies on the neighbouring Planters, it was found necessary to attempt to dislodge them . . . a small party of militia landed and attacked them, and killed three or four; but were at last obliged to retreat for want of ammunition, having four of their number wounded. Same evening, about sunset, 15 of the Savannah Light Infantry, and three or four others, drove in one of their out-guards; but the Negroes came down in such numbers, that it was judged advisable to retire to their boats from which the Negroes attempted to cut them off. Lieut. Elfe . . . had a field piece on board, which he discharged three times with grapeshot, and it is thought either killed or wounded some of them, as a good deal of blood was afterwards seen. . . . On Friday morning Gen. Jackson, with a party, proceeded to their camp, which they had quitted precipitately on his approach. He remained till Saturday afternoon, when he left the island having destroyed as much rough rice as would have made 25 barrels or more if beat out, and brought off about 69 bushels of corn, and 14 or 15 boats or canoes from the landing. He also burnt a number of the houses and huts, and destroyed about four acres of green rice. The loss of their provisions, it is expected, will occasion them to disperse about the country, and it is hoped will be the means of most of them being soon taken up.

THE saga of the black men, women, and children who sailed to Nova Scotia with the British deserves to be better known as part of the history of the African diaspora and the American revolution. Here is a brief account of a figure of some stature in that history.

Thomas Peters fought for his freedom in the service of the king, but that is only part of the saga of this black Moses—a cluster of fact and legend that relates him to the times

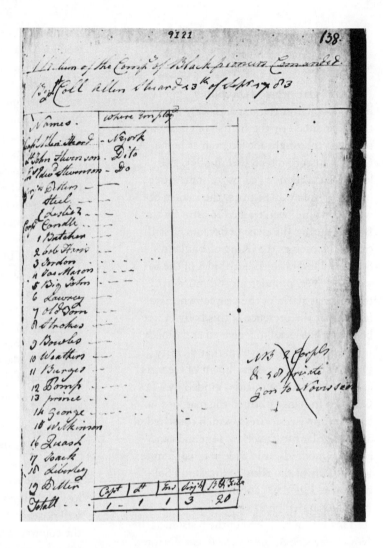

65. "A Return of the Comp^y of Black pioneers Commanded by Lt Col. Allen Steward," September 13, 1783. Public Records Office, London, photograph, Colonial Williamsburg Foundation.

of Martin Delany and Marcus Garvey. Peters was an Egba of the Yoruba tribe, of royal birth and "strong, far beyond the ordinary man," claim his descendants now living in Freetown, Sierra Leone. In the 1760s, he was kidnapped by the slave ship *Henri Quatre* and ended up on an American plantation, perhaps in Louisiana. He was then in his twenties. Legend has it that his master kept him shackled. After his first attempt to escape, he was forced to wear a broad iron belt from which hung two massive linked chains which connected the ankle bands. He

was whipped after each dash for liberty; the third time he was branded.

On the eve of the revolution, Peters was the slave of one William Campbell in Wilmington, North Carolina. When Lord Dunmore dangled the bait of freedom, he ran away into the British lines. Three years later, Sally, his wife-to-be, fled her master in Charleston, South Carolina. Peters fought with the British for the entire war and was twice wounded. No doubt his commitment to freedom, his courage, and his ability to lead brought him to the fore. His name ap-

66. List of the "Negroes [Black Pioneers], belonging to Captain Martin's Company," undated. The William L. Clements Library, The University of Michigan.

pears as "Petters" with the rank of sergeant in "a Return of the Companies of Black Pioneers" for September 13, 1783. He later described himself as "a free Negro and late Serjt. in the Regiment of Guides and Pioneers serving in North America under the Command of Genl. Sir Henry Clinton" [figs. 65 and 66].

The war over, Peters and his veteran comrades asked the British to keep their promises. In May 1784 the king's ships landed them in Nova Scotia. True, they were free, but where were the pledged farms? Peters hoped to work as a millwright. The reality was weasel words instead of farms, unclearable land for a few,

67. William Booth, *A Black Wood Cutter at Shelburne, Nova Scotia 1788,* watercolor. National Archives of Canada /C-40162.

slavelike apprenticeships to white Tories [fig. 67]. In August, Peters and Murphy Steel, another ex-sergeant in the Black Pioneers, petitioned the royal governor for an immediate grant of the promised acreage—to no avail. After six years of struggle, in which he was supported by his people, he determined to go to London. As he later wrote, the trip was one of "much Trouble and Risk"; he was fifty years old, carrying a complaint against the hostile governor, an ex-slave voyaging alone.

In London, after initial hardship, it is possible that he received his first help from a brother African, ex-slave Ottobah Cugoano, a Fanti who had been sold in the West Indies and brought to London as a servant. Four years earlier Cugoano had written a celebrated book, *Thoughts and Sentiments on the Evil and Wicked Traffic of Slavery and Commerce of the Human Species* [fig. 68]. It was Cugoano who probably introduced Peters to the great English abolitionists Granville Sharp, William Wilberforce, and Thomas Clarkson. Peters found his old commander-in-chief, Sir Henry Clinton, sympathetic to his cause. The upshot was that the aboli-

tionists agreed to support the petition that Peters had brought with him over the ocean, in which, "on Behalf of himself and others [of] the Black Pioneers and loyal Black Refugees" of Annapolis and New Brunswick, he demanded a "competent Settlement" [fig. 69]. He was "Attorney" for two groups: those "Black People . . . earnestly desirous of obtaining their due Allotment of Land and remaining in America," and those who were "ready and willing to go wherever the Wisdom of Government may think proper to provide for them as free Subjects of the British Empire." The British secretary of state endorsed the petition and ordered the governor of Nova Scotia to comply.

Meanwhile another path had opened up for Peters—a path back to Africa. A few years earlier, English abolitionists, appalled by the hard lot of the black poor in England, had helped some four hundred blacks begin a new life on the coast of Sierra Leone. A company had been formed to promote the idea. Why not offer the plan to the stranded, outraged black Nova Scotians—transportation to Sierra Leone and twenty

THOUGHTS AND SENTIMENTS

ON THE

EVIL AND WICKED TRAFFIC

OF THE

SLAVERY AND COMMERCE

OF THE

HUMAN SPECIES,

HUMBLY SUBMITTED TO

The INHABITANTS of GREAT-BRITAIN,

BY

OTTOBAH CUGOANO,

A NATIVE of AFRICA.

He that stealeth a man and selleth him, or maketh merchandize of him, or if he be found in his hand: then that thief shall die.　　　LAW OF GOD.

LONDON:

PRINTED IN THE YEAR

M.DCC.LXXXVII.

68. Ottobah Cugoano, *Thoughts and Sentiments . . .* (London, 1787). Courtesy of the Library of Congress.

69. Petition of Thomas Peters to William Wyndham Grenville, December 18, 1790. Public Records Office, London.

acres for each settler? Peters said yes, returned to Canada, and rounded up his own group of eighty-four emigrants, including his wife and six children. In January 1792 some twelve hundred settlers in fifteen ships sailed from Halifax for Freetown.

The rest belongs to the early history of the modern state of Sierra Leone. Although Thomas Peters died of fever only four months after returning to his native land, his name is imperishably linked to its history: kidnapped slave, branded fugitive, Tory soldier seeking his own freedom, early organizer of his own people for their return to the homeland, and finally, as his biographer noted, a founding father of Sierra Leone.*

*In the latest treatment of Thomas Peters, Gary B. Nash refers to him "as a leader of as great a stature as many a famous 'historical' figure of the Revolutionary era. Only because the keepers of the past are drawn from the racially dominant group in American society has Peters failed to find his way into history textbooks. . . ." The history of another colonial slave, Boston King of South Carolina, who fled to the British, is self-told. After the war, King struggled for a living on the land in Nova Scotia and as a crewman on an American whaler. He ended up as a cleric and schoolmaster in Sierra Leone. The story is told in "Memoirs of the Life of Boston King, a Black Preacher, Written by Himself . . ." (1798), published in his lifetime.

IV

The Black Clergy

It is probable that the earliest black pastors were exhorters in the slave quarters, preachers without churches—like two who turn up in advertisements for the return of fugitive slaves in Virginia: "Run away [in 1772] . . . a likely Virginia born Mulatto Lad named Primus, about nineteen or twenty Years of Age. . . . He has been a Preacher ever since he was sixteen . . . and has done much Mischief in his Neighborhood. . . ." Or: [in 1775] "Run away . . . a dark mulatto man named Jemmy . . . a very artful fellow . . . he is very fond of singing hymns and preaching. . . ." As late as the spring of 1793, a notice in the Baltimore *Maryland Journal* sought the return of a "Young negro man slave . . . named Sam. . . . He was raised in a Family of religious persons, commonly called methodists and has lived with some of them for years past, on terms of perfect equality; the refusal to continue him on these terms . . . has given him offence, and is the sole cause

of his absconding. Sam is about twenty-three years old, 5 feet 8 or 9 inches high, pretty square made, has a down look, very talkative among persons whom he can make free with, but slow of speech; he has been in the use of instructing and exhorting his fellow creatures of all colors in matters of religious duty. . . ."

The formation of the African-American church, north and south, under the tutelage of a handful of black apostles during the era of the revolution, was not solely a religious milestone. "I entreat you to consider the obligations we lie under to help forward the cause of freedom," cried Richard Allen, who in his old age was to be the country's first black bishop, in his "Address to the People of Colour" in 1794. As Charles H. Wesley has observed, the rise of the black church during the birthing time of the nation was an early assertion of "organized independence and self-expression" in the total life of revolutionary black America.

Founders of the African Baptist Church: David George, George Liele, Andrew Bryan

The determination of the southern slave to live his own religious life and to exploit the available forms of Christian association in order to construct a black solidarity beyond the slave quarters of a single plantation may be seen in the careers of three pioneer black Baptist preachers: David George, George Liele, and Andrew Bryan. At the close of the revolution, the first two stayed in the king's camp: George continued his work in Canada and Africa and Liele in the West Indies. Bryan built a church in Georgia [fig. 70].*

David George

The first black Baptist church in America was gathered among the slaves at Silver Bluff in South Carolina between 1773 and 1775 by David George. The lineaments of its first pastor, born in Virginia in 1742, must be discerned in his eventful life. A runaway to South Carolina, he eluded the

---

*Black Baptists were active in Virginia as well as in Georgia, as is shown by three advertisements for runaway slaves in the *Virginia Gazette:* "formerly the property of Rev. John Dixon . . . Nat . . . pretends to be very religious, and is a Baptist teacher . . ." [1778]; "Tim, about thirty . . . has a very smooth way of speaking . . . and pretends to be a Baptist preacher . . . lately seen near Williamsburg . . ." [1783]; and "a Negro man named Samuel . . . Virginia born, speaks plain . . . about twenty-six. . . . He is a Baptist preacher and very fond of what he calls preaching . . ." [1786].

Benjamin Quarles notes that black Peter Willis, born in South Carolina in 1762, moved westward in the 1790s, and as a licensed Baptist preacher delivered the first Protestant sermon west of the Mississippi at Vermilion, a village forty miles southwest of Baton Rouge in 1804.

70. John Rippon, "An Account of Several Baptist Churches, consisting chiefly of NEGRO SLAVES . . . ," excerpt, *The Baptist Annual Register* . . . (London, 1793). Courtesy of the Library of Congress.

bloodhounds for two years and then hid out with the Indians, first as a servant to Creek chief Blue Salt, later to Natchez chief King Jack, who in the early seventies sold him to a plantation on the Savannah River, twelve miles from Augusta. A Baptist slave, one Cyrus, awakened him to Christ and, helped by his master's children, he learned to read and write using the Bible as primer and text. Not long after, a few slaves baptized by a white minister formed a church. "Then I began to exhort in church, and learned to sing hymns," George later recorded. "I was appointed to the office of an elder. . . . I proceeded in this way till the American War was coming on. . . . I continued preaching at Silver Bluff, till the church, constituted with eight, increased to thirty or more. . . ." When the British occupied Savannah in 1778 and his patriot owner abandoned the plantation at Silver Bluff, George with his black flock—they had doubtless pondered Dunmore's offer of emancipation—took off for the British lines and freedom.

In Savannah during the next few years, George joined Liele and Bryan in preaching the word, but at the end of the war the three went their separate ways—Liele to establish the Baptist Church in Jamaica, Bryan in Savannah. George never returned to Silver Bluff but after the revolution his old church revived under the guidance of the slave pastor Jesse Peter. Instead, George and hundreds of his brothers sailed with the defeated British to Nova Scotia, where, for ten years, barely surviving lynch threat and arson ("they came one night and stood before the pulpit and swore how they would treat me if I preached again"), he exhorted Baptist congregations, at first made up of black and white. He opened the first Baptist church in Shelburne.

After a decade of selfless labor in the Canadian vineyard, George's story merges with that of Thomas Peters, the Tory corporal who with his Black Pioneers migrated in 1792 from Halifax to Freetown. David George also voyaged to Africa, where with Peters he became a founding father of Sierra Leone and planted the first Baptist church in West Africa.

George Liele

Of his origins, George Liele wrote: "I was born in Virginia, my father's name was Liele, and my mother's name Nancy; I can-

not ascertain much of them, as I went to several parts of America when young, and at length resided in New Georgia; but was informed both by white and black people, that my father was the only black person who knew the Lord . . ." [fig. 71]. In 1773 Liele moved with his master, a Baptist deacon by the name of Henry Sharp, to Burke County in Georgia, where a white minister brought him into the Baptist fold. He felt a call to preach. "Desiring to prove the sense I had of my obligations to God, I endeavoured to instruct the people of my own color in the word of God: the white brethren seeing my endeavours gave me a call at a quarterly meeting to preach before the congregation." Licensed as a probationer, for two years he carried the word to the slave quarters of the plantations on the Savannah River from Silver Bluff, where he exhorted David George's newly gathered church, to the suburbs of Savannah.

Sometime before the revolution, Deacon Sharp liberated the black preacher. In 1778, after Sharp had lost his life as a Tory officer, Liele joined the stream of black folk on their way to Savannah. There he met trouble when Sharp's heirs tried to reenslave him, but the British officer he served backed him up. Wasting no time, he began immediately to gather a church and for three years, during the British occupation of Savannah, he inspired a growing congregation of black Baptists, slave and free. David George and Andrew Bryan listened to George Liele and learned.

When the British evacuated Savannah in 1782, Liele sailed with them to Jamaica, paying his passage as an indentured servant. Two years later, settled in Kingston with his family and fully free, he began again to preach, at first in a private home. Then, as he recalled, "I formed the church with four brethren from America." The preaching went well "with the poorer sort, especially

71. The Reverend George Liele, illustration in Joel A. Rogers, *Africa's Gift to America* (New York, 1961).

the slaves," although whites "at first persecuted us both at meetings and baptisms." He fought back, drew up a "petition of our distresses," and wrung a promise of toleration from the Assembly. The church prospered. "I have baptized four hundred in Jamaica," he wrote in December 1791. "At Kingston I baptize in the sea, at Spanish Town in the river, and at convenient places in the country. We have nigh *three hundred and fifty members;* a few white people among them. . . ."

There is little protest against slavery in Liele's letters to his white Baptist colleagues. He is candid if joyless about the concessions he had been forced to make for the sake of survival. To guarantee that he was no fomenter of revolt, he submitted to the authorities for their inspection every scrap of prayer used in his service. The "chiefest part of our society are poor, illiterate slaves, some living on sugar estates, some on mountains, pens, and other settle-

ments . . . the free people in our society are but poor. . . . We receive none into the church without a few lines from their owners of their good behaviour towards them and religion. . . ." It is hard to decode the piety; the records are sparse. Is it significant that one of Liele's main interests was the promotion of "a *free school* for the instruction of children, both free and slave . . ."?

Looking back when he was forty, ten years after he had left Georgia with the British, George Liele, building a church on his own three acres at the east end of Kingston, seems to have been marking time: "I have a wife and four children. My wife was baptised by me in Savannah. . . . My occupation is a farmer. . . . I also keep a team of horses, and waggons for the carrying goods from one place to another, which I attend to myself, with the assistance of my sons. . . . I have a few books, some good old authors and sermons, and one large bible . . . a good many of our members can read, and are all desirous to learn. . . ."

Liele kept in touch with other pioneer black Baptists whom the stir of revolution had brought together. In his tally of their successes, is there a note of just pride in a collective enterprise, however limited by the powers that still ruled, as they struggled to pierce the white fog of slavery to a clearer day?

> The last accounts I had from Savannah were, that the Gospel had taken very great effect both there and in South Carolina. Brother Andrew Bryan, a black minister at Savannah, has two hundred members. . . . Also I received accounts from Nova Scotia of a black Baptist preacher, Brother David George, who was a member of the church at Savannah; he had the permission of the Governor to preach

in three provinces. . . . Brother Amos is at Providence [Bahamas], he writes me that . . . he has about three hundred members. Brother Jessy Gaulsing, another black minister, preaches near Augusta, in South Carolina, at a place where I used to preach . . . has sixty members; and a great work is going on there.

Andrew Bryan

Andrew Bryan was born a slave at Goose Creek, South Carolina, about sixteen miles from Charleston, in 1737. In Savannah, during the war, he harkened to the words of George Liele, who baptized him and his wife, Hannah, in 1782. Nine months after Liele had departed for Jamaica, Bryan took up his work and began to preach to small groups—mostly blacks with a few whites—at Yamacraw on the outskirts of Savannah. His master encouraged him, thought his influence on the slaves was "salutary," and allowed him to build a shack for worship, but hostile whites "artfully dispossessed" him. With the help of his brother Sampson, he gathered his flock in the swamps. On January 20, 1788, a white Baptist minister, Abraham Marshall of Kiokee, and the black minister Jesse Peter of Silver Bluff certified the congregation as "the Ethiopian church of Jesus Christ" and ordained "beloved Brother Andrew to the work of the ministry . . . to preach the Gospel, and administer the ordinances, as God in his providence may call." Thus was formed the First Bryan Baptist Church, which lives today in Savannah [figs. 72 and 73].

The organization of this church was an unhappy event for Georgia masters who feared slave uprisings. They quickly forbade their slaves to listen to Bryan's sermons. Even when a slave carried a pass, the whip of the patrol fell on his back; he was jailed and abused; meetings were heckled. In July 1790, Marshall wrote from Savannah: "The whites grew more and more inveterate; taking numbers of them before magistrates [about fifty, including Sampson]—they were imprisoned and whipped . . . particularly *Andrew, who was cut and bled abundantly* . . . he held up his hand, and told his persecutors that he rejoiced not only to be whipped, but *would freely suffer death for the cause of Jesus Christ.*" After his owner, Jonathan Bryan, protested to the magistrates, Andrew was released and resumed preaching at Brampton, three miles from Savannah, in a barn on the plantation. By the end of 1791 he had brought hundreds into his church, although he had been forced to confront a critical problem: there were, in fact, three hundred and fifty slaves, already "converted," who could not be baptized because their masters did not think Christianity "salutary" for blacks.

Bryan was a stubborn saint. In 1792 he appointed four deacons, while his brother Sampson, still a slave, helped as an assistant preacher. His church flourished: fifty of its members could read, three could write. When his master died, he bought himself free for fifty pounds, supported himself by his own labor, and built himself a home. In 1794, with the help of white Baptists, he raised enough money to erect a house of prayer.

A few days before Christmas 1800, the Reverend Andrew Bryan wrote to a white Baptist colleague:

With much pleasure, I inform you, dear sir, that I enjoy good health, and am strong in body, tho' 63 years old, and am blessed with a pious wife, whose freedom I have obtained, and an only daughter and child, who is married to a free man, tho' she, and consequently, under our laws, her seven children, five sons and two

72. The First African Baptist Church of Savannah, established in 1788, photograph by James M. Simms, *The First Colored Baptist Church in North America . . .* (Philadelphia, 1888).

daughters, are slaves. By a kind Providence I am well provided for, as to worldly comforts, (tho' I have had very little given to me as a minister) having a house and a lot in this city, besides the land on which several buildings stand, for which I receive a small rent, and a fifty-six acre tract of land, with all necessary buildings, four miles in the country. . . .

He owned "eight slaves"—members of his family—"for whose education and happiness, I am enabled thro' mercy to provide." His congregation now numbered about seven hundred blacks who "enjoy the rights of conscience to a valuable extent, worshiping in our families and preaching three times every Lord's-day, baptizing frequently from ten to thirty at a time in the Savannah, and administering the sacred supper, not only without molestation, but in the presence, and with the approbation and encouragement of many of the white people." Soon Andrew Bryan was writing about his "large church," which was "getting too unwieldy for one body." Before long there would be branches—the Second and Third Baptist churches in Savannah. The latter was guided by Henry Francis of Augusta, who

had been purchased and liberated so that, as Bryan put it, he could come to Savannah "to exercise the handsome ministerial gifts he possesses amongst us, and teach our youth to read and write."

When Bryan died in 1812 at a ripe seventy-five, the white Savannah Baptist Association eulogized the "pastor of the First Colored Church in Savannah": "This son of Africa, after suffering inexpressible persecutions in the cause of his divine Master, was at length permitted to discharge the duties of the ministry among his colored friends in peace and quiet, hundreds of whom, through his instrumentality, were brought to a knowledge of the truth as 'it is in Jesus.'"

THIS brief account of the three founders can give only passing notice to other men of mark who were also present during the birthing time of the African Baptist Church in the new nation. In Virginia—at Petersburg, Richmond, Charles City, Williamsburg, Gloucester, Isle of Wight—from 1776 to 1800, Baptist churches, some of them black and white, some all white, sprang up under the tutelage of black preachers. Of them little more is known

73. The Reverend Andrew Bryan, stained glass. First African Baptist Church, Savannah.

than their names: the Reverend Mr. Moses, Gowan Pamphlet, William Lemon, Uncle Jack, Thomas Armstead, and Josiah Bishop. Often even the name has been lost. Johann David Schoepf, traveling in Florida in 1784, noted in his journal as he stopped at St. Augustine: "Not far off an association of Negroes have a cabin, in which one of their own countrymen, who has set himself up to be their teacher, holds services. They are of the sect of the Anabaptists." Sometime before the turn of the century, Joseph Willis, a licensed black preacher born in South Carolina in 1762, headed for the western frontier. In November 1804, at Vermilion, a hamlet about forty miles southwest of Baton Rouge, he preached the first Baptist (and Protestant) sermon west of the Mississippi.

Founders of the African Methodist Church: Richard Allen, Absalom Jones, Peter Williams

A catalytic moment in the early struggle for black religious independence in the United States occurred on a Sunday morning in Philadelphia during the fall of 1792.* Years later the venerable Richard Allen, bishop of the African Methodist Episcopal Church, musing over his "trials and sufferings" in behalf of "Adam's lost race," recorded that moment:

A number of us usually attended St. George's Church in Fourth Street; and when the colored people began to get numerous in attending the church, they moved us from the seats we usually sat on, and placed us around the wall, and on Sabbath morning we went to church and the sexton stood at the door, and told us to go in the gallery. He told us to go, and we would see where to sit. We expected to take the seats over the ones we formerly occupied below, not knowing any better. We took those seats. Meeting had begun, and they were nearly done singing, and just as we got to the seats, the elder said, "Let us pray." We had not been long upon our knees before I heard considerable scuffling and low talking. I raised my head up and saw one of the trustees, H—— M——, having hold of the Rev. Absalom Jones, pulling him off of his knees, and saying, "You

*Gary B. Nash's recent chapter on the origins of the black church in Philadelphia is a valuable contribution to the subject (" 'To Arise Out of the Dust': Absalom Jones and the African Church of Philadelphia, 1785–95," in his *Race, Class, and Politics: Essays on American Colonial and Revolutionary Society* [Urbana, 1986]).

must get up—you must not kneel here." Mr. Jones replied, "Wait until prayer is over." Mr. H—— M—— said, "No, you must get up now, or I will call for aid and force you away." Mr. Jones said, "Wait until prayer is over, and I will get up and trouble you no more." With that he beckoned to one of the other trustees, Mr. L—— S—— to come to his assistance. He came, and went to William White to pull him up.

"By this time prayer was over," Allen recalled, "and we all went out of the church in a body, and they were no more plagued with us in the church." After that proud exit, "We were filled with fresh vigor to get a house erected to worship God in." It was not easy. They hired a storeroom in which to pray by themselves, but "bore much persecution" from white Methodists. "We will disown you all," the elder threatened again and again. "We told him we were dragged off our knees in St. George's church, and treated worse than heathens, and we were determined to seek out for ourselves, the Lord being our helper."

Richard Allen

He was born a slave in Philadelphia ten years before the Boston Massacre. His master was the Quaker lawyer Benjamin Chew, chief justice of Pennsylvania during the revolution. Chew sold the Allen family—father, mother, and four children—into Delaware, near the town of Dover, to one Stokeley, who, as Allen remembered, was "an unconverted man," but "a good master" and a "father" to his slaves. In 1777 seventeen-year-old Richard was converted to Methodism along with his mother, sister, and elder brother. Shortly after, he joined the Methodist Society in his neighborhood and began to attend class meetings in the forest:

> Our neighbors, seeing that our master indulged us with the privilege of attending meeting once in two weeks, said that Stokeley's negroes would soon ruin him; and so my brother and myself held a council together . . . so that it should not be said that religion made us worse servants; we would work night and day to get our crops forward. . . . At length, our master said he was convinced that religion made slaves better and not worse, and often boasted of his slaves for their honesty and industry.

When the Reverend Freeborn Garrettson, the Methodist circuit rider who had liberated his own slaves in 1775, preached from the text, "Thou art weighted in the balance, and art found wanting," Stokeley, conscience-stricken, "proposed to me and my brother buying our times" for sixty pounds hard cash or two thousand dollars in Continental paper. Somehow the Allen brothers raised their ransom: "I had it often impressed upon my mind that I would one day enjoy my freedom; for slavery is a bitter pill, notwithstanding we had a good master. But when we would think that our day's work was never done, we often thought that after our master's death we were liable to be sold to the highest bidder, as he was much in debt; and thus . . . I was often brought to weep between the porch and the altar."

Richard Allen now went to work for himself, sawing cordwood and making bricks. "I was after this employed in driving of wagon in time of the Continental war, in drawing salt from Rehobar, Sussex county, in Delaware. I had my regular stops and preaching places on the road. . . . After

74. Unknown artist, *Richard Allen,* pastel and chalk, 1784. Howard University Gallery.

peace was proclaimed, I then travelled extensively. . . ." From Delaware he made his way into west Jersey, preaching the Gospel at night and on Sundays, cutting wood for his bread on the weekdays. Like the Quaker abolitionist John Woolman, Allen wandered about the countryside. In east Jersey he was lamed by rheumatism; in Pennsylvania, "I walked until my feet became so sore and blistered the first day, that I scarcely could bear them to the ground." At Radnor, twelve miles from Philadelphia, strangers took him in and bathed his feet. "I preached for them the next evening" and "on Sabbath day to a large congregation of different persuasions." Staying on in Radnor for "several weeks," he inspired a small revival. "There were but few colored people in the neighborhood—the most of my congregation was white. Some said, 'this man must be a man

of God; I never heard such preaching before.' "

At the end of December 1784, when sixty preachers gathered in Baltimore for the first organizing conference of American Methodism, it is probable that Allen was present and that in 1785 he accompanied Bishop Asbury as a "helper" on the Baltimore circuit. "My lot was cast in Baltimore," he remembered, "in a small meeting-house called Methodist Alley . . . I had some happy meetings in Baltimore. . . . Rev. Bishop Asbury sent for me. . . . He told me he wished me to travel with him. He told me that in the slave countries, Carolina and other places, I must not intermix with the slaves, and I would frequently have to sleep in his carriage, and he would allow me my victuals and clothes. I told him I would not travel with him on these conditions." Is there a hint of this precious alloy of firm spirit and plain dignity in the chalk and pastel portrait of twenty-five-year-old Richard Allen limned by an unknown artist at about this time [fig. 74]? A later black Methodist bishop cherished this portrait and passed it on to his son, Henry Ossawa Tanner, the fine painter of scriptural themes who was Thomas Eakins's best pupil.

Rejecting Bishop Asbury's flawed offer, Allen continued to ride and preach on his own: "I received nothing from the Methodist connection. My usual method was when I would get bare of clothes, to stop travelling and go to work. . . . My hands administered to my necessities." It is possible to think of him at this time, wrote Charles H. Wesley, as "an unordained Methodist preacher . . . who could travel and preach without ministerial orders or authority from a conference." In the autumn of 1785 he returned to Radnor: "I killed seven beeves, and supplied the neighbors with meat; got myself pretty well clad through my own industry—thank God—and preached occasionally." The following year was a turning point. When, in February 1786, the Methodist elder in charge sent for him, he gave up his wanderings and journeyed to Philadelphia—where he would meet Absalom Jones.

Absalom Jones

He was born a slave in Sussex, Delaware (where Allen hauled salt) on November 6, 1746. As a child he learned to read, and with the pennies he managed to save he bought a speller and a Testament. When he was sixteen, his master took him to Philadelphia and put him to work in a shop where his job was "to store, pack up and carry out goods." A clerk taught him to write, and in 1766 he was permitted to study in night school. Four years later he married one of his master's slaves and bought her freedom with money the couple earned working evenings for wages. (Since a child's status followed its mother's, it was proper to liberate a wife first.) Working hard, they acquired a home. In 1784, while Allen was preaching in Pennsylvania and Maryland, Absalom Jones bought his own freedom. The couple continued in the employ of their old master and in time built two houses and rented them. When Richard Allen rode into Philadelphia to begin his historic work, Absalom Jones was already prominent among the black members of St. George's Methodist Episcopal Church.

For the next thirty-odd years, although they would seek the independence of the black church on different paths, Richard Allen and Absalom Jones would be coworkers and leaders in the striving of black people to achieve justice and equality.

When Allen arrived in Philadelphia, the Methodist elder in charge assigned him to preach at St. George's Church—at five in the morning. "I strove to preach as well as I could, but it was a great cross to bear. . . ." He had planned "to stop in Philadelphia a week or two," but his "labor was much blessed": "I soon saw a large field open in seeking and instructing my African brethren, who had been a long forgotten people and few of them attended public worship." He spread the Gospel all over the city, in the commons, and in the suburbs; "it was not uncommon for me to preach from four to five times a day." He "established prayer meetings" and "raised a society in 1786 of forty-two members," who "subscribed largely towards finishing St. George's church, in building the gallery and laying new floors. . . ."

Yet Allen felt "cramped." "I saw the necessity of erecting a place of worship for the colored people," he wrote, with a restraint that understated the historic nature of the decision. Indeed, no fanfare hailed the great idea. Ironically, when he proposed it to "the most respectable" blacks of the city, only three—all members of St. George's—agreed with him. One of them was Absalom Jones. The main opposition, however, came from the white Methodist clergy. The minister-in-charge in Philadelphia "was much opposed to an African church, and used very degrading and insulting language to us, to try and prevent us from going on." When the small group persisted in their desire for a separate place of worship and continued to recruit blacks for Methodism, the minister grew frantic and soon barred their meetings: "We viewed the forlorn state of our colored brethren . . . destitute of a place of worship. They were considered a nuisance."

It was at this point, even as they remained a harassed part of the Methodist Church, that Allen and Jones made a critical decision: it was also necessary to organize the blacks of Philadelphia outside the church. The decision, of course, was primarily a maneuver in the battle for religious autonomy, but it really went further and broke new ground. The Free African Society in Philadelphia, which came into being during the spring of 1787, was "the first evidence which history affords," wrote Wesley, "of an organization for economic and social cooperation among Negroes of the western world." Indeed, the opening sentence of its Articles of Association had the feeling of a great beginning: "We the free Africans and their descendants . . . do unanimously agree, for the benefit of each other. . . ." And the preamble rang out:

> Whereas Absalom Jones and Richard Allen, two men of the African race, who, for their religious life and conversation have obtained a good report among men, these persons, from a love to the people of their complexion whom they beheld with sorrow . . . often communed together . . . in order to form some kind of religious society, but there being too few to be found under the like concern, and those who were, differed in their religious sentiments; with these circumstances they labored for some time, till it was proposed, after a serious communication of sentiments, that a society should be formed, without regard to religious tenets, provided, the persons lived an orderly and sober life, in order to support one another in sickness, and for the benefit of their widows and fatherless children.

RICHARD ALLEN'S radical vision—"to seek out for ourselves"—was already the organized aim of the Free African Society, a wider sodality of the black community. Among its charter members were the first citizens of black Philadelphia—including Cyrus Bustill, once a slave but by then a prosperous baker. Bustill began as a Quaker and later joined the flock of Absalom Jones in the Protestant Episcopal Church of St. Thomas. After his retirement from business, he built a house for his family and in it organized a free school in which he was a teacher. Somewhat fatalistic in his religious ideas—as is evident in the manuscript of his address to "the Blacks in Philadelphia" in September 1787—he would nonetheless be a vigorous abolitionist for the rest of his life.

As time went on, the society, whose members "differed in their religious sentiments," seemed slow to inaugurate a separate black church. Allen grew restive, absented himself from meetings, and in June 1789 the society voted (Jones abstaining) to "discontinue" him as a member.

But Allen's view was really winning out. By the end of 1790, encouraged by Benjamin Franklin and Benjamin Rush, the society was ready to appoint a committee including Jones and a reinstated Allen to work on the problem. Writing to the abolitionist Granville Sharp in London, Rush told him of a plan to form "The African Church of Philadelphia," whose organizers had drawn up articles "so general as to embrace all and yet so orthodox in cardinal points as to offend none." Rush was right. The burgeoning black church belonged as yet to no sect. In August 1791, addressing "the Friends of Liberty and Religion," the "Representatives of the African Church in Philadelphia," terming themselves "the scattered and unconnected appendages of most of the religious societies of the city," sent out an appeal for funds. Allen was happy. "The first day the Rev. Absalom Jones and myself went out we collected three hundred and sixty dollars." Before long "[a] day was appointed" to break ground for the new church. "I arose early in the morning and addressed the throne of grace" and "as I was the first proposer of the African church, I put the first spade in the ground to dig a cellar for the same."

It was one thing to build a separate "African preaching-house," another to agree on what its doctrine should be. The question was debated at length in the Free African Society. "We then held an election, to know what religious denomination we should unite with." For Allen the vote was a disappointment—"there were two in favor of the Methodist, the Rev. Absalom Jones and myself, and a large majority in favor of the Church of England." Nor was his chagrin diminished when the "large majority" offered him the pastorate of a Protestant Episcopal church. He could not accept the call: "I was confident there was no religious sect or denomination would suit the capacity of the colored people as well as the Methodist; for the plain and simple gospel suits best for

any people. . . . The Methodist were the first people that brought glad tidings to colored people." When the majority made the same offer to Absalom Jones, he put aside doctrinal preference and accepted the pastorate.

IT was in this period of troubled groping for the correct religious way that an epidemic of yellow fever swept through the city during the summer of 1793 and ultimately killed five thousand Philadelphians, black and white, about a tenth of the population. In spite of their religious differences, the two black leaders got together (as they always would) to rally the city's blacks to fight the plague. Fifty physicians of Philadelphia, led by Dr. Rush, labored to stem death and panic. When, in early September, Rush published an appeal to the colored people of the city to assist in treating the sick and in burying the dead, Allen and Jones quickly responded: "We and a few others met and consulted how to act on so truly alarming and melancholy an occasion." After a conference with the mayor, they proceeded to their perilous tasks—Jones in charge of organizing the nursing of the sick, Allen of supervising the burial of the dead.

In their jointly written classic of 1794, *A Narrative of the Proceedings of the Black People, During the Late Awful Calamity in Philadelphia* [fig. 75], a magnificent rebuttal of slanderous misrepresentations of the black role during the crisis, Allen and Jones described the heroic service of the black community with a kind of laconic eloquence:

> Soon after, the mortality increasing, the difficulty of getting a corpse taken away, was such, that few were willing to do it, when offered great rewards. The black people were looked to. We then offered our services in the public papers, by advertising that we would

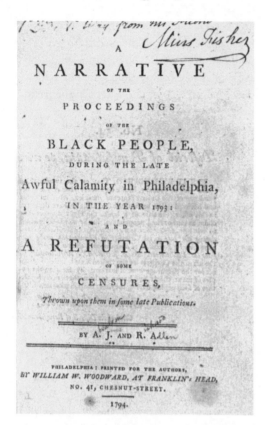

A
NARRATIVE
OF THE
PROCEEDINGS
OF THE
BLACK PEOPLE,
DURING THE LATE
Awful Calamity in Philadelphia,
IN THE YEAR 1793:
AND
A REFUTATION
OF SOME
CENSURES,
Thrown upon them in some late Publications.

BY A. J. AND R. Allen

PHILADELPHIA: PRINTED FOR THE AUTHORS,
BY WILLIAM W. WOODWARD, AT FRANKLIN's HEAD,
NO. 41, CHESNUT-STREET.
1794.

75. [Absalom Jones and Richard Allen], *A Narrative* . . . (Philadelphia, 1794). Courtesy of the Library of Congress.

remove the dead and procure nurses. Our services were the production of real sensibility;—we sought not fee nor reward. . . . It was very uncommon at this time, to find anyone that would go near, much more, handle a sick or dead person.

Of the group of prisoners in the town jail who "voluntarily offered themselves as nurses," two-thirds were "people of colour, who, on the application of the elders of the African church," had been liberated "to attend the sick at Bush-hill." When the

sickness became general, and several of the physicians died, and most of the survivors were exhausted by sickness or fatigue; that good man, Dr.

Rush, called us more immediately to attend upon the sick. . . . This has been no small satisfaction to us; for, we think that when a physician was not attainable, we have been the instruments, in the hand of God, for saving the lives of some hundreds of our suffering fellow mortals. . . . We have bled upwards of eight hundred people. . . .

There are unforgettable vignettes of the selfless "exercise of the finer feelings of humanity": an "elderly black woman nursed . . . with great diligence and attention; when recovered [her patient] asked what he must give for her services—she replied 'a dinner master on a cold winter's day. . . .' Caesar Cranchal, a black man, offered his services to attend the sick, and said, 'I will not take your money. I will not sell my life for money.' It is said he died with the flux."

The white delusion that blacks were immune to the contagion—initially advanced but later retracted by Dr. Rush—exasperated Allen and Jones:

Few have been the whites that paid attention to us while the blacks were engaged in the other's service. We can assure the public we have taken four and five black people in a day to be buried. In several instances when they have been seized with the sickness while nursing, they have been turned out of the house . . . they have languished alone, and we know of one who even died in a stable . . . as many coloured people died in proportion as others. In 1792, there were 67 of our colour buried, and in 1793 it amounted to 305; thus the burials among us have increased fourfold, was not this in a great degree the effects of the services of the unjustly vilified black people?

Outraged by such ingratitude—"It is unpleasant for us to make these remarks, but justice to our colour demands it"—the authors of *Narrative* seized the opportunity to castigate the racist ideology from which it flowed. Their "Address to those who keep Slaves, and approve the Practice," a short but powerful blast, is a green leaf from the early scripture of black liberation: "The judicious part of mankind will think it inreasonable, that a superior good conduct is looked for, from our race, by those who stigmatize us as men, whose baseness is uncurable, and may therefore be held in a state of servitude, that a merciful man would not doom a beast to; yet you try what you can to prevent our rising. . . ." Allen and Jones would have none of this slaveholder logic: "We can tell you . . . that a black man, although reduced to the most abject state . . . can think, reflect, and feel injuries. . . ." Try "the experiment of taking a few black children, and cultivate their minds with the same care, and let them have the same prospect in view, as to living in the world, as you would wish for your own children, you would find upon the trial, they were not inferior in mental endowments. . . . We wish you to consider, that God himself was the first pleader of the cause of slaves. . . . If you love your children, if you love your country, if you love the God of love, clear your hands from slaves, burden not your children or country with them."

The final note is portentous: "Will you, because you have reduced us to the unhappy condition our colour is in, plead our incapacity for freedom . . . as a sufficient cause for keeping us under the grievous yoke! . . . we appear contented . . . but the dreadful insurrections they [slaves] have made, when opportunity was offered, is enough to convince a reasonable man, that great uneasiness and not contentment, is the inhabitant of their hearts."

To far off Boston Allen's and Jones's fame would spread; in the *Massachusetts Magazine* of December 1793 an unknown admirer would publish a three-stanza "Eulogium in Honour of Absalom Jones and Richard Allen, Two of the Elders of the African Church, who Furnished Nurses to the Sick during the Late Pestilential Fever in Philadelphia":

> Brethren of man, and friend to human kind,
> Made of that blood which flow'd in Adam's vein!
> A muse who ever spurn'd at adulation's strains;
> Who rates not colour, but th'immortal mind,
> With transport guides the death redeeming plume;
> Nor leaves your names a victim to the tomb.

When five years later, in 1797 and 1798, the plague broke out again in Philadelphia, Richard Allen and his friend William Gray once more played an important part in fighting it. The Quaker philanthropist Samuel Coates wrote: "These two black men render'd very great Services . . . and I always thought it was reproachful to our City that they had not a *Reward* for their Labor— a thous'd dollars would have been a very Moderate Compensation for Grays labor— he died very poor & broken hearted."

THE plague at an end, Richard Allen and Absalom Jones turned their attention once more to the question of building the black church.

Rebuffed for the moment, Allen did not waiver in his conviction that the Methodist was the only right way for his people.

Working as a master shoemaker with jour-
neymen and apprentices in his employ, he
put enough aside to buy a lot for his church.
In early May 1794 a goodly number of the
city's blacks met with him "in order to con-
sult together . . . to provide for ourselves a
house to meet in for religious worship . . .
separate from our white brethren."—"I
bought an old frame," Allen recalled, "that
had been formerly occupied as a blacksmith
shop . . . and hauled it on the lot. . . . I
employed carpenters to repair the old frame,
and fit it for a place of worship. In July
1794, Bishop Asbury being in town I solicited him to open the church. . . . The
house was called Bethel"—its new pulpit
the work of Richard Allen's hands [fig. 76].

The house was called Bethel, but it
would require more than a score of years to
guarantee its independence, years of vig-
ilance for Allen as he tried to cope with the
hostility of Methodist "white preachers and
trustees." His gift of wise leadership was
soon recognized beyond the limits of his
church. In 1795 he opened a day school for
sixty pupils, and in 1804 he organized the
"Society of Free People of Colour for Promoting the Instruction and School Education of Children of African Descent." While
the country mourned the death of Washington, the *Philadelphia Gazette* printed Allen's Bethel sermon in which he stressed the
patriot who at the last had felt uneasy about
the sin of slavery: "If he who broke the yoke
of British burdens from the neck of the people of this land, and was called his country's
deliverer, by what name shall we call him
who secretly and almost unknown emancipated his bondmen and bondwomen, and
became to them a father, and gave them an
inheritance?" The Bethel Church prospered
and Allen was ordained deacon and elder by
Bishop Asbury. By 1810 there were almost
five hundred worshippers in his congregation; five years later there were more black

than white Methodists in Philadelphia.
Meanwhile Allen's message had spread.

Peter Williams

In New York City there was a black man
named Peter Williams who had been born
in a cow shed—"in as humble a place as my
Master," he would say with a smile
[fig. 77]. His owner was a tobacco merchant; the slave became an expert cigar
maker. As a youth, converted to Methodism, he listened to white preachers. Early in
1778 the trustees of the John Street Methodist Episcopal Church purchased him for
forty pounds sterling and made him sexton
of the church. In the spring, as the British
took over the city, he made off to New
Brunswick in Jersey, lived with a patriot
family, and met his wife, Molly, who later
presented him with a son, Peter Junior (who
would make his own mark in black religious
history). Local record has it that he saved an
outspoken white clergyman from a British
officer.

Williams was always proud of his patriotism. During the 1850s, his son sent Nell a
few reminiscences for his book:

In the Revolutionary War, my father was a decided advocate of American Independence, and his life was
repeatedly jeopardized in its
cause. . . . He was living in the State
of Jersey, and parson Chapman, a
champion of American liberty of
great influence throughout that part
of the country, was sought after by
the British troops. My father imme-
diatly mounted a horse and rode
round among his parishioners to no-
tify them of his danger, and to call on
them to help in removing him and his
goods to a place of safety. He then carried him to a private place, and as he
was returning, a British officer rode

76. Pulpit constructed by the Reverend Richard Allen. Mother Bethel African Methodist Episcopal Church, Philadelphia.

up to him, and demanded, in a most peremptory manner,—

"Where is parson Chapman?"

"I cannot tell," was the reply.

On that, the officer drew his sword, and, raising it over his head, said,—"Tell me where he is, or I will instantly cut you down."

Again he replied,—"I cannot tell."

Finding threats useless, the officer put up his sword, and drew out a purse of gold, saying,—"If you will tell me where he is, I will give you this."

The reply still was, "I cannot tell."

The officer cursed him and rode off.

This attachment to the country of his birth was strengthened and confirmed by the circumstance, that the very day on which the British evacuated New York was the same on which he obtained his freedom by purchase, through the help of some republican friends of the Methodist Church; and to the last year of his life, he always spoke of that day as one which gave double joy to his heart, by freeing him from domestic bondage, and his native city from foreign enemies.

In the fall of 1780, after the British evacuated New York, Williams and his wife returned to the John Street Church. They adopted an infant daughter. For the next sixteen years he performed the duties of sexton to the black and white congregation. He was a favorite of the white Methodists, for he was a hardworking and gentle man. Observe the black sexton standing "at his post" in the door of the John Street Church, as sketched in Joseph B. Smith's watercolor of 1817 [fig. 78].

Two years after Richard Allen opened the Bethel in Philadelphia something happened inside Peter Williams. There was no dramatic incident—nobody dragged him from his knees as he knelt in prayer—but one day, with a few of his black friends of the church, among them the future Bishop James Varick, he asked for a conference with Bishop Asbury. The blacks in the church had a "desire for the privilege of holding meetings of their own, where they might have an opportunity to exercise their spiritual gifts among themselves and thereby be

77. Unknown artist, *Peter Williams*, oil, ca. 1815. Courtesy of the New-York Historical Society, New York City.

more useful to one another." The bishop consented, and for the next three years they held separate meetings. Meanwhile Peter Williams, no longer sexton, was making good in his own tobacco business, acquiring a home and even some property. The legend is that he would not permit the racist name of a popular tobacco to be uttered in his shop. By 1799 the black Methodists of New York were ready to build their own house of

78. Joseph B. Smith, *The First Methodist Episcopal Church in America,* water-color, 1817. Museum of the City of New York.

worship, and on July 30, 1800, Peter Williams laid the cornerstone of the new church, called Zion. In his portrait, painted some time later by "a Frenchman from St. Domingo," he seems to exhibit a certain pride in the part he had played in planting the seed of the African Methodist Episcopal Zion Church of the future.

The Zion Church of Peter Williams was not the only offshoot of Richard Allen's Bethel. African Methodist Episcopal congregations would spring up in Baltimore, Maryland, and Wilmington, Delaware, as well as in Salem, New Jersey, and Attleboro, Pennsylvania, all of them suffering white Methodist harassment even as they flourished. In April 1816 the leaders of these congregations met with Allen in Philadelphia to launch the first fully independent black church in the United States. Elected as its first bishop, he composed a hymn to celebrate the event:

> The God of Bethel heard her cries,
> He let his power be seen;
> He stopp'd the proud oppressor's
> power. . . .

In the portrait of middle-aged Richard Allen engraved around this time, we can discern the black divine whom a later bishop of the same church, Daniel Payne, would de-

scribe as "a far-sighted churchman, modest without timidity, and brave without rashness. A lover of liberty, civil and religious . . ." [fig. 79].

DURING that summer of 1794 when Allen opened Bethel, Absalom Jones dedicated the St. Thomas African Episcopal Church of Philadelphia [fig. 80]. Ten years later, the rector of St. Thomas's would be the first black to be ordained an Episcopal priest in the United States. Although the church was always his base, Jones's interests and energies during the next quarter-century would be broadly enlisted in behalf of the welfare of his people. He would help organize a school for the black children of the city, found a society for the suppression of vice, create and direct an insurance company, and organize protest against the violation of black civil rights.

On December 30, 1799, the black community of Philadelphia, angered by kidnappings of free blacks on the coasts of Maryland and Delaware, made known their grievances to the president and Congress— "guardians of our rights, and patrons of equal and rational liberties." Signed by Absalom Jones and seventy-five other "people of Colour, free men" of Philadelphia, the petition argued that the "solemn compact"

79. Unknown artist, *Rev-
erend Richard Allen, Founder of the African Methodist
Episcopal Church in the
United States of America,
1779,* engraving, pub-
lished by J. Dainty, 1813.
Library Company of Phila-
delphia.

80. W. L. Breton, *The
African Episcopal Church of
St. Thomas, Philadelphia,*
lithograph, 1829. Histor-
ical Society of Pennsyl-
vania.

embedded in the preamble to the federal constitution was being "violated" by the slave trade—"poor helpless victims, like droves of cattle, are seized, fettered, and hurried into . . . dark cellars and garrets" and "transported to Georgia." Root out the evil, Jones admonished: "Undo the heavy burdens" of this "grossly abused part of the human species, seven hundred thousand of whom . . . are now in unconditional bondage in these states. . . ." Was the revolution real?—"if the Bill of Rights or the Declaration" is "of any validity, we beseech, that as we are men, we may be admitted to partake of the liberties and unalienable rights therein held forth." (Such anguish hardly touched the House, which saw in the petition a "tendency to create disquiet & jealousy.") Eight years later, in a sermon preached on January 1, 1808—when the African slave trade came to its legal end—Jones proposed that the day "be set apart in every year, as a day of publick thanksgiving," so that the children might remember the crime that dragged their "fathers from their native country, and sold them as bondmen in the United States of America." It was two years after this sermon during the winter of 1810 that Charles Willson Peale, the painter of the patriot fathers, visiting his son Raphaelle's studio, was happy to find that the younger man had "painted a Portrait in oil of Absalom Jones a very excellent picture of the Rev'd. Gentleman" [fig. 81].

Richard Allen and Absalom Jones, as they grew older, seemed to come even closer together and, with the revolutionary veteran James Forten, would form a kind of committee of leadership for the blacks of the city. When Jones and Forten decided to organize a Masonic Lodge for Pennsylvania, the local group of "white masons . . . refused to grant us a Dispensation, fearing that black men living in Virginia would get

to be Masons, too." It was Prince Hall, founder of black Masonry during the revolution, who journeyed from Boston in June 1797 to install Jones as Worshipful Master and Allen as treasurer of the new lodge. In 1808, marking its tenth birthday, the members of the lodge marched to St. Thomas's, where Richard Allen, occupying the pulpit of his good friend Absalom Jones, preached a sermon to the black Masons [fig. 82]. It is probable that the elegant Liverpoolware pitcher graced by Jones's silhouette and the mystic marks of Freemasonry was created to celebrate this anniversary [fig. 83].

Once again when Philadelphia was in the grip of crisis, Allen and Jones—long after they had collaborated to fight the yellow fever in 1793—were importuned to muster the aid of the black community. In 1814, as the British were threatening Philadelphia, the city's Committee of Defence called upon the two ministers to mobilize assistance. From the State House yard, twenty-five hundred black citizens marched to Gray's Ferry and toiled on the defenses for two days. A battalion of black troops—with revolutionary memories—was ready to march to the front when peace was declared.

THE Reverend Absalom Jones died in 1818. His friend Richard Allen lived on and worked for a dozen busy years as the antislavery movement gathered force. In November 1827, in the columns of *Freedom's Journal,* the country's first black newspaper, the "aged and devoted Minister of the Gospel" castigated the colonizationists who would ship free blacks to Liberia because their presence in America made "the slaves uneasy." Wrote Allen: "This land which we have watered with our *tears* and *our blood* is now our *mother country*. . . ." Three years later, the pioneer "Convention of the People of Colour of the United States"—the first of

81. Raphaelle Peale, *Absalom Jones,* oil, 1810. Delaware Art Museum.

many to follow—met in Bethel Church, presided over by Richard Allen, "Senior Bishop of the African Methodist Episcopal Churches" [figs. 84 and 85]. The convention recommended to the nation that the Fourth of July be observed as a day of fasting and prayer.

Side by side with Absalom Jones in the pantheon of early Afro-American history stands Richard Allen. Two years before his

THANKSGIVING SERMON,

PREACHED JANUARY 1, 1808,

In St. Thomas's, or the African Episcopal, Church,
Philadelphia:

ON ACCOUNT OF

THE ABOLITION

OF THE

AFRICAN SLAVE TRADE,

ON THAT DAY,

BY THE CONGRESS OF THE UNITED STATES.

BY ABSALOM JONES,
RECTOR OF THE SAID CHURCH.

PHILADELPHIA:
PRINTED FOR THE USE OF THE CONGREGATION.
FRY AND KAMMERER, PRINTERS.
1808.

82. Absalom Jones, *A Thanksgiving Sermon . . .*
(Philadelphia, 1808). The Historical Society of
Pennsylvania.

pression" of black people in America at the time of the revolution. But there were hundreds of others, nameless and faceless for the most part, charismatic preachers of the slave quarters, potential Gabriel Prossers and Nat Turners, or loners, like wayfaring John Marrant, missionary to the Indians and chaplain of the African Masons. Some felt the impulse to mold the Christian story into a message for their black brethren but, by accident of time and place, became stalwarts of the white church, where, by sheer force of their talent, they achieved eminence, even fame, and paid a price for it, perhaps. Such were the Reverend John Chavis, a Presbyterian in the south, and the Reverend Lemuel Haynes, a Congregationalist in the north.

John Marrant

"I, John Marrant, born June 15, 1755, in New-York, in North-America, wish these gracious dealings of the Lord with me to be published, in hopes they may be useful to others": so begins the autobiography of this black minister whose short life was full of remarkable happenings. "My father died when I was little more than four years of age," he continues, "and before I was five my mother removed from New York to St. Augustine. . . . Here I was sent to school, and taught to read and spell. . . ." Eighteen months later the family moved to Georgia. His schooldays over at eleven, John was then apprenticed to a trade. His mother packed him off to Charleston. One day, he wrote, "I passed by a school, and heard music and dancing. . . . I went home and informed my sister, that I had rather learn to play upon music than go to a trade." His mother objected, to no avail. After a year of study, the twelve-year-old boy could play the violin and French horn. He was "invited to all the balls and assemblies that were held in the town, and met

death, he was immortalized in David Walker's prophetic *Appeal:* "See him and his ministers in the states of New York, New Jersey, Pennsylvania, Delaware and Maryland, carrying the gladsome tidings of free and full salvation to the coloured people."

Three Black Ministers: John Marrant, John Chavis, Lemuel Haynes

David George, Andrew Bryan, George Liele, Richard Allen, Absalom Jones, Peter Williams—these six were the founders of the African-American church and shapers of the "organized independence and self-ex-

83. Masonic pitcher, Liverpoolware, presented to Absalom Jones, ca. 1808. National Portrait Gallery, Washington.

with the general applause of the inhabitants."

One evening, two years later, the Reverend George Whitefield came to town. Planning some mischief—the scheme was to break up Whitefield's meeting by a blast on the horn—young Marrant "was struck to the ground . . . speechless and senseless" by Whitefield's eloquence and could not deny the preacher's words: "Jesus Christ has got thee at last." He now began to "read the Scriptures very much." When his family ridiculed his happy faith, he "took up a small pocket Bible and one of Dr. Watts' hymn books" and ran away from home, wandering in field and forest, starving himself into religious ecstasy.

In the woods he met an Indian who befriended him. Hunting with the boy for ten weeks, the red man taught the black youth some of his language, and after the season was over the two headed for a village of the Cherokee Nation. Here there were trials in store for Marrant, who at moments seemed to hunger for Christian martyrdom. Jailed, strung up for torture, he turned to God: "I prayed in English a considerable time, and

THE

LIFE, EXPERIENCE,

AND

GOSPEL LABOURS

OF THE

Rt. Rev. RICHARD ALLEN.

TO WHICH IS ANNEXED

THE RISE AND PROGRESS OF THE AFRICAN
METHODIST EPISCOPAL CHURCH IN THE
UNITED STATES OF AMERICA.

CONTAINING A NARRATIVE OF THE YELLOW FEVER IN THE
YEAR OF OUR LORD 1793:

WITH AN ADDRESS TO THE

PEOPLE OF COLOUR IN THE UNITED STATES.

WRITTEN BY HIMSELF,
AND PUBLISHED BY HIS REQUEST.

Mark the perfect man, and behold the upright: for the end of
that man is peace.—Ps. xxxvii. 37.

PHILADELPHIA:
Martin & Boden, Printers.
1833.

84. *The Life, Experience, and Gospel Labours of
the Rt. Rev. Richard Allen . . . Written by Himself (1793)* (Philadelphia, 1833). Library Company of Philadelphia.

THE

DOCTRINES

AND

DISCIPLINE

OF THE

AFRICAN METHODIST

EPISCOPAL CHURCH.

FIRST EDITION.

PHILADELPHIA:

PUBLISHED BY RICHARD ALLEN AND JACOB TAPSICO,
FOR THE AFRICAN METHODIST CONNECTION
IN THE UNITED STATES.
John H. Cunningham, Printer.
1817.

85. Richard Allen and Jacob Tapisco, *The Doctrines and Discipline of the African Methodist Episcopal Church* (Philadelphia, 1817). Allegheny
College Library, Meadville, Pennsylvania.

about the middle of my prayer, the Lord impressed a strong desire upon my mind to
turn into their language, and pray in their
tongue." A miracle occurred—the king of
the Cherokees and his daughter were instantly converted. Cut down from the stake
and bedecked in fine garments, Marrant
lived well for nine weeks in the king's pal-
ace, where he "learnt to speak their tongue
in the highest stile."

Unattached, unordained, a prophet in
the wilderness, he now embarked upon his
mission to the Indians, accompanied by a
guard of fifty warriors, seeking out the
Creeks, the Catawars, and the Howsaws.
But the Indians he exhorted failed to respond to his Christian pleas: "When they

recollect" that Christians "drove them from
the American shores [they] have often
united, and murdered all the white people
in the back settlements. . . ." After six
months of failure, he returned to the Cherokees and, against the will of his friend the
king, made up his mind to return to
Charleston. Back home, at first no one recognized him: "My dress was purely in the
Indian stile; the skins of wild beasts composed my garments, my head was set out in
the savage manner, with a long pendant

down my back, a sash around my middle, without breeches, and a tomahawk by my side."

In Charleston he lived with his family "till the commencement of the American troubles." Then chance placed him on the British side: "I was pressed on board the Scorpion sloop of war, as their musician. . . . I continued in his majesty's service six years and eleven months. . . . I was at the siege of Charles Town and passed through many dangers." In August 1781 he was "in the engagement with the Dutch off the Dogger Bank, on board the *Princess Amelia,* of 84 guns," a bloody affair in which he was wounded so that he ended up in the hospital at Plymouth. Discharged from the navy, he found his way to London where he worked for a "pious" cotton merchant for the next three years.

During this time in England, he saw his "call to the ministry fuller and clearer" and began to feel a concern for his black "countrymen." One day he received a letter from his brother in Nova Scotia urging him to come over and preach, and he showed it to the evangelical, antislavery countess of Huntingdon, who had been a friend and sponsor of Phillis Wheatley, the black poet of Boston. He was not idle: in London he continued to exercise his "gifts . . . in prayer and exhortation." When the countess counseled him to carry the word to Canada and invited him to join her independent group of Calvinist Methodists, he gladly consented and was ordained a minister of the sect in the spring of 1785. For the next few months, preaching "many sermons in Bath and Bristol . . . many precious souls experienced great blessings" from his labors. In August, before he sailed, he told the story of his life to the Reverend William Aldridge, who "arranged, corrected, and published" it. "John's narrative," commented the *Monthly Review* of London with a pa-

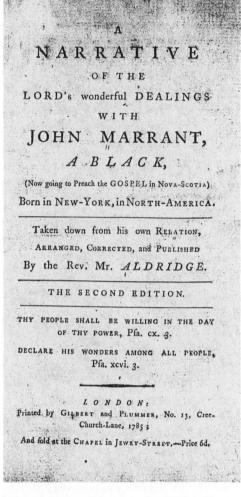

A
NARRATIVE
OF THE
LORD's wonderful DEALINGS
WITH
JOHN MARRANT,
A BLACK,
(Now going to Preach the GOSPEL in Nova-Scotia)
Born in NEW-YORK, in NORTH-AMERICA.

Taken down from his own RELATION,
ARRANGED, CORRECTED, and PUBLISHED
By the Rev. Mr. ALDRIDGE.

THE SECOND EDITION.

THY PEOPLE SHALL BE WILLING IN THE DAY
OF THY POWER, Pſa. cx. 3.

DECLARE HIS WONDERS AMONG ALL PEOPLE,
Pſa. xcvi. 3.

LONDON:
Printed by GILBERT and PLUMMER, No. 13, Cree-
Church-Lane, 1785;
And ſold at the CHAPEL in JEWRY-STREET,—Price 6d.

86. *A Narrative of the Lord's Wonderful Dealings with John Marrant, a Black,* 2d ed. (London, 1785). Courtesy of the Library of Congress.

tronizing flourish, "is embellished with a good deal of *adventure,* enlivened by the *marvellous,* and a little touch of the *miraculous. . . .*" The Narrative of the Life of John Marrant would be reprinted nineteen times during the next forty years {fig. 86}.

So, like David George, John Marrant went to Nova Scotia to spread the Gospel among his own people. At Birch Town he assembled a Huntingdonian congregation of forty members and carried the Bible to the wigwams of the Canadian Indians. Marrant's *Journal*, printed in London in 1790, is a chronicle of his selfless toil in Nova Scotia—of endless journeyings to remote places, of passionate sermons to gatherings of black, white, and red. After four years of spiritual wrestling and physical hardship, Marrant apparently felt that he had done his work in Canada, and in the winter of 1789 he embarked for a new field of endeavor in New England.

In Boston, resuming his preaching without delay, he at first had a hard time of it, although the liberal Baptist minister Dr. Samuel Stillman came to his aid. "I was preaching at the west end of the town," the *Journal* relates, "to a large concourse of people, there were more than forty that had made an agreement to put an end to my evening preaching . . . they came prepared that evening with swords and clubs. . . ." He was not deterred (a Boston judge admonished the hoodlums) but opened a school and went off preaching to black and white groups as far as Bridgewater and Shoreham. Meanwhile, he had struck up a friendship with Prince Hall, "one of the most respectable characters in Boston," and in the spring the black civic leader invited him to fill the post of chaplain to the African Lodge of the Honorable Society of Free and Accepted Masons of Boston, the first black lodge in America, of which Hall, its founder, was Grand Master.

On June 24, 1789, the Reverend Chaplain John Marrant, in celebration of the festival of St. John the Baptist, delivered a memorable sermon to the black Masons of Boston—a discourse studded with passages of such uncommon beauty and power, one wonders how and when this self-taught wanderer ever mastered the eloquence that suffuses it [fig. 87]. A jeremiad aimed against the "monsters" of white racism, it summons its hearers to a new sense of black worth and dignity:

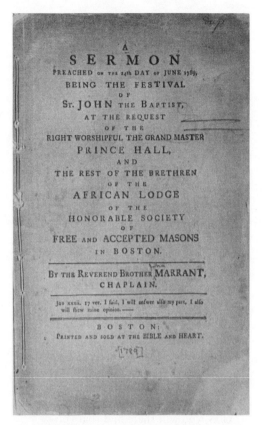

87. John Marrant, *A Sermon Preached on the 24th Day of June 1789* . . . (Boston, 1789). Courtesy, American Antiquarian Society.

Man is a wonderful creature, and not undeservedly said to be a little world, a world within himself, and containing whatever is found in the Creator.—In him is the spiritual and immaterial nature of God, the reasonableness of Angels, the sensitive power of brutes, the vegetative life of plants, and the virtue of all the elements he holds converse with in both worlds.—Thus man is crowned with glory and honour, he is the most remarkable workmanship of God. And is man such a noble creature and made to converse with his fellow men that are of his own order, to maintain mutual love and society, and to serve God in consort with each other?— then what can these God-provoking wretches think, who despise their fellow men, as tho' they were not of the same species with themselves, and would if in their power deprive them of the blessings and comforts of this life, which God in his bountiful goodness, hath freely given to all his creatures to improve and enjoy? Surely such monsters never came out of the hand of God. . . .

To his black audience he counsels a just pride in their African forebears—"Tertullian, Cyprian, Origen, Augustine, Chrysostom . . . and many others." There are some, he tells them, who "despise those they would make, if they could, a species below them, and as not made of the same clay with themselves":

> but if you study the holy book of God, you will there find that you stand on the level not only with them, but with the greatest kings on the earth, as Men and as Masons. . . . Ancient history will produce some of the Africans who were truly good, wise, and learned men, and as eloquent as any other nation whatever, though at present many of them are in slavery, which is not a just cause of our being despised; for if we search history, we shall not find a nation on earth but has at some period or other of their existence been in slavery, from the Jews down to the English Nation, under many Emperors, Kings, and Princes. . . .

The Reverend John Marrant's sermon, preached to the black Masons of Boston when he was thirty-four years old, may be the high point of his checkered career. He had not much longer to live, missed his English friends, and yearned to return to London. For the next six months he prayed and exhorted in Massachusetts. On February 5, 1790, a company of black Bostonians headed by Prince Hall walked with him "down to the ship, with very heavy hearts." A year later his coffin was lowered into a grave of the Burial Ground on Church Street in Islington, a borough of London.

John Chavis

The case of John Chavis, a black Presbyterian preacher and schoolmaster, is one of brilliance and aspiration thwarted and choked, then perhaps betrayed, as white racism fastened itself firmly on the south after the revolution. A recent study sees him as a perplex of unbearable social and psychic tensions [fig. 88].

Chavis was born free about 1763 in the West Indies or North Carolina and grew to manhood in Virginia. Almost nothing has been discovered to cast light on his early youth. When he was an old man, slighted by a few of his former pupils, he would declare proudly that he had been a "free born American and a revolutionary soldier." For ten years after the war the record is silent. Then, in September 1792, a brief entry on the rolls of the College of New Jersey (later Princeton University) reveals that "John Chavis a free Black man" of Virginia has been recommended for admission as a student by a Reverend John B. Smith. Tradition has it that Chavis's career was "the result of a wager that a Negro could not be educated" and that a few whites who perceived the extraordinary intellectual power of the man—he was now going on thirty— sent him to Princeton, which had permitted a few blacks and Indians to enter its classrooms. Chavis, it seems, became the pupil of old President John Witherspoon, who tutored him privately. For reasons unknown

88. Unknown artist, *John Chavis,* reproduced in Joel A. Rogers, *Africa's Gift to America* (New York, 1961), 239.

he never graduated from Princeton but continued his studies at an academy that after the Civil War was transformed into Washington and Lee University. There he completed a "regular course of Academical Studies."

Apparently he had been preparing himself in the usual subjects, classical and theological, for a career in the church; at its regular meeting in the fall of 1799 the Presbytery of Lexington, Virginia, was asked to ponder the request of "John Chavis, a black man, personally known . . . of unquestionably good fame, & a communicant" to

be ordained to the ministry. The reply was favorable and careful: "considering that they, like their heavenly Father, should be no respecter of persons, being satisfied with his narrative," the Presbytery "agreed, notwithstanding his colour, to take him under their care, for further trials in the usual form." In November 1800, at Timber-Ridge Meetinghouse, Chavis preached a sermon on the assigned text: "Believe on the Lord Jesus Christ & thou shalt be saved." Later the same year, the Presbytery saw fit "to license him to Preach the Gospel . . . hoping as he is a man of colour he may be peculiarly useful to those of his own complexion." Accordingly, in 1801, using cautious phrases that exude a sense of anxiety, the Presbytery directed that "Mr. John Chavis, a black man of prudence and piety . . . be employed as a missionary among people of his own colour; and that for his better direction in the discharge of duties which are attended with many circumstances of delicacy and difficulty, some prudential instructions be issued to him by the assembly, governing himself by which, the knowledge of religion among that people may be made more and more to strengthen the order of society. . . ." It is quite clear that the Presbyters had no consuming desire to send abroad another Gabriel Prosser, who, during the summer of the previous year, with his brother Martin, a people's preacher, had organized an insurrection at religious gatherings and planned to take over Richmond for the slaves.

For the next thirty years, on and off, John Chavis rode his horse up and down country roads in Virginia, Maryland, and North Carolina as a Presbyterian missionary "under the Direction of the General Assembly," repeatedly instructed "to employ himself chiefly among the blacks and people of colour," and always performing to the satisfaction of his superiors, who praise him for executing his mission with "great diligence, fidelity and prudence." He was also an "acceptable preacher" now and then to white congregations, one of whose members recollected that his sermons abounded "in strong common sense views and happy illustrations, without any effort at oratory or sensational appeals to the passions of his hearers."

In 1805 or thereabouts, settled in North Carolina as a minister of the Orange Presbytery and continuing his work as a riding missionary, Chavis decided to open a school where he could employ his correct English, good Latin, and fair Greek for the collegiate preparation of the sons of the white gentry. Recalling his own struggle for an education, it is probable that at the start he admitted to his classes the children of free blacks. That he could not for long resist the mounting intolerance of the times is evidenced by a notice he placed in the *Raleigh Register* during the summer of 1808: "John Chavis takes this method of informing the citizens of Raleigh" that he will "open an evening school for the purpose of instructing children of colour; as he intends, for the accomodation of some of his employers, to exclude all children of colour from his day school." And that he was still compelled to employ the strategy of "accomodation," doubtless behind a mask of irony, is evidenced again twenty years later in the same newspaper. "On Friday last," wrote Joseph Gales, its Whig editor, in an issue of April 1830, "we attended an examination of the free children of colour, attached to the school conducted by *John Chavis,* also colored, but a regularly educated Presbyterian minister. . . ."

To witness a well regulated school, composed of this class of persons—to see them setting an example both in behavior and scholarship, which their *white* superiors might take pride in imitating, was a cheering spectacle to a philanthropist. The exercises throughout, evinced a degree of attention and assiduous care on the part of the instructor, highly creditable, and of attainment on the part of his scholars almost incredible.

Gales was much pleased with Chavis's "sensible address," which closed the examination: "The object of the respectable teacher, was to impress on the scholars, the fact, that they occupied an inferior and subordinate station in society, and were possessed but of limited privileges; but that even *they* might become useful in their particular sphere by making a proper improvement of the advantages afforded them." One shudders at the anguish Chavis must have suffered as he paid the price of protecting his black school from destruction. Years later—long after the school had ceased to exist—he would implore his white friend Senator Willie P. Mangum to refute the charge that "in going to Raleigh to Teach the children of the free people of colour" he had really intended to preach the abolitionist creed.

The uprising led by the self-taught black preacher, Nat Turner, in Southampton County, Virginia, during the summer of 1831 put an end to John Chavis's career as Presbyterian minister and classical schoolmaster. In North Carolina an "act for the better regulation of the conduct of Negroes" prescribed "thirty-nine lashes on his bare back" for any black "under any pretense" who preached to his brothers. When Chavis complained of the "difficulties and embarassments" he suffered by this law, the Presbyters counseled him to comply "until God in his Providence" showed another way and at the same time discouraged him from publishing—since he could no longer speak—an exegesis on the reconciliation of God and man by the sufferings of Christ.

As Sterling Brown has observed, "It is ironic that at the moment of John Calhoun's epigram, 'If a Negro could be found who could parse Greek or explain Euclid, I should be constrained to think that he had human possibilities'—a classically trained Negro schoolmaster was operating a private academy for boys of aristocratic white families of North Carolina." Indeed, in the official history of North Carolina the Reverend John Chavis retains a certain fame as the greatly gifted teacher of the sons of the slavocracy—of future statesmen, among them a governor and a senator. He seemed to cherish a relationship of intimacy with some of the first families of the state. "In my boyhood life at my father's home," recalled a judge's son, "I often saw John Chavis . . . he was received by my father and treated with kindness and consideration, and respected as a man of education, good sense and most estimable character." A Granville County lawyer remembered: "I have heard him read and explain the Scriptures to my father's family repeatedly. His English was remarkably pure . . . his manner was impressive, his explanations clear and concise, and his views . . . entirely orthodox." With Willie Mangum, Chavis maintained a long friendship, as his letters to the senator, full of family news and sharp political counsel, demonstrate. But again, it would seem, at the high price of a grim accommodation. Writing to Mangum in April 1836 he declared his annoyance with the abolition petitions then stirring up the House and the country; but as he goes on, the tense rhetoric discloses the complex artifice of his uncomfortable position: "That Slavery is a national evil no one doubts, but what is to be done? It exists and what can be done with it? All that can be done, is to make the best of a bad bargain. For I am clearly of the opinion that immediate emancipation would be to entail the greatest earthly curse upon my brethren according to the flesh that could be conferred upon them especially in a country like ours." And he concludes with tragic candor: "I suppose if they knew I said this, they would be ready to take my life, but as I wish them well I feel no disposition to see them any more miserable than they are." Perhaps, as John Hope Franklin has noted, "Chavis had no counterparts during the ante-bellum period. . . ."

When he was seventy, the Presbytery resolved to support him as a "superannuated licentiate." In 1837, a year before his death, although barred from preaching, he managed to publish on his own an undelivered sermon, *The Extent of the Atonement.*

Lemuel Haynes

A few years after the death of that eminent divine, the Reverend Lemuel Haynes, A.M., the first black minister of the Congregational Church in America—an octogenarian whose years had stretched from the French and Indian War to the presidency of Andrew Jackson—Harper's published a full-scale memoir of his life and thought. His biographer, Timothy Mather Cooley, D.D., a white colleague in the church, drawing on the Abbé Henri Grégoire's history of illustrious Negroes, began his account with a eulogy that linked his hero to history: "In various periods of time there have been Africans whose intellectual powers and attainments would be an ornament to any age or country. Among warriors few have held a higher rank than Hanno and Hannibal. The poetic works of Terence were admired in the Augustan age, and have survived the devastations of two thousand years. Cyprian, bishop of Carthage, whose memory is dear to all Christendom, and Augustine, bishop of Hippo, the successful defender of the church from Pelagius and his heresies, were sons of Africa." It was in this distinguished company that the Reverend

Lemuel Haynes belonged—a "sanctified genius" whose life story could "hardly fail to
mitigate the unreasonable prejudices
against the Africans in our land" [fig. 89].

Lemuel Haynes was born in 1753 at
West Hartford, Connecticut. His father
(whom he never knew) was "of unmingled
African extraction"; his mother, "a white
woman of respectable ancestry in New England." Someone gave him a name. "When
I was five months old," Haynes wrote, "I
was carried to Granville, Massachusetts,
and bound out as a servant to Deacon David
Rose till I was Twenty-one. He was a man of
singular piety. I was taught the principles of
religion. His wife, my mistress, had a peculiar attachment to me: she treated me as
though I was her own child." (One painful
day the lad had met his mother by accident
in a nearby town. She had tried to elude
him. "Vexed and mortified at such an instance of unnatural contempt," observed
Dr. Cooley, "he accosted her in the language
of severe but merited rebuke.") The deacon,
one of Granville's pioneers, had to carve a
farm out of the forest; for him Lemuel
wielded the ax and guided the plow. There
was a little time left over for education. "As
I had the advantage of attending a common
school equal with the other children," he remembered, "I was early taught to read, to
which I was greatly attached, and could vie
with almost any of my age." People said that
"Lemuel Haynes got his education in the
chimney-corner," where by the light of blaz-
ing pine knots he devoured speller, psalter,
and Bible. "At the age of fifty," a friend recalled, "he could repeat nearly the whole of
Young's *Night Thoughts,* Milton's *Paradise
Lost,* Watts's *Psalms and Hymns,* and large
unbroken passages from different authors,
and more of the sacred Scriptures than any
man I ever knew." When Haynes was an old
man, he often used to say, "If I were to live

89. Lemuel Haynes, frontispiece in Timothy
Mather Cooley, *Sketches of the Life and Character
of the Reverend Lemuel Haynes, A.M.* (New York,
1837).

my life over again, I would devote myself to
books."

Theology fascinated the Bible-struck
youth. One evening, "greatly alarmed by
the *Aurora Borealis*" as a "presage of the day
of judgment," he experienced conversion.
In the deacon's family on Saturday nights—
a time of religious instruction—Lemuel
usually read aloud a sermon by some worthy
of the church. "One evening being called
upon to read . . . he slipped into the book
his own sermon . . . and read it to the family." The deacon was highly edified:
"Lemuel, whose work is that which you
have been reading? Is it Davies's sermon, or
Watts's, or Whitefield's?" When the youth
answered, "It's Lemuel's sermon," that moment was the start of a career. Since the parish at this time lacked a minister, Lemuel
was frequently called upon to conduct the

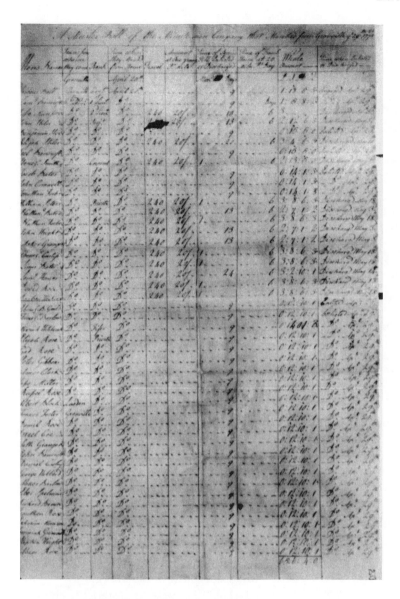

90. *A Muster Roll of the Minutemen that Marched from Granville ye 29th Apr. 1775.* Massachusetts Archives, Revolutionary Rolls, 14: 40.

service and to read an approved sermon. Sometimes he read one of his own.

In 1774, at the age of twenty-one, his period of service to the deacon completed, Lemuel enlisted as a minuteman and spent a day a week training on the village green. Soon after the skirmish at Lexington, he joined the army at the siege of Boston with Captain Lebbeus Ball's militia company [figs. 90 and 91].

It was about this time that the revolutionary soldier wrote a ballad-sermon of thirty-seven quatrains. This has survived in the manuscript he was still revising, possibly intended for a printed broadside [fig. 92]. There is a certain pride in these stanzas by the patriot and former indentured servant in arms against British tyranny, which can be seen in his title and epigraph:

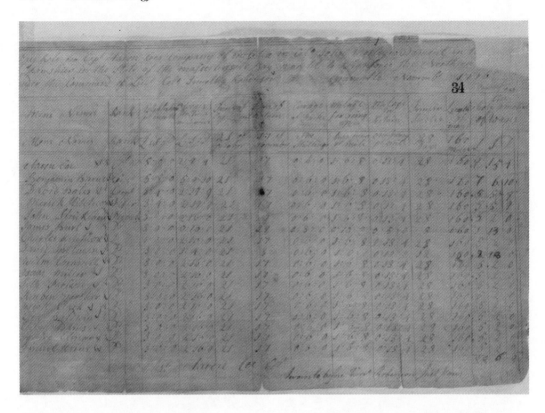

91. *Pay Role for Cap' Aaron Coe's Company of Militia . . . Granville Novemb' 1776.* Massachusetts Archives, Revolutionary Rolls, 18:34.

THE BATTLE OF LEXINGTON
A POEM on the *inhuman* Tragedy perpetrated on the 19th of April 1775 by a Number of the British Troops under the Command of Thomas Gage, which Parricides and Ravages are shocking Displays of ministerial & tyrannic Vengeance. . . .

At the center of the poem is the clash between freedom and slavery:

> For liberty each Freeman strives
> As its a Gift of God
> And for it, willing yield their Lives
> And Seal it with their Blood.

> Twice happy they who thus resign
> Into the peacefull Grave
> Much better those in Death Consign
> Than a Surviving Slave.

This Motto may adorn their Tombs
(Let Tyrants come and view)
"We rather seek these silent Rooms
"Than live as Slaves to You."

Although Haynes does not yet explore the paradox implicit in the struggle of slaveholders against "ministerial tyranny," he surely touches on it when he names himself "Lemuel a young Mollato" as the poet, "who obtained what little knowledge he possesses, by his own Application to Letters."

A document in Haynes's hand has come to light which confirms that toward the end of the war he wished to speak out boldly against black slavery. The manuscript of forty-six small pages, apparently a draft of a "Small *Treatise*"—unfinished, never printed

92. Lemuel Haynes, *The Battle of Lexington,* excerpt. By permission of Houghton Library, Harvard University.

or uttered—is one of the earliest, most passionate and astute sociotheological statements in our history, ranking high with those of Samuel Sewall, John Woolman, and Anthony Benezet. Its title page, citing the Declaration of Independence, rings out: "Liberty Further Extended: Or Free thoughts on the illegality of Slave-keeping; Wherein those arguments that Are used in its vindication Are plainly confuted. Together with an humble Address to such as are Concearned in the practise." The author's name is now plainly written out: "Lemuel Haynes" [fig. 93].

Haynes's "main proposition" is "That an *African,* or, in other terms, *that a Negro may Justly Chalenge, and has an undeniable right to his Liberty:* Consequently, the practise of Slave-keeping, *which so much abounds in this Land is illicit."* And his conclusion, pointing up slavery as a sin, exposes the irony of men fighting for their own political freedom while they themselves own slaves as a portent of blood and doom: "for this is God's way of working, Often he brings the Same

Judgements or Evils upon men as they unriteously Bring upon Others. . . . Some gentlemen have Determined to Contend in a Consistant manner: they have *Let the oppressed go free.* . . ."*

In 1775 Haynes marched in the expedition to Ticonderoga, where, with Ethan Allen and the Green Mountain Boys, he helped take the fort from the British. Over forty years later, in a sermon preached on George Washington's birthday, he would remind his listeners of his service in the revolution: "Perhaps it is not ostentatious in the speaker to observe, that in early life he de-

*Ruth Bogin, who a few years ago discovered the manuscript, notes its "virtuosity of argument" and raises a valid question: "Future appraisals of Haynes must consider not only his reluctance to speak out publicly on slavery and race prejudice but also his vigorous arguments for the extirpation of slavery as well as the circumstances that may have influenced his decision to suppress his views . . ." (" 'Liberty Further Extended': A 1776 Antislavery Manuscript of Lemuel Haynes," *William and Mary Quarterly,* 3d ser., 40 [January 1983]: 85–105). The text of Haynes's "Small *Treatise"* is printed in the above article.

93. Lemuel Haynes, "Liberty Further Extended. . . ." By permission of the Houghton Library, Harvard University.

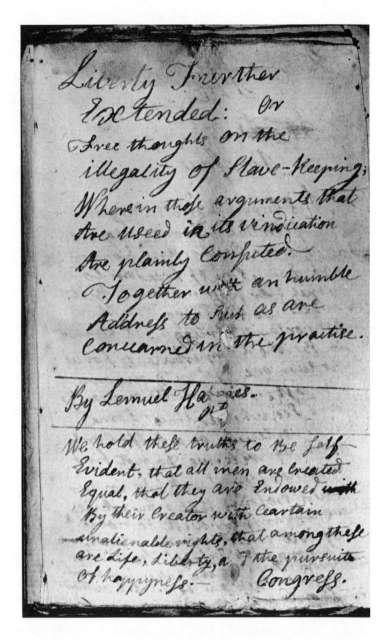

voted all for the sake of freedom and independence, and endured frequent campaigns in their defence. . . ."

Back home from the front, white friends in Granville encouraged him to consider a life in the church. "I was solicited by some to obtain a collegiate education with a view to the gospel ministry. A door was opened for it at Dartmouth College, but I shrunk at the thought." At last he was persuaded to study "the learned languages" and in 1779 was invited by a clergyman in Canaan, Connecticut, to live with him and learn Latin. Now he felt a "quenchless ardor" to master Greek as well, so that he might read the New Testament in the original. A well-wishing pastor got him a position as a teacher in Wintonbury, and after school hours he tutored Haynes in Greek. In the fall of 1780 the pastor thought he was ready; several ministers of "high respectability," after examining him "in the languages and sciences, and with respect to his knowledge of the doctrines of the gospel, and practical and experimental religion, recommended him as qualified to preach the gospel." His first official sermon was on the text "The Lord reigneth, let the earth rejoice," preached in a new house of worship to a white congregation in Middle Granville, which had unanimously invited him to supply its vacant pulpit. Three years later he married a young white schoolteacher of the town, Elizabeth Babbit, whom he had helped to convert. "Looking to Heaven for guidance," remarked Dr. Cooley, "she was led with a consistent and justifiable delicacy, to make him the overture of her heart. . . . He consulted a number of ministers and . . . received their unanimous advice and sanction." (There were ten children, seven daughters and three sons: at the time of Elizabeth's death in 1836, two sons lived in New York, one a farmer, the other a physician; the third son was a law student in Massachusetts.) In November 1785 Haynes was officially ordained by an Association of Ministers in Litchfield County, Connecticut, in response to the unanimous request of his Granville congregation signed by Deacons Aaron Coe and Timothy Robinson, the latter his commander ten years earlier in the war and later a governor of Vermont.

Haynes's first call to fill a pulpit came from Torrington, Connecticut—the town in which fifteen years later John Brown was born—and after a preaching tour of Vermont during the summer of 1785 he settled down to his work. Although his sermons soon began to pack the meetinghouse, there were intolerant diehards in the congregation who were less than pleased with his dark skin. Dr. Cooley has preserved the memoir of one churchgoer who did not at first approve:

> He was disaffected that the church should employ him, and neglected meeting for a time. At length curiosity conquered prejudice. . . . He took his seat in the crowded assembly, and, from designed disrespect, sat *with his hat on.* Mr. Haynes gave out his text, and began with his usual impassioned earnestness, as if unconscious of anything amiss in the congregation. "The preacher had not proceeded far in his sermon . . . before I thought him the *whitest* man I ever saw. My hat was instantly taken off and thrown under the seat, and I found myself listening with the most profound attention."

Others in Haynes's flock did not conquer their prejudice, and the "designed disrespect" of a clique forced him to leave Torrington after two years to seek another pulpit.

In March of 1788, he received his second call, from a church in the west parish of Rutland, Vermont, which probably had a few "poor Africans" enrolled in its congregation. Here for the next thirty years he would try to save souls, preserve doctrine untainted by liberal theology, and enlighten the backward on political questions. In Vermont, where freethinkers "extensively circulated Allen's 'Oracle of Reason,' and other infidel books," the thirty-five-year-old black minister would achieve a transatlantic reputation as a ruthless polemicist in theological dispute. Writing from Rutland in 1796 he observed that he had never known "infidelity more prevalent. . . . Paine has advocates. I have attended to all his writings on theology, and can find little else but invective and the lowest kind of burlesque."

The years of the turn of the century, when the animated frontispiece portrait in Cooley's memoir was probably executed, seem his most vigorous and productive. "Many, on seeing him in the pulpit," the biographer records, "have been reminded of the inspired expression, 'I am black, but comely' . . . the remarkable assemblage of graces which were thrown around his semi-African complexion, especially his eye, could not fail to prepossess the stranger in his favour." The papier-mâché tray that shows Haynes exhorting from the pulpit of his white church might illustrate this passage. During these years, he defended the gospels according to Jonathan Edwards and George Washington in a barrage of eloquent discourse. In 1798 two of his sermons were printed for wider notice, one religious, the other political—although these blend at times. The first was a manifesto, *The Important Concerns of Ministers,* the second, an anti-Jeffersonian defense of the quasi-war with "atheistical" France. "I am preparing another political discourse for the press," he informed a friend in September 1801. Its title is imposing: *The Nature and Importance of True Republicanism: with a Few Suggestions Favorable to Independence. Delivered at Rutland, Vermont, the Fourth of July, 1801. It Being the 25th Anniversary of American Independence* [fig. 94]. What is remarkable in this oration is not so much its passionate praise of the revolution and "the rights of men" as its castigation of "monarchal government," where the "people are commonly ignorant . . . and know but little more than to bow to despots, and crouch to them for a piece of bread," for the truth of his argument is illustrated by the sin of American slavery:

The propriety of this idea will appear strikingly evident by pointing you to the poor Africans, among us. What

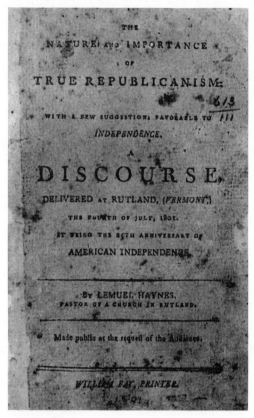

94. Lemuel Haynes, *The Nature and Importance of True Republicanism* . . . (Rutland, 1801). Courtesy of the Library of Congress.

has reduced them to their present pitiful, abject state? Is it any distinction that the God of nature hath made in their formation? Nay—but being subjected to slavery, by the cruel hands of oppressors, they have been taught to view themselves as a rank of beings far below others, which has suppressed in a degree, every principle of manhood, and so they become despised, ignorant, and licentious. This shows the effects of despotism and should fill us with the utmost detestation against every attack on the rights of men. . . .

A few lines later, he asks: "On the whole, does it not appear that a land of liberty is favourable to peace, happiness, virtue, and religion, and should be held sacred by mankind?" The answer is a resounding yes—and that is all. Nowhere else during the next thirty years of utterance from pulpit or press does Lemuel Haynes make a public statement on the subject of race or slavery.

His fame flourished. He had close friends on the faculty of Middlebury College, whose trustees in 1804 conferred on him the honorary degree of Master of Arts—the first ever bestowed on a black in America. It was in the following year that his name became known beyond rural Vermont. The scene had a certain drama. Unknown to Haynes, who had planned to visit a remote part of his parish on that day, Hosea Ballou, the distinguished champion of the doctrine of universal salvation, had been invited to preach from his pulpit in the west parish of Rutland. When Ballou learned that Haynes would not be present for his sermon, he remarked that "the orthodox gentry generally *scud*" when he appeared to preach. Haynes decided to attend. He "had been repeatedly solicited to hear and dispute" with the Universalist, he tells us, "and had been charged with dishonesty and cowardice for refusing. He felt that some kind of testimony, in opposition to . . . error, ought to be made. . . ." Ballou lectured and Haynes—with little or no preparation—immediately replied. The result was the sermon called *Universal Salvation, a Very Ancient Doctrine (of the Devil)*, which, during the next quarter century, as Dr. Cooley relates, was "printed and reprinted, both in America and Great Britain, till no one pretends to give any account of the number of editions" [fig. 95]. If the gentle Ballou felt that Haynes had identified him with the Serpent, he had every reason to think so, and in the sharp exchange of letters of the following two years Haynes does not abate a jot. His wrath was leveled against a Universal-

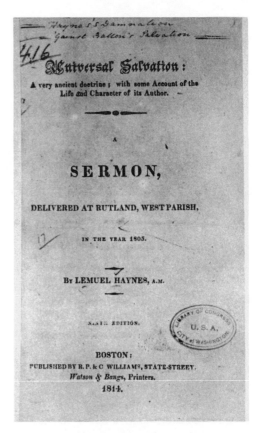

95. Lemuel Haynes, *Universal Salvation* . . . (Boston, 1814). Courtesy of the Library of Congress.

ism that he saw as a doctrine that preached heaven for all and hell for none.

> Blest all who hunger and who thirst
>   to find
> A chance to plunder and to cheat
>   mankind;
> Such die in peace—for to them God
>   has given,
> To be unjust on earth, and go to
>   heaven.

So runs a parody of Ballou's creed which Haynes appended to his sermon. Would the sin of slavery be rewarded rather than punished? The sermon is silent on this question.

MEANWHILE, life went on in a routine way. Haynes found himself in great demand as a speaker at ordinations, dedications, and funerals [fig. 96]. He proved himself from time to time a magnetic revivalist. "His very colour," thought a brother cleric, "which marks the neglect and servitude of his race in this country, associated, as it was . . . with his high qualifications to entertain and instruct, became the means of increasing his celebrity and enlarging the sphere of his influence." In 1809 he was appointed field secretary of the Vermont Missionary Society. And all the while he labored on his farm, his early training standing him in good stead, in order to feed his large family.

The year 1814 was memorable for Haynes. As delegate of the General Convention of Ministers in Vermont, he attended the meeting of the General Association of Connecticut which gathered at Fairfield. On the way, there was an opportunity to visit New Haven and stop for a talk with the Reverend Doctor Timothy Dwight, president of Yale. Haynes's fame had in fact preceded him. In the Blue Church of New Haven, he preached to a full house. Professor Silliman was impressed with his "dignity and feeling," and President Dwight was moved to tears. At Fairfield, addressing one hundred ministers, the Reverend Mr. Humphrey, then pastor of the church in the town and later president of Amherst College, recalled that Haynes used "no notes, but spoke with freedom and correctness." The sermon was so "rich in Scriptural thought . . . there was so much of truth and nature in it . . . hundreds were melted into tears." Did the black pastor perhaps feel lonely among his hundred white colleagues? "In meetings of councils and associations," wrote Dr. Cooley, without a smile, "where it was necessary to put two in one bed, one and another would say, '*I will sleep with Mr. Haynes!*' " And what would have been Haynes's reaction, one wonders, to the benevolent appraisal of a Vermont governor's wife, who was a member of his flock: "He ever held the station of man without blemish—never appearing to repine that God had not made him without a stain upon his skin: nor was he often called upon to remember it, unless more than ordinary tenderness, manifested by others in their intercourse with him, should have reminded him of it."

New Haven and Fairfield were triumphs, but all was not going as smoothly back in Rutland. A partisan of the Federalists who did not mince his words in the pulpit, Haynes found himself in increasing conflict with most of his parishioners. In a manuscript written by an unknown contemporary, the conflict may have been a matter of racism: "The people in Rutland, where he preached for thirty years, at length began to think they would appear more respectable with a white pastor than a black one, and therefore, or at least measurably on that account, dismissed him. Attending to this, he subsequently used to say 'he lived with the people of Rutland thirty years, and they were so sagacious that at the end of that time they found out that he was *a nigger,* and so turned him away.' "

Opposing the War of 1812, he nevertheless scorned the threat of New England secession, but his activity in the conservative Washington Benevolent Society, as well as his biting sarcasm in urging his political views, at last brought matters to a crisis. Thus it was that during the spring of 1818 the pastoral relation between Lemuel Haynes and his Rutland church came to an end. The farewell letter of the black minister—he was now sixty-five—is far from pathetic:

It was thirty years ago . . . since I took the pastoral care of this church

96. Unknown artist, *Reverend Lemuel Haynes in the Pulpit,* papier-mâché tray, 1800–1820. Museum of Art, Rhode Island School of Design. Gift of Miss Lucy T. Aldrich.

and people; the church then consisted of forty-two members; since which time, there have been about three hundred and twelve added to it. . . . I have preached about five thousand five hundred discourses: four hundred of them have been funeral sermons. I have solemnized more than a hundred marriages. During this period we have had two remarkable seasons of the outpourings of the Spirit. . . .

"Never was a greater degree of stupidity discovered among us," he wrote to a friend, "I expected it. . . . It was mutual agreement. No impeachment of my moral or ministerial character was pretended. I fully acquiesce in

the event. I have many calls to labor elsewhere."

The third call, which he now responded to, was from Manchester, on the west side of the Green Mountains. It was there in 1820 that he became involved in the celebrated case of the allegedly murdered Russell Colvin, a "wandering maniac" of the town. In 1813 Colvin had suddenly disappeared. Years passed and a charge of murder was pressed against his wife's two brothers, who were finally sentenced to hang. Haynes spent many hours with the doomed men, grew convinced of their innocence, but despaired of saving them. Seven years after the supposed crime and thirty-seven days before the time appointed for the execution, Russell Colvin, alive and well, wandered back to town. The event was the sensation of the day. Haynes's sermon on the facts and meanings of the case under the title *Mystery Developed* broadened into an interesting disquisition on religion and prisons; packaged with his "narrative of the whole transaction" and the trial records, it was a bestseller for a decade [fig. 97].

Two years later, in 1822, when the excitement was over, he learned to his dismay that his flock in Manchester felt the need for a younger pastor. There was regret on both sides. In Vermont he had made good friends: Richard Skinner, congressman, judge, and antislavery governor; Joseph Burr, patron of the American Colonization Society; Stephen Bradley, who had introduced into the Senate the bill that abolished the African slave trade; and Chief Justice Royall Tyler, poet and playwright. Now, once again, Lemuel Haynes, at three score and ten, resumed his pilgrimage. This time it took him over the border into New York, where, in the town of Granville, revered as Father Haynes, he spent the last eleven years of his life. There were preaching trips to New York City, Albany, and Troy, and a trip back to the first church he had led, in Massachusetts. He was a firm Federalist to the end. When Jackson was elected president in 1828, celebrating Democrats forced him to toast the victor. He responded: "Andrew Jackson. Psalm 109th, 8th verse." The toast was drunk before anyone could look up the passage: "Let his days be few; and let another take his office." When, on September 28, 1833, at an even eighty, he breathed his last, he left in his own hand "an epitaph to be put upon my tombstone": "Here lies the dust of a poor hell-deserving sinner, who ventured into eternity trusting wholly on the merits of Christ for salvation. In the full belief of the great doctrines he preached while on earth, he invites his children, and

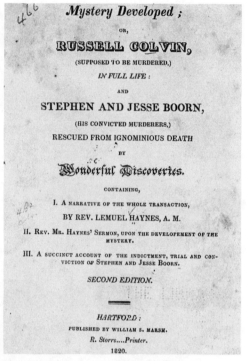

97. Lemuel Haynes, *Mystery Developed; or, Russell Colvin . . .* (Hartford, 1814). Courtesy of the Library of Congress.

all who read this, to trust their eternal interest on the same foundation."

When Samuel E. Cornish, editor of the New York *Colored American,* one of the earliest black newspapers in the country, received a copy of Dr. Cooley's biography of Lemuel Haynes for review, it is probable that he was not quite sure what he ought to make of the "very interesting and useful memoir of Father Haynes . . . one of the Lord's worthies . . . published for the benefit of his children." How could this miracle have come to pass in the United States? Sixty years after the Declaration of Independence, the black editor struggled for an answer: "He is the only man of *known* African descent, who has ever succeeded in overpowering the system of American *caste.* And this he did by wisdom and piety, aided also by the more favorable state of the times in which he lived."

V

The Emergence of Gifts and Powers

On the Fourth of July 1791, at a public meeting of the Maryland Society for the Abolition of Slavery, a physician named George Buchanan delivered "An Oration Upon the Moral and Political Evil of Slavery." The young doctor was a member of the American Philosophical Society, had studied medicine in Edinburgh and Paris, practiced in Baltimore, and would succumb to the yellow fever in Philadelphia while ministering to the victims of the plague, but his justest claim to fame is this remarkable oration, a rare jeremiad of the white revolutionary conscience uttered in a stronghold of slavery only a few years after the adoption of the Constitution of the United States:

> Deceitful men! Who could have suggested that American patriotism would at this day countenance a conduct so inconsistent; that while America boasts of being a land of freedom, and an asylum of the oppressed of Europe, she should at the same time foster an abominable nursery of slaves to check the shoots of her growing liberty? Deaf to the clamors of criticism, she feels no remorse. . . . Not even the sobs and groans of injured innocence which reek from every state can excite her pity, nor human misery bend her heart to sympathy. Cruel and oppressive she wantonly abuses the rights of man, and willingly sacrifices her liberty upon the altar of slavery.

"What! will you not consider that the Africans are men?" Buchanan cries out, "that they have human souls to be saved? that they are born free and independent? . . . the Africans, whom you despise, whom you more inhumanly treat than brutes, and whom you unlawfully subject to slavery, with the tyrannizing hands of Despots, are equally capable of improvements with yourselves":

> Things pleasing rejoice them, and melancholy circumstances pall their

appetites for amusements. They brook no insults, and are equally prone to forgiveness as to resentment; they have gratitude also, and will even expose their own lives, to wipe off the obligation of past favours; nor do they want the refinements of taste, so much the boast of those who call themselves Christians.

And now Buchanan becomes more specific. "Neither is their genius for literature to be despised; many instances are recorded [of] persons of eminence among them." He would cite a few: "Phillis Wheatley, who distinguished herself as a poetess—The physician of New Orleans—The Virginia calculator—Banneker, the Maryland Astronomer. . . ."

These were but a handful who, in the time of transition from colony to nation, here and there emerged, almost heroically, with a wide range of gifts and powers—poignant reminders of black creative genius that had not been free to flower, blighted for a century and a half by the pall of slavery. The impassioned orator had not had the time to speak of "many others whom it would be needless to mention." Here are some who managed to breach the racist wall: first, a scientist, a colonizer, a frontiersman, a revolutionary veteran, a doctor, a mathematical prodigy; then a medley of poets and writers, including the celebrated Phillis Wheatley, and a few artists, dimly discerned.

Benjamin Banneker

In the era of the revolution, Benjamin Banneker of Maryland—astronomer, mathematician, and defender of black dignity against the aspersions of Thomas Jefferson—was a primary symbol of the self-evident truth that all men are created equal.

Banneker achieved transatlantic fame. In Paris, his name and work would be cited by the revolutionary Abbé Henri Grégoire. In London, Pitt, Fox, and Wilberforce would flourish his almanac in the House of Commons while the benches rang "with much Applause." Yet Jefferson never really forgave the sable scientist for speaking out. Who in this historic encounter finally emerged as the finer champion of the cause of humanity may be clarified in the following notes.

A FEW pages must suffice to sketch in the first fifty years of Banneker's rich but simple life. In 1683 an English dairymaid named Molly Welsh, falsely accused of pilfering a bucket of milk, found herself part of a cargo of convicts and was sold as an indentured servant to a tobacco farmer on the Patapsco River in tidewater Maryland. After working out her seven years, she rented some land on the nearby frontier and farmed it alone for a number of years. Then, "from a ship anchored in the Bay," she purchased two African slaves. One, who had the name of Bannke or Bannaka, said he was the son of a chief, never gave up his African religion, and is described in tradition as "a man of bright intelligence, fine temper, with a very agreeable presence, dignified manners, and contemplative habits." A few years later, Molly Welsh liberated both her slaves, and—despite the laws against miscegenation—took Bannaka for her husband. Mary, one of the daughters of this marriage, married a man from Guinea, the slave of a neighboring planter who had baptized him Robert and then set him free. Robert took the name of Banneky, or Banneker.

Robert and Mary Banneker's first child was Benjamin, born in 1731. Six years later, for seventeen thousand pounds of tobacco, Robert bought a farm of a hundred acres located ten miles from Baltimore, a village of thirty houses. The free Bannekers were an unusual family in Baltimore County, where fifteen years later there were, roughly, only two hundred free blacks in a population of four thousand slaves and thirteen thousand whites. Benjamin's grandmother Molly Welsh taught him, via the Bible, to read and write and sent him for a while to a one-room, interracial school presided over by a Quaker master. A black classmate recalled that young Benjamin was not fond of play—"all his delight was to dive into his books." He grew up a farm boy grumbling at his share of the chores, but even then he displayed an interest in things mechanical and mathematical, long before he fell in love with the stars. The elaborate process of tobacco production fascinated the lad—he once tallied the number of steps in the operation—thirty-six from seed to cigar.

When he was twenty-two, Benjamin took it into his head to make with his own hands a clock that would strike the hours. His tools were primitive and up to this time he had never seen a book on the subject, perhaps not even a clock. "This first scientific achievement," writes Silvio A. Bedini in his biography of Banneker, "was associated with a theme that preoccupied him during the major part of his life. This was the theme of Time":

> In all of his young life he had seen but two timepieces. One was a sundial; the other was a pocket watch. . . . Banneker conveyed his memories of the wheelwork of the watch into drawings, then he applied his natural mathematical skill into calculating the relative size and number of teeth of the wheels. First he drew a diagram of the wheels and gears, balance regulator, and spring barrel, then converted these into three dimensional parts . . . carving the wheels and

pinions from selected pieces of hard-grained wood. . . . At last the movement was finished, and it was a successful striking clock . . . this miracle of untutored craftsmanship actually worked. . . . His fame spread rapidly throughout the valley. . . .

Completed in 1753, this clock, made almost entirely of wood, continued to strike the hours for more than half a century until its maker's death.

He was twenty-eight when his father died and willed him the farm, and for the next decade he lived alone with his mother. He was a good farmer, owned two horses and a few cows, sold honey from his beehives, cultivated a large garden for table and sale, and raised wheat and corn for his own use. Tobacco was his main market crop. He bought a book now and then when he could—a quarto Bible in 1763. He was the proud possessor of a flute, a violin, and some music books. He loved to devise mathematical puzzles, sometimes in verse. Now and then his neighbors came to marvel at his clock or to ask for help in arithmetic and letter writing. He favored the Quakers but never formally became a Friend.

In 1772 two brothers named Ellicott came to the valley and in a few years built a complex of well-designed grist mills, which became the focus of a busy settlement with a post office and a general store. Banneker, now in his early forties, closely observed all the work—the details of construction, the semi-automated operation that converted wagons of grain into sacks of flour—and his farm helped supply food for the laborers. The black farmer got to know the Ellicotts and on his visits to the store there was palaver about politics and other matters. Banneker was restrained in his manner, but "when he could be prevailed upon to set this reserve aside," those within earshot discovered that he had "a great store of traditional lore which he had gathered from listening to others and particularly from the books he had read," and that he could tell "anecdotes which fitted the current subject under discussion." One of his favorite topics was "the history of the early settlement of the North American continent"—no doubt he pondered the role of the kidnapped Africans in that history. Occasionally he would talk about his own life and his struggle for knowledge. He was a regular reader of the *Maryland Gazette* and the *Baltimore Advertiser,* two newspapers he could find in the Ellicott store.

Although Congress met briefly in Baltimore in 1776, the war touched the county only slightly—the Quakerish Banneker, in his late forties, physically not at all. By the spring of 1781 free blacks were subject to the draft and the idea of a regiment of slaves was discarded only because Maryland lawmakers felt that the blacks were needed for production and that it was risky to put guns in their hands. The Ellicotts went to war and the mills suffered, especially from floods, but when they returned they rebuilt better than before.

Banneker's best friend among the Ellicotts was young George, almost thirty years his junior, an enthusiast of science and especially astronomy, who had imported from London a collection of texts, instruments, and globes. George Ellicott was "one of the best mathematicians, and also one of the finest amateur astronomers of the time," wrote his daughter Martha, "and was fond of imparting instruction to every youthful inquirer after knowledge who came to his house. As early as the year 1782, during the fine clear evenings of autumn, he was in the habit of giving gratuitous lessons on astronomy to any of the inhabitants of the village who wished to

hear him. To many of these, his celestial globe was an object of great interest and curiosity." Banneker became intoxicated with astronomy. In the autumn of 1788 George lent him some texts, a sturdy table, and a few pieces of apparatus—"a pedestal telescope and a set of drafting instruments for making observations of the times of the stars in the meridian, of their southing, and of their rising and setting." Using his logarithmic tables, Banneker ambitiously attempted a projection of an eclipse of the sun and sent the results to Ellicott, who found a trifling error but was amazed at the feat, for he had given Banneker no instruction on the procedure to be used [fig. 98]. When Banneker learned of his error, he was chagrined and went over his work. The fault, he found to his joy, was not his, but had stemmed from a disparity in two of his sources, the leading English authorities on astronomy, "the Learned Leadbetter" and the "wise Author Ferguson." Although he counted himself among the "young Tyroes in Astronomy," he confessed to George, his confidence had not been destroyed: "I Doubt not being able to Calculate a Common Almanack."

Was Banneker planning to become a black Poor Richard? A colonial institution as early as 1639, the almanac was a popular compendium of practical data—astronomical, meteorological, medical, agricultural, and almost everything else—seasoned with proverb, poem, and jest. "No one who would penetrate to the core of early American literature," commented Moses Coit Tyler, " . . . may by any means turn away, in lofty literary scorn, from the almanac— most despised, most prolific, most indispensable of books . . . the supreme and only literary necessity even in households where the Bible and newspaper were still undesired and unattainable luxuries." But the heart of the almanac was the ephemeris,

98. Benjamin Banneker
to George Ellicott,
October 13, 1789.
Maryland Historical
Society, Baltimore.

calculated by the astronomer, as Bedini explains, "from a series of basic computations required to establish the positions of the sun, moon and planets each year, from which other calculations may be made: the solar and lunar eclipses, the times of rising and setting of the sun and moon, identification of remarkable days, weather forecasting on a daily basis, tide tables for the region, and similar data." Probably before he thought of publishing an almanac, encouraged by George Ellicott, Banneker had hit

upon the idea of constructing an ephemeris, as he says later, "at the request of Several Gentlemen." George's young wife, Elizabeth, who had lent Banneker her own precious text on astronomy, called on him with a few of her friends early in 1790:

His door stood wide open, and so closely was his mind engaged that they entered without being seen. Immediately upon observing them he arose and with much courtesy invited them to be seated. The large oval table at which Banneker sat was strewn with works on astronomy and with scientific appurtenances. He alluded to his love of the study of astronomy and mathematics as quite unsuited to a man of his class, and regretted his slow advancement in them, owing to the laborious nature of his agricultural engagements, which obliged him to spend the greater portion of his time in the fields. . . .

At last, in the spring of that year, the calculations for the twelve months of 1791 were completed, and Banneker decided on his own to send off the ephemeris to the Baltimore printer John Hayes. There was no prompt answer; he chafed with impatience. When the printer finally replied that he had dispatched the ephemeris to Philadelphia for review by the well-known surveyor Major Andrew Ellicott, Banneker could not wait. In May he wrote to the major: "I beg that you will not be too Severe upon me but favourable in giving your approbation . . . knowing well the difficulty that attends long Calculations and especially with young beginners in Astronomy. . . ." Whether Ellicott ever replied to Banneker is unknown; Hayes did not publish Banneker's ephemeris that year. The black astronomer was, of course, deeply disappointed, but he was determined to persevere. Perhaps the next year would be a luckier one. He continued his calculations for 1792.

But now something else, an interlude of some importance in Banneker's life, interrupted his work for a few months.

FROM the Declaration of Independence to the inauguration of George Washington, eight cities had furnished sites for the meetings of Congress. It was time to establish a national capital. During the winter of 1791, the president appointed Major Andrew Ellicott to survey the district chosen for the new federal city on the Potomac that would later be known as the District of Columbia. When the major asked George Ellicott to serve as his "scientific assistant," George strongly recommended the sixty-year-old Banneker for the position. The major, who had seen Banneker's ephemeris, knew that he was qualified, and Thomas Jefferson, the secretary of state, approved the appointment. As the two were preparing to proceed on horseback to Georgetown, Elizabeth Ellicott busied herself with getting her husband's black friend ready for the journey: "Under the impression that Banneker would fall under the notice of the most eminent men of the country, whilst thus engaged," recalled her daughter Martha, she "paid a visit to his cottage [and] was careful to direct the appointments of his wardrobe, in order that he might appear in respectable guise, before the distinguished personages likely to be assembled there."

In early February they reached Alexandria and went on to Georgetown to begin their task. Banneker worked closely with Ellicott, kept notes on the progress of the survey, made the necessary calculations, and handled the astronomical instruments for establishing the base points. "It was the work, also, of Major Ellicott," wrote Martha, "under the orders of General Washington . . . to locate the sites of the Capitol, president's house, treasury, and other public buildings. In this, also, Banneker was his assistant":

> Banneker's deportment throughout the whole of this engagement, secured their respect, and there is good authority for believing, that his endowments led the commissioners to overlook the color of his skin to con-

verse with him freely, and to enjoy the clearness and originality of his remarks on various subjects. . . . He was invited to sit at table with the engineer corps, but, as his characteristic modesty induced him to decline this, a separate table was prepared for him in their dining room; his meals being served at the same time as theirs.

Banneker, in fact, spent most of his time in the observatory tent, where he also slept. It was only after Ellicott and his black "scientific assistant" were well under way in the survey that Jefferson appointed Major Pierre Charles L'Enfant to prepare drawings of the site and of specific government buildings.

In early March the *Georgetown Weekly Ledger* printed a notice, widely copied in the newspapers of Maryland and elsewhere:

> Some time last month arrived in this town Mr. *Andrew Ellicott,* a gentleman of superior astronomical abilities. He was employed by the President of the United States of America, to lay off the tract of land, ten miles square, on the Potowmack, for the use of Congress;—is now engaged in this business, and hopes soon to accomplish the object of his mission. He is attended by *Benjamin Banneker,* an Ethiopian, whose abilities, as a surveyor, and an astronomer, clearly prove that Mr. Jefferson's concluding that race of men were void of mental endowments, was without foundation.

Whenever Banneker had time, he labored on his ephemeris for the coming year. At the end of April, when the major's two brothers arrived to assist him, Banneker was not sorry to start for home. He had learned something about practical astronomy from Major Ellicott and he was eager to resume

full-time work on his calculations. And there was the farm. Elizabeth remembered the day he got back. "On his return home, he called at the house of his friend George Ellicott to give an account of his engagements. He arrived on horseback, dressed in his usual costume, a full suit of drab cloth, surmounted by a large beaver hat." He was in fine spirits, seeming to have been reanimated by the kindness of the distinguished men with whom he had mingled. With his usual humility he estimated his own services at a low rate.

BENJAMIN Banneker published six almanacs, for the years 1792 to 1797, in twenty-eight editions, printed in Baltimore, Philadelphia, Petersburg, Richmond, Wilmington, and Trenton. The achievement was a notable one for at least two reasons: it was a scientific feat by a self-taught polymath in his sixties; it was a bold polemic aimed at those who denied equal intellect and humanity in black and white. "His notes remain as a monument to his love of astronomy and to his unflagging determination to master every aspect of the task he had set himself," Bedini observes. Was there something else that drove the black astronomer to the herculean effort embodied in his six years of ceaseless toil? ("A vast amount of work was required to calculate a single eclipse," adds Bedini, "which makes Banneker's accomplishment in this field all the more impressive. He had to make at least sixty-eight mathematical calculations to produce the ten elements required to construct a single eclipse diagram.") There is a clue, perhaps, in the letter he had sent to Major Andrew Ellicott during the spring of 1790 as he breathlessly awaited his verdict on the first ephemeris: "The Calculations was made more for the Sake of gratifying the Curiosity of the public, than for any view of profit, as I suppose it to be the first attempt of the kind that ever was made in America by a person of my Complection."

Inevitably the trail leads to Thomas Jefferson. It was in 1788 that the American edition of his *Notes on the State of Virginia* was published in Philadelphia. It is hardly possible that the Ellicotts did not own a copy of the book and more than probable that Banneker, either directly or through the press, was painfully aware of its slurs on the intellectual capacities of the blacks. "Comparing them by their faculties of memory, reason, and imagination, it appears to me," wrote Jefferson, "that in memory they are equal to the white; in reason much inferior, as I think one could scarcely be found capable of tracing and comprehending the investigations of Euclid; and that in imagination they are dull, tasteless, and anomalous . . . never yet could I find that a black had uttered a thought above the level of plain narration. . . ." In Georgetown, in the *Weekly Ledger,* Banneker had already seen himself cited as "an Ethiopian" who was the living rebuttal of Mr. Jefferson's opinion that blacks were "void of mental endowments." Now, back home in Maryland, his historic task was clear. *Banneker's Almanacs* would drive the point home.

When the ephemeris for 1792 was at last ready for the press, he quickly lined up a few printers in Georgetown and Baltimore, but his particular wish was to publish it in Philadelphia, where the stalwarts of the Society for the Abolition of Slavery—already aware of his work—saw eye to eye with his concept of an almanac that would combine scientific data with antiracist argument. Everything went well, the ubiquitous Ellicotts assisting. George sent the ephemeris to his brother Elias in Baltimore, who in turn

wrote to James Pemberton, the wealthy Quaker abolitionist and friend of John Woolman, Anthony Benezet, and Captain Paul Cuffe. "He is a man of strong Natural parts," wrote Elias, "and by his own Study hath made himself well Acquainted with the Mathematicks. About three Years ago he began to study Astronomy . . . became so far a proficient as to Calculate an Almanac. . . . He hath a Copy now ready for the Press for the Year 1792." Then he added what all the Ellicotts knew was uppermost in Banneker's mind—"he is a Poor man & Would be Pleased With having something for the Copy but if the Printer is not Willing to give any thing He would rather let him have it for nothing than not to have it Published. He thinks as it is the first performance of the kind ever done by One of his Complection that it might be a means of Promoting the Cause of Humanity as many are of the Opinion that the Blacks are Void of Mental Endowments."

Pemberton lost no time. He immediately dispatched a copy of Banneker's ephemeris to David Rittenhouse, the nation's foremost scientist, who had recently been appointed to succeed Benjamin Franklin as president of the American Philosophical Society. (Before that same society in 1775, in his famous oration on the wonders of astronomy, Rittenhouse had defended the equality of the blacks, who, "degraded from their native dignity, have been doomed to endless slavery by us in America, merely because *their* bodies may be disposed to reflect or absorb the rays of light, in a way different from *ours*.") A "very extraordinary performance," replied Rittenhouse, " . . . Every Instance of Genius amongst the Negroes is worthy of attention, because their oppressors seem to lay great stress on their supposed inferior mental abilities."

It was at this moment, during the summer of 1791, that Benjamin Banneker, feeling that the time was now ripe for spelling out his grand idea, wrote to Secretary of State Thomas Jefferson a letter that deserves to be enshrined as a classic document of our literature—the black democratic challenge put to the chief ideologist of the American Revolution [figs. 99 and 100]. No treatment of the black presence in that era would be complete without all of this manifesto, no future edition of *Notes on the State of Virginia* should ever omit it.

Sir I am fully sensible of the greatness of that freedom which I take with you on the present occasion; a liberty which Seemed to me scarcely allowable, when I reflected on that distinguished, and dignifyed station in which you Stand; and the almost general prejudice and prepossession which is so prevalent in the world against those of my complexion.

I suppose it is a truth too well attested to you, to need of proof here, that we are a race of Beings who have long laboured under the abuse and censure of the world, that we have long been looked upon with an eye of contempt, and that we have long been considered rather as brutish than human, and Scarcely capable of mental endowments.

Sir, I hope I may Safely admit, in consequence of that report which hath reached me, that you are a man far less inflexible in Sentiments of this nature, than many others, that you are measurably friendly and well disposed towards us, and that you are willing and ready to Lend your aid and assistance to our relief from those many distresses and numerous calamities to which we are reduced.

Now Sir if this is founded in truth, I apprehend you will readily embrace every opportunity to eradicate that train of absurd and false ideas and oppinions which so generally prevail with respect to us, and that your Sentiments are concurrent with mine, which are that one universal Father hath given being to us all, and that he hath not only made us all of one flesh, but that he hath also without partiality afforded us all the Same Sensations, and endued us all with the same faculties, and that however variable we may be in Society or religion, however diversified in Situation or colour, we are all of the Same Family, and Stand in the Same relation to him.

Sir, if these are Sentiments of which you are fully persuaded, I hope you cannot but acknowledge, that it is the indispensible duty of those who maintain for themselves the rights of human nature, and who profess the obligations of Christianity, to extend their power and influence to the relief of every part of the human race, from whatever burthen or oppression they may unjustly labour under; and this I apprehend a full conviction of the truth and obligation of these principles should lead all to.

Sir, I have long been convinced, that if your love for your Selves and for those inesteemable laws which preserve to you the rights of human nature, was founded on Sincerity, you could not but be Solicitous, that every Individual of whatsoever rank or distinction, might with you equally enjoy the blessings thereof, neither could you rest Satisfyed, short of the most active diffusion of your

Maryland. Baltimore County. Near Ellicotts Lower Mills August 19th 1791.

Thomas Jefferson Secretary of State.

Sir

I am fully sensible of the greatness of that freedom which I take with you on the present occasion; a liberty which seemed to me scarcely allowable, when I reflected on that distinguished, and dignifyed station in which you stand; and the almost general prejudice and prepossession which is so prevalent in the world against those of my complexion.

I suppose it is a truth too well attested to you, to need a proof here, that we are a race of Beings who have long laboured under the abuse and censure of the world, that we have long been looked upon with an eye of contempt; and that we have long been considered rather as brutish than human, and scarcely capable of mental endowments.

Sir I hope I may safely admit, in consequence of that report which hath reached me, that you are a man far less inflexible in Sentiments of this nature, than many others, that you are measurably friendly and well disposed towards us; and that you are willing and ready to Lend your aid and assistance to our relief from those many distresses, and numerous calamities to which we are reduced.

Now Sir if this is founded in truth, I apprehend you will readily embrace every opportunity to eradicate that train of absurd and false ideas and opinions which so generally prevails with respect to us; and that your Sentiments are concurrent with mine, which are that one universal Father hath given being to us all, and that he hath not only made us all of one flesh, but that he hath also without partiality afforded us all the same Sensations, and endued us all with the same faculties, and that however variable we may be in Society or religion, however diversifyed in Situation or colour, we are all of the Same Family, and Stand in the Same relation to him.

Sir, if these are Sentiments of which you are fully persuaded, I hope you cannot but acknowledge, that it is the indispensible duty of those who maintain for themselves the rights of human nature, and who profess the obligations of Christianity, to extend their power and influence to the relief of every part of the human race, from whatever burthen or oppression they may unjustly labour under, and this I apprehend a full conviction of the truth and obligation of these principles should lead all to.

Sir, I have long been convinced, that if your love for your Selves and for those inestimable laws which preserve to you the rights of human nature, was founded on Sincerity, you could not but be Solicitous, that every Individual of whatsoever rank or distinction, might with you equally enjoy the blessings thereof, neither could you rest Satisfyed, short of the most active diffusion of your exertions, in order to their promotion from any State of degradation, to which the unjustifyable cruelty and barbarism of men may have reduced them.

Sir I freely and Chearfully acknowledge, that I am of the African race, and in that colour which is natural to them of the deepest dye; and it is under a Sense of the most profound gratitude to the Supreme Ruler of the universe, that I now confess to you, that I am not under that State of tyrannical thraldom, and inhuman captivity, to which too many of my brethren are doomd; but that I have abundantly tasted of the fruition of those blessings which proceed from that free and unequalled liberty with which you are favored and which I hope you will willingly allow you have received from the immediate hand of that Being from whom proceedeth every good and perfect gift.

Sir, Suffer me to recall to your mind that time in which the Arms and tyranny of the British Crown were exerted with every powerful effort in order to reduce you to a State of Servitude; look back I intreat you on the variety of dangers to which you were exposed, reflect on that time in which every human aid appeared unavailable, and in which even hope and fortitude wore the aspect of inability to the Conflict, and you cannot but be led to a Serious and grateful Sense of your miraculous and providential preservation; you cannot but acknowledge, that the present freedom and tranquility which you enjoy you have mercifully received, and that it is the peculiar blessing of Heaven.

This Sir, was a time in which you clearly saw into the injustice of a State of Slavery, and in which you had just apprehensions of the horrors of its condition, it was now Sir, that your abhorrence thereof was so excited, that you publickly held forth this true and invaluable doctrine, which is worthy to be recorded and remembred in all Succeeding ages. "We hold these truths to be Self evident, that all men are created equal, and that they are endowed by their creator with certain unalienable rights, that among these are life, liberty, and the pursuit of happyness".

Here Sir, was a time in which your tender feelings for your selves had engaged you thus to declare, you were then impressed with proper ideas of the great valuation of liberty, and the free possession of those blessings to which you were entitled by nature; but Sir how pitiable is it to reflect, that altho you were so fully convinced of the benevolence of the Father of mankind, and of his equal and impartial distribution of those rights and privileges which he had conferred upon them, that you should at the same time counteract his mercies, in detaining by fraud and violence so numerous a part of my brethren under groaning captivity and cruel oppression; that you should at the same time be found guilty of that most criminal act, which you ~~professedly~~ professedly detested in others, with respect to yourselves.

Sir, I suppose that your knowledge of the situation of my brethren is too extensive to need a recital here; neither shall I presume to prescribe methods by which they may be relieved; otherwise than by recommending to you and all others, to wean yourselves from those narrow prejudices which you have imbibed with respect to them and as Job proposed to his friends " Put your souls in their souls stead"; thus shall your hearts be enlarged with kindness and benevolence toward them, and thus shall you need neither the direction of myself or others in what manner to proceed herein.

And now, Sir, altho my sympathy and affection for my brethren hath caused my enlargement thus far, I ardently hope that your candour and generosity will plead with you in my behalf, when I make known to you, that it was not originally my design; but that having taken up my pen in order to direct to you as a present, a copy of an Almanack which I have calculated for the succeeding year, I was unexpectedly and unavoidably ~~was~~ led thereto.

This calculation, Sir, is the production of my arduous study in this my advanced stage of life; for having long had unbounded desires to become acquainted with the secrets of nature I have had to gratify my curiosity herein thro my own assiduous application to Astronomical study, in which I need not to recount to you the many difficulties and disadvantages which I have had to encounter.

And altho I had almost declined to make my calculation for the ensuing year, in consequence of that time which I had allotted therefor being taking up at the Federal Territory by the request of Mr Andrew Ellicott, yet finding myself under several engagements to printers of this state to whom I had communicated my design, on my return to my place of residence, I industriously applied ~~myself thereto which I~~ have accomplished with correctness and accuracy, a copy of which I have taken the liberty to direct to you, and which I humbly request you will favourably receive, and altho you may have the opportunity of perusing it after its publication, yet I chose to send it to you in manuscript previous thereto, that thereby you might not only have an earlier inspection, but that you might also view it in my own hand writing.

And now Sir, I shall conclude
and subscribe myself with the most profound respect
your most Obedient humble Servant

Benjamin Banneker

NB any communication to me
may be had by a direction to
Mr Elias Ellicott merchant
in Baltimore Town
☞

As an Essay of my calculation is put into the hands of
~~of~~ Mr Cruickshank of Philadelphia, for publication I
would wish that you might neither have this ~~published~~
~~a~~Almanack copy published nor give any printer an opportunity
thereof, as it might tend to disappoint Mr Joseph Cruickshank
in his sale
☞

100. *Copy of a Letter from Benjamin Banneker, to the Secretary of State . . .* (Philadelphia, 1792). Courtesy, American Antiquarian Society.

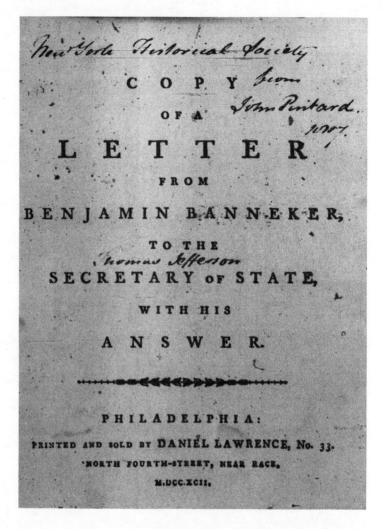

New York Historical Society

COPY from

OF A John Pintard.

1807

LETTER

FROM

BENJAMIN BANNEKER,

TO THE

Thomas Jefferson

SECRETARY OF STATE,

WITH HIS

ANSWER.

PHILADELPHIA:

PRINTED AND SOLD BY DANIEL LAWRENCE, No. 33.

NORTH FOURTH-STREET, NEAR RACE.

M.DCC.XCII.

exertions, in order to their promotion from any State of degradation, to which the unjustifyable cruelty and barbarism of men may have reduced them.

Sir I freely and Chearfully acknowledge, that I am of the African race, and in that colour which is natural to them of the deepest dye,* and it is under a Sense of the most profound gratitude to the Supreme Ruler of the universe, that I now confess to you, that I am not under that State of ty-

*My Father was brought here a Slave from Africa. [Banneker's note]

rannical thraldom, and inhuman captivity, to which too many of my brethren are doomed; but that I have abundantly tasted of the fruition of those blessings which proceed from that free and unequalled liberty with which you are favoured and which I hope you will willingly allow you have received from the immediate Hand of that Being from whom proceedeth every good and perfect gift.

Sir, Suffer me to recall to your mind that time in which the Arms and tyranny of the British Crown were exerted with every powerful effort in order to reduce you to a State of Servitude; look back I intreat you on the variety of dangers to which you were exposed, reflect on that time in which every human aid appeared unavailable, and in which even hope and fortitude wore the aspect of inability to the Conflict, and you cannot but be led to a Serious and grateful Sense of your miraculous and providential preservation; you cannot but acknowledge, that the present freedom and tranquility which you enjoy you have mercifully received, and that it is the peculiar blessing of Heaven.

This Sir, was a time in which you clearly saw into the injustice of a State of Slavery, and in which you had just apprehensions of the horrors of its condition, it was now Sir, that your abhorrence thereof was so excited, that you publickly held forth this true and invaluable doctrine, which is worthy to be recorded and remembered in all Succeeding ages. "We hold these truths to be Self evident, that all men are created equal, and that they are endowed by their creator with certain unalienable rights, that amongst these are life, liberty, and the persuit of happiness."

Here Sir, was a time in which your tender feelings for yourselves engaged you thus to declare, you were then impressed with proper ideas of the great valuation of liberty, and the free possession of those blessings to which you were entitled by nature; but Sir how pitiable is it to reflect, that altho you were so fully convinced of the benevolence of the Father of mankind, and of his equal and impartial distribution of those rights and privileges which he had conferred upon them, that you should at the Same

time counteract his mercies, in detaining by fraud and violence so numerous a part of my brethren under groaning captivity and cruel oppression, that you should at the Same time be found guilty of that most criminal act, which you professedly detested in others, with respect to yourselves.

Sir, I suppose that your knowledge of the situation of my brethren is too extensive to need a recital here; neither shall I presume to prescribe methods by which they may be relieved; otherwise than by recommending to you, and all others, to wean yourselves from those narrow prejudices which you have imbibed with respect to them, and as Job proposed to his friends "Put your Souls in their Souls stead," thus shall your hearts be enlarged with kindness and benevolence towards them, and thus shall you need neither the direction of myself or others in what manner to proceed herein.

And now, Sir, altho my Sympathy and affection for my brethren hath caused my enlargement thus far, I ardently hope that your candour and generosity will plead with you in my behalf, when I make known to you, that it was not originally my design; but that having taken up my pen in order to direct to you as a present, a copy of an Almanack which I have calculated for the Succeeding year, I was unexpectedly and unavoidably led thereto.

This calculation, Sir, is the production of my arduous study, in this my advanced Stage of life; for having long had unbounded desires to become Acquainted with the Secrets of nature, I have had to gratify my curiosity herein thro my own assiduous application to Astronomical Study, in which I need not to recount to you the many difficulties and disadvantages which I have had to encounter.

And altho I had almost declined to make my calculation for the ensuing year, in consequence of that time which I had allotted therefor being taking up at the Federal Territory by the request of Mr. Andrew Ellicott, yet finding myself under Several engagements to printers of this state to whom I had communicated my design, on my return to my place of residence, I industriously apply'd myself thereto, which I hope I have accomplished with correctness and accuracy, a copy of which I have taken the liberty to direct to you, and which I humbly request you will favourably receive, and altho you may have the opportunity of perusing it after its publication, yet I chose to send it to you in manuscript previous thereto, that thereby you might not only have an earlier inspection, but that you might also view it in my own hand writing.

And now Sir, I Shall conclude and Subscribe mySelf with the most profound respect, your most Obedient humble Servant

BENJAMIN BANNEKER

Five days after Banneker had dispatched this letter to Jefferson with a manuscript copy of his forthcoming almanac, George Ellicott wrote to James Pemberton: "Inclosed is a Coppy of a Letter which Benjamin Banaker wrote to Thos. Jefferson Secretary of State which he wrote himself and desired Me to send to thee it is his wish to have it put into the Allmanacke if its thought proper or in to the publick papers." (It is to be noted

that Banneker was not being "used" by the Quaker abolitionists; the initiative was his own; the letter was to be printed, if possible, in the almanac—the printers were finally responsible for the insertion of editorial materials—or in the newspapers.) "Their is a small piece of poetry inclosed of Banaker's composing," Ellicott continued, "which he desires may be put under the Letter if its published." How eager Banneker was to ram home his humanitarian point may be sensed in these verses, which never got into print:

> Behold ye Christians! and in pity see
> Those Afric sons which Nature
>   formed free;
> Behold them in a fruitful country
>   blest,
> of Nature's bounties see them rich
>   possest,
> Behold them here from town by cruel
>   force,
> And doomed to slavery without re-
>   morse,
> This act, America, thy sons have
>   known;
> This cruel act, relentless have they
>   done.

Jefferson received Banneker's ephemeris and letter at Philadelphia, and replied on August 30 [fig. 101]:

SIR, I Thank you sincerely for your letter of the 19th instant and for the Almanac it contained. No body wishes more than I do to see such proofs as you exhibit, that nature has given to our black brethren, talents equal to those of the other colors of men, and that the appearance of a want of them is owing merely to the degraded condition of their existence, both in Africa and America. I can add with truth, that no body wishes more

101. Thomas Jefferson to
Benjamin Banneker, August 30, 1791. Courtesy
of the Library of Congress.

ardently to see a good system commenced for raising the condition both of their body & mind to what it ought to be, as fast as the imbecility of their present existence, and other circumstances which cannot be neglected will admit.

I have taken the liberty of sending your Almanac to Monsieur de Condorcet, Secretary of the Academy of Sciences at Paris, and member of the Philanthropic society, because I considered it as a document to which your whole colour had a right for their justification against the doubts which have been entertained of them.

On the same day, Jefferson forwarded the

ephemeris—but not Banneker's letter—to Condorcet, with a covering note:

I am happy to be able to inform you that we have now in the United States a negro, the son of a black man born in Africa, and a black woman born in the United States, who is a very respectable mathematician. I procured him to be employed under one of our chief directors in laying out the new federal city of the Potowmac, & in the intervals of his leisure, while on that work, he made an Almanac for the next year, which he sent me in his own handwriting, & which I inclose to you. I have seen very elegant solutions of Geometrical problems by

him. Add to this that he is a very
worthy & respectable member of society. He is a free man. I shall be delighted to see these instances of moral
eminence so multiplied as to prove
that the want of talents observed in
them is merely the effect of their degraded condition, and not proceeding
from any difference in the structure of
the parts in which intellect depends.

Did Condorcet reply? We do not know.
But seventeen years later, another distinguished Frenchman, the Abbé Henri Grégoire, sent to Jefferson a copy of his recent
book, *De la littérature des Negres,* which
would shortly be translated and published
in Brooklyn under the impressive title *An
Enquiry concerning the Intellectual and Moral
Faculties and Literature of Negroes; Followed
with an Account of the Life and Works of Fifteen
Negroes and Mulattoes* [fig. 102]. There were
some writers, observed the revolutionary
priest, who believed that nature had denied
to black people "deep reflection, genius and
reason. . . . We regret to find the same
prejudice in a man, whose name is not pro-
nounced amongst us, but with the most
profound esteem or merited respect—we
mean Jefferson in his 'Notes on Virginia.' "
To Grégoire, Jefferson responded, as
Winthrop Jordan puts it, with "his usual
protestations of inconclusiveness":

> Be assured that no person living
> wishes more sincerely than I do, to
> see a complete refutation of the
> doubts I have myself entertained and
> expressed on the grade of understand-
> ing alloted to them by nature, and
> that to find that in this respect they
> are on a par with ourselves. My
> doubts were the result of personal ob-
> servation on the limited sphere of my
> own State, where the opportunities
> for the development of their genius

102. Henri Grégoire, *An Enquiry Concerning the
Intellectual and Moral Faculties and Literature of
Negroes . . .* (Brooklyn, 1810). Courtesy of the
Library of Congress.

> were not favorable, and those of ex-
> ercising it still less so. I expressed
> them therefore with great hesita-
> tion . . . but whatever be their de-
> gree of talent it is no measure of their
> rights. . . .

But to his friend Joel Barlow, Jefferson confessed that he had given Grégoire "a very
soft answer." It is in this letter, with its in-
accuracies and innuendo, that his original
opinion of Banneker and his achievement—
and of the equality of the black intellect—
comes clear:

Bishop Grégoire wrote to me on the doubts I had expressed five or six and twenty years ago, in the *Notes on Virginia,* as to the grade of understanding of the negroes. His credulity had made him gather up every story he could find of men of color (without distinguishing whether black, or of what degree of mixture), however slight the mention, or light the authority on which they are quoted. The whole do not amount in point of evidence, to what we know ourselves about Banneker. We know he had spherical trigonometry enough to make almanacs, but not without the suspicion of aid from Ellicott, who was his neighbor and friend, and never missed an opportunity of puffing him. I have a long letter from Banneker, which shows him to have had a mind of very common stature indeed. . . .

The black astronomer was three years in his grave when Jefferson wrote these nervous lines.

ALTHOUGH Banneker was eager to print his correspondence with Jefferson as a preface to his first almanac, a misunderstanding among the printers delayed its inclusion until the almanac for 1793. Almost at the same time, to ensure wider distribution by the Abolition Society, he published the letters as a separate pamphlet, which sold out rapidly and had to be reprinted in a second edition. In place of the letters, *Benjamin Banneker's Pennsylvania, Delaware, Maryland and Virginia Almanack and Ephemeris, for the Year of Our Lord, 1792 . . . and the Sixteenth Year of American Independence* opened with a preface by the printer-editors, who presented to the public *"an extraordinary Effort of Genius"*

Calculated by a sable Descendant of Africa, who, by this Specimen of Ingenuity, evinces, to Demonstration, that mental Powers and Endowments are not the exclusive *Excellence of* white people, *but the Rays of Science may alike illumine the Minds of Men of every Clime, (however they may differ in the Colour of their Skin) particularly those whom Tyrant-Custom hath too long taught us to depreciate as a Race inferior in intellectual Capacity.*

There followed a short biography of Banneker—the earliest sketch of his life, reprinted again and again at home and abroad during the next few years—by the senator from Maryland, Dr. James McHenry of Baltimore, whom he had asked for help. (The senator, who had come over from Ireland in 1771, had studied medicine under Dr. Benjamin Rush, served as secretary to Washington and Lafayette during the war, and then spent three years in the Continental Congress.) "I cannot but wish on this occasion," wrote McHenry, "to see the Public patronage keep pace with my black friend's merit":

I consider this Negro as a fresh proof that the powers of the mind are disconnected with the colour of the skin, or, in other words, a striking contradiction to Mr. *Hume's* doctrine, that "Negroes are naturally inferior to the whites and unsusceptible of attainments in arts and sciences." In every civilized country we shall find thousands of whites, liberally educated, and who have enjoyed greater opportunities of instruction than this Negro, his inferior in those intellectual acquirements and capacities that form the most characteristic feature in the human race.

The almanacs themselves, aside from the ephemerides of Banneker, were an innovation in the old genre, bringing together, as they did, the usual variety of useful science and general information, but adding humanitarian politics. There were extracts from the *Columbian Magazine,* "On Negro Slavery, and the Slave Trade," which cited a comment on skin pigmentation by David Rittenhouse, passages from the debates in Parliament on the slave trade with an abstract of William Pitt's great speech, stanzas from "Wilkinson's Appeal to England in Behalf of the Abused Africans," Cowper's poem "On Liberty," and a typical filler to the effect that needles were "first made in London, by a Negro from Spain, in the reign of Q Mary." Phillis Wheatley's twelve lines from "On the Works of Providence" in the almanac for 1794 are introduced by the editors with the remark "that Africans and their Descendants are capable of attaining a Degree of Eminence in the Liberal Sciences BENJAMIN is not the only proof." Most notable, except for the letter of Jefferson that had been in the almanac of 1793, was the first version of Benjamin Rush's "A Plan of a Peace-Office, for the United States," a landmark in the history of the search for alternatives to war and an argument for peace with which Banneker no doubt fully concurred [fig. 103]:

> The labours of the justly celebrated *Bannaker* will likewise furnish you with a very important lesson, courteous reader, which you will not find in any other Almanac, namely that the Maker of the Universe is no respecter of colours; that the colour of the skin is in no ways connected with strength of mind or intellectual powers. . . . To the untutored Blacks, the following elegant lines of GRAY may be applied—

A PLAN OF A *PEACE-OFFICE,* FOR THE UNITED STATES.

AMONG the many defects which have been pointed out in the federal constitution by its antifederal enemies, it is much to be lamented that no person has taken notice of its total silence upon the subject of an office of the utmost importance to the welfare of the United States, that is, an *office* for promoting and preserving perpetual *peace* in our country.

It is to be hoped that no objection will be made to the establishment of such an office, while we are engaged in a war with the Indians, for as the *War-Office* of the United States was established in the *time of peace,* it is equally reasonable that a *Peace-Office* should be established in the *time of war.*

The plan of this office is as follows:

I. Let a Secretary of Peace be appointed to preside in this office, who shall be perfectly free from all the present absurd and vulgar European prejudices upon the subject of government; let him be a genuine republican and a sincere Christian, for the principles of republicanism and Christianity are no less friendly to universal and perpetual peace, than they are to universal and equal liberty.

V. To inspire a veneration for human life, and an horror at the shedding of human blood, let all those laws be repealed which authorise juries, judges, sheriffs, or bangmen to assume the resentments of individuals, and to commit murder in cold blood in any case whatever. Until this reformation in our code of penal jurisprudence take place, it will be in vain to attempt to introduce universal and perpetual peace in our country.

VI. To subdue that passion for war, which education, added to human depravity, have made universal, a familiarity with the instruments of death, as well as all military shews, should be carefully avoided. For which reason, militia laws should every where be repealed, and military dresses and military titles should be laid aside: reviews tend to lessen the horrors of a battle by connecting them with the charms of order; militia laws generate idleness and vice, and thereby produce the wars they are said to prevent; military dresses fascinate the minds of young men, and lead them from serious and useful professions; were there no *uniforms,* there would probably be no armies; lastly, military titles feed vanity, and keep up ideas in the mind which lessen a sense of the folly and miseries of war.

103. Benjamin Rush, "A Plan of a *Peace-Office,* for the United States," in Banneker's *Almanack* (Philadelphia, 1793). Courtesy of the Library of Congress.

> Full many a gem of purest ray serene,
> The dark unfathom'd caves of ocean
> bear:
> Full many a flower is borne to blush
> unseen.
> And waste its fragrance on the desert
> air.

So ends the preface to the almanac for 1796, to which the editors added another quatrain:

104. *Benjamin Bannaker's
. . . Almanac . . . 1795*
(Baltimore, 1795). Mary-
land Historical Society,
Baltimore.

Nor you ye proud, impute to these
    the blame
If Afric's sons to genius are unknown,
For Banneker has prov'd they may ac-
    quire a name
As bright, as lasting as your own.

THE portrait cut on wood that adorns the
cover of the almanac of 1795 shows Banneker at sixty-four (he looks younger) in the
plain Quaker garb he always wore

[fig. 104]. There would be two more almanacs, in 1796 and 1797, and then his work
would be done. His health had begun to decline. A young friend of the Ellicotts from
Philadelphia, Susannah Mason, visiting the
old man in the summer of 1796, "found the
venerable star-gazer under a wide-spreading
pear tree laden with delicious fruit. He
came forward to meet us, and bade us welcome to his lowly dwelling. It was built of
logs, one story in height, and was sur-

rounded by an orchard. In one corner of the room was a clock of his own construction. . . . He took down from a shelf a little book, wherein he registered the names of those by whose visits he felt particularly honored. . . ." When Susannah, in a rhymed letter of admiration, praised him as a "man exalted high,"

> Conspicuous in the world's keen eye,
> On record now thy name's enrolled;
> And future ages will be told
> There lived a man named
> BANNEKER
> An African Astronomer!

he replied with thanks in a note penned "with trembling hands."

Banneker never married, lived alone on his farm, cooked his own meals. As his infirmities increased, he sold and rented parts of his land, then gave the rest of it to the Ellicotts in exchange for a twelve-pound annuity guaranteed for his life. He puttered in his garden and orchard, watched the stars at night, went to sleep at dawn, studied his bees endlessly, made original observations on the seventeen-year locusts, hunted a bit, sat under his chestnut tree in the dooryard and played his violin and flute, drank a little too much at times, attended Quaker meetings now and then. The journal that he always kept was not abandoned. In its pages he recorded his observations of nature, new mathematical puzzles in verse, his dreams, and the continuing calculations for new ephemerides that were never published. "The contents of Banneker's Manuscript Journal and his commonplace book," notes Bedini, "are unique records of an eighteenth-century almanac-maker . . . with a clear exposition of the method by which almanacs were calculated during this period of American scientific history."

About Banneker in his old age there was the aura of a sage. All who knew him at this time remembered his "very venerable and dignified appearance." One found it curious that "the statue of Franklin at the Library in Philadelphia" was "the perfect likeness of him." A young clerk who worked in the store at Ellicott's Mills in 1800 could never forget him: "After hearing him converse, I was always anxious to wait upon him. After making purchases, he usually went to the part of the store where George Ellicott was in the habit of sitting, to converse with him about the affairs of our Government and other matters. He was very precise in conversation and exhibited deep reflection . . . he seemed to be acquainted with every thing of importance that was passing in the country. . . ."

"I remember Benjamin Banneker's personal appearance very well," wrote Thomas Ellicott, "he was quite a black man, of medium stature, of uncommonly soft and gentlemanly manners, and pleasant colloquial powers, and like *other* gentlemen of that day had not abstained from the use of intoxicating drink—though I think I never saw him improperly influenced by it." As a young woman, George Ellicott's daughter, Martha, frequently saw Banneker at the Elkridge Quaker Meeting House: "His raiment was always scrupulously neat; that for summer wear, being of unbleached linen, was beautifully washed and ironed by his sisters. . . . In cold weather he dressed in light colored cloth, a fine drab broadcloth constituting his attire when he designed appearing in his best style: His ample forehead, white hair, and reverent deportment, gave him a very venerable appearance, as he leaned on the long staff (which he always carried with him) in contemplation. . . . The countenance of Banneker had a most benign and thoughtful expression. . . . His figure was perfectly erect, showing no inclination to stoop as he advanced in years." The end came in October 1806 when he was almost seventy-five. Two days after his death, as his body was being lowered into the grave, his house, a few yards away, caught fire. The clock that he made with his own hands forty years before was consumed in the flames.

On October 28, 1806, the *Federal Gazette and Baltimore Daily Advertiser* printed a brief but pithy obituary:

> On Sunday, the 9th instant, departed this life at his residence in Baltimore County, Mr. Benjamin Banneker, a black man, and immediate descendant of an African father. He was well known in his neighborhood for his quiet and peaceful demeanor, and, among scientific men, as an astronomer and mathematician.
>
> In early life he was instructed in the most common rules of arithmetic, and thereafter, with the assistance of different authors, he was enabled to acquire a perfect knowledge of all the higher branches of learning. Mr. Banneker was the calculator of several almanacs, published in this as well as several of the neighboring States; and, although of late years none of his almanacs have been published, yet he never failed to calculate one every year, and left them among his papers.
>
> Preferring solitude to mixing with society, he devoted the greater part of his time to reading and contemplation, and to no book was he more attached than the Scriptures.
>
> At his death, he bequeathed all his astronomical and philosophical books and papers to a friend.
>
> Mr. Banneker is a prominent instance to prove that a descendant of Africa is susceptible of as great mental improvement and deep knowledge of the mysteries of nature as that of any other nation.

Forty years later, the Reverend Daniel Alexander Payne, pastor (later bishop) of the African Methodist Church, who had lauded Banneker as a model for the young men of his Baltimore parish, organized a committee to raise money for a monument to his memory. He tried to find the grave. At Ellicott's Lower Mills an old-timer led him to the site of the family burying ground: "Beneath two tulip-trees, so grown as to seem one, lay the mortal remains of the black astronomer of Maryland. A few yards to the north-west of the grave was the site of his house, not a vestige of which could then be seen. It was marked only by a shallow cavity, at the southeastern end of which stood a tall Lombardy poplar, said to be that which overshadowed the gable end of his house."

Captain Paul Cuffe

On February 10, 1780, seven freemen, "Chiefly of the African Extract," living in the seacoast town of Dartmouth, Massachusetts, sent a protest to the legislature in Boston [fig. 105]. Their grievance had a familiar ring—taxation without representation:

> by Reason of Long Bondag and hard Slavery we have been deprived of Injoying the Profits of our Labouer or the advantage of Inheriting Estates from our Parents as our Neighbouers the white peopel do . . . & yet . . . we have been & now are Taxed both in our Polls and that small Pittance of Estate which through much hard Labour & Industry we have got together to Sustain our selves. . . .

Not only does such taxation "Reduce us to a

105. Petition of Paul Cuffe and "Several poor Negros & Molattors" of Dartmouth, Massachusetts, to the General Court, March 14, 1780. Massachusetts Archives, 186: 134.

State of Beggary," they claimed, but "we are not allowed the Privilage of freemen of the State having no vote or Influence in the Election of those that Tax us . . . we are not alowed in voating in the town meating . . . nur to chuse an oficer . . . & we have not an Equal Chance with white people Neither By Sea nur By Land. . . ." And the final irony: "Yet many of our Colour (as is well known) have cheerfully Entered the field of Battle in the defence of the Common cause and that (as we conceive) against a similar Exertion of Power (in Regard to taxation) too well known to need a recital in this place."

One of the seven signers and possibly the petition's author was twenty-one-year-old Paul Cuffe, destined to make his mark in the world as master mariner, merchant, shipbuilder, philanthropist, and African colonizer. Like the ship's compass he left be-

hind, Captain Paul Cuffe's life had many points and directions [fig. 106].

CUFFE'S father, Cuffe Slocum, was an Ashanti of Akan ancestry; his name was Kofi, "born on Friday." He purchased his own freedom from his Quaker Dartmouth master, married a Gayhead Wampanoag woman, Ruth Moses, in 1746, acquired a hardscrabble farm on Martha's Vineyard, and raised a family of ten children. The seventh was Paul, born in 1759 on the island of Cuttyhunk, nine miles off New Bedford. When Paul was nineteen, two years after the Declaration of Independence, he and his brothers discarded the slave name of Slocum and adopted the first name of their father. It was about this time that he wrote out his name and lineage on a page of the notebook in which he was teaching himself the three R's: "Paul Cuffee of Dartmouth in the Province Plantations of America the Comtey[?] of Massachusetts Bay and living in the Border of R.I. and mustee [African/Indian] is my nation."

A boy of thirteen at the time of his father's death, he scarcely knew the letters of the alphabet, but with the aid of a tutor he learned to read and write. From the start, salt was in his blood. He studied navigation and mastered the rudiments of "latitude, lead, and lookout." At sixteen, when the acres his father had willed him proved worthless, like many other lads, black and red, he shipped as a hand on a whaler bound for the Gulf of Mexico. (In the century to follow, men of color, including a few in his own family, would play a big part in the American whale fishery—as seamen, mates, harpooners, and, occasionally, captains; an Afro-American blacksmith of New Bedford, Lewis Temple, would revolutionize the technique of the whale hunt with his invention of the toggle harpoon. John Mashow would design and build a goodly number of

106. Paul Cuffe's compass. New Bedford Whaling Museum.

the best whale ships in the same region.) Cuffe's second voyage was to the West Indies. On the third, in 1776, he was captured by the British and spent three months in a New York prison.

After his release he settled down on the Massachusetts coast at Westport, worked a farm, and for the next two years resumed his study of navigation. The war still raged and it was hazardous to go to sea, but he could not wait. With an older brother he built an open boat to trade with towns on the Connecticut shore. When rough seas, pirates, and privateers time and again thwarted his enterprise, he returned to the plow.

It was around this time that Paul and his brother John, with five others of "African Extract," would berate the elected worthies of the state house for violating revolutionary doctrine. "[We petitioned] for relief from Taxation in the days of our distress," John noted. "But we received non." The Cuffe brothers persisted, and late in the year took

their case to the Court of General Sessions in Bristol County. For three years the brothers had refused to pay taxes. When the collectors arrived to seize their property, there was none. In December 1780 the brothers found themselves in the common jail in Taunton and from there they fought their case. During the following spring, putting the issue squarely before town meeting, they demanded a vote as to "whether all free Negroes and molattoes shall have the same Privileges . . . as the white People having Respecting Places of profit choosing of officers and the Like together with all other Privileges in all cases . . . or that we have Reliefe granted us Joyntly from Taxation. . . ." The Cuffes finally had to pay—but by forcing the issue they hastened the day when taxation without representation, for any man, would be declared unconstitutional in the Bay State.

Fighting for his people's rights, Paul Cuffe was at the same time planning a career as mariner-merchant. His struggle to carry a cargo to Nantucket showed his mettle. First, he built a deckless boat "from keel to gun-wale." Tory pirates captured it. He built another, borrowed money for a cargo, foiled the pirates in the night, hit a rock and had to limp back and refit. When he finally made Nantucket, he could not sell his goods. On the second try there was a bit of profit, but on his way home the pirates stole all but the boat and, for good measure, beat him up. A third trip was so well rewarded that he procured a craft of eighteen tons and took on a hand to help.

In 1784 Alice Pequit, a woman of the Wampanoags like his mother, chose Paul Cuffe for her husband. The war was over, the sea safer. Cuffe rented a small house on the Westport River and in his new boat sailed to Saint George for a haul of codfish—and thus founded a fishing industry that was to thrive in his neighborhood for years to come. This was a turning point for the black captain. (Sally Loomis has noted that "of 11 black captains in Harold Lewis' manuscript list of black seamen in the area, 7 were related to Cuffe.) There would be partnerships with his Indian brother-in-law, Michael Wainer, a seasoned seaman. The vessels would get bigger, the voyages better. A new twenty-five-ton ship, the *Sunfish,* made two trips to the Straits of Belle Isle and Newfoundland, and the profits were invested in a forty-two-ton schooner, the *Mary.* In 1793, with a crew of ten black whale men, the *Mary,* cruising the Atlantic, encountered some trouble from a few white whale ships. It was on this voyage that Captain Cuffe himself hurled the harpoon that accounted for two of the leviathans. Back home, laden with oil and bone, the *Mary* proceeded to Philadelphia to exchange its goods for hardware to build a new and larger vessel. In 1795 Cuffe launched the *Ranger,* a sixty-nine-ton schooner, sold two

smaller boats to buy a cargo, and sailed to Norfolk. This was probably his initial visit to the south, where at firsthand he could view slavery as a flourishing institution. At Vienna on the Nanticoke River, where the *Ranger* dropped anchor to buy Indian corn, his *Memoir* relates that

> the people were filled with astonishment and alarm. A vessel owned and commanded by a black man, and manned with a crew of the same complexion, was unprecedented and surprising. The white inhabitants were struck with apprehensions of the injurious effects . . . on the minds of their slaves, suspecting that he wished secretly to kindle the spirit of rebellion, and excite a destructive revolt among them.

(To be sure, four years earlier the slaves had risen in San Domingue, and five years later Gabriel Prosser would rise up in Virginia.) A lynch-minded gang tried to stop him "from entering his vessel or remaining among them." Somehow, by smile and guile, he disarmed the suspicious, sold his cargo, and carried three thousand bushels of corn back to Westport. When, after a second trip south, the corn market thinned out, he set his sails for the north to fetch gypsum from Maine to Delaware, thus opening up another new line of trade.

In between voyages he was rooting himself in the Westport community as a benefactor of the town. Westport had no school—he proposed to his neighbors that they establish one, but, tired of the squabbles that arose, he built the schoolhouse with his own money on his own land and donated it "freely . . . to the use of the public." His parents had always gone to Quaker meeting and so had he. In 1808 he became a formal member of the Friends and sent one of his sons to a Quaker school in

Philadelphia; later he was the main contractor in the rebuilding of a new meetinghouse in Westport. To the end of his life, his manner of body and soul was reminiscent of Woolman and Benezet.

Things continued to prosper for the black Yankee trader. He acquired an interest in a bark of 162 tons, the *Hero,* which rounded the Cape of Good Hope, and he would later build the 268-ton *Alpha,* which, with a black crew of seven, sailed south to Wilmington and Savannah, thence across the ocean to Helsingør and Göteborg, returning to Philadelphia with passengers and freight. His last and favorite vessel, the *Traveller,* would carry him to Africa. Nearing the half-century mark, Captain Paul Cuffe was a merchant-mariner of substance: he owned one ship, two brigs, and several smaller vessels—a small fleet—as well as considerable property in houses and land.

I F the narrative thus far has the sound of an early American success story with Captain Paul Cuffe cast in the role of an Afro-Indian Benjamin Franklin, let it be said that all of it was but prelude to the serious saga of his remaining years. How could this son of a freed slave take his ease in a society that shackled his people? A few blacks—by talent, toil, and luck—might survive prejudice and statute to become men of property in the new nation. But what of the rest— the slaves and poor freemen? Anger and despair gnawed at his heart. Once in New York, after he was well known, a white Methodist preacher asked Cuffe, "Do you understand English?" He replied that some of the language was difficult for him: "That many persons who profess being enlightened with the true light, yet had not seen the evil of one brother professor making merchandise of and holding his brother in bondage."

The "true light" that he worked out for his own people, born of a profound disillusionment with the unfulfilled pledges of the revolution, was an exodus of free blacks to Africa. If whites, as they said, refused to liberate their slaves only because they feared masses of inferior and dangerous freemen in their midst, then let these freemen, present and future, of their own free choice depart from America for a better life in their native Africa. Thereby, in time, a number of worthy aims might be achieved: accelerated manumission and the doom of slavery in America; independent and free black societies in Africa; the economic development of Africa; the abolition of the slave trade; the "civilizing" of Africa by antislavery black Christians. The last was crucial to the devout Quaker. "The travail of my soul," he would often say, "is that Africa's inhabitants may be favored with reformation." Although he did not reject the idea of an additional colony of blacks somewhere in the United States, in Cuffe's evangelical vision the logic of black exodus seemed clear enough. For him it did not mean, as some would later charge, the abandonment of the slaves by their free brothers nor the weeding out of potential organizers of black liberation. On the contrary, the colonization of Africa, conducted by Christian blacks of talent, was the precondition in the long run for the ultimate emancipation of the slaves. To this idea, with all his resources of spirit and wealth, he would single-mindedly dedicate the last years of his life.

For Cuffe, to think was to act—the most immediate task was to discover a fruitful place in Africa to begin the historic process. In Philadelphia he discussed the matter with James Pemberton. "Since thy last being in this city," the Quaker merchant wrote him in June 1808, "the remembrance of thee has so frequently occupied my mind as to excite an inclination to write to thee, and particularly of thy sympathy expressed with the poor afflicted Inhabitants of Africa." From London Pemberton had news of an association for "promoting the civilizations of the people" of Africa, whose members had "raised a considerable sum of money to engage persons of sobriety and other necessary qualifications" to go to Sierra Leone to offer instruction "in the art of Agriculture and other employments." Among the members of the African Institution were Thomas Clarkson, William Wilberforce, and Granville Sharp. He had also heard that Zachariah Macaulay, the late governor of the colony, had said "that if Captn Cuffey should incline to make a voyage to Sierra Leone," he would be welcomed with open arms. By September, Pemberton was more insistent. Clarkson and the rest were "anxious to receive all the assistance and encouragement they can from the friends of humanity" in America: "Now if thy concern for the good of the poor untutored people continues and finds the mind impressed with a sense that any portion of the work is alloted for thee to perform, I hope and trust thou wilt give it thy most serious consideration." Cuffe's response was quick. Although he felt "very feebel and all most worn out in hard service and uncapable of doing much for my brethren of the African Race," if God was pleased to choose him as an instrument "for that service," he was ready and willing.

Cuffe had been speaking with Quaker modesty. By the spring of 1809, his plans for going to Africa were well under way. Since Pemberton was no longer alive, he sought help from two other merchant Friends in Philadelphia, John James and Alexander Wilson:

I have for some years had it impressed on my mind to make a voyage to Sierra Leon in order to inspect the situation of the country, and feeling a real desire that the inhabitants of Africa might become an enlightened people. . . . And as I am of the African race I feel myself interested for them and if I am favored with a talent I think I am willing that they should be benefited thereby.

Could a letter be dispatched to London to find out, "in case I engage in the whale fishery whether I could have encouragement such as bounty, or to carry the productions of the country duty free to England?" He was eager to make the trip by the next fall with "several families of good credit that may like to go." A year went by. Impatient, he laid his plans for the voyage before a committee of Westport Friends, whose enthusiastic letter of endorsement stated that the black captain was worth £5,000 and was "highly respected" by the Friends of Philadelphia. Unable to wait any longer, he rented his farm and asked his brother to look after his family. Paul would be gone for a year or two, wrote John to their sister, Freelove, in New York, on a "religious visit amongst the inhabitants of that Land, our own nation."

In the fall of 1810, Captain Cuffe sailed the *Traveller* out of Westport bound for Sierra Leone with a crew of nine black seamen. In Philadelphia, he conferred with Friends at the Arch Street meetinghouse, but when John James urged him to carry a cargo of corn to Cádiz, he replied that "it was not for profit or gain" that he "had undertaken this voyage." He departed from Philadelphia on New Year's Day of 1811, and fifty-two days later he recorded in his journal, with a sense of history: "The dust of Africa lodged on our riggings."

For three months, Cuffe took notes on the possibilities of Sierra Leone as the land of promise for the blacks of America. There were conferences with the governor on the economic state of the colony, the control of the slave trade, and problems of settlement. He looked at things for himself—visited a school of thirty girls, went to Methodist meetings, distributed Bibles, recorded without further comment that the "Mendingo men have the Scriptures in their tongue, viz the old testament, but deny the new testament. They own Mahomet a prophet." The longest entries in his journal reflect his eagerness to meet the local chieftains:

> King Thomas came on board to see me. He was an old man, gray headed, appeared to be sober and grave. I treated him with civility, and made him a present of a bible, a history of Elizabeth Webb, a Quaker, and a book of essays on War: together with several other small pamphlets accompanied with a letter of advise from myself . . . for the use and encouragement of the nations of Africa. He and retinue were thirteen in number. I served him with victuals . . . but it appeared that there was *rum* wanting, *but none was given.*

A few days later there was a visit to the "Bullion Shore" to visit King George, who had earlier brought a gift of three chickens and who now "treated us very cordially."

In mid-May, invited by Wilberforce, Cuffe headed the *Traveller* for Liverpool, carrying with him a young African whom he had "taken as an apprentice . . . to instruct in navigation." The pages of his English journal are pervaded by a sense of excitement and discovery. During a busy month, he took in the sights of London, Liverpool, and Manchester. "We went over London Bridge to Lancaster's School, where were taught one thousand scholars by one master . . . the greatest gratification that I met

with." In Manchester he spent a day in the factories, marveling at a woman who spun 150 threads at a time "under gaslight extracted from sea coal." In Liverpool, on a tour of the "blind school," it was "wonderful to see the . . . spinning, weaving, matting, carpeting, of many colors." There was a visit to Parliament, conferences with Wilberforce, Clarkson, William Dillwyn, who gave him Clarkson's book on the slave trade, and William Allen, whom he told that he planned "to build a house in Sierra Leone." His conversation with William Roscoe, the famous historian and author of *The Wrongs of Africa*—"he being a very warm friend for the abolishing the slave trade, many subjects took place between us"—focused on a question that would shortly become crucial, as war between England and America threatened the African project:

> He stated the necessity, and propriety of condemning all nations, that might be found in the trade. I likewise was favored to state to him the necessity there was of keeping open a communication between America, Africa and England in order to assist Africa in its civilization . . . the two powers to countenance it even if they were at variance, and to consider it as a neutral path.

A high point was his meeting with members of the African Institution, who praised him for "maintaining the good cause," following which he presented to its president, the duke of Gloucester, who was a nephew of the king, "an African robe, a letter box, and a dagger to show that the Africans were capable of mental endowment." Cuffe's "simplicity and strong natural good sense made a great impression upon all parties," noted William Allen in his diary. He found himself a celebrity of a sort and in October could read in the *Liverpool Mercury* that his efforts were "gratifying to humanity" [fig. 107]. "Who that justly appreciates human character," asked the editor, "would not prefer Paul Cuffe, the offspring of an African slave, to the proudest statesman that ever dealt out destruction amongst mankind?"

In November the *Traveller* sailed back to Africa, and for another three months Cuffe investigated Sierra Leone for its economic potential. Waterpower was abundant. He noted thriving crops—pineapples, Indian corn, and buckwheat. The Guinea grass grew so tall he could barely reach the top with the tip of his umbrella. He distributed seeds and silkworm eggs and arranged for the indenture of four African apprentices to return with him to Westport.

Back home in the spring of 1812, Cuffe was reminded once more of what it meant to be a black man in America. The *Traveller,* arriving in American waters at the beginning of the war, had been condemned by a revenue cutter for bringing in a British cargo. Cuffe journeyed to Washington to speak personally with the secretary of war and President Madison. The day after the president ordered the release of the *Traveller,* he started home. In the Baltimore coach he took a seat—and ran into trouble:

> In came a blustering powder-headed man with stern countenance. "Come away from that seat." I . . . sat still. . . . He then said, "You must go out of this for there is a lady coming in." I entered into no discourse with him, but took my seat; he took his beside me but showed much evil contempt. . . . When I arrived in Baltimore they utterly refused to take me in at the tavern or to get me a dinner unless I would go back among the

MEMOIR OF CAPTAIN PAUL CUFFEE.

Written for the Liverpool Mercury.

" On the first of the present month of August, 1811, a vessel " arrived at Liverpool, with a cargo from Sierra Leone, the " owner, master, mate, and whole crew of which are free " Negroes. The master, who is also owner, is the son of an " American Slave, and is said to be very well skilled both in " trade and navigation, as well as to be of a very pious and " moral character. It must have been a strange and ani- " mating spectacle to see this free and enlightened African " entering, as an independent trader, with his black crew, " into that port which was so lately the *nidus* of the Slave " Trade."—*Edinb. Review, August,* 1811.

We are happy in having an opportunity of confirming the above account, and at the same time of laying before our readers an authentic memoir of Capt. Paul Cuffee, the master and owner of the vessel above referred to, who sailed from this port on the 20th ult. with a licence from the British Government, to prosecute his intended voyage to Sierra Leone.

THE father of Paul Cuffee, was a native of Africa, whence he was brought as a Slave into Massachussetts.—He was there purchased by a person named Slocum, and remained in slavery a considerable portion of his life.—He was named Cuffee, but as it is usual in those parts took the name of Slocum, as expressing to whom he belonged. Like many of his countrymen he possessed a mind superior to his condition, and although he was diligent in the business of his Master and faithful to his interest, yet by great industry and economy he was enabled to purchase his personal liberty.

At this time the remains of several Indian tribes, who originally possessed the right of soil, resided in Massachusetts; Cuffee became acquainted with a woman descended from one of those tribes, named Ruth Moses, and married her.—He continued in habits of industry and frugality, and soon afterwards purchased a farm of 100 acres in Westport in Massachusetts.

Cuffee and Ruth had a family of ten children.—The three eldest sons, David, Jonathan, and John are farmers in the neighbourhood of Westport, filling respectable situations in society, and endowed with good intellectual capacities.—They are all married, and have families to whom they are giving good educations.—Of six daughters four are respectably married, while two remain single.

Paul was born on the Island of Cutterhunkker, one of the Elizabeth Islands near New Bedford, in the year 1759; when he was about 14 years of age his father died leaving a considerable property in land, but which being at that time unproductive afforded but little provision for his numerous family, and thus the care of supporting his mother and sisters devolved upon his brothers and himself.

At this time Paul conceived that commerce furnished to industry more ample rewards than agriculture, and he was conscious that he possessed qualities which under proper culture would enable him to pursue commercial employments with prospects of success; he therefore entered at the age of 16 as a common hand on board of a vessel destined to the bay of Mexico, on a Whaling voyage. His second voyage was to the West Indies; but on his third he was captured by a British ship during the American war about the year 1776: after three months detention as a prisoner at New York, he was permitted to return home to Westport, where owing to the unfortunate continuance of hostilities he spent about 2 years in his agricultural pursuits. During this interval Paul and his brother John Cuffee were called on by the Collector of the district, in which they resided, for the payment of a personal tax. It appeared to them, that, by the laws of the constitution of Massachusetts, taxation and the whole rights of citizenship were united.—If the laws demanded of them the payment of personal taxes, the same laws must necessarily and constitutionally invest them with the rights of representing, and being represented, in the state Legislature. But they had never been considered as entitled to the privilege of voting at Elections, nor of being elected to places of trust and honor.—Under these circumstances, they refused payment of the demands.—The Collector resorted to the force of the laws, and after many delays and vexations, Paul and his brother deemed it most prudent to silence the suit by payment of the demands. But they resolved, if it were possible, to obtain the rights which they believed to be connected with taxation.

107. "Memoir of Captain Paul Cuffee," *Liverpool Mercury,* October 4–11, 1811. Courtesy of the Library of Congress.

108. *Captain Paul Cuffee,* wood engraving by Mason and Maas after drawing by John Pole, 1812. Courtesy of the Library of Congress.

servants. This I refused, not as I thought myself better than the servants, but from the nature of the case. I found my way to a tavern where I got my dinner.

One imagines him, at these moments, standing tall in his dignity. On the trip to the capital, from Providence to Washington, men of stature, black and white, had been eager to listen to his words. It was about this time that an obscure artist drew the captain's portrait in silhouette and sketched beneath it his good ship *Traveller,* the ark of colonization {fig. 108}. "In his

person," wrote a black friend, "Capt. Cuffe was large and well proportioned. His countenance was serious, but mild. His speech and habit, plain and unostentatious. His deportment, dignified and prepossessing; blending gravity with modesty and sweetness, and firmness with gentleness and humility."

For the moment, he seemed a bit tired. Had he done his proper share of the work in preparing the exodus to the promised land? Was it time for others to carry the torch? He had intimated to William Allen a plan to settle in Sierra Leone. Now he decided against it, although this meant no slackening in his zeal. "Paul Cuffee doth not at present go to Africa," he informed Allen, "but shall send such characters as confidence may be placed in. At present it is thought that I may be as serviceable towards the promotion of the colony, as though I was to remove. However, as my wife is not willing to go, I do not feel at liberty to urge, but feel in duty bound to escort myself to the uttermost of my ability for the good cause of Africa." His plan, in fact, was to make a trip to Sierra Leone once a year, transporting settlers and cargo, and returning with African products. But there were difficulties. The voyage of the *Traveller* had lost money; the *Alpha* had just returned with a huge deficit; an uninsured bark on a whaling voyage around Cape Horn had disappeared.

The war, of course, was the great obstacle. He was ready to send over plows, wagons, and a sawmill. His four apprentices were schooled and seemed eager to return. The idea of a whale fishery off the African coast seemed more feasible than ever. People were clamoring to be taken to Sierra Leone. He wanted to get going again. In June 1813 he sent a memorial to Congress requesting a license for the voyage; the Senate approved but the House refused to permit any commerce with a colony of the enemy [fig. 109].

His spirit would not down. One wintry day in 1815, as soon as the war was over, with thirty-eight black emigrants and a cargo of goods that pioneers could use, Captain Cuffe steered the *Traveller* for Africa [fig. 110]. Only eight of the future settlers could pay for their passage. He made little of it, although the trip would cost him a small fortune; "all this was done," he wrote, "without fee or reward—my hope is in a coming day." Ashore in Sierra Leone, he was not idle. With the governor he inspected schools, compiled data on captured slave ships for the Abolition Society in Phila-

109. Bill authorizing Paul Cuffee to take cargo to Sierra Leone, January 10, 1814. National Archives, Washington, D.C.

delphia, assailed the license houses that trafficked in slaves, and urged that houses be built on the farms of the settlers. In the spring, the *Traveller* returned to Westport.

It was his final trip to Africa, and he seemed to know it. But there was work yet to be done in America. He kept in close touch with the organizers of the African Institution in New York and Philadelphia, wrote frequently to the colonists he had carried over, experienced moments of despair when he felt that the seed he had planted in Africa might perish. When the American Colonization Society, among whose first officers were Henry Clay and Andrew Jackson, began to be active early in 1817, its chief organizers went to Cuffe for information and

110. List of passengers aboard Paul Cuffe's *Traveller,* bound for Sierra Leone in 1815. New Bedford Free Public Library.

advice. He gave freely of his knowledge of Africa, perhaps never suspecting that many of its founders saw the chief aim of the Colonization Society as a greater security for the institution of slavery in the United States. Perhaps, knowing this, he thought that he might cooperate with certain elements of the Society to further his own grand plan of colonization as the road to general emancipation. It is difficult to know. He had only a short time to live, and others would have to take up the problem.

Is there anything in the record to show that Captain Paul Cuffe, toward the end of his life, ever doubted the validity of his back-to-Africa idea? After his second voyage to Sierra Leone he had boasted that two thousand pleas for passage to Africa had reached him from the city of Boston. But Boston was not America. In Richmond in January 1817 "a respectable portion of the free people of color" would resolve that they preferred being "colonized in the most remote corner of the land of our nativity, to being exiled" in Africa. It is possible that Cuffe never heard of the Virginia protest, but during that same month the post brought a letter from Philadelphia that must have shaken his confidence. "I must mention to you," wrote his friend James Forten, "that the whole continent seems to be agitated concerning Colonising the People of Colour." When, during the previous month, the American Colonization Society had published its program, "the People of Colour here was very much fritened at first. They were afrade that all the free people would be Compelled to go, particularly in the southern States." There had been "a large meeting of Males at the Rev. R. Allens Church the other evening. Three thousand at least atended, and there was not one sole that was in favour of going to Africa. They think that the slave holders want to get rid of them so as to make their property more secure."

Indeed, Forten himself had chaired the meetings and with Richard Allen and Absalom Jones had signed his name to the document that boldly affirmed—"we never will separate ourselves voluntarily from the slave population of the country; they are our brethren by the ties of consanguinity, of suffering, and of wrong." Although Forten had transmitted this repudiation of deportation to his congressman from Philadelphia, he was deeply troubled; the way for him was no longer "strate and clear." While his unalterable opinion was that blacks would "never become a people until they com out from amongst the white people . . . as the majority is decidedly against me I am determined to remain silent. . . ." (Before the year was out he would denounce colonization as a weapon of the slavocracy and would persuade William Lloyd Garrison to do likewise.)

How did Cuffe react to Forten's shattering news? There is perhaps a hint of doubt in his advice to his brethren to wait a year before coming to final judgment on the issue [fig. 111]. A few months later, in the spring, his health began to fail. How sacred the cause of Africa continued to be for him may be gauged by a curious letter he wrote during his last sick days to a black confidence man who had masqueraded as his son and had fleeced the unwary from New Bedford to Albany: "The great evil that thou has embarked upon is not only against me as an individual. It is a national concern. It is a stain to the whole community of the African race. Wilt thou consider, thou imposter, the great number thou hast lifted thy hand against. . . . Let me tell thee that the manumission of 1,500,000 slaves depends on the faithfulness of the few who have obtained their freedom, yea, it is not only those who are in bondage, but the whole community of the African race. . . ."

Seven months later Captain Paul Cuffe was buried with honors in the Quaker cemetery of Westport. From the pulpit of the Zion Church in New York, his coworker, the Reverend Peter Williams, Jr., delivered a discourse in praise of a great and saintly lover of his people, whose "thoughts ran deep" [fig. 112]. If, in his peroration, the preacher departed cautiously from the text of his eulogy to make a plea of forbearance, he was no doubt trying to answer a question that burned in the minds of his black audience: "Oh! what honor to the son of an African slave, the most respectable men in Great Britain and America, were not ashamed to seek to him for counsel and advice. Moreover brethren, he was our friend. Let us not then hastily condemn a measure to which every fibre of his heart clung, and from which it could only be separated by the strong hand of death. . . ." The "measure" of which the preacher spoke was, of course, the colonization of Africa. "Let us suspend our judgments of it," he concluded, "until we see its further develop-

111. Letter from Paul
Cuffe to James Forten,
1816. New Bedford Free
Public Library.

ment. . . ." The injunction was prophetic. If it was the failure of the revolutionary promise that stirred a segment of the black people to seek another way, there is a sense in which the standpoint first formulated by Captain Paul Cuffe—who saw himself as the champion of "the whole community of the African race"—has been a black thread running through American history to the present day.

Jean Baptiste Point du Sable

Benjamin Banneker and Paul Cuffe loom large and clear in the early annals of Afro-America. It is otherwise with Jean Baptiste Point du Sable. There is a mythic quality about this black pioneer who founded Chicago during the time of the revolution, a reminiscence of Estevanico, the African explorer in the party of the Spaniard Cabeza de Vaca, who in 1524 set out to conquer the Floridas. First of all, what was his real name—Sable, Saible, Sabre, Dessables? And what were his origins? Was he the son of a black maidservant and white master who had emigrated from Bourges to French Canada, or had he been born in Haiti, his parents a white planter and a free black woman?

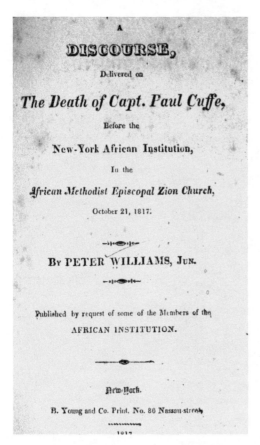

A

DISCOURSE,

Delivered on

The Death of Capt. Paul Cuffe,

Before the

New-York African Institution,

In the

African Methodist Episcopal Zion Church,

October 21, 1817.

By PETER WILLIAMS, Jun.

Published by request of some of the Members of the
AFRICAN INSTITUTION.

New-York.

B. Young and Co. Print. No. 86 Nassau-street

1817

112. Peter William, Jun., *A Discourse Delivered on The Death of Capt. Paul Cuffe* . . . (New York, 1817). Courtesy of the Library of Congress.

Du Sable's name makes its first appearance in the historical record in the journal of the British commandant at Mackinaw, a New York Tory, one Colonel Arent Schuyler de Peyster, who, in an entry for July 4, 1779, describes him as "a handsome negro, (well educated and settled in Eschecagou) but much in the French interest." De Peyster tried to win him over to the royal cause. In August, Lieutenant Thomas Bennett of the King's Regiment wrote from St. Joseph's: "Baptiste Point au Sable I have taken into custody, he hopes to make his conduct to you spotless. . . ." Du Sable ap-

parently had little interest in the issues of the war. He gave the lieutenant some information on the movements of hostile Indians. In September, Bennett reported to De Peyster that the Potawatomi were strongly disaffected. As for the black trader, he no longer distrusted him: "I had the Negro Baptiste point au Sable brought Prisoner from the River Du Chemin, Corporal Tascon who commanded the Party very prudently, prevented the Indians from burning his house, or doing him any injury, he secured his Packs &c which he takes with him from Michilimakinac." Since his imprisonment, he had behaved in a manner becoming a man in his situation and had many friends, "who gave him a good character." Du Sable was a big man in the area. In "Speech to the Western Indians," which he later put into verse, De Peyster threatens a council of "Great Chiefs" that he has convened: they must become allies of the British

Or, he will send them *tout au diable,*
As he did Baptist *Point de Saible.*

Du Sable did not long remain a prisoner. During the summer of 1780, a delegation of Indians from a settlement of the British on the St. Clair River south of Port Huron demanded that the governor of the territory, Patrick Sinclair, oust their French overseer and appoint du Sable to replace him. Sinclair ordered his immediate release from the stockade and sent him in a sloop to take over the job.

The war over, du Sable hastened back to Chicago, where years before he had built a trading post and a house—the first in the city. The house was no rude hut. Perched on the north bank of the Chicago River, it measured forty feet long by twenty-two feet wide and was more than comfortably furnished. There were four tables and seven chairs, a French walnut cabinet with four glass doors, a bureau, a couch, a stove, a large featherbed, mirrors, lanterns, candlesticks, and, at one time, twenty-three pictures. In addition to the house there were two barns, a dairy, a mill, a bakehouse, a poultry house, a workshop, as well as forty-four hens, thirty-eight hogs, thirty head of cattle, two calves, and two mules. And tools: eight axes, eight sickles, seven scythes, a variety of saws, a plow.

Du Sable and an Indian woman named Catherine lived together with their children for some time, and in 1788 a parish priest at Cahokia officially made them man and wife. Their daughter, Suzanne, married a Catholic. Their son, Jean Baptiste, Jr., left home and settled at Saint Charles in Missouri.

Du Sable was general merchant, fur trader, farmer, and man of affairs in the frontier community he had fashioned in the wilderness. He also owned property elsewhere; in 1773 he had purchased thirty acres and a house in Peoria; eighteen years later he received a grant of another four hundred acres from the government. A visitor from Wisconsin who was in Chicago about 1794 later recalled that du Sable "was a large man; that he had a commission for some office, but for what particular object, or from what Government, I can not now recollect; he was a trader, pretty wealthy, and drank freely."

Suddenly, in 1800, du Sable sold everything he owned in Chicago to a white trader for twelve hundred dollars [fig. 113]. Why? People invented all sorts of reasons. One story was that before he had settled on the banks of the Chicago River he had lived among the Peorias with a friend named Glamorgan, a brother San Domingan, who held vast Spanish land grants near Saint Louis; he now planned to return to Glam-

organ and the Peorias to spend his last days. Another story had it that he had always aspired to become chief of the Potawatomis; now he had joined them, but they denied him the headship.

The documents are more prosaic. From Chicago, he went to Saint Charles to live with his son. They owned property together in the city and county. His wife was dead; his son died in 1814. He went to live with his granddaughter, to whom he gave his house in Saint Charles on condition that she take care of him in his old age (she did not) and bury him in the Catholic cemetery of the town. Sixteen months later he had to apply for relief as a pauper; after that he did not last long.

These are the bare facts with a bit of lore about Jean Baptiste Point du Sable.

A recent news item in the *New York Times* reveals that du Sable has not been forgotten in Chicago: "Mayor Harold Washington and a group of black aldermen say the [official] seal is racist because it includes a depiction of a high-masted sailing ship that city documents once described as 'emblematic of the approach of white man's civilization and commerce' back in the 17th century. 'The ship represents institutionalized racism in this country,' said Alderman Robert Shaw, who also believes that the vessel bears a resemblance to the slave ships that plied the coast of Africa. As a result, Mr. Shaw and Alderman Allan Streeter last week asked the City Council to alter the seal by replacing the ship with a likeness of Jean Baptiste Point du Sable, a black who, as a fur trader, in 1779 became the city's first permanent non-Indian settler."

There is a tradition that the Potawatomis, who were there when the black frontiersman arrived, used to say: "The first white man to settle in Chicago was a Negro."

113. Bill of sale of Jean Baptiste du Sable's Chicago property, May 1800. Original unlocated. *Ebony* 26 (November 1970).

Dick Pointer: He Saved the Fort

Anne Newport Royall, sometimes called the first American newspaper woman, lived through the revolution and in 1826 wrote an interesting account of her journeying on the frontiers of the new nation. She visited almost every settlement of importance in the west, collecting fact and folklore of the revolution from those who still lived and remembered it. In Lewisburg, West Virginia, in 1824, she talked with old settlers, among them Dick Pointer, who recalled the Battle of Fort Donnally in May 1778.

About two hundred Wyandots and Mingoes, allies of the British, were on their way to Lewisburg:

> The inhabitants flew to Donnally's Fort, to the amount of three hundred souls. It was late in the evening before they were all fairly in, principally women and children: there were but four men besides Col. Donnally, and a negro man belonging to him, and three or four guns in the fort. The negro's name was Dick Pointer, and Dick saved the fort! On the same night the Indians drew near, old Dick (as he now is, for he is still living,) and the four men, were standing guard. Col. Donnally's house made a part of the fort, the front of it forming a line with the same, the door of the house being the door of the fort. Near this door, Dick and his companions were stationed, and about midnight Dick espied, through a porthole, something moving, but the night was so dark, and the object making no noise, it was long before he discovered it to be an Indian, creeping up to the door on all fours. The negro pointed it out to his companions, and asked "if he might shoot;" "no," they replied, not yet. In about twenty minutes after this a large force was at the door, thundering it to pieces with tomahawks, stones, and whatever weapon offered. The door being of the stoutest sort, resisted their efforts for some time; at length they forced one of the planks. Dick, (who, from every account, is as brave as Cesar,) had charged his musket well with old nails, pieces of iron, and buck shot; when the first plank dropped, he cried out to his master, "May I shoot now, sir?" "Not yet, Dick:" he stood ready, with his gun cocked. The Indians, meanwhile,

were busy, and the second plank began to tremble. "O master, may I shoot now?" "Not yet," his master replied. The second plank falls; "Now Dick," said his master; he fired, killed three, and wounded several; the Indians ran into some rye, with which the fort was surrounded, leaving the dead bodies at the door. . . . Had it not been for Dick Pointer's well-timed shot, every soul in the fort must have been massacred. I have had the relation from several persons, and from old Dick himself. The poor old creature wanders about very shabby: the country does allow him something, but his principal support is derived from donations by gentlemen, who visit this place and admire his character. He does not know how old he is, he thinks he was twenty-five at the attack of Donnally's Fort. His head is as white as wool, which, contrasted with his black keen eye, gives him a singular appearance. His master, some years after the signal service he rendered his country, set him free.

Colonel John Stuart, in charge of the fort at the time of the attack, left another, slightly different version of Dick Pointer's last days: "Dick is now upwards of eighty years old, has long been abandoned by his master, as also his wife, as aged as himself, and they have made out to support their miserable existence, many years past, by their own endeavors. This is the negro to whom our assembly, at its last session, refused to grant a small pension to support the short remainder of his wretched days, which must soon end, although his humble petition was supported by certificates of the most respectable men in the county, of his meritorious service on this occasion, which

saved the lives of many citizens then in the house."

Dr. James Derham and Thomas Fuller

Back east in Philadelphia, a year after ratification of the Constitution, the Abolition Society received a request from London to send over "accounts of mental improvement, in any of the blacks . . . in order the better . . . to contradict those who assert, that the intellectual faculties of the negroes are not capable of improvement equal to the rest of mankind." The redoubtable Dr. Benjamin Rush, friend of Richard Allen, Absalom Jones, and Benjamin Banneker, responded at once, supplying biographies of two extraordinary black men. One was a young New Orleans physician, Dr. James Derham, once a slave. "I expected to have suggested some new medicines to him," remarked Dr. Rush after their first meeting, "but he suggested many more to me." The other was an aged "African slave, living in Virginia," one Thomas Fuller, called "Negro Tom" in his obituary, which appeared in the *Columbian Centinel* during the winter of 1790 [fig. 114]. "This man possesses a talent for arithmetical calculation," thought Dr. Rush, "the history of which, I conceive, merits a place in the records of the human mind." The biographies of Derham and Fuller, subsequently published in the *American Museum* for January 1789, are the earliest existing sources for the lives of these gifted men.

Philadelphia, Jan. 4, 1789. At a meeting of the Pennsylvania Society for promoting the abolition of slavery, and the relief of free negroes, unlawfully held in bondage—ordered, that the following certificates, communicated by Dr. Rush, be published.

DIED]—Lately, at *Alexandria*, in *Virginia*, Mr. JOHN SUMMERS, in the 103d year of his age. He was born within thirty miles of that place, in the State of *Maryland*, and settled in the year 1715 in *Alexandria*, where he has resided ever since. He has left children, grand children, great grand-children, and great-great grand children to the number of near four hundred.

—— NEGRO TOM, the famous *African Calculator*, aged 80 years. He was the property of Mrs. Elizabeth Cox of *Alexandria*. Tom was a very black man. He was brought to this Country at the age of 14, and was sold as a slave with many of his unfortunate Countrymen.

This man was a prodigy. Though he could neither read nor right, he had perfectly acquired the art if enumeration. The power of recollection and the strength of memory were so complete in him, that he could multiply seven into itself, that product by 7, and the product, so produced, by seven, for seven times. He could give the number of months, days, weeks, hours, minutes and seconds in any period of time that any person chose to mention, allowing in his calculation for all the leap-years that happened in the time; and would give the number of poles, yards, feet, inches and barley-corns in any given distance, say the diameter of the earth's orbit; and in every calculation he would produce the true answer in less time than ninety-nine men in an hundred would take with their pens: And, what was, perhaps, more extraordinary, though interrupted in the progress of his calculation, and engaged in discourse upon any other subject, his operations were not thereby in the least deranged, so as to make it necessary for him to begin again, but he would go on from where he had left off, and could give any, or all, of the stages through which the calculation had passed. His first essay in numbers was counting the hairs in the tails of the cows and horses which he was set to keep. With little instruction he would have been able to cast up plats of land. He took great notice of the lines of land which he had seen surveyed. He drew just conclusions from facts: surprisingly so, for his opportunities. Thus died Negro Tom, this self-taught Arithmetician, this untutored Scholar!—Had his opportunities of improvement been equal to those of thousands of his fellow-men, neither the Royal Society of London, the Academy of sciences at Paris, nor even a NEWTON himself, need have been ashamed to acknowledge him a Brother in Science.

114. Obituary of Thomas Fuller, *Columbian Centinel* (Boston), December 1790. Courtesy of the Library of Congress.

There is now in this city [Philadelphia], a black man, of the name of James Derham, a practitioner of physic, belonging to the Spanish settlement of New Orleans, on the Mississippi. This man was born in a family in this city, in which he was taught to read and write, and instructed in the principles of christianity. When a boy, he was transferred by his master to the late dr. John Kearsly, jun. of this city, who employed him occasionally to compound medicines, and to perform some of the more humble acts of attention to his patients.

Upon the death of dr. Kearsly, he became (after passing through several hands) the property of dr. George West, surgeon to the sixteenth British regiment, under whom, during the late war in America, he performed many of the menial duties of our profession. At the close of the war, he was sold by dr. West to dr. Robert Dove, of New Orleans, who employed him as an assistant in his business: in which capacity he gained so much of his confidence and friendship, that he consented to liberate him, after two or three years, upon easy terms. From dr. Derham's numerous opportunities of improving in medicine, he became so well acquainted with the healing art, as to commence practitioner at New Orleans, under the patronage of his last master. He is now about twenty-six years of age, has a wife, but no children, and does business to the amount of three thousand dollars a year.

I have conversed with him upon most of the acute and epidemic diseases of the country where he lives, and was pleased to find him perfectly acquainted with the modern simple mode of practice in those diseases. . . . He is very modest and engaging in his manners. He speaks

French fluently, and has some knowledge of the Spanish language. By some accident, although born in a religious family, belonging to the church of England, he was not baptised in his infancy; in consequence of which he applied, a few days ago, to bishop White, to be received by that ordinance into the episcopal church. The bishop found him qualified, both by knowledge and moral conduct, to be admitted to baptism, and this day performed the ceremony, in one of the churches in this city.

Philadelphia, November 14, 1788. Account of a wonderful talent for arithmetical calculations, in an African slave, living in Virginia.

There is now living, about four miles from Alexandria, in the state of Virginia, a negro slave of seventy years old, of the name of Thomas Fuller, the property of mrs. Elizabeth Coxe. . . . He is a native of Africa, and can neither read nor write. Two gentlemen, natives of Pennsylvania, viz. William Harthorne and Samuel Coates, men of probity and respectable characters, having heard, in travelling through the neighborhood in which this slave lived, of his extraordinary powers in arithmetic, sent for him, and had their curiosity sufficiently gratified by the answers which he gave to the following questions.

First. Upon being asked how many seconds there are in a year and a half, he answered in about two minutes, 47,304,000.

Second. On being asked, how many seconds a man lived, who is seventy years, seventeen days and twelve hours old, he answered in a minute and a half, 2,210,500,800.

One of the gentlemen, who employed himself with his pen in making these calculations, told him he was wrong, and that the sum was not so great as he had said—upon which the old man hastily replied, "Top, massa, you forget de leap year." On adding the seconds of the leap years to the others, the amount of the whole in both their sums agreed exactly.

Third. The following question was then proposed to him: suppose a farmer has six sows, and each sow has six female pigs, the first year, and they all increase in the same proportion, to the end of eight years, how many sows will the farmer then have? In ten minutes, he answered, 34,588,806. The difference of time between his answering this, and the two former questions, was occasioned by a trifling mistake he made from a misapprehension of the question.

In the presence of Thomas Wistar and Benjamin W. Morris, two respectable citizens of Philadelphia, he gave the amount of nine figures multiplied by nine. . . .

At the time he gave this account of himself, he said his memory began to fail him—he was grey-headed, and exhibited several other marks of the weakness of old age—he had worked hard upon a farm during the whole of his life, but had never been intemperate in the use of spiritous liquors. He spoke with great respect of his mistress, and mentioned in a particular manner his obligations to her for refusing to sell him, which she had been tempted to do by offers of large sums of money, from several curious persons.

One of the gentlemen (mr. Coates) having remarked in his presence, that it was pity he had not had an education equal to his genius; he said, "no massa—it is best I got no learning; for many learned men be great fools."

Phillis Wheatley

"I doubt not God is good, well-meaning, kind," muses Countee Cullen in the opening line of the great sonnet that ends with a couplet of doubt.

> Yet do I marvel at this curious thing:
> To make a poet black, and bid him
>   sing.

It was so from the beginning in America. The first black poets who sang in print during the time of the revolution, Phillis Wheatley and Jupiter Hammon, lucky to have humane owners, thanked God for snatching them from heathen Africa and never doubted that He would free the virtuous slave in heaven. Yet, here and there, the anguish that Cullen knew so well breaks through the facade of their comforting piety. Given the time and the place, it is no small miracle that in their finest passages these gifted slaves, even in a muffled way, could speak out as blacks in charged, poetic lines.

IT has often been noted that Phillis Wheatley—"*Afric's* muse," as she called herself in her "Hymn to Humanity"—was the first black, the first slave, and the third woman in the United States to publish a book of poems [fig. 115]. The editor of the recent edition of her complete works is of the opinion that her "poems are certainly as good as or better than those of most of the poets usually included and afforded fair treatment in a discussion of American poetry before 1800." Add to all this that she was probably the first truly American poet in our literary history, for in some of the best passages of

Boston's "Ethiopian poetess" her strong and graceful line plucked a uniquely American chord—what it meant to be black in white revolutionary America. (Were the poems of Anne Bradstreet and Edward Taylor written in New or Old England? It is hard to tell.) And, of course, there is the unparalleled tale of her short, radiant life, of her early flowering genius.

Phillis Wheatley was born in Africa, Senegal perhaps. She liked to recall that her mother "poured out water before the sun at his rising" and in one of her major poems she would mourn with Niobe for her lost children. In 1761, when she was about seven, she was put up for sale in a Boston slave market. Susannah, the wife of John Wheatley, a prosperous tailor, wanted a black girl to train as a domestic, although the Wheatleys already owned several household slaves. There, on the block, Mrs. Wheatley saw an African child, "of a slender frame, and evidently suffering from a change of climate," naked except for a piece of dirty carpet [fig. 116]. She was shedding her front teeth. The girl quickly became a favorite. "She was not devoted to menial occupations, as was at first intended"; wrote her first biographer in 1834, "nor was she allowed to associate with the other domestics of the family, who were of her own color and condition, but was kept constantly about the person of her mistress." It is related that "her anxious mistress, fearful of the effects of cold and damp upon her already delicate health, ordered Prince (also an African and a slave) to take the chaise, and bring home her *protegee*. When the chaise returned, the good lady drew near the window, as it approached the house, and exclaimed—'Do but look at the saucy varlet—if he hasn't the impudence to sit upon the same seat with my Phillis!'" It is almost incredible that, as time went on, in the face of this tender assault on her African iden-

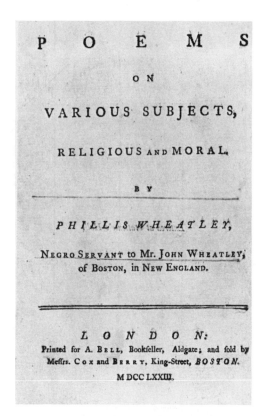

115. Phillis Wheatley, *Poems on Various Subjects Religious and Moral* (London, 1773). Library, University of Massachusetts, Amherst.

tity, the child could think of herself as a black among blacks. The Wheatleys' home was on King Street. Nine years later, through her window, Phillis would probably hear the guns of the Boston Massacre.

Her new owners quickly discovered that they had purchased a prodigy. The Wheatleys' daughter, Mary, found the slave an apt student of theology and literature. "Without any assistance from school education, and by only what she was taught in the family," wrote her master, "she, in sixteen months' time from her arrival, attained the English language . . . to such a degree as to read any, the most difficult parts of the Sacred Writings, to the great astonishment of all who heard her." She was eager to write— "her own curiosity led her to it"—and she tried the alphabet on the wall with chalk or

charcoal. All this "she learned in so short a time, that in the year 1765 she wrote a letter" to the Reverend Samson Occum, the Indian minister, who, something of a poet himself, would later publish a hymnal for his people.

In 1767, when she was fourteen, she wrote her first poem, "To the University of Cambridge," thirty-two competent lines of blank verse which admonished unruly college boys to shun sin and follow Christ [fig. 117]. The first stanza set a pattern for the next dozen years:

While an intrinsic ardor bids me
  write
The muse doth promise to assist my
  pen.
'Twas but e'en now I left my native
  shore

TO BE SOLD,

A Parcel of Likely Ne-groes, imported from *Africa*, enquire of *John Avery* at his Houſe next door to the White-Horſe, or at a Store adjoining to ſaid *Avery's* Diſti!l Houſe, at the South-End, near the South Market :—Alſo if any Perſons have any Negro Men, ſtrong and hearty, tho' not of the beſt moral character, which are proper Subjects for Tranſportation, may have an Exchange for ſmall Negroes.

116. *Boston News Letter,* July 30, 1761. Courtesy, American Antiquarian Society.

117. Phillis Wheatley, "To the University of Cambridge," 1767. Courtesy, American Antiquarian Society.

The sable Land of error's darkest
    night.
There, sacred Nine! for you no place
    was found.
Parent of mercy, 'twas thy Powerful
    hand
Brought me in safety from the dark
    abode.

The evidence is clear that the Wheatleys had done a good missionary job on the child—to her, Africa is a pagan inferno and she is well out of it, thankful to be a slave in a good Christian household. Her final counsel to the students at Harvard is to avoid all "hateful vice":

Suppress the sable monster in its
    growth,
Ye blooming plants of human race,
    divine.
An Ethiop tells you, tis your greatest
    foe,
Its transient sweetness turns to end-
    less pain,
And brings eternal ruin on the Soul.

("An Ethiop tells you"—is it significant that six years later, when she revised the poem for the press, "The sable Land of error's darkest night" became "the land of errors, and *Egyptian* gloom," while "the sable

On the death of Mr Snider Murder'd by Richardson

In heavens eternal court it was decreed
How the first martyr for the cause should bleed
To clear the country of the hated brood
He whet his courage for the common good
Long hid before, a vile infernal here
Prevents Achilles in his mid career
Where'er this fury darts his Poisonous breath
All are endanger'd to the Shafts of death.
The generous Sires beheld the fatal wound
Saw their young champion gasping on the ground
They rais'd him up, but to each present ear
What martial glories did his tongue declare
The wretch appal'd no longer can despise
But from the Shrinking victim turns his eyes —
When this young martial genius did appear
The Tory chiefs no longer could forbear.
Ripe for destruction, see the wretches doom
He waits the curse of the age to come
In vain he flies, by Justice Swiftly chaced
With unexpected infamy disgraced
Bo Richardson for ever banish'd here
The grand Usurpers bravely vaunted Heir:
We bring the body from the watry bower
To lodge it where it shall remove no more.
Snider behold with what Majestic Love
The Illustrious retinue begins to move
With Secret rage fair freedoms foes beneath
See in thy corse ev'n Majesty in Death

Phillis

118. Phillis Wheatley,
"On the death of Mr
Snider [Seider], Murder'd
by Richardson," 1770.
The Library Company of
Philadelphia.

monster" changed into "the deadly serpent"?)

The muse kept her promise to Phillis Wheatley. During the next three years she wrote a sheaf of poems, two of them short pieces: "On Friendship" and "On Atheism." There is a salute to King George, who is praised for repealing the Stamp Act and is promised God's blessing if he cherishes the liberty of the people—

And may each clime with equal gladness see
A monarch's smile can set his subjects free!

More outspoken is a threnody on the murder by a Tory custom's officer of Christopher Seider, a youth who, in an angry crowd, had protested the presence of the redcoats in Boston a year before the Massacre [fig. 118]:

In heaven's eternal court it was decreed
Thou the first martyr for the cause
should bleed
To clear the country of the hated
brood
He whet his courage for the common
good.

Christopher Seider has sometimes been
called the first martyr of the American Revolution. His corpse was placed under a "Liberty Tree" and Sam Adams excoriated the
assassin. At the funeral, reported the *Evening Post,* fifty schoolboys headed the proces-
sion of two thousand marchers "of all ranks,
amid a crowd of spectators." Six youths
chosen by Seider's parents carried the coffin.

An elegy on the death of her revered pastor, the Reverend Doctor Joseph Sewall of
the Old South Church (whose father, the re-
canting witch-trial judge, had written New
England's first antislavery tract, *The Selling
of Joseph*) was to be the first in a succession of
occasional poems hailing or lamenting the
births and deaths of Boston's elite. Most
deeply felt, her eight lines, "On Being
Brought from Africa to America," are worth
repeating here—the first attempt of the
young black poet to struggle for a position:

'Twas mercy brought me from my
Pagan land,
Taught my benighted soul to under-
stand
That there's a God, that there's a *Sav-
iour* too:
Once I redemption neither sought nor
knew.
Some view our sable race with scorn-
ful eye,
"Their colour is a diabolic die."
Remember, *Christians, Negroes,* black
as *Cain,*
May be refin'd and join th' angelic
train.

A black voice in the Christian white wilderness cries out in these lines. After all the ob-
vious comments are duly made—she rejects
her heritage, she accepts the myth of Cain,
she expects her soul to be whitewashed in
heaven—there is still much undiminished
spirit to be found in this little poem. The
charged voice of the outraged girl, defending "our sable race" against a "scornful eye,"
is rightfully stored in the mind.

These lines are not the only affirmation
of her "sable race." Probably at about the
same time, she wrote an anti-Tory "Ode, on
the [thirtieth] Birth Day of Pompey Stockbridge." Undated and unsigned but indu-
bitably hers, it is a small broadside printed
as a gift for a friend (slave or freeman we do
not know) [fig. 119], whose virtues
"stamped him *real* man," she will not imi-
tate those "hireling scribblers" who "pros-
titute their pen,"

Creating virtues for abandon'd men,
Ascribing merit to the vicious great,
And basely flatter when they ought to
hate—
Be mine the just, and grateful task to
scan
Th'effulgent virtues of a *sable*
man . . .

The italics—"*real*" and "*sable*"—are her
own.

No doubt, after she wrote out these early
poems in her own pleasing hand, they circulated beyond the Wheatleys' family circle.
Her name spread. When the Reverend
George Whitefield died at Newburyport in
September 1770, the *Massachusetts Spy* advertised for sale *An Elegiac Poem, On the
Death of that celebrated Divine . . . By PHIL-
LIS, a Servant girl of 17 years of Age, Belonging to Mr. J. WHEATLEY . . . but 9 Years
in this Country from Africa* [fig. 120]. To
many blacks, Whitefield, although he did
not preach abolition, was a crusading friend

An ODE,

On the *BIRTH DAY* of POMPEY STOCKBRIDGE.

WHILE hireling fcribblers proftitute their pen,
  Creating virtues for abandon'd men,
Afcribing merit to the vicious great,
And bafely flatter whom they ought to hate—
Be mine the juft, the grateful tafk to fcan
Th' effulgent virtues of a *fable* man ;
Trace the good action to its fource fublime,
And mark its progrefs to the death of time.
Alternate feafons quickly pafs away,
And the *fixth* luftre crowns this natal day,
Since firft my POMPEY, humble, modeft, wife,
Shot the bright dawn of reafon from his eyes :
Nor was his morn o'ercaft by folly's cloud ;
Ne'er prefs'd his footfteps 'mong the giddy crowd :
E'en the gay feafon of luxuriant youth
Was wifely fpent to afcertain the truth.
Religious precepts form'd his darling plan,
And virtue's dictates ftamp'd him *real* man.——
Long may my POMPEY live, long live to prove
The fweets of virtue, and the joys of love ;
And when thefe happy annual feafts are paft,
That day be happieft which will be his laft :
Then may his foul triumphantly afcend,
Where *perfect blifs* fhall never know an end.

119. Phillis Wheatley, "An Ode, On the *Birth Day* of Pompey Stockbridge." Moorland-Spingarn Research Center, Howard University.

who spoke of a savior equally available to black and white. Thus, Phillis:

> Take him [Christ] my dear *Americans,*
>   he said,
> Be your complaints on his kind
>   bosom laid:
> Take him, ye *Africans,* he longs for
>   you,
> *Impartial Saviour* is his title due:
> Wash'd in the fountain of redeeming
>   blood,
> You shall be sons, and kings, and
>   priests to God.

This was her second published poem and it launched her quickly into transatlantic fame. Another Massachusetts poet, Jane Dunlap, who saw herself as "a Daughter of Liberty and lover of Truth" and the next year also paid tribute to the renowned Whitefield in a pamphlet of *Poems* on his sermons preached in Boston, was one of the first to praise in print her sister Wheatley's verses [fig. 121]:

> Shall his due praise be so loudly sung
> By a young Afric damsel's virgin
>   tongue?
> And I be silent!

The Whitefield broadside was reprinted almost immediately in Boston, Newport, New York, and Philadelphia, and it found its way to England the following year in Pemberton's *Heaven the Residence of Saints.*

Phillis Wheatley was becoming a person of eminence in the literary capital of the colonies, and she was pleased when she read in Dr. Benjamin Rush's *Address upon Slave-Keeping* that in Boston there was a "Negro Girl about 18 years of age, who has been but 9 years in the country, whose singular genius and accomplishments are such as not only do honor to her sex, but to human nature." People lent her books. Ministers, merchants, and scholars—"the most respectable Characters" of the town—visited and talked with her, read her poems. Eighteen of them later attested [fig. 122]:

> We whose Names are under-written,
> do assure the World, that the POEMS
>   . . . were (as we verily believe) written by *Phillis,* a young Negro Girl,
> who was but a few Years since,
> brought an uncultivated Barbarian
> from *Africa,* and has ever since been,
> and now is, under the Disadvantage
> of serving as a Slave in a Family in
> this Town. She has been examined by

120. Phillis Wheatley, "An Elegiac Poem on the Death of . . . George Whitefield," broadside, 1770. The Library Company of Philadelphia.

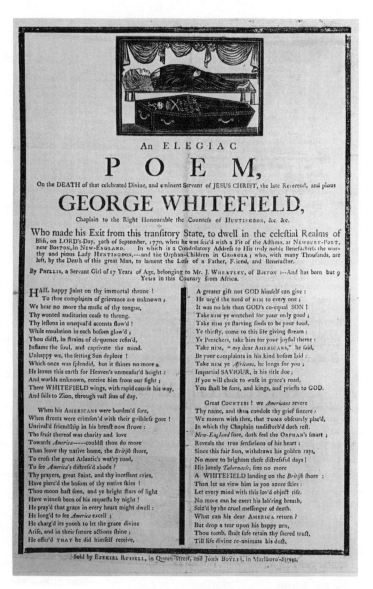

An ELEGIAC

POEM,

On the DEATH of that celebrated Divine, and eminent Servant of JESUS CHRIST, the late Reverend, and pious

GEORGE WHITEFIELD,

Chaplain to the Right Honourable the Countess of HUNTINGDON, &c. &c.

Who made his Exit from this transitory State, to dwell in the celestial Realms of Bliss, on LORD's-Day, 30th of September, 1770, when he was seiz'd with a Fit of the Asthma, at NEWBURY-PORT, near BOSTON, in NEW-ENGLAND. In which is a Condolatory Address to His truly noble Benefactress the worthy and pious Lady HUNTINGDON,---and the Orphan-Children in GEORGIA; who, with many Thousands, are left, by the Death of this great Man, to lament the Loss of a Father, Friend, and Benefactor.

By PHILLIS, a Servant Girl of 17 Years of Age, belonging to Mr. J. WHEATLEY, of BOSTON:---And has been but 9 Years in this Country from Africa.

HAIL happy Saint on thy immortal throne !
To thee complaints of grievance are unknown;
We hear no more the music of thy tongue,
Thy wonted auditories cease to throng.
Thy lessons in unequal'd accents flow'd !
While emulation in each bosom glow'd;
Thou didst, in strains of eloquence refin'd,
Inflame the soul, and captivate the mind.
Unhappy we, the setting Sun deplore !
Which once was splendid, but it shines no more;
He leaves this earth for Heaven's unmeasur'd height,
And worlds unknown, receive him from our sight;
There WHITEFIELD wings, with rapid course his way,
And sails to Zion, through vast seas of day.

When his AMERICANS were burden'd sore,
When streets were crimson'd with their guiltless gore !
Unrival'd friendship in his breast now strove:
The fruit thereof was charity and love
Towards America-----couldst thou do more
Than leave thy native home, the British shore,
To cross the great Atlantic's wat'ry road,
To see America's distress'd abode ?
Thy prayers, great Saint, and thy incessant cries,
Have pierc'd the bosom of thy native skies !
Thou moon hast seen, and ye bright stars of light
Have witness been of his requests by night !
He pray'd that grace in every heart might dwell:
He long'd to see America excell;
He charg'd its youth to let the grace divine
Arise, and in their future actions shine;
He offer'd THAT he did himself receive,

A greater gift not GOD himself can give :
He urg'd the need of HIM to every one;
It was no less than GOD's co-equal SON !
Take HIM ye wretched for your only good;
Take HIM ye starving souls to be your food.
Ye thirsty, come to this life giving stream;
Ye Preachers, take him for your joyful theme:
Take HIM, "my dear AMERICANS," he said,
Be your complaints in his kind bosom laid:
Take HIM ye Africans, he longs for you;
Impartial SAVIOUR, is his title due;
If you will chuse to walk in grace's road,
You shall be sons, and kings, and priests to GOD.

Great COUNTESS ! we Americans revere
Thy name, and thus condole thy grief sincere:
We mourn with thee, that TOMB obscurely plac'd,
In which thy Chaplain undisturb'd doth rest.
New-England sure, doth feel the ORPHAN's smart;
Reveals the true sensations of his heart;
Since this fair Sun, withdraws his golden rays,
No more to brighten these distressful days!
His lonely Tabernacle, sees no more
A WHITEFIELD landing on the British shore:
Then let us view him in yon azure skies:
Let every mind with this lov'd object rise.
No more can he exert his lab'ring breath,
Seiz'd by the cruel messenger of death.
What can his dear AMERICA return ?
But drop a tear upon his happy urn,
Thou tomb, shalt safe retain thy sacred trust,
Till life divine re-animate his dust.

Sold by EZEKIEL RUSSELL, in Queen-Street, and JOHN BOYLES, in Marlboro'-Street.

some of the best Judges, and is thought qualified to write them.

Among the judges were a royal governor, Thomas Hutchinson, and two future governors, James Bowdoin and John Hancock; the Reverend Charles Chauncey, pastor of the First Church, a Unitarian who rejected Whitefield's emotional style; Mathew Byles, poet and wit; and the Reverend Samuel Mather, son of Cotton. It was about this

time that she became a baptized communicant and began to worship at Old South Meeting House. "Whenever she was invited to the houses of individuals of wealth and distinction, (which frequently happened)," recalled a grandniece of Susannah Wheatley, "she always declined the seat offered her at their board, and, requesting that a side-table might be laid for her, dined modestly apart from the rest of the company." (Benjamin Banneker would do likewise in

Georgetown. In either case, was it modesty or a complex pride that prompted the action?) A legend attached to the genesis of her first poem to be published in a magazine adds a detail to the scene. This "young *Negro woman* . . . a compleat sempstress, an accomplished mistress of her pen . . . a most surprising genius," a reader informs the editor of the *London Magazine* for March 1772, "being in company with some young ladies of family, when one of them said she did not remember, among all the poetical pieces she had seen, ever to have met with a poem upon RECOLLECTION, the *African* . . . took the hint," returned to her master's house, and invoking the muse—

> Mneme, begin; inspire, ye sacred
> Nine!
> Your vent'rous *Afric* in the deep de-
> sign.

—the next day sent to the suggestor the elegant tour de force in Popean couplets called "Recollection."

THE winter of 1772 would be unkind to Phillis Wheatley and in the spring she was still "in a very poor state of health." The trouble was asthma and the Wheatleys packed her off to the country "for the benefit of its more wholesome air," although she returned to the city "to spend the Sabbath" with the family. Her illness did not keep her from her desk. To her friend Obour Tanner, a young black woman living in Newport, Rhode Island, she wrote of her "great pleasure to hear of so many of my nation, seeking with eagerness the way of true felicity." She studied hard and went on with her reading in literature, sacred and profane. "She has a great Inclination to learn the Latin Tongue," John Wheatley noted, "and has made some Progress in it." In her precocious advice to the students at Harvard, she had in fact revealed her own hunger for learning.

> Students, to you 'tis giv'n to scan
> the heights
> Above, to traverse the ethereal space,
> And mark the systems of revolving
> worlds. . . .
> Improve your privileges while they
> stay,
> Ye pupils, and each hour re-
> deem. . . .

So, under Mary Wheatley's tutelage and with the help of friends, she set herself the task of acquiring what amounted to a Harvard education, classical and neoclassical. She read voraciously—Christian scripture, ancient history and mythology, the classics (especially Vergil, Ovid, and Horace), Milton, Pope (she loved his translation of Homer and used his meter and rhyme in most of her verse), Gray, Addison, and Isaac Watts. She picked up as much as she could of geography and astronomy. All was grist for her poetic mill—sources of image, theme, and style in her varied work. And as she read, the couplets flowed. The story has come down that her "kind mistress indulged her with a light, and in the cold season with a fire, in her apartment during the night. The light was placed upon a table at her bed-side, with writing materials, that if anything occurred to her after she had retired, she might, without rising or taking cold, secure the swift-winged fancy, ere it fled."

Growing up in Boston during the decade that began with the martyrdom of Attucks, she followed political events with the zeal of an incipient patriot who "worshipped at Freedom's shrine." David was the hero and Goliath the villain of her longest poem. In August 1772, the earl of Dartmouth was appointed secretary of state for the colonies.

POEMS,
Upon several SERMONS, Preached
by the Rev'd, and Renowned,
GEORGE WHITEFIELD,
while in BOSTON.

"The Righteous shall be in everlasting Remembrance;
and they that turn many to Righteousness, as the
Stars for ever and ever."

A New-Years Gift, from a Daughter of
Liberty and lover of Truth.

Boston: Printed and Sold, next to the Writing-School
in Queen-Street. 1771.

4   A new Years Gift.
POEMS &c.

THE holy psalmist he did sing
   Of Saul, the Lord's anointed king,
And of his dearest Jonathan,
After they both were dead and gone.

Most worthy man, of thy dear name,
In love I'll mention make,
Both for thine own, and for thy works ;
And for thy masters sake.

Dear Whitefield's name I'll not forget,
That name to me so dear,
That's made me glad, and also sad,
And cost me many a tear.

Glad for good tidings, which thou brought'st,
Of Gospel-grace, in store :
And sad, because thy lovely voice,
I ne'er shall hear no more.
       Another.
Shall his due praises be so loudly sung
By a young Afric damsels virgin tongue ?
And I be silent ! and no mention make
Of his blest name, who did so often speak.

To us, the words of life,
Fetch'd from the fountain pure,
Of God's most holy sacred truths ;
Which ever shall endure.

But Oh ! should I attempt the praise
Of that most blessed man,
I should but darken his bright rays,
Which none in justice Can.

121. From [Jane Dunlap's] *Poems* (Boston, 1771). Courtesy, American Antiquarian Society.

As soon as the news arrived in Boston, the ailing black poet seized on the event—for Dartmouth had been Whitefield's friend and was close to the antislavery countess of Huntingdon—as a good omen for the end of British tyranny in America.

> Hail, happy day, when, smiling like
>   the morn,
> Fair *Freedom* rose *New-England* to
>   adorn.

Thus she saluted Dartmouth in her opening lines, and went on:

> No more *America,* in mournful
>   strain

> Of wrongs, and grievance unredress'd
>   complain,
> No longer shalt thou dread the iron
>   chain,
> Which wanton *Tyranny* with lawless
>   hand
> Had made, and with it meant t'en-
>   slave the land.

Her three key words here—*"America," "Tyranny"* and *"t'enslave"*—lead strategically to the next stanza, as splendid a statement of one facet of the black patriot position, three years before Bunker Hill, as can be found in the literature of the time.

A New Years Gift.   17

O seek the Lord, while in your youth,
And remember your Creator ;
And he will guide you in the truth,
Who is the best of teachers.

O may the Holy Spirit descend,
With grace inspire your breasts ;
That you may follow your dear Friend,
As he has follow'd Christ.

The Ethiopians shall Stretch out their hands to God,
Or a call to the Ethiopians.

POOR Negroes flee, you'l welcome be,
Your colour's no exception ;
But fly to Christ, he's paid the price,
Meet for your Souls redemption.

And though your souls made black with sin,
The Lord can make them white ;
And cloath'd in his pure righteousness,
They'l shine transparent bright.

A few Reflections on the prevailing Sins of
the Times.

HOW does iniquity abound,
And transgressions manifold ;
And unto all that's good how does,
The love of most grow cold.

No doubt our sins, are the true cause,
Of all the evils sent ;
Which now we feel, and still may fear,
Unless that we repent.

How

Should you, my lord, while you
  peruse my song,
Wonder from whence my love of *Free-*
  dom sprung,
Whence flow these wishes for the
  common good,
By feeling hearts alone best understood,
I, young in life, by seeming cruel fate
Was snatch'd from *Afric's* fancy'd
  happy seat:
What pangs excruciating must mo-
  lest,
What sorrows labour in my parent's
  breast?

Steel'd was that soul and by no misery
  mov'd
That from a father seiz'd his babe be-
  lov'd . . .

Where, in these lines, is the notion of an earlier poem—" 'Twas mercy brought me from my *Pagan* land"? There is a new, independent note in the stanza's final couplet:

Such, such my case. And can I then
  but pray
Others may never feel tyrannic sway?

IT was about this time, in the winter of 1772, that the idea of gathering her verse into a book first entered the young poet's mind, and an advertisement asking for subscribers to "a Collection of POEMS" soon appeared in a few Boston newspapers [fig. 123]. The manuscript was a sheaf of almost forty poems, some already in print, others known to a circle of friends and admirers. All that was needed was a poem to head the list—an ode of aspiration, in which she might implore the Muses to let her join the epic company, and at the same time an ode of identity, in which she might define herself and her world. "To Maecenas," the piece that would begin the book, is, of course, her grateful nod to the generous Wheatleys, but it is also a bold, initial statement of the blackness of the poet. After Homer and Vergil,

The happier *Terence** all the choir
  inspir'd,
His soul replenish'd, and his bosom
  fir'd;
But say, ye *Muses,* why this partial
  grace,
To one alone of *Afric's* sable race;
From age to age transmitting thus his
  name
With the first glory in the rolls of
  fame?

To the PUBLICK.

AS it has been repeatedly fuggefted to the Publifher, by Perfons, who have feen the Manufcript, that Numbers would be ready to fufpect they were not really the Writings of PHILLIS, he has procured a following Atteftation, from the moft refpectable Characters in Bofton, that none might have the leaft Ground for difputing their Original.

WE whofe Names are under-written, do affure the World, that the POEMS fpecified in the following Page, * were (as we verily believe) written by PHILLIS, a young Negro Girl, who was but a few Years fince, brought an uncultivated Barbarian from Africa, and has ever fince been, and now is, under the Difadvantage of ferving as a Slave in a Family in this Town. She has been examined by fome of the beft Judges, and is thought qualified to write them.

His Excel'ency THOMAS HUTCHINSON, *Governor,*

The Hon. ANDREW OLIVER, *Lieutenant-Governor.*

The Hon. Thomas Hubbard,	*The Rev.* Charles Cheuney, D. D.
The Hon. John Erving,	*The Rev.* Mather Byles, D. D.
The Hon. James Pitts,	*The Rev.* Ed. Pemberton, D.D.
The Hon. Harrifon Gray,	*The Rev.* Andrew Elliot, D.D.
The Hon. James Bowdoin,	*The Rev.* Samuel Cooper, D.D.
John Hancock, *Efq;*	*The Rev.* Mr. Samuel Mather,
Jofeph Green, *Efq;*	*The Rev.* Mr. Joen Moorhead,
Richard Carey, *Efq;*	Mr. John Wheatley, *her Mafter.*

N. B. The original Atteftation, figned by the above Gentlemen, may be feen by applying to *Archibald Bell,* Bookfeller, No. 8, *Aldgate-Street.*

---

* The Words " *following Page,*" allude to the Contents of the Manufcript Copy, which are wrote at the Back of the above Atteftation.

122. "To the Publick," from Phillis Wheatley, *Poems on Various Subjects* (London, 1773). Courtesy of the Library of Congress.

PROPOSALS

For Printing in *London* by SUBSCRIPTION, A Volume of POEMS, DEDICATED by Permiffion to the Right Hon. the COUNTESS of HUNTINGDON, Written by PHILLIS, A NEGRO SERVANT to Mr. WHEATLEY, Bofton in New-England. Terms of Subfcription.

I. The Book to be neatly printed in 12mo. on a new Type and a fine Paper, adorned with an elegant Frontifpiece, reprefenting the Author.

II. That the Price to Subfcribers fhall be Two Shillings fewed, or Two Shillings and Six-pence neatly bound.

II. That every Subfcriber depofit One Shilling at the Time of fubfcribing ; and the Remainder to be paid on the Delivery of the Book.

. Subfcriptions are received by COX & BERRY, in *Bofton*.

123. "Proposals" for Phillis Wheatley's *Poems* . . . (London, 1773), *Boston Censor,* February 29, 1772. Courtesy, American Antiquarian Society.

It was Phillis who placed the asterisk after the name of Terence to make sure the reader got the point—her footnote read: "*He was an African by birth."

In November 1772, with a covering letter containing a few biographical notes, John Wheatley had dispatched the manuscript to Archibald Bell, the London bookseller. News came from a London friend early in January 1773. Bell had "waited upon the Countess of Huntingdon with the poems, who was greatly pleas'd with them, and pray'd him to read them; and often would break in upon him, and say, 'Is not this, or that, very fine? Do read another,'

and question'd him much, whether she was *real,* without a deception?" Moreover, the countess was "fond of having the book dedicated to her; but one thing she desir'd . . . to have Phillis' picture in the frontispiece. So that if you would get it done, it can be engraved here." The excitement in the Wheatley house must have been intense. A "deception"? There were eighteen Boston worthies who had signed a testimonial that she was indeed *"real."* The dedication to the antislavery countess would be a distinct pleasure. The picture? The poet had a friend who would do the job. One of the "worthies," the Reverend John Moorhead, pastor of the Church of the Presbyterian Strangers, owned a slave who not only turned out verse himself but also painted pictures. Scipio Moorhead's portrait of Phillis, quill in hand, demure, definite, and thoughtful, was on the next ship out of Boston harbor, to be engraved in London as a frontispiece to the *Poems.* Susannah Wheatley said it was a fine likeness. What happened to Moorhead's original, we do not know. (Could it have been one of the "Fifty

To S. M. a young *African* Painter, on seeing
his Works.

TO show the lab'ring bosom's deep intent,
    And thought in living characters to paint,
When first thy pencil did those beauties give,
And breathing figures learnt from thee to live,
How did those prospects give my soul delight, 5
A new creation rushing on my sight?
Still, wond'rous youth! each noble path pursue,
On deathless glories fix thine ardent view:
Still may the painter's and the poet's fire
To aid thy pencil, and thy verse conspire! 10
And may the charms of each seraphic theme
Conduct thy footsteps to immortal fame!
High to the blissful wonders of the skies
Elate thy soul, and raise thy wishful eyes.
Thrice happy, when exalted to survey 15
That splendid city, crown'd with endless day,
Whose twice six gates on radiant hinges ring:
Celestial *Salem* blooms in endless spring.

Calm

Calm and serene thy moments glide along,
And may the muse inspire each future song! 20
Still, with the sweets of contemplation bless'd,
May peace with balmy wings your soul invest!
But when these shades of time are chas'd away,
And darkness ends in everlasting day,
On what seraphic pinions shall we move, 25
And view the landscapes in the realms above?
There shall thy tongue in heav'nly murmurs flow,
And there my muse with heav'nly transport glow:
No more to tell of *Damon's* tender sighs,
Or rising radiance of *Aurora's* eyes, 30
For nobler themes demand a nobler strain,
And purer language on th' ethereal plain.
Cease, gentle muse! the solemn gloom of night
Now seals the fair creation from my sight.

P 2   To

124. Phillis Wheatley, "To S.M. [Scipio Moorhead] a young *African* Painter . . ." from *Poems on Various Subjects* (London, 1773). Courtesy of the Library of Congress.

elegant Portrait Paintings [drawn from life]," titled "Phillis Wheatley, the celebrated African Poetess of Boston," noticed for sale in the *Columbian Gazeteer* ten years after her death?) What remains is Phillis's tribute "To S. M. a young *African* painter, on seeing his Works" [fig. 124]:

> To show the lab'ring bosom's deep intent,
> And thought in living characters to paint,
> When first thy pencil did those beauties give,
> And breathing figures learnt from thee to live,
> How did those prospects give my soul delight,
> A new creation rushing on my sight?
> Still, wond'rous youth! each noble path pursue,
> On deathless glories fix thine ardent view:
> Still may the painter's and the poet's fire
> To aid thy pencil, and thy verse conspire!

She waited eagerly for the book. But as her health continued to fail, the family doctor advised a voyage—the sea air might be good for her lungs. Why not send her to London, thought the Wheatleys, with their son, Nathaniel, who had already planned a business trip, where she might be on hand the day the volume came off the press? In May she wrote her "Farewel to America" and in June was on the high seas.

London, for Phillis Wheatley, whose fame had preceded her, was in a small way a triumphal progress. The countess of Huntingdon, who a decade later would sponsor the black preacher John Marrant, introduced her to the reform-minded society of the day, where her conversational acuteness won her new friends. In July, Brook Watson, later a lord mayor of London, gave her a fine edition of *Paradise Lost,* which the earl of Dartmouth matched with Smollett's new translation of *Don Quixote.* That same month Benjamin Franklin called, reporting to his cousin Jonathan Williams: "Upon your recommendation I went to see the black poetess and offered her any services I could do her." (A few years later she would dedicate to Franklin her second, never-to-be printed volume of poems and letters.) Her English friends pressed her to stay on in London for presentation at St. James to George III, but at the end of summer Susannah Wheatley, ill in Boston, asked her to return.

Most important of all, as she was crossing the Atlantic her *Poems on Various Subjects, Religious and Moral* was being sought in London bookshops. By October she was back in Boston, writing to Obour Tanner that England had been a great experience: "The friends I found there among the nobility and gentry, their benevolent conduct toward me, the unexpected civility and complaisance with which I was treated by all, fills me with astonishment. I can scarcely realize it." Would Obour solicit subscriptions in Newport for her *Poems?* In January the books arrived from London and were placed on sale on King Street, each volume, as the *Boston Gazette* put it, "Adorn'd with an Elegant Engraving of the Author." The poet lost no time in posting seventeen copies to the Reverend Samuel Hopkins, the disciple of Jonathan Edwards who preached New Divinity and the eman-

cipation of the slaves in the First Church of Newport, at the same time applauding his plan of helping "two negro men, who are desirous of returning to their native country to preach the Gospel." She hoped that the prophecy of the psalmist was "now on the point of being accomplished, namely, Ethiopia shall now stretch forth her hands unto God." More certain was the fact that a goodly number of readers, both white and black, would stretch forth their hands toward the Ethiopian poetess of Boston. Although the *London Magazine* denied her the "astonishing power of genius," it printed her "Hymn to the Morning" in "admiration of talents so vigorous and lively." The *Poems* would be twice republished in England before the century was out. In America, during the next thirty years, at least seven editions would make Phillis Wheatley's name and face familiar in Pennsylvania, New York, Connecticut, and New Hampshire.

IN March 1774, when Phillis was twenty-one, her beloved Susannah Wheatley died. She had been more a mother and a friend than a mistress, as Phillis explained to Obour, and her departure signaled a new epoch in the poet's life [fig. 125]. Whether she stayed on in the Wheatley home is not clear. What is certain is that her muse did not desert her after the publication of the book. A few months after her return from London, there was another broadside for sale in Boston, an elegy on the death of the artist Scipio's master, the Reverend John Moorhead. In May, she informs Obour Tanner that three hundred copies of *Poems,* possibly the second London edition, have just come off the ship. In the *Royal American Magazine* of Boston for December there is a poem (and a reply) addressed "To Lieut R—— of the Royal Navy" by *"Phillis, (a young* Affrican, *of surprising genius),"* with a Swiftian note by

125. Phillis Wheatley to Obour Tanner, March 21, 1774. Massachusetts Historical Society.

the editor that anticipates the answers that Jefferson would receive a decade later:

> By this single instance may be seen, the importance of education.—Uncultivated *nature is much the same in every part of the globe. It is probable* Europe *and* Africa *would be alike* savage *or* polite *in the same circumstances; though, it may be questioned, whether men who have no ar-*

tificial *wants, are capable of becoming so
ferocious as those, who, by faring* sump-
tuously every day, *are reduced to a habit
of thinking it necessary to* their *happiness,
to plunder the whole human race.*

There is some sentimental persiflage in the
exchange between Phillis and the officer.
"Paris, for Helen's bright resistless charms,"
she sings, "Made Illion bleed and set the
world in arms," and in his "Answer" he re-
plies to the "lovely virgin's praise"—"Behold with reverence, and with joy adore; /
the Lovely daughter of the Affric shore."
One wonders whether Captain John Paul
Jones's mysterious note, written to a brother
officer from the *Ranger* on an undated Friday, refers to an exchange of this sort: "I am
on the point of sailing . . . pray be so good
as put the Inclosed into the hands of the
Celebrated Phillis the African Favorite of
the Nine and of Apollo, should she Reply, I
hope you will be the bearer" [fig. 126].
More interesting, perhaps, than any roman-
tic speculation about this literary affair is
Phillis's attempt in her "Reply to the Answer" to recapture a memory of her African
childhood in the poetic conventions of the
day:

> And pleasing Gambia on my soul re-
>   turns,
> With native grace in spring's lux-
>   uriant reign,
> Smiles the gay mead, and Eden
>   blooms again,
> The various bower, the tuneful flow-
>   ing stream,
> The soft retreats, the lovers golden
>   dream,
> Her soil spontaneous, yields exhaust-
>   less stores;
> For phoebus revels on her verdant
>   shores
> Whose flowery births, a fragrant train
>   appear,

> And crown the youth throughout the
>   smiling year. . . .

As the arguments of the revolution
reached the stage of arms, she found herself
trapped in the crossfire of events, and after
the Battle of Bunker Hill fled British-oc-
cupied Boston to join Obour Tanner in
nearby Rhode Island. When Washington arrived in Cambridge to take command of the
American army, it was from Providence that
she sent him a letter and a paean in verse.
"Sir," wrote the poet and patriot, "I have
taken the freedom to address your Excellency in the enclosed poem, and entreat
your acceptance, though I am not insensible
of its accuracies. Your being appointed by
the Grand Continental Congress to be Gen-
eralissimo of the armies of North America,
together with the fame of your virtues, excite sensations not easy to suppress." Her
poem, too, was a weapon in "the great
cause."

It is easy to understand why the Virginia
general liked the poem. Unlike her prerevolutionary address to the earl of
Dartmouth, in which the poet-slave yoked
British tyranny to black bondage, the ode to
Washington is indited by a raceless champion of Columbia—a name she invented for
the new "land of freedom's heaven-defended
race." For the aristocrat who owned slaves or
for the general who at this point barred
blacks from the army, there was no discor-
dant note in her hymn to independence.

> Celestial Choir! enthron'd in realms
>   of light,
>   Columbia's scenes of glorious
>   toils I write.
> While freedom's cause her anxious
>   breast alarms,
>   She flashes dreadful in refulgent
>   arms.

Nor was the general embarrassed by the offer of her final couplet:

126. John Paul Jones to Hector McNeill, not dated. The Pierpont Morgan Library, New York.

A crown, a mansion, and a throne
   that shine,
With gold unfading,
  WASHINGTON! be thine.

"At first, with a view of doing justice to her great poetical genius," the general in early February confided to a friend, "I had a great mind to publish the poem; but not knowing whether it might not be considered rather as a mark of my own vanity, than as a compliment to her, I laid it aside. . . ." At the end of the month he wrote to "Miss Phillis":

> a variety of important occurrences, continually interposing to distract the mind and withdraw the attention, I hope will apologize for the delay, and plead my excuse for the seeming but not real neglect. I thank you most sincerely for your polite notice of me, in the elegant lines you enclosed; and however undeserving I may be of such encomium and panegyric, the style and manner exhibit a striking proof of your poetical talents; in honor of which, and as a tribute justly due to you, I would have published the poem, had I not been apprehensive, that, while I only meant to give the world this new instance of your genius, I might have incurred the imputation of vanity. This, and nothing else, determined me not to give it place in the public prints.

If you should ever come to
Cambridge, or near head-quarters, I
shall be happy to see a person so favored by the Muses, and to whom nature has been so liberal and
beneficient in her dispensations.

In fact, a month later both letter and poem
found their way into the "Poetical Essays"
section of the *Pennsylvania Magazine,* whose
editor, Thomas Paine, presented them to
the public as *"written by the famous* Phillis
Wheatley, *The African Poetess"* [fig. 127].
When later in the year she visited Washington at his headquarters, she was cour-
teously received.

Two years later, on April 1, 1778, Phillis
Wheatley married John Peters, whose dim
figure, it would seem, has been somewhat
besmirched by her early white biographers.
(The tone may be gauged by a passage in the
first *Memoir* of 1834: "he wore a wig, carried
a cane, and quite acted out *'the gentleman'* . . . he is said to have been both too
proud and too indolent to apply himself to
any occupation below his fancied dignity.")
Both are recorded as free Negroes in the
Boston marriage records. It is indeed difficult to reconstruct the six years of their
wedded life. In 1805, when Grégoire was
writing his book entitled *Literature of
Negroes,* he asked the French consul at
Boston to gather some data on Wheatley's
last years. She "married a man of colour,"
the consul replied, notable for "the superi-
ority of his understanding." Starting out as
a grocer, he went on to become "a lawyer
under the name of Doctor Peter, and plead
before tribunals the cause of the blacks. The
reputation he enjoyed procured him a fortune." What seems to emerge from the
mélange of posthumous gossip and hearsay
is that John Peters, possibly a friend of
Obour Tanner's, was a "respectable" citizen

127. Phillis Wheatley, "Letter and Verses . . .
presented to his Excellency Gen. Washington,"
October 26, 1775, *Pennsylvania Magazine,*
April 1776. The Historical Society of Pennsylvania.

of Boston. In the 1830s, a granddaughter of
Susannah Wheatley remembered that he
"was not only a very remarkable looking
man, but a man of talents and information,
and that he wrote with fluency and propriety, and at one period read law." She "admitted, however, that he was disagreeable
in his manners, and that on account of his
improper conduct, Phillis became entirely
estranged from the immediate family of her
mistress. . . ." Nowhere does Phillis
breathe a word of complaint against her
husband. He seems to have been a black
man of dignity, who valued himself, did not
kowtow to patronizing whites, struggled to
climb the educational and economic ladder,
and failed.

One thing is clear. The marriage did not quench her poetic fire. On the front page of the *Evening Post and General Advertiser* for October 30, 1779, Phillis Wheatley, a *"female African,"* outlined her "Proposals" for publishing by subscription a new three-hundred-page volume of "Poems & Letters on various subjects, dedicated to the Right Hon. Benjamin Franklin Esq: One of the Ambassadors of the United States at the Court of France," to be printed "as soon as a sufficient Number of Encouragers offer" [fig. 128]. The book was to contain thirty-odd poems—among the titles: "Thoughts on the Times," "Ocean," "Niagara," "Chloe to Calliope"—and thirteen letters, including one to Dr. Benjamin Rush and three to the countess of Huntingdon. The war was still in progress and "Encouragers" did not flock to her standard. Yet her reputation did not fade, and her portrait, crudely copied from the frontispiece of her *Poems,* adorned the cover of *Bickerstaff's Boston Almanac* for 1782, in the "Sixth Year of Independency" [fig. 129]. Life was bitter for the Peters. At one point John sat in jail for debt while Phillis scrubbed and washed in a cheap lodging house. There were three children—two died, a third lived on precariously. Always delicate, she found herself sick, poor, and unable to find a printer willing to risk the new book. Yet she continued to write—a broadside elegy for the Brattle Street Church on the death of one of her old supporters, the "Learned Dr. Samuel Cooper," and a published four-page pamphlet in verse on *Liberty and Peace* [fig. 130], which shows her frayed and tired. Her last piece in print, in the *Boston Magazine* of September 1784 [fig. 131], is a consolation on the death of an infant son, which perhaps reflected the loss of her own last child. "This Poem," noted the editor, "was selected from a manuscript Volume of Poems, written by PHILLIS PETERS, formerly PHILLIS

128. "Proposals for Printing by Subscription, A Collection of poems, wrote . . . by Phillis, a Negro Girl . . . ," *Boston Evening Post & General Advertiser,* October 30, 1779. Courtesy, American Antiquarian Society.

WHEATLEY—and is inserted as a specimen of her Work."

That winter she ceased to invoke the Muse. "Last Lord's day died, Mrs. PHILLIS PETERS, (formerly Phillis Wheatley), aged 31, known to the literary world by her celebrated miscellaneous Poems," so reads her obituary in the *Massachusetts Centinel* of December 8, 1784 [fig. 132]. In the same

129. *Bickerstaff's Boston Almanack . . . 1782,* woodcut portrait of Phillis Wheatley, Boston, 1781. Courtesy, American Antiquarian Society.

newspaper a few months later the following notice appeared: "The person who borrowed a volume of manuscript poems etc of Phillis Peters . . . would very much oblige her husband, John Peters, by returning it immediately, as the whole of her works are intended to be published." When the first American edition of her book of 1773 was published in 1786, none of the thirty-odd new poems graced its pages. One of these days the manuscript may turn up. When it does, we will be able to read "the whole of her works."

DURING the era of the revolution, the "vent'rous Afric" was a critical image in the ongoing polemic between equalitarian and elitist. That she was black and a woman somewhat sharpened the issue. Jefferson's reservations sparked the debate, as they did with Benjamin Banneker. (Recall how the black astronomer printed Wheatley's poetry with the stars in his almanac.) "Misery is often the parent of the most affecting touches in poetry," begins the author of *Notes on Virginia,* who some years later would say that "of all men living I am the last who should undertake to decide as to the merits of poetry": "Among the blacks is misery enough, God knows, but no poetry. Love is the peculiar oestrum of the poet. Their love is ardent, but it kindles the senses only, not the imagination. Religion indeed has produced a Phillis Wheatley; but it could not produce a poet. The compositions published under her name are below the dignity of criticism." (The innuendo of fraudulent authorship would also be aimed at Banneker and Ignatius Sancho.)

Jefferson, of course, did not go unanswered. Gilbert Imlay, the revolutionary captain whose name is linked to that of Mary Wollstonecraft, recorded in his *Topographical Description of the Western Territory of North America* (1792), that he was "ashamed, in reading Mr. Jefferson's book, to see, from one of the most enlightened and benevolent of my countrymen, the disgraceful prejudices he entertains against the unfortunate negroes," and singled out Wheatley in his rebuttal: "I will transcribe part of her poem on Imagination, and leave you to judge whether it is poetical or not. It will afford you an opportunity, if you have never met with it, of estimating her genius and Mr. Jefferson's judgment; and I think, without any disparagement to him, that, by comparison, Phillis appears much the superior. Indeed, I should be glad to be informed that a white upon this continent has written more beautiful lines." Grégoire, in Paris, reprinting three of her poems, was outraged: "If we were disposed to cavil, we might say, that to an assertion, it is sufficient to oppose a contrary assertion . . . but a more direct refutation may be made, by selecting some portions of her works, which will give us an idea of her talents. . . ." Dr. Samuel Stanhope Smith, member of the American Philosophical Society and president of the College of New Jersey, as late as 1810, discoursing in his *Causes of the Variety of Complexion and Figure on the Human Species,* echoing Imlay, was still demanding of "Mr. Jefferson, or any other man who is acquainted with American planters, how many of those masters could have written poems equal to those of Phillis Wheatley?"

There were others beside Jefferson whom Phillis Wheatley made uneasy. One Richard Nisbet, who in the year of her *Poems* published his tract, *Slavery Not Forbidden by Scripture,* was impatient with Dr. Benjamin Rush for citing "a single example of a negro girl writing a few silly poems, to prove that the blacks are not deficient to us in understanding," and two years later, Bernard Romans in his natural history of Florida went out of his way to argue that "against the Phillis of Boston (who is the *Phaenix* of her race)," he could "bring at least twenty well known instances of the contrary effect of education on this sable generation."

But these were ineffectual voices drowned out by the wave of international acclaim. In 1774 Voltaire, who did not think highly of blacks, wrote to a friend: "Fontanelle was wrong to say there never would be Negro poets: there is right now a Negress who writes excellent verse in English," and five years later his countryman the marquis de Barbé-Marbois, secretary of the French legation in Boston, recorded in his diary that Phillis was a prodigy, "one of the strangest creatures in the country and perhaps in the whole world." In Göttingen, the anthropologist John Friedrich Blumenbach, defending the unity of mankind in 1806, cited blacks "who have distinguished themselves by their talents for poetry." He knew "English, Dutch, and Latin poems" by black poets, "above all, those of Phillis Wheatley of Boston, who is justly famous. . . ." Her volume of verse was a "collection which scarcely any one who has any taste for poetry could read without pleasure." And Thomas Clarkson, in his essay on slavery that shook the world, citing three of her poems went on to remark that "if the authoress was *designed for slavery* . . . the greater part of the inhabitants of Britain must lose their claim to freedom."

At home she stirred tribute from other poets, black and white. In his second published poem, Jupiter Hammon, the black bard of Long Island, greeted her in a broadside *Address*. The month she died, a pseudonymous "Horatio" of State Street sent to the *Boston Magazine* an "Elegy on the Death of a late celebrated Poetess":

> As Orpheus play'd the list'ning
>   herds among,
> They own'd the magic of his powerful
>   song;
> Mankind no more their savage nature
>   kept,
> And foes to music, wonder'd how
>   they wept.
> So PHILLIS tun'd her sweet
>   mellifluous lyre;
> (Harmonious numbers bid the soul
>   aspire)
> While AFRIC's untaught race with
>   transport heard,
> They lov'd the poet, and the muse re-
>   ver'd.

During the summer of 1786 Dr. Joseph Ladd, a young New Englander practicing medicine in Charleston, South Carolina (where a few months later he would die in a duel), published a long poem, "The Prospects of America," in which the glory of the new nation is illustrated by its greatest citizens, among them the poets Freneau and Barlow—and "a negress . . . the authoress of some ingenious poems . . . entitled to a remembrance. . . ."

> Here the fair volume shows the far-
>   spread name
> Of Wondrous Wheatley, Afric's heir
>   to fame,
> Well is it known what glowing ge-
>   nius shines,
> What force of numbers, in her po-
>   lished lines:
> With magic power the grand descrip-
>   tions roll

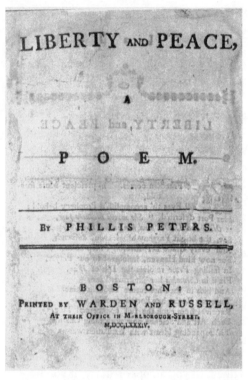

130. Phillis Peters, *Liberty and Peace,*

> Thick on the mind, and agitate the
>   soul.

A decade later in an issue of the *New York Magazine* for 1796, one "Matilda"—apparently a man—moved to create his own verse, "On Reading the Poems of Phillis Wheatley, the African Poetess," ended his tribute with a stanza that echoed her insight into the twofold meaning of liberty in the American Revolution:

> 'Tis done! at length the long-with-
>   held decree
> Goes forth, that Afric shall be blest
>   and free;
> A PHILLIS rises, and the world no
>   more
> Denies the sacred right to mental
>   pow'r;
> While, Heav'n-inspir'd, she proves
>   *her Country's* claim

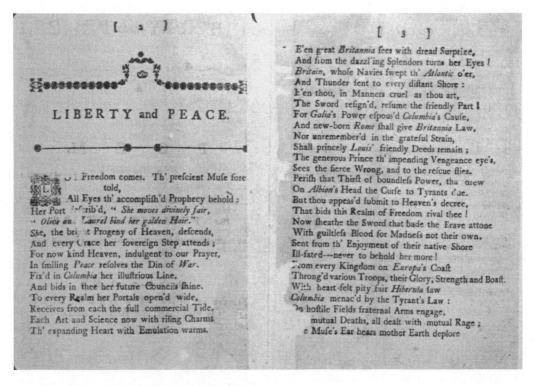

A Poem (Boston, 1784). Courtesy of The New-York Historical Society.

To Freedom, and *her own* to deathless Fame.

Long after her untimely death, another talented young black woman, sixteen-year-old Charlotte L. Forten, daughter of the well-known revolutionary veteran and abolitionist of Philadelphia, recorded in her journal on a Friday in July 1854: "This evening read 'Poems of Phillis Wheatly,' an African slave, who lived in Boston at the time of the Revolution. She was a wonderfully gifted woman, and many of her poems are very beautiful. Her character and genius afford a striking proof of the falseness of the assertion made by some that hers is an inferior race. . . ." Only the other day, two centuries after Phillis Wheatley's *Poems* first saw the light, another "vent'rous" young black poet, Nikki Giovanni, tracing her roots, was moved to say: "We have a line of strong poets. Wheatley, by her life style, was a strong woman intent on survival."

Jupiter Hammon

The first published poem by a black American actually preceded Phillis Wheatley's book by a dozen years. It was printed in 1760 as a broadside in double column with the title *An Evening Thought. Salvation by Christ, with Penetential Cries: Composed by Jupiter Hammon, a Negro belonging to Mr. Lloyd, of Queen's-Village, on Long Island* [fig. 133].* "Believe me now my Christian

---

*In the same year appeared the first Afro-American slave narrative—by another Hammon: *A Narrative of the Uncommon Sufferings, and Surprizing Deliverance of Briton Hammon, A Negro Man.—Servant to General Winslow, of Mansfield, in New-England; Who returned to Boston, after having been absent almost Thirteen Years* (Boston, 1760).

friends," exhorted the poet-preacher over twenty years later in a stanza of the last poem he was to write:

> Believe your friend call'd Hammon:
> You cannot to your God attend,
>   And serve the God of Mammon.

A few sparse notes, scraped together from some faded letters and printed lines, will have to serve as a life of this black puritan of New York.

JUPITER Hammon was born a slave on October 17, 1711. His masters were the Lloyds, manorial landlords and merchants of Long Island's north shore near Oyster Bay, and he served them his whole long life. It is possible that as a child he was allowed to attend the village school and later to read his master's books; in one of his discourses he refers to the English divines Burkitt and Beveridge, whose works were in Henry Lloyd's library. In May 1733, when Hammon was twenty-two, he purchased from his master for seven shillings and six pence a Bible with psalms. In his seventies, he claimed that he was still "able to do almost any kind of business"—which may indicate that he was a valued servant in house and market, a skilled farmhand and artisan, and able to save a bit by doing extra jobs for pay. When he was thirty, there occurred in nearby New York City an event that must have made a deep impression on him: the discovery of an alleged conspiracy by the blacks of the city, with a few whites, to rise against their masters and the government. Thirteen slaves were burned at the stake, eighteen hanged (two in chains), and seventy banished to the West Indies.

When the revolution came, the patriot Lloyds fled Long Island as the British and Hessians took over, and Hammon went with them to Connecticut. All his poems and discourses composed during the war

To Mr. and Mrs. * * * * * * *, on the Death of their Infant Son. By Phillis Wheatly.

O DEATH! whose sceptre, trembling realms obey,
And weeping millions mourn thy savage sway;
Say, shall we call thee by the name of friend,
Who blasts our joys, and bids our glories end?
Behold, a child who rivals op'ning morn,
When its first beams the eastern hills adorn;
So sweetly blooming once that lovely boy,
His father's hope, his mother's only joy,
Nor charms nor innocence prevail to save,
From the grim monarch of the gloomy grave!
Two moons revolve when lo! among the dead
The beauteous infant lays his weary head:
For long he strove the tyrant to withstand,
And the dread terrors of his iron hand;
Vain was his strife, with the relentless power,
His efforts weak; and this his mortal hour;
He sinks --he dies---celestial muse, relate,
His spirit's entrance at the sacred gate.
Methinks I hear the heav'nly courts resound,
The recent theme inspires the choirs around.

131. Phillis Wheatley, "To Mr. and Mrs. ***, on the Death of their Infant Son," *Boston Magazine*, September 20, 1784. Courtesy, American Antiquarian Society.

MARRIED, at her Father's Manſion, in Dux-
bury, by the Rev. Mr. Sanger, the amiable Miſs
NABBY ALDEN, youngeſt Daughter of Colonel
Briggs Alden, of that Place, to Mr. BEZA HAY-
WARD, of Bridgewater.

Laſt Lord's day died, Mrs. PHILLIS
PETERS, (formerly Phillis Wheatly)
aged 31, known to the literary world by
her celebrated miſcellaneous Poems. Her
funeral is to be this afternoon, at 4 o'clock,
from the houſe lately improved by Mr.
Todd, nearly oppoſite Dr. Bulfinch's, at
Weſt-Boſton, where her friends and acquaintance are deſired to attend.

132. Obituary, Phillis
Wheatley, *Massachusetts
Centinel*, December 8,
1784. Courtesy, American
Antiquarian Society.

A N

Evening THOUGHT.

SALVATION BY *CHRIST*,

WITH

PENETENTIAL CRIES:

Compoſed by Jupiter Hammon, a Negro belonging to Mr Lloyd, of Queen's-
Village, on Long-Iſland, the 25th of December, 1760.

133. Jupiter Hammon,
"An Evening Thought,"
broadside, December 25,
1760. Courtesy of the
Library of Congress.

SALVATION comes by Jeſus Chriſt alone,
  The only Son of God ;
Redemption now to every one,
  That love his holy Word.
Dear Jeſus we would fly to Thee,
  And leave off every Sin,
Thy tender Mercy well agree ;
  Salvation from our King.
Salvation comes now from the Lord,
  Our victorious King ;
His holy Name be well ador'd,
  Salvation ſurely bring.
Dear Jeſus give thy Spirit now,
  Thy Grace to every Nation,
That han't the Lord to whom we bow,
  The Author of Salvation.
Dear Jeſus unto Thee we cry,
  Give us thy Preparation ;
Turn not away thy tender Eye ;
  We ſeek thy true Salvation.
Salvation comes from God we know,
  The true and only One ;
It's well agreed and certain true,
  He gave his only Son.
Lord hear our penetential Cry :
  Salvation from above ;
It is the Lord that doth ſupply,
  With his Redeeming Love.
Dear Jeſus by thy precious Blood,
  The World Redemption have :
Salvation comes now from the Lord,
  He being his captive Slave.
Dear Jeſus let the Nations cry,
  And all tne People ſay,
Salvation comes from Chriſt on high,
  Haſte on Tribunal Day.
We cry as Sinners to the Lord,
  Salvation to obtain ;
It is firmly fixt his holy Word,
  Ye ſhall not cry in vain.
Dear Jeſus unto Thee we cry,
  And make our Lamentation :
O let our Prayers aſcend on high ;
  We felt thy Salvation.

Lord turn our dark benighted Souls ;
  Give us a true Motion,
And let the Hearts of all the World,
  Make Chriſt their Salvation.
Ten Thouſand Angels cry to Thee,
  Yea louder than the Ocean.
Thou art the Lord, we plainly ſee ;
  Thou art the true Salvation.
Now is the Day, excepted Time ;
  The Day of Salvation ;
Increaſe your Faith, do not repine :
  Awake ye every Nation.
Lord unto whom now ſhall we go,
  Or ſeek a ſafe Abode ;
Thou haſt the Word Salvation too
  The only Son of God.
Ho ! every one that hunger hath,
  Or pineth after me,
Salvation be thy leading Staff,
  To ſet the Sinner free.
Dear Jeſus unto Thee we fly ;
  Depart, depart from Sin,
Salvation doth at length ſupply,
  The Glory of our King.
Come ye Bleſſed of the Lord,
  Salvation gently given ;
O turn your Hearts, accept the Word,
  Your Souls are fit for Heaven.
Dear Jeſus we now turn to Thee,
  Salvation to obtain ;
Our Hearts and Souls do meet again,
  To magnify thy Name.
Come holy Spirit, Heavenly Dove,
  The Object of our Care ;
Salvation doth increaſe our Love ;
  Our Hearts hath felt thy fear.
Now Glory be to God on High,
  Salvation high and low ;
And thus the Soul on Chriſt rely,
  To Heaven ſurely go.
Come Bleſſed Jeſus, Heavenly Dove,
  Accept Repentance here ;
Salvation give, with tender Love ;
  Let us with Angels ſhare.

F I N I S.

were printed at Hartford. In 1782, when Prince William Henry, later King William IV, stopped over at the Lloyd's manor house, the black poet wrote a poem to celebrate the visit.

It is altogether possible that Jupiter Hammon was a preacher to the slaves in the communities of Long Island and Connecticut where he labored for the Lloyds. *An Evening Thought,* an antiphonal poem echoing the word "Salvation" in twenty-three of its eighty-eight lines, has all the ringing ecstatic hope for heavenly freedom with "tender love" that charges the earliest spirituals of the enslaved. The preacher calls and the flock responds—thus the "Penetential Cries":

> Dear Jesus unto Thee we cry,
>   Give us the Preparation;
> Turn not away thy tender Eye;
>   We seek thy true Salvation. . . .
> Lord hear our penetential Cry:
>   Salvation from above;
> It is the Lord that doth supply
>   With his Redeeming Love.

Jupiter Hammon wrote this hymn on Christmas Day 1760, and for the next forty years, whenever he cried out in print to his black brothers and sisters, his theme, more or less, was always salvation. Yet there are hints toward the end of his career of a certain impatience, a feeling that freedom was possible—and desirable—in the Here as well as in the After.

It seems significant that his next poem of record, printed as a broadside eighteen years later when he was sixty-seven years old, is *An Address to Miss Phillis Wheatly* in twenty-one scripture-glossed quatrains, "published by the Author, and a number of his friends, who desire to join with him in their best regards" to "the Ethiopian Poetess" [fig. 134]. Five years after Phillis Wheatley's *Poems of*

1773, Hammon echoes her sense of miracle in being rescued from pagan Africa:

> God's tender mercy brought thee
>   here;
>   Tost o'er the raging main;
> In Christian faith thou hast a share,
>   Worth all the gold of Spain. . . .
> That thou a pattern still might be,
>   To youth of Boston town,
> The blessed Jesus set thee free,
>   From every sinful wound.

But did Hammon detect in Wheatley an occasional note of frustration, even protest (which he took pains to conceal in his own poems)?

> Thou, Phillis, when thou hunger
>   hast,
>   Or pantest for thy God;
> Jesus Christ is thy relief,
>   Thou hast the holy word.

The "holy word" of this stanza is tagged to Psalm 13, in which "David complaineth of delay in help":

> How long wilt thou forget me O Lord? for ever? how long wilt thou hide thy face from me?
>
> How long shall I take counsel in my soul, *having* sorrow in my heart daily? how long shall mine enemy be exalted over me?
>
> Consider *and* hear me, O Lord my God: lighten my eyes, lest I sleep the *sleep* of death.

HAMMON'S next piece, of the following year, *An Essay on the Ten Virgins,* has not yet turned up, although it was advertised in the *Connecticut Courant* for December 4, 1779, "To be sold at the Printing-Office in Hartford" [fig. 135]. There has survived, however, a work published three years later

134. Jupiter Hammon, "An Address to Miss Phillis Wheatley . . . ," broadside, Hartford, August 4, 1778. Courtesy, The Connecticut Historical Society.

in the same town, Hammon's first sermon in print, *A Winter Piece: Being a Serious Exhortation, with a Call to the Unconverted: and a Short Contemplation on the Death of Jesus Christ.* "As I have been desired to write something more than Poetry," the black preacher began, "I shall endeavour to write from these words, Matthew xi, 28. Come unto me all ye that labour and are heavy laden." Although this sermon is very far from being a call to revolt, neither is it an exhortation to slaves to obey their masters.

In places, it has the heat of a certain friction. Some whites had apparently objected to Hammon's preaching the word:

But it may be objected by those who have had the advantage of studying, every one is not calculated for teaching of others. To those I answer, Sirs, I do not attempt to teach those I know are able to teach me, but I shall endeavour by divine assistance to enlighten the minds of my brethren; for

135. *Connecticut Courant*, December 4, 1779. Courtesy of the Library of Congress.

we are a poor despised nation, whom God in his wise providence has permitted to be brought from their native place to a christian land, and many thousands born in what are called christian families, and brought up to years of understanding. In answer to the objectors, Sirs, pray give me leave to enquire into the state of those children that are born in those christian families, have they been baptised, taught to read, and learnt their catechism? Surely this is a duty incumbent on masters or heads of families. Sirs, if you had a sick child, would you not send for a doctor?

Then he turns to his "Brethren for whom this discourse is designed"—some of whom, apparently, have looked at him askance as an upholder of slavery:

My dear Brethren, as it hath been reported that I had petitioned to the court of Hartford against freedom, I now solemnly declare that I never have said, nor done any thing, neither directly nor indirectly, to promote or to prevent freedom; but my answer hath always been I am a stranger here and I do not care to be concerned or to meddle with public affairs, and by this declaration I hope my friends will be satisfied, and all prejudice re-

moved, Let us all strive to be united together in love, and to become new creatures.

His message was simply this: everything was in God's hands. If freedom of body or soul was to be the fate of black or white, it must be bestowed as a gift from God:

Come my dear fellow servants and brothers, Africans by nation, we are all invited to come, Acts x, 34. Then Peter opened his mouth and said, of a truth I perceive that God is no respecter of persons, verse 35. But in every nation he that feareth him is accepted of him. My Brethren, many of us are seeking a temporal freedom, and I wish you may obtain it; remember that all power in heaven and on earth belongs to God; if we are slaves it is by the permission of God, if we are free it must be by the power of the most high God. Stand still and see the salvation of God, cannot that same power that divided the waters from the waters for the children of Israel to pass through, make way for your freedom?

The emphasis of Hammon's doctrine is that it applies equally to all:

My brethren, it is not we servants only that are unworthy, but all mankind by the fall of Adam, became guilty in the sight of God. . . . But how art we to forget that God spoke these words, saying, I am the Lord thy God, which brought thee out of the land of Egypt and out of the house of bondage. Exod. xx, 1. Thus we see how the children of Israel were delivered from the Egyptian service.

Both freedoms will come, must come, he concludes: "But the scripture hath told us, that we must not depend on the use of means alone. . . . Here we see if we are saved, it must be by the power of God's holy spirit. But my dear Brethren the time is hastening when we must appear." But then, as if to mute the string of protest, he appends seventeen quatrains of his *Poem for Children with Thoughts on Death*—another series of pious homilies strung together in Hartford on New Year's Day 1782.

Soon after *A Winter Piece* there followed, during the revolution, another earnest discourse, *An Evening's Improvement. Shewing, the Necessity of beholding the Lamb of God . . . Printed for the Author, by the Assistance of his Friends.* "And now my brethren," Hammon begins, "seeing I have had an invitation to write something more to encourage my dear fellow servants and brethren Africans, in the knowledge of the Christian religion"—

let us behold the Lamb of God as having the power to make the blind to see, the dumb to speak, and the lame to walk, and even to raise the dead; But it may be objected and said by those that have had the advantage of studying, are we to expect miracles at this day? . . . Others may object and say, what can we expect from an unlearned Ethiopian? . . . Sirs, I know we are not to expect miracles at this day.

It is in this discourse that the "unlearned Ethiopian" has something to say about the war:

And now my dear brethren, I am to remind you of a most melancholy scene of Providence; it hath pleased the most high God, in his wise providence, to permit a cruel and unnatural war to be commenced. . . . Have we not great cause to think this is the just deserving of our sins. . . . Here we see that we ought to pray, that God may hasten the time when the people shall beat their swords into ploughshares and their spears into pruning-hooks, and nations shall learn war no more.

In fact, the poem that concludes the sermon "A Dialogue, Entitled, The Kind Master and Dutiful Servant"—a duet on Christian virtue rather than an injunction of holy obedience—is more than half devoted to the theme of "*the present* war." Hammon does not pray for the victory of either side; rather, he admonishes:

Lay up the sword and drop the spear,
    And Nations seek for peace.

LOOKING back in 1786, Jupiter Hammon wrote: "When I was at Hartford in Connecticut, where I lived during the war, I published several pieces which were well received, not only by those of my own colour, but by a number of white people, who thought they might do good among their servants."

Hammon's last recorded work, *An Address to the Negroes in the State of New-York*, was printed in his seventy-sixth year from a "manuscript, wrote in his own hand," with an unsolicited dedication to the members of the African Society in the City of New York [fig. 136]. It has the feeling of a final utterance, a tone of legacy, to his "nation":

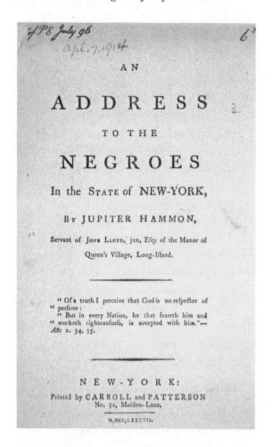

AN

ADDRESS

TO THE

NEGROES

In the STATE of NEW-YORK,

By JUPITER HAMMON,

Servant of JOHN LLOYD, jun, Efq; of the Manor of
Queen's Village, Long-Ifland.

"Of a truth I perceive that God is no refpecter of
"perfons:
"But in every Nation, he that feareth him and
"worketh righteoufnefs, is accepted with him,"—
Act x. 34, 35.

NEW-YORK:

Printed by CARROLL and PATTERSON
No. 32, Maiden-Lane,

M,DCC,LXXXVII.

136. Jupiter Hammon, *An Address to the Negroes in the State of New-York* (New York, 1787). Courtesy of The New-York Historical Society.

> I think you will be more likely to listen to what is said, when you know it comes from a negro, one of your own nation and colour. . . . My age, I think, gives me some right to speak to you. . . . I have passed the common bounds set for man, and must soon go the way of all the earth.

One can understand from its opening pages why some "white people" thought Hammon's writings "might do good among their servants," for his first injunction is Paul's: "Servants be obedient to them that are your masters according to the flesh." He will not go into the question of "whether it is right, and lawful, in the sight of God, for them to make slaves of us or not"—but he is "certain that while we are slaves, it is our duty to obey our masters, in all their lawful commands, and mind them unless we are bid to do that which we know to be sin. . . ."

One wonders about the reactions at this point of the members of the African Society who noted Hammon's confession: "I have great reason to be thankful that my lot has been so much better than most slaves have had. I suppose I have had more advantages and privileges than most of you, who are slaves, have ever known, and I believe more than many white people have enjoyed, for which I desire to bless God, and pray that he may bless those who have given them to me." Were the unfree happy as they read Hammon's diatribes against swearing, stealing, and loitering? ("Some of you to excuse yourselves, may plead the example of others, and say that you hear a great many white people, who know more than such poor ignorant Negroes as you are, and some who are rich and great gentlemen, swear, and talk profanely; and some of you may say this of your masters, and say no more than is true.") Yet masters, sinful as they may be, must be served honestly by their servants. True, slavery is never condoned as a good— it is God's mystery, like an earthquake or a flood. The main force of Hammon's argument is to maintain the absolute equality of all men in what matters as infinitely important for him—the hereafter, which black and white can attain only by a life free of sin:

> He will bring us all, rich and poor, white and black, to his judgment seat. If we are found among those who *feared his name,* and *trembled at his word,* we shall be called good and faithful servants. Our slavery will be at an end, and though ever so mean,

low and despised in this world, we shall sit with God in his kingdom, as Kings and Priests, and rejoice for ever and ever.

Thus, the faultless logic of his advice—"to become religious, and to make religion the great business of your lives."

Hammon does not fault freedom: "Now I acknowledge that liberty is a great thing, and worth seeking for, if we can get it honestly" and "by our good conduct prevail on our masters to set us free. . . ." To "those Negroes who have liberty," his counsel is to be exemplary Christians, so that masters cannot use their sinfulness as a reason for refusing to free their own slaves.

Yet there are some lines in which Hammon seems to reject "Penetential Cries" and speaks out as a man of the revolution:

That liberty is a great thing we may know from our own feelings, and we may likewise judge so from the conduct of the white people in this war. How much money has been spent, and how many lives have been lost to defend their liberty! I must say that I have hoped that God would open their eyes, when they were so much engaged for liberty, to think of the state of the poor blacks, and to pity us. He has done it in some measure, and has raised us up many friends; for which we have reason to be thankful, and to hope in his mercy. What may be done further, he only knows. . . .

The lines leap out of the text—and ring like those of Banneker and Cuffe. But only for a moment: "This, my dear brethren, is by no means the greatest thing we have to be concerned about. Getting our liberty in this world is nothing to our having the liberty of the children of God. . . . What is forty, fifty, or sixty years, when compared to eter-

nity?" And for further consolation: "There are but two places where all go after death, white and black, rich and poor; those places are Heaven and Hell." Make no mistake: Hammon may have had the luck to be owned by a "good" master, but he will not therefore argue that the lot of the slave is a happy one. As a matter of fact, the misery of slavery is another argument for faith in eternity, "for God hath not chosen the rich of this world. Not many rich, not many noble are called, but God hath chosen the weak things of this world. . . ."

Now, my brethren, it seems to me that there are no people that ought to attend to the hope of happiness in another world so much as we. Most of us are cut off from comfort and happiness here in this world, and can expect nothing from it. Now seeing this is the case, why should we not take care to be happy after death? Why should we spend our whole lives in sinning against God; and be miserable in this world, and in the world to come? If we do thus, we shall certainly be the greatest fools. We shall be slaves here, and slaves for ever.

Yet the final note, it must be admitted, is passive faith. Yes, "liberty is a great thing"—and this is what the revolution might have meant for black people, too—but the whole question must be left in God's hands:

If you become Christians, you will have reason to bless God for ever, that you have been brought into a land where you have heard the gospel, though you have been slaves. If we should ever get to Heaven, we shall find nobody to reproach us for being black, or for being slaves. Let me beg of you, my dear African brethren, to

think very little of your bondage in
this life; for your thinking of it will
do you no good. If God designs to set
us free, he will do it in his own time
and way. . . .

THE minutes of a meeting of the Acting
Committee of the Pennsylvania Society for
Promoting the Abolition of Slavery held on
June 30, 1787, contained the following
paragraph:

> A Pamphlet wrote by Jupiter Ham-
> mon, servant to John Lloyd, jun. Esq.
> Queen's Village, Long-Island, and ad-
> dressed to the African descendants in
> General, was laid before them. Im-
> pressed with a lively sense of the good
> effects that may result from a re-pub-
> lication thereof, to those persons to
> whom it is particularly addressed, Or-
> dered, that Daniel Humphreys be di-
> rected to print five hundred copies,
> for the purposes above mentioned.

Can it be that the Abolition Society, the
sponsor of Banneker and Cuffe, thought
that Hammon's message might serve as a
weapon of the antislavery movement? Or
was it simply that the virtuosity of mind
displayed in the *Address* was still another
disproof of Jefferson's doubt about the ability of blacks to achieve intellectual equality
with whites? The final impression is perhaps
one of sheer waste. For Jupiter Hammon
was a genius of a sort and no time-serving
hypocrite. He pursued his argument, for
what it was worth, with skill and conviction. Who cannot respond to the tragic ten-
sion between the two utterances: "Liberty is
a great thing" and "If we should ever get to
Heaven, we shall find nobody to reproach us
for being black, or for being slaves"? What
finally remains is the sense of his titanic
struggle for a position as a black and a slave
in a white world that called itself Christian.

Wentworth Cheswill of Newmarket, New Hampshire

During the winter of 1820, Senator David
Lawrence Morril of New Hampshire, argu-
ing the antislavery side in the debate on the
Missouri Compromise, went back to the
time of the revolution in order to make a
point: "In New Hampshire, there was a
yellow man by the name of Cheswell, who,
with his family, was respectable in point of
abilities, property, and character. He held
some of the first offices in the town . . . and
was perfectly competent to perform with
ability all the duties of his various offices. . . ."

The "yellow man" (elsewhere referred to
as "mulatto") was Wentworth Cheswill of
Newmarket in Rockingham County, not far
from Portsmouth. He was born in 1746, the
grandson of a slave. His father, Hopestill
Cheswill, a freeman, was a noted builder in
the area who framed the gambrel roofs of
some of Portsmouth's finest houses. Young
Wentworth (he probably had been named
after the ruling family of colonial governors)
was educated at Dummer Academy, a good
school; he was apparently a first-rate student. In 1767, at the age of twenty-one, he
married Mary Davis of nearby Durham; in
their long life together they would have
thirteen children.

In 1768, Cheswill was appointed justice
of the peace for the county; he dealt with
wills, deeds, and other legal papers, while
acting as judge in the trial of causes. Seven
years later, in October 1775, the town of
Newmarket, voting to dispatch forty-three
minutemen to Portsmouth, chose him to
mount his gray horse and carry the message
to patriots in Exeter. In April 1776, the
New Hampshire Committee of Safety, responding to the call of the Continental Congress, collected the signatures of those
citizens who "at the Risque of . . . Lives

137. Wentworth Cheswill's signature on his will, April 14, 1807. Registry of Probate, Exeter, New Hampshire.

and Fortunes" pledged themselves to take up arms to resist the British. Wentworth Cheswill was one of the signers. The following year, during the fall of 1777, he served as a private in a company of volunteers under Captain John Langdon, who ten years later was to be a delegate to the Constitutional Convention in Philadelphia. The volunteers made the 250-mile march to Saratoga to join the Continental Army under General Horatio Gates. Cheswill was not the only black man to serve at Saratoga. A few months before he arrived, General Philip Schuyler, writing from Saratoga, had complained to John Hancock and others that one-third of the troops sent from New England were too old, too young, or "Negroes."

Back home after the surrender of Burgoyne, during the spring of 1778, the black veteran was elected by the town as a delegate to a convention in Concord gathered to draw up a constitution for the state. Apparently he never made the trip and the journal of the convention has been lost. Two years later, in March 1780, the people of Newmarket elected him to the post of selectman.

After the war, the career of Wentworth Cheswill was a remarkable one, especially for a black man. From 1783 to 1787 he served Newmarket three times as selectman, four times as assessor; on various other occasions he was moderator, auditor, and coroner. The records reveal that in 1806 he was the overwhelming choice of the town for state senator, but he failed to carry the district. Following the craft of his father, he became a prosperous builder and landowner. He was a shareholder in the Newmarket Social Library. In 1807, at sixty, a sense of mortality came over him and he wrote out his own will and signed it [fig. 137]: "In the Name of God, Amen! I Wentworth Cheswill of Newmarket . . . considering Death as a certain Event, at an uncertain Time; do therefore now in the Calm of Life and whilst of sound Mind, make this my Last Will and Testment, in my own hand Writing. . . ." One item of the document tells something of his mind: "I also order and direct that my Library and collection of Manuscripts be kept safe and altogether, by my said Wife, for her own use during Life . . . if any Posterity should desire the Use of any of the Books and give Caution to return the same again in reasonable Time, they may be lent out to them, provided that only one Book be out of said Library in the Hands of any one Heir at the same Time—." After he died in 1817, at three score and ten, the "Widow Cheswill" lived on in the "mansion" he had built.

Three years after Wentworth Cheswill's death, the senator from New Hampshire, castigating the proslavery compromise that had just become the law of the land, remarked that the black ministers Lemuel Haynes and Thomas Paul, if they were alive, as well as the exemplary citizen Wentworth Cheswill, would be "forbidden to enter and live in Missouri."

Prince Hall: Organizer

Prince Hall, Boston's most prominent black in the era of the revolution, devoted his whole life to grappling, in a refractory world, with a problem of the future, still unsolved. He was the founder of the world's first lodge of black Freemasonry. But more than that, he was, in a sense, the first organizer in American history of a black society for social, political, and economic improvement. Prince Hall was not the only organizer of this kind of society. South of Boston they sprang up before the turn of the century. There was an African Union Society not only in Boston (where its membership overlapped the Masonic lodge) but also in New York, Philadelphia, Newport, and Providence. In 1790 in Charleston, South Carolina, a group of "free brown men," as they called themselves in the "Preamble" to their "Rules and Regulations," facing "the unhappy situation of our fellow creatures, and the distresses of our widows and orphans, for the want of a fund to relieve them in the hour of their distresses, sickness and death; and holding it an essential of mankind to contribute all they can towards relieving the wants and miseries, and

promoting the welfare and happiness of one another," organized themselves into the Brown Fellowship Society.*

The impulse toward unity surfaced in Massachusetts between the martyrdom of Attucks and the Battle of Bunker Hill in the black petitions addressed to the General Court. Although the name of Prince Hall is not signed to any of these petitions, it can be said, from one point of view, that the idea of African Lodge No. 1 was an outgrowth of the black solidarity fostered by these first bold attempts to force the Commonwealth to confront the anomaly of racism in the struggle for liberty. In fact, the first appearance of Prince Hall in the public record, two years after he had become a Free and Accepted Mason, was as a signer of a "petition of A Great Number of Blackes detained in a State of slavery in the Bowels of a free & Christian Country," demanding of the General Court that slavery cease in Massachusetts.

THE prerevolutionary life of Prince Hall is still something of a mystery, although black Masonic historians and others have tried to unravel it. Ten years ago, the late Charles G. Wesley, in his definitive biography, *Prince Hall: Life and Legacy,* tried valiantly to sort

---

*Broadly speaking, churches, lodges, and benevolent societies were the earliest forms of public organization by black people for their own welfare. Another form of organization, especially in New England during the second half of the eighteenth century, where an innovative slave or freeman assumed a leader's role in the African tradition, was the institution of "Negro Election Day," when black communities elected "Governors," "Kings," and other officials who acted as judges throughout the year. There are two excellent studies of the subject: Joseph P. Reidy, " 'Negro Election Day' and Black Community Life in New England, 1750–1800," *Marxist Perspectives* 3 (1978): 102–17, and William D. Piersen, *Black Yankees: The Development of an Afro-American Subculture in Eighteenth-Century New England* (Amherst, Mass., 1988), 117–40.

out the truth in the voluminous, often con-
tentious, literature of lore and legend.

Prince Hall was born in 1735; his parents and birthplace are unknown. His name
is first seen during the 1740s as the slave of
one William Hall of Boston. In 1756 he fa-
thered a son, Primus, whose mother, Delia,
was a servant in another household. (Primus
would be a soldier in the war for independence and thereafter lead a long and useful
life as a citizen of Boston.) Six years later,
when Prince was twenty-seven, he joined
the Congregational Church "in full communion"; shortly thereafter, presumably a wid-
ower, he married Sarah Ritchie, a slave.
During the spring of 1770, a month after
the Boston Massacre, his master presented
him with a certificate of manumission
which attested to the fact that he was "no
longer Reckoned a slave, but [had] been always accounted as a free man." That summer, Sarah dead, he took to wife Flora
Gibbs of Gloucester.

Prince Hall is first listed as a voter in
1780, and for the next decade he appears on
the tax lists as Grandmaster of the Masonic
lodge, leather dresser, and black huckster
with a small house and leather workshop.
During this period he conducted a business
as a caterer and leather dresser at the "sine of
the Golden Fleece," which was also a meeting place for the African Lodge.

Did Prince Hall fight in the revolution?
George Washington Williams and Carter
Woodson state he did and with credit. Others have held that with Peter Salem and
Salem Poor he fired a round at Bunker Hill.
But military records of the time reveal at
least six black Prince Halls of Massachusetts
in the army and navy of the revolution. It is
probable that the future Worshipful Master
of the black Masons was one of these. What
is sure is that, whether or not he fought in
the revolution as a front-line soldier, he did
render it a service as a skilled craftsman, for

there still exists a bill he sent to Colonel
Crafts of the Boston Regiment of Artillery
on April 24, 1777, for five leather drumheads [fig. 138].

This ends the speculative part of Prince
Hall's biography. The rest of his life, to his
death at seventy-two in 1807, is fairly clear
in its larger outlines.

ON March 6, 1775, six weeks before the
skirmishes at Lexington and Concord,
Prince Hall and fourteen other free blacks
became members of an army lodge of Free
and Accepted Masons attached to a British
regiment stationed in Boston. When the
British left the city, the black Masons who
remained behind were given a qualified permit to meet as a lodge. They would have to
wait until the end of the war for a permanent charter. Given their need to get together, why did Prince Hall and his friends
choose to join the Masons? Recall the five
petitions of Boston's blacks to the General
Court in 1773 and 1774. (When James
Swan, Son of Liberty in the tea party caper,
reprinted his argument against slavery in
1773, contending that "no country can be
called free where there is one slave," he revealed that he had done so "at the earnest
desire of the Negroes in Boston.") Recall
that these petitions had been fruitless, and
that Abigail Adams had written John of a
"conspiracy of the negroes," who had drawn
up a "petition to the [British] Governor,
telling him that they would fight for him
provided he would arm them, and engage to
liberate them if he conquered." Was this
Prince Hall's mood as he listened to the
white British officers inviting him to become a member of the army lodge? Or was
it simply that "true Masonry," as he often
repeated, had "something in it Divine and
Noble and Diffuses Universal love to all
Mankind"? One thing seems certain: searching for a form of solidarity that might struc-

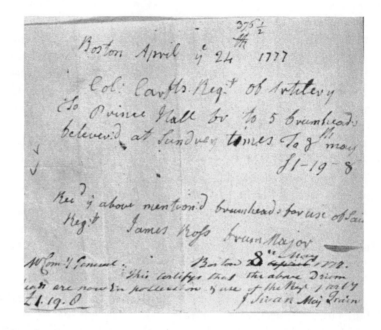

138. Bill of sale for drumheads, Prince Hall to Boston Regiment of Artillery, April 24, 1777. Massachusetts Archives, 151:375½.

ture the efforts of the petitioners, when the offer came from the British Masons, his organizing mind saw it as a possibility of a sort. Seize the day!

Two years later, on January 13, 1777, eight blacks of Boston and nearby signed a petition to the General Court "humbly" demanding the abolition of slavery. The four signers heading the list—Lancaster Hill, Peter Bess, Brister Slenser, and Prince Hall—were Masons. What they signed was, in fact, an almost exact copy of the petition rejected by Governor Gage on May 25, 1774—with a few additional sentences that updated it to the second year of the revolution. Abolish slavery and restore "the Natural Right of all Men," Hall and his fellow petitioners beseeched the legislature, so that the "Inhabitanc of these Stats" might no longer be "chargeable with the inconsistancey of acting themselves the part which thay condem and oppose in others. . . ." Although Hall and his friends were not alone in making the demand—a few white allies drew up a bill to abolish the nefarious

practice—in the end the legislature passed the buck by referring the matter to the Congress of the Confederation. The abolition of slavery in Massachusetts, by judicial construction, would have to wait until the close of the war.

For the next five years the town records list Hall as taxpayer and voter, but there is no news of the lodge. No doubt many of its members were away, serving in the ranks on land and sea. But the lodge survived. When, in December 1782, the black Masons celebrated their traditional Feast of St. John, a Boston newspaper reporting the event facetiously referred to the "St. Blacks Lodge of Free and Accepted Masons." The reply was restrained but angry: "with due submission to the public, our title is not St. Black's Lodge; neither do we aspire after high titles. But our only desire is that the Great Architect of the Universe would diffuse in our hearts the true spirit of Masonry, which is love to God and universal love to all mankind. These I humbly conceive to be the two grand pillars of Masonry. Instead of a splendid entertainment, we had an agreeable one in brotherly love." The letter was signed—"Prince Hall, Master of the African Lodge No. 1, Dedicated to St. John."

The African Lodge, however, was still without a charter. Two years later, in March 1784, Hall wrote to London: "this Lodge hath been founded almost eight years and we have had only a Permit to Walk on St. John's Day and to Bury our Dead in manner and form . . . we hope [you] will not deny us nor treat us Beneath the rest of our fellowmen, although Poor yet Sincere Brethren of the Craft." London was eager to grant the charter, but red tape delayed its delivery for three years. Finally, Captain James Scott, a brother-in-law of John Hancock, carried it over the ocean in the spring of 1787. African Lodge No. 1, renumbered 459, was now formally organized with Prince Hall as Master.

THE years 1786 and 1787 were a time of trouble in Massachusetts. The sound of the auctioneer's hammer was loud in the land. A new revolution had broken out on the mortgaged farms in the western half of the state. In the county conventions and in the guerrilla bands, veterans of the war, like black Moses Sash of Worthington, who had returned to debt-ridden fields, demanded of the legislature a moratorium on sales and evictions, emergency grants of paper money, the curbing of the courts, and abolition of the lawyers. It was only after a pitched battle at Springfield Arsenal in January 1787, when the army of Governor Bowdoin routed the insurgent troops under Captain Daniel Shays, that the men of property and standing in the state were able to quiet their fears about agrarians and levelers taking over the State House in Boston.

What stand would Prince Hall and the African Lodge take on Shays Rebellion? The white Masons supported the government against the rebels. In an appraisal of their own interests, could the black city folk of Boston find much in common with the tax-laden farmers of the west? Among the few blacks who lived west of the Connecticut, were there even a handful who owned farms? Although slavery had already been abolished in Massachusetts as a result of court decisions, white hostility still abounded, and the battle for full citizenship had yet to be won. No doubt there was sympathy for the dispossessed of the countryside in the hearts of urban and maritime blacks, but there was also the problem of the survival of the black community in Boston. When, in the fall of 1786, a call went out for volunteers to march to the west, the black organizer made up his mind: "We, by the Providence of God, are members of a fraternity that not only enjoins upon us to be peaceable subjects to the civil powers where we reside," Prince Hall wrote to Governor Bowdoin at the end of November,

but it also forbids our having concern in any plot of conspiracies against the state where we dwell; and as it is the unhappy lot of this state at the present date, and as the meanest of its members must feel that want of a lawful and good government, and as we have been protected for many years under this once happy Constitution, so we hope, by the blessing of God, we may long enjoy that blessing; therefore, we, though unworthy members of this Commonwealth, are willing to help and support, as far as our weak and feeble abilities may become necessary in this time of trouble and confusion, as you in your wisdom shall direct us. That we may, under just and lawful authority, live peaceable lives in all godliness and honesty, is the hearty wish of your humble servants, the members of the African Lodge. . . .

Nine years later, the historian-minister Jeremy Belknap, after a conversation with Prince Hall, wrote to St. George Tucker in Virginia: "In time of the insurrection, 1786, they offered their service to Governor Bowdoin, to go against the insurgents, to the number of 700; but the council did not advise to send them, and indeed there was no necessity for their services." Seven hundred black troops seem a very large number—perhaps Prince Hall was speaking not only for the lodge, but also for the whole black community of coastal Massachusetts. Why did Governor Bowdoin and his council turn down Hall's offer? In November there was a great need for government troops—the crisis at Springfield Arsenal was a month in the future. Judge James Winthrop of Cambridge, writing in 1795, was of the opinion that "the Council did not think fit to accept of their aid, as the white officers might be unwilling to serve with them." Were the upper classes of the state still fearful of black conspiracy, a bit nervous about the idea of putting arms on the shoulders of seven hundred blacks?

PRINCE Hall's reaction to Bowdoin's rejection of his services may be illuminated by a subsequent communication he signed and sent a month later to the State House—a petition to the General Court by seventy-three "African Blacks," whose mood and message strike a note very different from that of their offer in November to join the fight against Shays [fig. 139]. This petition of January 4, 1787, is a remarkable document. During the spring of 1773, four Boston slaves had organized a movement to persuade the General Court to legislate for

a.

b.

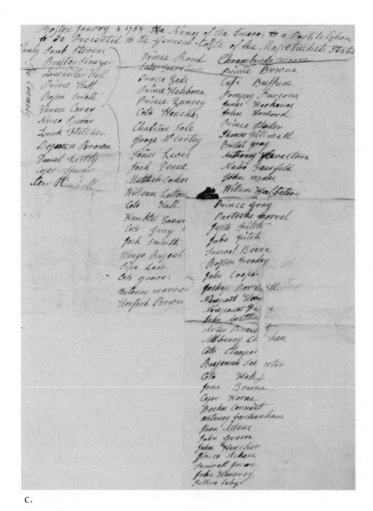

c.

139a–c. Petition to the General Court of Massachusetts, January 4, 1787, the African Petition. Massachusetts Archives, Unenacted Legislation; House Document #2358.

the "*Africans* . . . one day in a week to work for themselves" in order to earn enough to buy freedom and "leave the province . . . as soon as we can from our joynt labours procure money to transport ourselves to some part of the coast of Africa, where we propose a settlement." Now, fourteen years later, a committee of twelve of the African Lodge, headed by its Grand Master, Prince Hall, spelled out the idea of a return to the motherland in passionate detail, five years before the Tory black veterans sailed from Canada to Africa, twenty-three years before Captain Paul Cuffe's first voyage to Sierra Leone. The first major statement on the subject in Afro-American history—yet never printed from the original manuscript—it deserves to be better known:

. . . we, or our ancestors have been taken from all our dear connections, and brought from Africa and put into a state of slavery in this country; from which unhappy situation we have been lately in some measure delivered by the new constitution which has been adopted by this State, or by a free act of our former masters. But we yet find ourselves, in many respects, in very disagreeable and disadvantageous circumstances; most of which must attend us, so long as we and our children live in America.

This, and other considerations, which we need not here particularly mention, induce us earnestly to desire to return to Africa, our native country, which warm climate is much more natural and agreable to us; and, for which the God of nature has formed us; and, where we shall live among our equals, and be more comfortable and happy, than we can be in our present situation; and, at the same time, may have a prospect of usefulness to our brethren there.

This leads us humbly to propose the following plan to the consideration of this honourable Court. The soil of our native country is good, and produces the necessaries of life in great abundance. There are large tracts of uncultivated lands, which, if proper application were made for them, it is presumed, might be obtained, and would be freely given for those to settle upon, who shall be disposed to return to them. When this shall be effected by a number of Blacks, sent there for this purpose, who shall be thought most capable of making such an application, and transacting this business; then they who are disposed to go and settle there shall form themselves into a civil society, united by a political constitution, in which they shall agree. And those who are disposed, and shall be thought qualified, shall unite, and be formed into a religious society, or christian church; and have one or more blacks ordained as their pastors or Bishops: And being thus formed, shall remove to Africa, and settle on said lands.

These must be furnished with nec-

essary provisions for the voyage; and with farming utensils necessary to cultivate the land; and with the materials which cannot at present be obtained there, and which will be needed to build houses and mills.

The execution of this plan will, we hope, be the means of inlightening and civilizing those nations, who are now sunk in ignorance and barbarity; and may give opportunity to those who shall be disposed, and engaged to promote the salvation of their heathen brethren, to spread the knowledge of Christianity among them, and perswade them to embrace it. And schools may be formed to instruct their youth and children, and christian knowledge be spread through many nations who now are in gross darkness; and christian churches be formed, and the only true God and Saviour be worshiped and honoured through that vast extent of country, where are now the habitations of cruelty under the reign of the prince of darkness.

This may also lay a happy foundation for a friendly and lasting connection between that country and the united States of America, by a mutual intercourse and profitable commerce, which may much more than overbalance all the expence which is now necessary in order to carry this plan into effect.

This leads us to observe, that we are poor and utterly unable to prosecute this scheme or to return to Africa, without assistance. Money is wanted to enable those who shall be appointed, to go to Africa, and procure lands to settle upon; and to obtain a passage for us and our families; and to furnish us with necessary provisions, and the utensils and articles that have been mentioned.

We therefore humbly and earnestly apply to this honourable Court, hoping and praying that in your wisdom and goodness, you concert and prosecute the best method to relieve and assist us either by granting a brief for a collection in all the congregations in this State, or in any other way, which shall to your wisdom appear most expedient.

The House accepted the petition—and quickly buried it in committee: yet Boston blacks for a time were hopeful that the General Court would look with favor upon their back-to-Africa plan. The Court, they thought, "will grant us all we Require of them if we find a place to settle in."

It was not only a Boston plan, but a network of plans. One of the earliest efforts to achieve a minimum of collective security had been made at Newport, Rhode Island, during the fall of 1780, when Newport Gardner and a few friends established a Free African Union Society in that slave-trading town. At first, a prime aim of the society was to ensure the sheer survival of the black community's historic identity—to keep a record of births, deaths, and marriages, to assist members in time of distress, to find apprenticeships for young men seeking a trade. Three weeks after the Boston petition to return to Africa, the Newport Union negotiated a similar scheme with a friend of George Washington's, the philanthropist William Thornton, who was also in touch with black Masons in Boston. And there were links elsewhere. "We hartly agree with you in sending surcular Letters to our free Black to all States, as it will Strengthen our Number," wrote Samuel Stevens, a leading signer of the Boston petition, to Anthony Tyler in Newport on June 1, 1787. (In this letter, Stevens states that the Boston group does not want Thornton to arrange the exodus: "we think it would be better to charter a Vessel, and send some of our own Blacks.")

A return to Africa might seem the only solution in times of deepest despair. Meanwhile for Prince Hall and his friends there were battles to be fought on the home front. Nine months after the petition, in October 1787, he was ready with another "petition of a great number of blacks, freemen of this Commonwealth," this time an assault on the system of racist discrimination in education. Taxed as citizens, and

> willing to pay our equal part of these burdens, we are of the humble opinion that we have the right to enjoy the privileges of free men. But that we do not will appear in many instances, and we beg leave to mention one out of many, and that is of the education of our children which now receive no benefit from the free schools in the town of Boston, which we think is a great grievance, as by woful experience we now feel the want of a common education. We, therefore, must fear for our rising offspring to see them in ignorance in a land of gospel light . . . and for no other reason can be given [but] this [that] they are black. . . .

Denial of free schools for black freemen was indeed "a great grievance," but during the following winter the institution of slavery flourishing in the rest of the country struck a harder blow at their very existence. In early February 1788, three black Bostonians, named Wendham, Cato, and Luck (a Mason), were decoyed by Captain Solomon Babson aboard his sloop *Ruby* with the promise of work. While they were toiling in the hold, the ship set sail for Salem, where,

according to the *American Herald,* "he invei-
gled a number more of unfortunate blacks
on board." Prince Hall lost no time in rallying the Masons to protest the outrage. On
February 27, once more a "greet Number of
Blacks" addressed a petition to the General
Court. "It is a truly original and curious
performance," confided the Reverend
Jeremy Belknap to a friend, "written by the
Grand Master of the Black Lodge," and
signed by twenty-two of its members,
"justly Allarmed at the enhuman and cruel
Treetment that Three of our Brethren free
citizens of the Town of Boston lately Re-
ceved":

> What then are our lives and Lebeties
> worth if they may be taken a way in
> shuch a cruel & unjust manner . . .
> we are not uncensebel that the good
> Laws of this State forbedes all such
> base axones: Notwithstanding we can
> aseuer your Honners that maney of
> our free blacks . . . have Entred on
> bord of vessels as seamen *and* have
> been sold for Slaves . . . maney of us
> who are good seamen are oblidge to
> stay at home thru fear. . . .

The grievance went beyond the incident to
the source of the outrage—the slave trade
itself:

> your Petetioners have for sumtime
> past Behald whith greef ships cleared
> out from this Herber for Africa and
> there they ether steal or case others to
> steal our Brothers & sisters fill there
> ships holes full of unhappy men &
> women crouded together, then set out
> to find the Best markets seal them
> there like sheep for the slarter and
> then Returne hear like Honest men;
> after haven sported with the Lives and
> Lebeties fello men and at the same
> time call themselves Christions:
> Blush o Hevens at this.

The previous year the Quakers of Boston
had urged the legislature to put an end to
the slave trade. The petition of the black
Masons now spurred the Boston clergy to do
likewise. The threefold pressure in the General Court was effective: on March 26 the
Court passed an act "to prevent the Slave
Trade, and for granting Relief to the Families of such unhappy Persons as may be
Kidnapped or decoyed away from this Commonwealth."

Meanwhile, Governor Hancock and the
French consul in Boston had sent letters to
the governors of all the islands of the West
Indies advising them of the crime. The outcome was an unexpectedly happy one. "I
have one piece of good news to tell you,"
wrote Belknap, in high spirits:

> The Negroes who were kidnapped
> from hence last winter are returned.
> They were carried to St. Bar-
> tholomew's and offered for sale. One
> of them was a sensible fellow, and a
> Free mason. The merchant to whom
> they were offered was of this frater-
> nity; they were soon acquainted; the
> negro told his story, they were carried
> before the governor, with the ship
> master and the supercargo. . . .

When, at the end of July, the three kidnapped men returned to Boston, the African
Lodge arranged the festivities. "The morning after their arrival here," Belknap continued, "they made me a visit, being
introduced by Prince Hall, who is one of the
head men among the blacks in this town.
The interview was affecting—There, said
Prince, this is the gentleman who was so
much your friend, and petitioned the Court
for us—alluding to the share which I had in
the petition against the slave trade. They
joined in thanking me. . . ."

A battle had been organized and won; it
was a glad morning for Hall. But there was

a flaw in the victory. While the gentlemen of the General Court were willing to stifle the slave trade with Africa, they were not yet ready to treat people of color as full citizens. Thus, a day after the Court had closed the ports of the state to slave ships from Africa, the same Court, ostensibly to reduce the cost of pauperism, ruled that blacks who fled slavery would no longer be tolerated in the land of the free. Indeed, any "African or Negro" resident of the Commonwealth who could not produce "a certificate from the Secretary of State" in which he had formerly lived as a "citizen" would be jailed and whipped if, after legal warning, he did not get out. Whether the state enforced this draconian measure, the record does not disclose. Doubtless, it forced many fugitives to take up their travels once more. If, under the new federal constitution, the Commonwealth was to be legally obligated to cooperate with slave catchers, the Massachusetts act might be interpreted, from one point of view, as premature compliance with the nation's new systemic slavery.

When, during the following year, Prince Hall's friend John Marrant, the new chaplain of the African Lodge, delivered his sermon at the annual Festival of St. John, his excoriation of the sins of white chauvinism was doubtless directed against this inhuman law. (In 1800, fourteen years after the Shays Rebellion, when news arrived in Boston that Gabriel Prosser had tried to organize an insurrection of the slaves in Virginia, a "Notice to Blacks" appeared in the newspapers of Massachusetts listing the names and places of two hundred and forty "Africans or Negroes . . . Indians and Mulattoes," warning them "to depart out of this commonwealth." One-fourth of the banished blacks were members of the African Society of Boston. In Philadelphia, *The Gazette of the United States* reprinted the news item with this remark: "The following

notice has been published in the Boston papers: It seems probable, from the nature of the notice, that some suspicions of the design of the negroes are entertained, and we regret to say there is too much cause.")

IN 1792 Prince Hall gave the discourse in Charlestown celebrating the Festival of St. John, duly published as *A Charge Delivered to the Brethren of the African Lodge on the 25th of June, 1792* [fig. 140]. Careful, as usual, to proclaim that black Masons had had "no hand in any plots or conspiracies or rebellion," he was impatient that black taxpayers were still denied free schools for their children. Four years later, he would memorialize the selectmen of Boston on that subject and finally establish a school for black children in his own house. Still irked by the decree of expulsion, which Marrant had blasted in his annual sermon in 1789, and further irritated by the hostility of white Masons to the African Lodge, he traced the early history of Freemasonry from the defense of Jerusalem by the Order of St. John to the establishment of Christianity south of the Mediterranean by "our Fathers," the African saints—and focused his points in a "Query":

> Whether at that day, when there was an African church, and perhaps the largest Christian church on earth, whether, if they were all whites, they would refuse to accept them as their fellow Christians and brother Masons; or whether there were any so weak, or rather foolish, as to say, because they were blacks, they would make their lodge or army too common or too cheap? Sure this was not our conduct in the late war; for then they marched shoulder to shoulder, brother soldier and brother soldier, to the field of battle. . . .

A

CHARGE

Delivered to the Brethren of the

AFRICAN LODGE

On the 25th of June, 1792.

At the Hall of Brother WILLIAM SMITH,

IN CHARLESTOWN.

By the Right Worshipful Master

PRINCE HALL.

Printed at the Request of the Lodge.

Printed and Sold at the Bible and Heart, Cornhill, Boston.

140. Prince Hall, *A Charge Delivered to the Bretheren of the African Lodge on 25th of June, 1792* (Boston, 1792). Courtesy of the Library of Congress.

The answer is clear: "he that despises a black man for the sake of his colour, reproacheth his Maker. . . ."

The abrasive attitudes of white Masons continued to rankle. Belknap, investigating the situation in 1795, asked "a white gentleman of the craft, of good information and candour" for his opinion. "The African Lodge, though possessing a charter from England," he replied, "meet by themselves; and white masons not more skilled in geometry, will not acknowledge them. . . . The truth is, they are *ashamed* of being on *equality* with blacks." When Belknap queried

Prince Hall, his answer was circumspect, but closed on a taut, ironic note:

> Harmony in general prevails between us as citizens, for the good law of the land does oblige every one to live peaceably with all his fellow citizens, let them be black or white, We stand on a level, therefore no preeminence can be claimed on either side. As to our associating, there is here a great number of worthy good men and good citizens, that are not ashamed to take an African by the hand; but yet there are to be seen the weeds of pride, envy, tyranny, and scorn, in this garden of peace, liberty and equality.

Life was hard for black Bostonians, not only because of the violations of their rights as citizens, but also because it was hard for them to make a living. In 1796, twenty years after Hall had pioneered the African Lodge, there was a felt need for another association "for the mutual benefit of each other"—to find jobs for the children, support the widowed, attend the sick, and bury the dead. The new African Society of Boston would print its *Laws* for all to see. Among its forty founders was Ceazer Fayerweather, who in 1777, like James Forten, had been a powder boy on a revolutionary frigate. In 1808 one of its members would publish for the society an eloquent tract: *The Sons of Africans: An Essay on Freedom . . .* [fig. 141].

IN June 1797 in West Cambridge, the "Right Worshipful Prince Hall" again addressed the African Lodge at the Feast of St. John [fig. 142]. After recalling those brethren who had departed "to the Grand Lodge above" and flaying the merchants who traded in human flesh, he described certain "weeds of pride, envy, tyranny, and

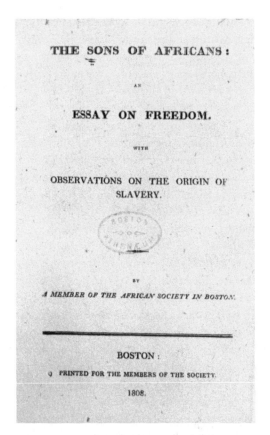

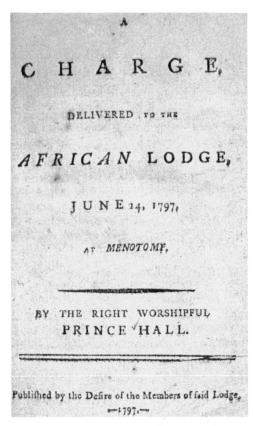

141. *The Sons of Africans: An Essay on Freedom* . . . (Boston, 1808). Library of the Boston Athenaeum.

142. Prince Hall, *A Charge Delivered to the African Lodge, June 24, 1797, at Menotomy* (Boston, 1797). Courtesy of the Library of Congress.

scorn, in this garden of peace, liberty and equality":

> Patience I say, for were we not possess'd of a great measure of it you could not bear up under the daily insults you meet with in the streets of Boston: much more on public days of recreation, how are you shamefully abus'd, and that at such a degree that you may truly be said to carry your lives in your hands, and the arrows of death are flying about your heads; helpless old women have their clothes torn off their backs, even to the exposing of their nakedness; and by

whom are these disgraceful and abusive actions committed, not by the men born and bred in Boston, for they are better bred; but by a mob or horde of shameless, low-lived, envious, spiteful persons, some of them not long since, servants in gentlemen's kitchens, scouring knives, tending horses, and driving chaise . . . many in town who hath seen their behaviour to you, and that without provocation—twenty or thirty cowards fall upon one man—have wonder'd at the patience of the Blacks: 'tis not for want of courage in you, for they know that they dare not face you man for man, but in a mob, which we despise. . . .

Yet, all was not gloom. In Haiti, black leaders had arisen to change the course of imperialist history:

> My brethren, let us not be cast down under these and many other abuses we at present labour under: for the darkest is before the break of day. My brethren, let us remember what a dark day it was with our African brethren six years ago, in the French West-Indies. Nothing but the snap of the whip was heard from morning to evening; hanging, broken on the wheel, burning, and all manner of tortures inflicted on those unhappy people for nothing else but to gratify their masters pride, wantonness, and cruelty: but blessed by God, the scene is changed; they now confess that God hath no respect of persons, and therefore receive them as their friends, and treat them as brothers. Thus doth Ethiopia begin to stretch forth her hand, from a sink of slavery to freedom and equality.

If genuine liberty had begun "to dawn in some of the West-Indian islands, then, sure enough, God would act for justice in New England too, and let Boston and the World know, that He hath no respect of persons; and that that bulwark of envy, pride, scorn and contempt, which is so visible to be seen in some . . . shall fall, to rise no more." This, in fact, was the message of the great organizer and lawgiver Moses, who had been "instructed by his father-in-law, Jethro, an Ethiopean" in "the first and grandest lecture that Moses ever received from the mouth of man. . . ." It was in this mood during the same month that Prince

Hall headed for Philadelphia to charter its first African Lodge and to install the Reverend Absalom Jones—who had just launched the benevolent Friendly Society of his St. Thomas's African Church—as its Worshipful Master [fig. 143].

The charge delivered to the lodge at West Cambridge was Prince Hall's last published utterance. He still had ahead of him a decade of useful work. In June 1807, testifying in a legal process, he stated that he was "a leatherdresser and labourer aged about seventy years," but the Reverend William Bentley, Hall's good friend, in his diary entry for September 20 of the same year, referred to him as "the leading African of Boston & author of several masonic addresses." A fortnight later, he was dead. Six Boston newspapers printed the obituary of "Mr. Prince Hall, aged 72, Master of the African Lodge." His funeral was a Masonic one. The following year his brethren of the lodge honored the great black organizer and servant of his people by changing its name to the "Prince Hall Grand Lodge."

On January 1, 1808, President Jefferson signed a bill that put an end to American participation in the Atlantic slave trade. At a celebration of the historic event, two hundred black Bostonians marched through the streets to the African Meeting House for a service of thanksgiving.

Olaudah Equiano: The Image of Africa

The first name that comes to my mind is Olaudah Equiano, better known as Gustavus Vassa, the African. Equiano was an Ibo, I believe from the village of Iseke in the Orlu division of Eastern Nigeria. . . . In 1789 he published his life story, a beautifully written document which, among other things, set down for the Europe of his time something of the

CONSTITUTION

AND

R U L E S

TO BE

O B S E R V E D AND K E P T

BY THE

FRIENDLY SOCIETY

OF

St. Thomas's African Church,

OF

P H I L A D E L P H I A.

PHILADELPHIA:

PRINTED BY W. W. WOODWARD, No. 17, CHESNUT-
STREET.

1797.

143. *Constitution and Rules . . . the Friendly Society of St. Thomas's African Church of Philadelphia* (Philadelphia, 1797). The Library
Company of Philadelphia.

life and habit of his people in Africa in an
attempt to counteract the lies and slander
invented by some Europeans to justify the
slave trade.

CHINUA ACHEBE, *Morning Yet on
Creation Day*

Even as white America fought for its own
nationhood, it carried on a war against the
nations of Africa, shipping across the ocean
cargoes of captives, each a member of a nation and a culture in the black motherland.
The paradox troubled not a few patriots,

but by 1776 the apologists of slavery had
easily resolved it as they fashioned a grand
strategy for the suppression of white guilt
and black revolt. Let the "Dark Continent"
be construed as actual Hell, the abode of the
devil and total depravity—a nonplace in-
habited by nonpeople—and let this be believed as gospel truth. Ergo, was it not
right to destroy the memory of the motherland—of its tongues, its arts, its wis-
doms—in the minds of the enslaved, to
erase all sense of an honorable and historic
identity, to obliterate the very image of Africa, so that the kidnapped, robbed of their
heritage, might be divided, ruled, and de-
nationalized by the new nation? How else
explain the fact that during the first two
centuries of slavery in America only a few
black voices, furnishing images of a real Africa and real Africans, were permitted in
print to demolish the myth of a nonpast?

MOST eloquent of these voices was that of a
black man who in his boyhood had been the
subject of an African king and who lived the
rest of his days as slave and freeman in Europe and America [fig. 144]. When in 1789
he gave to the world *The Interesting Narrative
of the Life of Olaudah Equiano, or Gustavus
Vassa,* he was careful to complete his title
with the words, *the African, Written by Himself* [fig. 145]. The added phrase gives the
timbre of his voice, for the writer, neither
Afro-American nor Anglo-African, was indeed an African, speaking for the black family of the pan-African world. Not long after
Phillis Wheatley's death, he too became a
transatlantic celebrity* when the twelve

---

*In 1813 the names of Olaudah Equiano and Phil-
lis Wheatley would be linked in an edition of his *Narrative* and her *Poems,* published in Halifax [fig. 147].
In 1829 an illustrated juvenile edition of the *Narrative*
with antislavery poems by the English poet William
Cowper was published in New York, edited by

144. Unknown artist, *Portrait of Olaudah Equiano (Gustavus Vassa)*, oil, 18th C. English School, ca. 1780. Royal Albert Memorial Museum, Exeter.

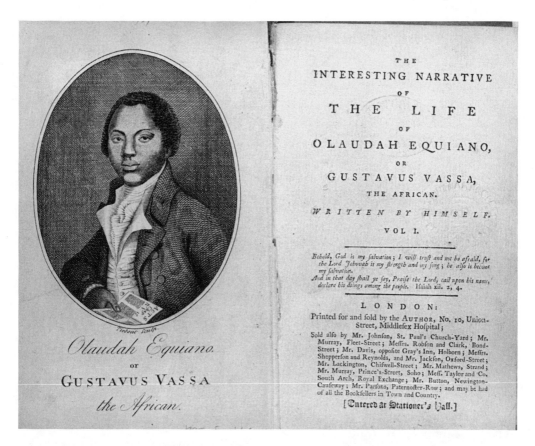

145. *The Interesting Narrative of the Life of Olaudah Equiano, or Gustavus Vassa, the African, Written By Himself,* 2 vols. (London, 1789). The Library Company of Philadelphia.

chapters of his *Narrative,* printed first in London and then, in 1791, in New York—with his bold ebony face looking out of the frontispiece—ran through eight editions in five years [fig. 146]. One of "the rarest historical documents," Charles H. Nichols has

Abigail Mott, a white abolitionist, for use as a text in the African Free Schools [fig. 148]. Olaudah Equiano's *Narrative* was widely read. In an old cemetery on Nantucket Island still stand the weatherbeaten gravestones of the black Boston family of mariners, whose most celebrated member was Captain Absalom F. Boston, who in 1822 made a famous whaling voyage in a vessel manned by black officers and an all-black crew. The carving on one of the stones reads: "Olaudo H. / Son of / Wm M. Boston / Died Nov. 21 / 1836, aged / 10 Years."

rightly called it in his compendious study of the slave narrative. A classic of its genre, probing a wide range of deeply human themes and recounting the evolution of a bewildered, exiled slave into a statesman of his people, it surely ranks with the autobiographies of Benjamin Franklin and Frederick Douglass. Concrete and vigorous in the style of Defoe, there is a Swiftian quality in the tale of this black Gulliver who explores white worlds and opens wide his eyes in wonder and horror.

Olaudah Equiano, whose book, as he put it, was "the history of neither a saint, a hero, nor a tyrant," is a complex figure still awaiting a full-length portrait. What can be

146. *The interesting Narrative of the Life of Olaudah Equiano or Gustavus Vassa, the African, Written by himself,* 1st American ed. (New York, 1791). The Library Company of Philadelphia.

147. Olaudah Equiano, *The Interesting Narrative . . . To which are added Poems on Various Subjects,* by *Phillis Wheatley* (Halifax, 1813). Courtesy of the Library of Congress.

offered here is the merest sketch of his rich life with a few scattered passages, in his own good words, from *The Interesting Narrative.*

Equiano was born in the nation of Benin, eastern Nigeria, where the language was Ibo. "This Kingdom," he begins, "is divided into many provinces or districts: in one of the most remote and fertile of which, I was born, in the year 1745, situated in a charming fruitful vale, named Essaka. . . . I had never heard of white men or Euro-

peans, nor of the sea; and our subjection to the king of Benin was little more than nominal." His father, in whose household there were "many slaves," was an *enbrenche* or chief, and Essaka was ruled by its chiefs, who "decided disputes and punished crimes." In most cases, the trials were short and "the law of retaliation" prevailed: "Adultery, however, was sometimes punished with slavery or death; a punishment which I believe is inflicted on it throughout most of the nations of Africa: so sacred among them is the honour of the marriage bed. . . . The men, however, do not preserve the same constancy to their wives,

THE
LIFE AND ADVENTURES
OF
OLAUDAH EQUIANO;
OR
GUSTAVUS VASSA,
THE AFRICAN.
FROM AN ACCOUNT WRITTEN BY HIMSELF.

ABRIDGED
BY A. MOTT.

TO WHICH ARE ADDED
SOME REMARKS ON THE SLAVE TRADE, &c.

" AM I NOT A MAN AND A BROTHER."

" Ah pity human mis'ry, human wo!
" 'Tis what the happy to the unhappy owe."

NEW YORK:
PUBLISHED BY SAMUEL WOOD & SONS,
No. 261 Pearl-street.

R. & G. S. WOOD, PRINTERS.
1829.

148. *The Life and Adventures of Olaudah Equiano* . . . Abridged by A. Mott . . . (New York, 1829). Courtesy, American Antiquarian Society.

which they expect from them; for they indulge in a plurality. . . ." The "mode of marriage" was a happy ritual; at the end of the ceremony there was a festival "celebrated with bonfires and loud acclamations of Joy, accompanied with music and dancing." Equiano says:

> We are almost a nation of dancers, musicians and poets. Thus every great event such as a triumphant return from battle or other cause of public rejoicing is celebrated in public dances. . . . The assembly is separated into four divisions, which dance either apart or in succession, and each with a character peculiar to itself. The first division contains the married men, who in their dances frequently exhibit feats of arms and the representation of a battle. To these succeed the married women, who dance in the second division. The young men occupy the third: and the maidens the fourth. Each represents some interesting scene of real life, such as a great achievement, domestic employment, a pathetic story, or some rural sport. . . . This gives our dances a spirit and variety which I have scarcely seen elsewhere. We have many musical instruments, particularly drums of different kinds, a piece of music which resembles a guitar, and another much like a stickado. These last are chiefly used by betrothed virgins, who play on them on all grand festivals.

The land was a happy and equal one—and its people beautiful:

> Every one contributes something to the common stock; and as we are unacquainted with idleness, we have no beggars. . . . Those benefits are felt by us in the general healthiness of the people, and in their vigour and activity; I might have added too in their comeliness. Deformity is indeed unknown amongst us, I mean that of shape . . . in regard to complexion, ideas of beauty are wholly relative. I remember while in Africa to have seen three negro children who were tawny, and another quite white, who were universally regarded by myself,

and the natives in general, as far as related to their complexions, as deformed. Our women too were in my eye, at least uncommonly graceful, alert, and modest to a degree of bashfulness. . . .

It was this kind of society that shaped the mind of Olaudah Equiano, the youngest and favorite son of his family: "I was trained up from my earliest years in the art of war: my daily exercise was shooting and throwing javelins; and my mother adorned me with emblems, after the manner of our greatest warriors." But the idyll came to an early, abrupt close: "In this way I grew up till I was turned the age of eleven when an end was put to my happiness. . . ."

Kidnapped by native raiders, carried southward in a sack, sold and resold (and observing, in the process, a variety of black societies), pampered as a slave in an African household, the young boy was eventually marched to the deck of a slave ship riding at anchor, waiting for cargo:

> I was immediately handled and tossed up to see if I were sound by some of the crew. . . . When I looked round the ship too and saw a large furnace or copper boiling and a multitude of black people of every description chained together, every one of their countenances expressing dejection and sorrow, I no longer doubted of my fate. . . . In a little time after, amongst the poor chained men I found some of my own nation, which in a small degree gave ease to my mind. . . .

The middle passage was a nightmare he could never shake off:

> The stench of the hold while we were on the coast was so intolerably loathsome, that it was dangerous to remain there for any time. . . . The closeness of the place, and the heat of the climate, added to the number in the ship, which was so crowded that each had scarcely room to turn himself, almost suffocated us. This produced copious perspirations, so that the air soon became unfit for respiration, from a variety of loathsome smells, and brought on a sickness among the slaves, of which many died. . . . This wretched situation was again aggravated by the galling of the chains, now become insupportable, and the filth of the necessary tubs, into which the children often fell. . . .

The experience decimated the boy, he wanted to die, and had to be force-fed with a whip. He had "never seen among any people such instances of brutal cruelty."

There was slavery in his own country, he later reflected, but the differences were crucial. When the traders passed through his village, "Sometimes indeed we sold slaves to them, but they were only prisoners of war, or such among us as had been convicted of kidnapping, or adultery, and some other crimes which we esteemed heinous. . . ."

> When a trader wants slaves he applied to a chief for them and tempts him with his wares. It is not extraordinary if on this occasion he yields to the temptation with as little firmness, and accepts the price of his fellow creatures liberty with as little reluctance as the enlightened merchant. Accordingly he falls on his neighbors and a desperate battle ensues. If he prevails and takes prisoners, he gratifies his avarice by selling them; but if his party be vanquished and he falls into the hands of the enemy, he is put to death . . . no ransom can save

him. . . . The spoils were divided according to the merit of the warriors. Those prisoners which were not sold or redeemed we kept as slaves: but how different was their condition from that of the slaves in the West Indies! With us they do no more work than other members of the community, even their master; their food, clothing and lodging were nearly the same as theirs, (except that they were not permitted to eat with those who were freeborn), and there was scarce any other difference between them. . . . Some of these slaves have even slaves under them as their own property and for their own use. . . .

ARRIVING at Bridge-Town, Barbados, Equiano was "conducted immediately to the merchant's yard, where we were all pent up together like so many sheep in a fold." A few days after, at the auction, he began to understand the slave masters' strategy of divide and rule: "I remember . . . there were several brothers, who in the sale were sold in different lots." Their "cries at parting" moved him thirty years later to cry out:

O, ye nominal Christians! might not an African ask you, learned you this from your God, who says unto you, Do unto all men as you would men should do unto you? Is it not enough that we are torn from our country and friends, to toil for your luxury and lust of gain? . . . Are the dearest friends and relations, now rendered more dear by their separation from their kindred, still to be parted from each other, and thus prevented from cheering the gloom of slavery with the small comfort of being together and mingling their sufferings and sorrows?

Shipped to a Virginia plantation, "constantly grieving and pining, and wishing for death," he was summoned from the fields to the big house one hot day and ordered to fan his master. What he saw in the kitchen turned his stomach: "A black woman slave . . . was cooking the dinner, and the poor creature was cruelly loaded with various kinds of iron machines; she had one particularly on her head, which locked her mouth so fast that she could scarcely speak; and could not eat nor drink. . . ." This contrivance was called "the iron muzzle."

One day Pascal, a lieutenant in the royal navy which was visiting Virginia, purchased Equiano for thirty sterling pounds and gave him a new name, Gustavus Vassa. His life for the next few years as the lieutenant's slave opened up new vistas for the precocious lad. He stayed from time to time in the houses of the lieutenant's friends, went to school at odd moments and gathered the knowledge that would later help him as shipping clerk and navigator, began to think about the Christian religion, and got himself baptized. With Pascal, he served in the expedition against Louisbourg and in the maneuvers of Admiral Boscawen in the Mediterranean during the Seven Years War. When the British sailed from Halifax to Cape Breton, he remembered, "We had the good and gallant General Wolfe on board our ship, whose affability made him highly esteemed and beloved by all the men. He often honoured me, as well as other boys, with marks of his notice, and saved me once a flogging for the fighting with a young gentleman."

But at the end of the war, Pascal, who had promised to free his intrepid servant, betrayed him and sold him to James Doran, master of the *Sally,* on his way to the West Indies. For the next three years, from 1763 to 1766, Equiano had the bitter chance to

observe and analyze the nature of bondage
in the Caribbean. At Montserrat, Captain
Doran sold the eighteen-year-old youth to
"Mr. Robert King, a Quaker, and the first
merchant in the place," who promised to
send him to school in order to improve his
arithmetic and train him as a clerk. Equiano's portrait of this tight-fisted Quaker
dealer in all sorts of goods, including black
flesh and blood—he was no John Woolman
or Anthony Benezet—is a small master-
piece:

> Mr. King dealt in all manner of mer-
> chandises, and kept from one to six
> clerks. He loaded many vessels in a
> year; particularly to Philadelphia,
> where he was born, and was con-
> nected with a great mercantile house
> in that city. He had besides many ves-
> sels and droggers, of different sizes,
> which used to go about the island;
> and others, to collect rum, sugar, and
> other goods. I understood boats very
> well . . . and this hard work . . . in
> the sugar seasons used to be my con-
> stant employment. I have rowed the
> boat, and slaved at the oars, from one
> hour to sixteen in the twenty-
> four. . . .

And as he toiled to enrich his master, he observed the misery of his brother slaves. As
bad as King was, other masters were worse:
"In going about the different estates on the
island, I had all the opportunity I could
wish for to see the dreadful usage of the poor
men; usage that reconciled me to my situation, and made me bless God for the hands
into which I had fallen." Indeed, King had
found a good thing in Equiano:

> There was scarcely any part of his
> business, or household affairs, in
> which I was not occasionally engaged.
> I often supplied the place of a clerk,

> in receiving and delivering cargoes to
> the ships in tending stores, and deliv-
> ering goods: and besides this, I used
> to shave and dress my master when
> convenient, and take care of his
> horse. . . . I worked likewise on
> board of different vessels of his . . .
> and saved him, as he used to acknowl-
> edge, above a hundred pounds a year.

Longing to purchase his liberty, cruising the
islands, he began trading in small articles to
amass the sum that King would demand;
but at times, the inhumanity of white to
black in the islands nearly drove him ber-
serk: "The reader cannot but judge of the
irksomeness of this situation to a mind like
mine, in being daily exposed to new hard-
ships and imposition, after having seen
many better days, and been as it were, in a
state of freedom and plenty; added to
which, every part of the world I had hitherto been in seemed to me a paradise in
comparison of the West-Indies."

Equiano was never a Gabriel Prosser or a
Nat Turner—indeed, in his earlier years,
while he strove stubbornly for his own freedom, there is at times in the *Narrative* a certain fatalism in his thinking about the
possibility of general emancipation:

> My mind was . . . hourly replete
> with inventions and thoughts of
> being freed, And, if possible, by hon-
> est and honourable means; for I al-
> ways remembered the old adage . . .
> that "Honesty is the best policy";
> [from Poor Richard?] And likewise
> that other golden precept—"To do
> unto all men as I would they should
> do unto me." However, as I was from
> early years a predestinarian, I thought
> whatever fate had determined must
> ever come to pass, and therefore, if
> ever it were my lot to be freed
> nothing could prevent me, although I

should at present see no means or hope to obtain my freedom; on the other hand if it were my fate not to be freed I never should be so, and all my endeavours for that purpose would be fruitless. In the midst of these thoughts I therefore looked up with prayers anxiously to God for my liberty; and at the same time used every honest means, and did all that was possible on my part to obtain it.

Yet, even as he "became master of a few pounds" of freedom money, "dishonest" means were not entirely excluded:

I determined to make every exertion to obtain my freedom and to return to Old England. For this purpose I thought a knowledge of navigation might be of use to me; for, though I did not intend to run away unless I should be ill used; yet, in such a case, if I understood navigation, I might attempt my escape in our sloop, which was one of the swiftest sailing vessels in the West Indies, and I could be at no loss for hands to join me . . . but this, as I said, was only to be in the event of my meeting with any ill usage. I therefore employed the mate of our vessel to teach me navigation, for which I agreed to give him twenty-four dollars. . . .

In the Caribbean, however, a black seaman who was a slave might find himself ferrying his manacled brothers from market to market. Thus, at the end of 1764, Equiano's captain sailed for South Carolina with "a load of new slaves"—"live cargo" they were called—and a little later "took slaves on board for St. Estatia, and from thence to Georgia." Back in Montserrat, "we took in, as usual, some of the poor oppressed natives

of Africa" and "set off again for Georgia and Charles Town."

He had a narrow escape in Savannah. One Sunday night, as he exchanged pleasantries with a few black friends,

it happened that their Master, one Doctor Perkins, who was a very severe and cruel man, came in drunk; and not liking to see any strange negroes in his yard, he and a ruffian of a white man, he had in his service, beset me in an instant, and both of them struck me with the first weapons they could get hold of. I cried out as long as I could for help and mercy; but, though I gave a good account of myself. . . . They beat and mangled me in a shameful manner, leaving me near dead. I lost so much blood from the wounds I received, that I lay quite motionless, and was so benumbed that I could not feel anything for many hours. Early in the morning they took me away to the jail.

In Philadelphia—a heaven compared with Savannah—where all Friends were not of Robert King's caliber, he sold his own goods "chiefly to the Quakers," who "always appeared to be a very honest discreet sort of people, and never attempted to impose" on him. It was there that he heard the inspired George Whitefield preach: "When I got into the church I saw this pious man exhorting the people with the greatest fervour and earnestness, and sweating as much as I ever did in slavery on Montserrat beach."

At last, during the summer of 1766, the great day dawned. Equiano, just twenty-one, with forty pounds in his pocket to buy himself free, shamed his unwilling master into keeping his promise—King was forced to admit that he had been clearing one hundred pounds a year on his slave's labor—and then taking him on as a free "able-bodied sailor at thirty-six shillings per month." Although Equiano was overjoyed to return to his "original free African state," he had few illusions about the good life for a black freeman in America. Even in Philadelphia,

> were it not for the benevolence of the Quakers in that city many of the sable race who now breathe the air of liberty would, I believe, be groaning indeed under some planter's chains. . . . Hitherto, I had thought only slavery dreadful, but the state of a free negro appeared to me now equally so at least, and in some respects even worse, for they live in constant alarm for their liberty; and this is but nominal, for they are universally insulted and plundered without the possibility of redress. . . .

"In this situation," he asked, "is it surprising that slaves, when mildly treated, should prefer even the misery of slavery to such a mockery of freedom?"

Farther south, in Georgia, the situation of the free black was even more perilous. During the summer of his liberation, on a Savannah street the slave of a merchant, egged on by his owner, insulted him. When he dealt the slave a blow, the merchant threatened to have him "flogged all around the town." There is no fatalism in Equiano's reaction: "There was a free black man, a carpenter, that I knew, who, for asking a gentleman that he worked for for the money he had earned, was put into gaol; and afterwards this oppressed man was sent from Georgia, with false accusations, of an intention to set the gentleman's house on fire, and run away with his slaves." He would not allow himself to be flogged:

> I dreaded of all things, the thoughts of being striped as I never in my life had the marks of violence of that

kind. At that instant a rage seized my soul, and for a little I determined to resist the first man that should offer to lay violent hands on me, or basely use me without a trial; for I would sooner die like a free man, than suffer myself to be scourged by the hands of ruffians, and my blood drawn like a slave.

By good luck he foiled his torturers but swore never to go back to Savannah: "I thus took a final leave of Georgia; for the treatment I had received in it disgusted me very much against the place."

The West Indies were even more intolerable. The young black mariner had been building a reputation in the islands for his seamanship. On a voyage from Georgia, the captain died during a storm, the mate proved himself a bungler, and Equiano had to navigate the vessel back to Montserrat. "Many were surprised," he notes with pride, "when they heard of my conducting the sloop into the port, and I now obtained a new appelation, and was called Captain." Yet this was scant compensation for the systematic white brutality of the Caribbean. Returning to Georgia with a cargo of slaves in January 1767, an ignorant captain wrecked the boat on the shoals of the Bahamas:

> The captain immediately ordered the hatches to be nailed down on the slaves in the hold, where there were about twenty, all of whom must unavoidably have perished if he had been obeyed. . . . I asked him why? He said that every one would endeavour to get into the boat, which was but small, and thereby we should be drowned; for it would not have carried above ten at the most. I could no longer restrain my emotion and I told him he deserved drowning for not

knowing how to navigate the vessel . . . the hatches were not nailed down. . . .

"I was disgusted with the West Indies," he concludes, "and thought I never should be entirely free until I left them."

Equiano's acute observations of slavery in the Caribbean are an important source for the historical study of the system in its nuances of depravity. The quality of his outraged commentary may be judged by gathering a few of his passages on an aspect of the institution that interested him deeply—the miscegenation of black and white in the West Indies. Working on the vessels of his Quaker master, Robert King, he was "often a witness to cruelties of every kind, which were exercised" on his "unhappy fellow slaves":

> I used frequently to have different cargoes of new negroes in my care for sale; and it was almost a constant practice with our clerks, and other whites, to commit violent depredations on the chastity of the female slaves; and these I was, though with reluctance, obliged to submit to at all times, being unable to help them. . . . I have known our mates to commit these acts most shamefully, to the disgrace, not of Christians only, but of men. I have even known them gratify their brutal passions with females not ten years old; and these abominations some of them practised to such scandalous excess, that one of our captains discharged the mate and others on that account.

As against this literal rape of Africa, in Montserrat he saw

> a negro man staked to the ground, and cut most shockingly, and then his ears cut off bit by bit, because he had been connected with a white woman who was a common prostitute: as if it were no crime in the whites to rob an innocent African girl of her virtue, but most heinous in a black man only to gratify a passion of nature, where the temptation was offered by one of a different colour, though the most abandoned woman of her species.

For killing his own slave, whatever the reason, a law enacted by the Assembly of Barbados fined the murderer the sum of fifteen pounds:

> Mr. James Tobin . . . gives an account of a French planter of his acquaintance in the island of Martinique who showed him many mulattoes working in the fields like beasts of burden, and he told Mr. Tobin they were all the produce of his own loins! And I myself have known similar instances. Pray, reader, are these sons and daughters of the French planter less his children by being gotten on a black woman? And what must be the virtue of those legislators and the feelings of those fathers, who estimate the lives of their sons, however begotten, at no more than fifteen pounds. . . .

"But is not the slave trade," he asks, "entirely a war with the heart of man?" And then, a little later, an instance of the absurd:

> While I was in . . . St. Kitt's, a very curious imposition on human nature took place: A white man wanted to marry in the church a free black woman that had land and slaves in Montserrat, but the clergyman told him it was against the law of the place to marry a white and a black in the church. . . . The man then asked to be married on the water, to which the

parson consented, and the two lovers went in one boat and the parson and clerk in another, and thus the ceremony was performed.

When, in January 1767, Equiano climbed aboard the *Andromache,* bound for London, there were sad partings with black friends, but no regrets:

> I had free dances, as they are called, with some of my countrymen, previous to my setting off. . . . With a light heart I bade Montserrat farewell . . . and with it I bade adieu to the sound of the cruel whip, and all other dreadful instruments of torture; adieu to the offensive sight of the violated chastity of the sable female, which has too often accosted my eyes; adieu to oppressions, although to me less severe than most of my countrymen. . . .

So, a year after he had bought himself free, Olaudah Equiano quit America once and for all, as he then thought, to take up another kind of life in a more liberal place. But, now and then, as if driven by an anthropologist's zeal to add fresh data to his case, he would return to the land of the "cruel whip." In the spring of 1771 he shipped as a steward on a vessel bound for Madeira and Barbados—"once more to try my fortune in the West Indies"—and in the winter he voyaged to Jamaica, "a very fine large island, well peopled," where he was intrigued by the persistence of African mores:

> When I came to Kingston, I was surprised to see the number of Africans who were assembled together on Sundays; particularly at a large commodious place, called Spring Path. Here each different nation of Africa meet and dance after the manner of

their own country. They still retain most of their native costumes; they bury their dead, and put victuals, pipes and tobacco, and other things, in the grave with the corpse, in the same manner as in Africa.

But Jamaica, "the most considerable of the West Indian islands," was also a "scene of roguery":

> I saw many cruel punishments inflicted on the slaves in the short time I stayed there. In particular I was present when a poor fellow was tied up and kept hanging by the wrists at some distance from the ground, and then some half hundred weights were fixed to his ankles, in which posture he was flogged unmercifully. There were also, as I heard, two different masters noted for cruelty on the island, who had staked up two negroes naked, and in two hours the vermin stung them to death.

London was a world of absorbing interest to Equiano—he learned the art of the hairdresser, mastered the French horn, went to night school, and in the daytime assisted the scientist Dr. Charles Irving, "so celebrated for his successful experiments in making sea water fresh." Displaced so early from his own culture, baptized without conviction, there was a hunger within him to settle the large philosophical questions for his peace of mind. Searching for religious light, he sat and listened in a variety of churches. Quaker, Catholic, and Jew had no answer to gladden his heart. "I really thought the Turks were in a safer way of salvation than my neighbours," he felt at one point, and "determined at last to set out for Turkey, and there to end" his days. When the Calvinist Methodists seemed to offer the best solution to the knottiest problem in his mind—"the difference between human works and free election"—he ended his soul-searching, joined the fellowship of Westminster Chapel, composed twenty-eight quatrains called "Miscellaneous Verses" on the "benefits of Christianity" reminiscent of Jupiter Hammon's, and printed them in the pages of the *Narrative*.

He was still a struggling member of the black poor of London; the cupboard was often bare. From time to time, he "thought it best, therefore, to try the sea again in quest" of bread—a quest that he did not resist, for he was "still of a roving disposition, and desirous of seeing as many different parts of the world" as he could. Curious to see the East, he signed up as an able seaman on a Turkeyman headed for Smyrna. The ancient splendor, cheap wine, luscious fruits, and women with veiled faces—some of them "out of curiosity uncovered them to look at me"—delighted him, but it was the racial openness of the Turks, who treated him "always with great civility," that fascinated the African observer: "In general I believe they are fond of black people; and several of them gave me pressing invitations to stay amongst them. . . . I was surprised to see how the Greeks are, in some measure, kept under by the Turks, as the negroes are in the West-Indies by the white people." There were voyages also as seaman or steward to other parts of the Mediterranean, to Genoa, where everything pleased, except that all the "grandeur" was in his "eyes disgraced by the galley slaves, whose condition both there and in other parts of Italy is truly piteous and wretched." Later in Portugal and Spain, the convert who had struggled for an acceptable Christian doctrine was tempted by the Church of Rome. At the bullring in Cádiz, he encountered a Father Vincent, to whom he expressed his dislike of the sport as a "great scandal of Christianity and morals":

I had frequent contests about religion with the reverend father. . . . In his zeal for my conversion, he solicited me to go to one of the universities in Spain, and declared that I would have my education free; and told me, if I got myself made a priest, I might in time become even pope; and that Pope Benedict was a black man. As I was ever desirous of learning, I paused for some time upon this temptation . . . we parted without conviction on either side.

A voyage westward to the Mosquito Shore of Honduras and Nicaragua, stemming from Equiano's missionary zeal to convert "four Musquito Indians, who were Chiefs in their own country, and were brought here by some English traders for some selfish ends," opened up other insights into the ways of the world. He took a special interest in the eighteen-year-old son of the king of Mosquitia, tutoring him at sea in English and scripture via "Fox's Martyrology with cuts." The whole enterprise, which involved the cultivation of a plantation hacked out of the wilderness with slave labor, turned out to be a fiasco, except perhaps in the opportunity it gave the African to record and analyze a new array of data on comparative racial and social systems. "The natives," he wrote, "are well made and warlike; and they particularly boast of never having been conquered by the Spaniards." These unchristian Indians seemed to him "to be singular, in point of honesty, above any other nation I was ever amongst." Living under an open shed, with all their goods, "we slept in safety . . . if we were to lie in that manner in Europe we should have our throats cut at first sight." Fed up with the debauched white colonizers, he finally managed to slip off; his only regret was the part he played in the recruitment of blacks to man the plantation: "All my poor countrymen, the slaves, when they heard of my leaving them, were very sorry, as I had always treated them with care and affection, and did every thing I could to comfort the poor creatures, and render their condition easy."

It was on the trip back to England that Equiano in a casual paragraph made his single reference to the American Revolution: "We had many very heavy gales of wind in our passage; in the course of which no material incident occurred, except that an American privateer, falling in with the fleet, was captured and set fire to by his Majesty's ship the Squirrel."

Equiano's travels even included a voyage to the Arctic. Back home in London after the Mosquito debacle, "now tired of the sea," he returned to his job with Irving, the purifier of seawater. But when the good doctor, the following spring, was invited by Constantine Phipps to join him in an expedition to seek a "north-east passage" to the Orient, Irving suggested that his black assistant come along. Aroused "by the sound of fame, to seek new adventures, and find, towards the north pole . . . a passage to India," Equiano was happy to accept the offer. During the four-month adventure his main task on the H.M. sloop-of-war *Race Horse* was to turn salt water into fresh with Irving's machine, but at times when the floes crushed the wooden ships, he felt, with the rest, that his end would be an icy grave. He never reached India—had he looked forward to observing a new code of race and morality in that fabulous place?—but, with Dr. Irving, he felt glad that they had sailed nearer to the Pole "than any navigator had ever ventured before."

THE antislavery activity carried on by Equiano in England during the 1780s as a leading representative of the African diaspora, culminating with the publication of the *Narrative* at the end of the decade, was the crowning achievement of his life. His mind seems to have been set on going to Africa either as an explorer for the African Association or as a Christian missionary "in hope of doing good, if possible, among his countrymen." Sponsored by influential friends, he sought ordination by the lord bishop of London—"your memorialist is a native of Africa, and has a knowledge of the manners and customs of the inhabitants of that country"—but "from scruples of delicacy," he reported, the lord bishop "declined to ordain me."

As the effort to halt the slave trade gathered strength, Equiano emerged as London's chief black abolitionist. When, in September 1781, the notorious Captain Luke Collingwood, master of the *Zong,* transporting 440 slaves from Africa to Jamaica, jettisoned almost a third of the sick and dying in order to collect their insurance, it was Equiano who initiated the movement that made the atrocity on the *Zong* an international cause célèbre. "Gustavus Vassa called on me with an account of 132 Negroes being thrown alive into the sea from on board an English slave ship," Granville Sharp recorded in his journal, and later Sharp demanded that the Admiralty act quickly on the case—"having been earnestly solicited and called upon by a poor negro for my assistance to avenge the blood of his slaughtered countrymen."

Equiano's thirst to see new places was not easily slaked and even in the midst of organizing the antislavery cause he planned excursions at home and abroad. For a time he served a nobleman in the Dorsetshire militia encamped at Coxheath; in 1783, "from motives of curiosity," he toured eight counties of Wales. The land seemed to burn his feet; he "thought of visiting old ocean again," and in the spring of 1785 he embarked as a steward on a ship sailing to Philadelphia: "I was very glad to see this favorite old town once more; and my pleasure was much increased in seeing the worthy Quakers freeing and easing the burthens of many of my oppressed African brethren. It rejoiced my heart when one of these friendly people took me to see a free-school they had erected for every denomination of black people. . . ." In October, back in London, "accompanied by some of the Africans," he presented an "address of thanks" for their abolitionist labors to the Friends of the Grace-Church-Court in Lombard Street on behalf of "the poor, opressed, needy and much degraded Negroes"—a "captivated . . . people."

In 1786 another opportunity to go to Africa turned up. "On my return to London in August," he wrote:

> I was very agreeably surprised to find that the benevolence of government had adopted the plan of some philanthropic individuals to send the Africans from hence to their native quarter; and that some vessels were then engaged to carry them to Sierra Leona . . . a select committee of gentlemen for the black poor . . . sent for me . . . they seemed to think me qualified to superintend part of the undertaking, they asked me to go with the black poor to Africa. . . . I expressed some difficulties on the account of the slave dealers, as I would certainly oppose their traffic in the human species by every means in my power.

But once again nothing came of his high hopes. Appointed commissary of stores for the black poor going to Africa, he became enmeshed in a web of white duplicity and negligence. The controversy was hot and Equiano did not mince words. Some of the black poor feared a British plot to lead them back into chains, and his friend Ottobah Cugoano, a Fanti and former slave in London, expressed his doubts in print. In the *Public Advertiser* for 1787, Equiano exposed the "great villains" who "mean to serve (or use) the blacks the same as they do in the West Indies," while his opponents accused him of "advancing falsehoods as deeply black as his jetty face," of inciting blacks to mutiny—quoting the Reverend Mr. Fraser, one of Equiano's "villains," who charged him with urging the settlers to boycott his sermons "for no other reason whatever than that I am *white*." As Paul Edwards has noted, the authorities finally vindicated Equiano and awarded him fifty pounds for his services: "On the whole, Equiano appears to have been in the right, and to have been dismissed as a troublemaker because he was not prepared to turn a blind eye to corrupt procedures and the neglect of the black settlers. Equiano's worst crime appears to have been his anxiety to see that justice was done to his own people. . . ."

Although Equiano did not get to Africa, the fiasco did not blunt his zeal "to assist in the cause" of his "much injured countrymen." The *Narrative* comes to an end in 1788 with his petition to the queen "in behalf of my African brethren":

> I do not solicit your royal pity for my own distress; my sufferings, although numerous, are in a measure forgotten. I supplicate your Majesty's compassion for millions of my African countrymen who groan under the lash of tyranny in the West Indies. . . . [I] implore your interposition with your royal consort, in favour of the wretched Africans, that . . . a period may now be put to their misery—and that they may be raised from the condition of brutes, to which they are at

present degraded, to the rights and situation of freemen. . . .

"May the time come—at least the speculation to me is pleasing," is his final word, "when the sable people shall gratefully commemorate the auspicious era of extensive freedom."

THE *Interesting Narrative* came off the press in 1789 when Equiano was forty-four, and although the writer had only another eight years to live, he had the joy of its quick and solid success on both sides of the ocean. During the spring of 1792, the *Gentleman's Magazine* of London carried a notice of the marriage of "Gustavus Vassa, the African, well known as the champion and advocate for procuring the suppression of the slave trade" to a Miss Cullen of Ely. The same magazine recorded his death in London on April 31, 1797. In his last moments he was visited by his friend and coworker, the great Granville Sharp, with whom he had petitioned king and Parliament. Some years later, Sharp's niece, Jemima, avidly reading the *Narrative,* asked her uncle about the character of its author. "He was a sober, honest man," Sharp replied—"and I went to see him when he lay upon his death bed, and had lost his voice so that he could only whisper. . . ." Of course, Olaudah Equiano, whose book imaged forth a real African during the era of the American Revolution, would never lose his voice.

The Burgeoning of Art and Craft

Fortune was on Phillis Wheatley's side— when her portrait had to be done, she found nearby the black artist, Scipio Morehead, to do it. (Hers was the first black face identified by name to be portrayed in the United States.) Sheer miracle that in those early days a few black Americans, transcending

caste, began to paint pictures rather than fences.

We know, by brief report, a few facts about a handful of black artists and artisans of the revolutionary era, sketched here at random.

In southern newspapers during the years of the revolution, an endless stream of advertisements for the return of runaway slaves often revealed the varied talents of black artisans who toiled for the slavocracy. Carpenters, joiners, carvers, weavers, seamstresses, shoemakers, toolmakers, wheelwrights, coopers, bricklayers, millwrights—all take to their heels in their search for freedom. Among these advertisements, a frequent figure is the blacksmith in flight from plantation and forge, like the "Negro Fellow named Elijah" described in the *Virginia Gazette* during the autumn of 1776 as having "a yellow Complexion . . . about 22 or 23 Years of Age, by Trade a Blacksmith, and an excellent Workman at that Business."

As is well known, blacksmiths in bondage created splendid iron gates and grilled balconies in Louisiana. Not long ago, in Alexandria, Virginia, during a dig at the site of an old smithy near the slave quarters of a plantation, there came to light the buried image of a man wrought in iron, only a foot high yet monumental in its impact—as Malcolm Watkins has said, a "remarkable example of African expression in ironwork" [fig. 149]. For some viewers, the wrought-iron man seems to resemble the sculpture of blacksmiths in Mende Senegambia. The nameless slave who fashioned this piece in Virginia had not forgotten the art that he or his father had practiced in Africa.

One of the most gifted of the artisans who ornamented the powderhorns carried by New England soldiers in the French and Indian War was one John Bush, born in Shrewsbury, Massachusetts. Bush fought in a regiment at Lake George during the campaigns of 1755 and 1756. When, in the summer of 1757, Fort William Henry fell to the French, he was captured. His father, a free black landowner (although there were Bushes who were slaves in Shrewsbury) wrote to Governor Thomas Pownal the following year asking for help in locating his son—"a Mullater Fellow about 30 years of Age." He found that John and two of his brothers had fallen on the battlefield. Before he died, John Bush had carved at least eight powderhorns. Only one is signed—the superb horn he made for Thomas Campbell, inscribed "Lake George. The Battle 8th of Sepr 1755 . . . John Bush: Fecit" {fig. 150}. The powderhorn was a popular American art form. Bush, who described himself in his will as "Negro," was one of the earliest and most ingenious of its carvers, a founder of the Lake George School of horn engravers.

Isaiah Thomas, in his *History of Printing,* relates that in the Boston shop of Thomas Fleet, as early as 1724, slaves did much of the work:

> He owned several negroes, one of which worked at the printing business, both at the press and at setting types; he was an ingenious man, and cut, on wooden blocks, all the pictures which decorated the ballads, and small books of his master. Fleet had also two negro boys born in his house; sons, I believe, to the man just mentioned, whom he brought up to work at press and case; one named Pompey and the other Cesar; they were young when their master died; but they remained in the family, and continued to labor regularly in the printing house with the sons of Mr. Fleet, who succeeded their father, until the constitution of Massachusetts,

149. Unknown artist, *Wrought-Iron Figure,* late eighteenth century, ht. 12″. Collection of Adele Earnest, Stony Point, New York.

150. Powderhorn made by John Bush for Thomas Williams at the Battle of Lake George, September 8, 1775. Drawing by Geo. H. Harris of Rochester, New York, September 1888. Courtesy of The New-York Historical Society, Grider Collection, New York City.

adopted in 1780, made them free-men.

And Sinclair Hamilton adds: "We find some editions of that well-known chapbook *The Prodigal Daughter* issued from the Heart and Crown . . . with a woodcut bearing the initials 'P.F.' and it is possible that this is the work of Pompey Fleet, or perhaps the work of that ingenious Negro himself, Pompey's father . . ." [fig. 151]. (In April 1758, Fleet tried to sell one of his black printers: " . . . a Negro Man about thirty years

old. . . . He has worked at the Printing Business Fifteen or Sixteen years.")

Toward the turn of the century, David and John Fowle employed in their two printing shops in Boston at least one black pressman. "This negro was named Primus," wrote Thomas. "He was an African. I well remember him; he worked at press with or without an assistant; he continued to do press work until prevented by age. He went to Portsmouth with his master, and there died, being more than ninety years of age; about fifty of which he was a pressman."

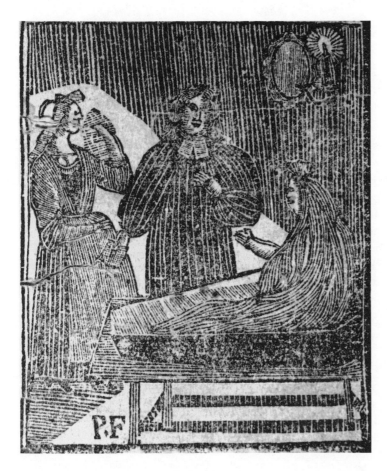

151. Woodcut by "P.F." from *The Prodigal Daughter* (Boston: Printed at the Heart and Crown, 1768). Princeton University Library.

Not only in Boston were there "ingenious" blacks who set type, operated the handpress, and cut blocks. In Philadelphia there was "a negro pressman named Andrew Cain," who was "a good workman." In Richmond, the *Virginia Independent Chronicle* carried a plea for the return of one of its fugitive slaves: "Ran-Away . . . a mulatto fellow named Tom . . . who for the last two years has been employed in this office as a Pressman." In Charleston, Robert Wells, the "principal bookseller for both the Carolinas" and "one of the principal [slave] auctioneers in the city . . . owned a number of negroes; two or three of whom were taught to work at press. It was a common custom in the Carolinas, and in the West Indies, to have blacks for pressmen."

In Charleston also, the *South Carolina and American General Gazette,* June 3, 1771, carries the notice of John Fisher, "cabinet and chair maker," that he has in his shop slaves "brought up to the business."

A notice in the *Massachusetts Gazette* of January 7, 1773, reads as follows: "At Mr. M'Lean's, Watch-Maker near the Town House, is a Negro Man whose extraordinary Genius has been assisted by one of the best Masters in London; he takes Faces at the lowest rates. Specimens of his Performances may be seen at said Place" [fig. 152].

In March 1773 in Charleston, South Carolina, an artist-artisan, John Allwood, on departing from the province, advertised in the *South Carolina Gazette:* "WILL DISPOSE OF HIS NEGRO FELLOWS,

At Mr. *M'Lean's*, Watch-Maker near the Town-House, is a Negro Man whose extraordinary Genius has been assisted by one of the best Masters in *London*; he takes Faces at the lowest Rates. Specimens of his Performances may be seen at said Place.

152. *Massachusetts Gazette*, January 7, 1773. Courtesy of the Library of Congress.

Painters. . . . As to their Abilities, he thinks them evident, they have transacted the Whole of his Business, without any hired Assistance; and he has taken no little Pains in initiating them in the true Principles of their Profession. . . . He has also a few well-painted Pictures to dispose of. . . ." Thus far we have neither their names nor their works [fig. 153].

A few other dim names have survived in the record.

In Newbury, Massachusetts, it is remembered that Phebe Cash, a black child, fourteen years old, owned by the widow of Dudley Atkins, Esq., worked an unusual sampler in 1789. With varied cross-stitch and two alphabets it depicted home, shed, trees, and birds.

In Newport there was a black man of talent who hammered staves for his master. It was said—so reported a historian of Rhode Island in 1853—that Gilbert Stuart "derived his first impression of painting from witnessing Neptune Thurston, a slave, who was employed in his master's cooper-shop, sketch likenesses on the heads of casks, and remarked that if he had an instructor he would make quite a celebrated artist." It was in Newport also that Newport Gardner composed his hymns and anthems.

In the *Pennsylvania Gazette* for July 5, 1770, George Dowig, jeweller and goldsmith, advertised for sale "a Negroe man, by trade a silversmith" [fig. 154]. Eight years later, in the Charleston *South-Carolina and American General Gazette* for February 5,

The SUBSCRIBER, Intending to leave the Province in APRIL next, *WILL DISPOSE OF* His NEGRO FELLOWS, *Painters*, On WEDNESDAY *the* Seventh *of April* next, At his Yard in Queen-Street, directly opposite Mr. CANNON'S.

AS to their Abilities, he thinks them evident, they having transacted the Whole of his Business, without any hired Assistance; and he has taken no little Pains in initiating them in the true Principles of their Profession.

LIKEWISE, A good HOUSE-WENCH, Who can wash and iron exceeding well, and is a tolerable Cook. He has also a few well-painted Pictures to dispose of; some good Prints, framed and glazed; with a little Household-Furniture.—The Conditions will be made known on the Day of Sale.

⁎⁎⁎ He begs those to whom he is indebted to send in their Accompts for Payment;—and requests the Favour of those who are indebted to him, to discharge their Accompts; by which Means he hopes to give his Creditors general Satisfaction. JOHN ALLWOOD.

153. *South Carolina Gazette*, March 8, 1773. Courtesy of the Library of Congress.

1778, one Jacob Vale offered a reward of £250 for the return of his runaway, twenty-one-year-old Joe, "brought up to the goldsmith business [who] may perhaps pass himself for a free fellow." In the *Pennsylvania Packet* for May 1, 1784, one Benjamin Halsted of New York City offered a reward of eight dollars for the return of a valuable slave: "*RAN-AWAY* . . . *a negro man, named* John Frances, *but commonly called* Jack: *he is about* 40 *years of age, five feet ten inches high, slender built, speaks good English, by trade a goldsmith; he generally affects to be very polite, and it's more than probable he may pass for a freeman.* . . . *All masters of vessels and others are forbid to harbour or carry him off at their peril*" [fig. 155].

NEW ADVERTISEMENTS.

ON Friday, the 13th of July, will be SOLD by public VENDUE, at the City-Vendue-Store, in Front-ftreet, all the JEWELLERY, and SILVER WARE, belong-ing to GEORGE DOWIG, Jeweller and Goldfmith; confifting of garnet ear-rings, fet in gold, chryftal ditto, fet in ditto, clufter ditto, fet in filver, gold ftone rings of all kinds, gold locket but-tons, plain gold ditto, gold lockets, beft chryftal buttons, fet in filver, a variety of plate and buckles, likewife a filverfmith's flatting-mill, all his jewellery and filverfmith's tools, a Negroe man, by trade a filverfmith, a variety of unfet ftones, garnets for ear-rings, ditto for rings, chryftals for ear and finger rings, chryftals for buttons, &c. &c. Alfo all his houfhold and kitchen furniture. The fale to begin at 9 o'clock in the morning.

All perfons indebted to faid DOWIG, are requefted to make immediate payment; and thofe that have any demands againft him, are requefted to bring in their accounts, in order to be ad-jufted, as he intends to leave the province foon. ¶

154. "For Sale, a Negro silversmith," *Pennsylvania Gazette,* July 5, 1770. Courtesy, American Antiquarian Society.

In Burlington, New Jersey, in the Friends' Burial Ground is the grave of a black clockmaker, Peter Hill, who probably knew John Woolman. In 1795, when he was twenty-seven years old, Hill won his freedom and married Tenah, who also had been a slave. When his former master re-tired, Hill took over his shop. A century later a few of his timepieces were still tick-ing away in houses of the area. The dial of one of his handsome tall case clocks features a moonface, maps of the world, and his sig-nature [fig. 156].

It is well known, especially from news-paper notices offering rewards for the return of runaways, that black fiddlers, banjoists, and fifers were everywhere, north and south, in the late colonial period—like Zelah of Groton in Massachusetts who fought in the

Philadelphia, April 27.

Eight Dollars Reward.

RAN-AWAY from the fubfcriber, a negro man, named JOHN FRANCES, but commonly called JACK: he is about 40 years of age, five feet ten inches high, flender built, fpeaks good English, by trade a goldfmith; he generally affects to be very po-lite, and it's more than probable he may pafs for a freeman. Said negro was carried to New York and left in charge of Mr. Ephraim Brafher, goldfmith, from whom he abfconded, and returned to me after fkulking about this city for a confiderable time: had on when he went away, an old green coat, fuftian waiftcoat and breeches, a pair of half boots, but may probably change his drefs. All mafters of vef-fels and others are forbid to harbour or carry him off at their peril. Whoever takes up faid negro and delivers him to John Le Telier, goldfmith in Mark-et ftreet, or to the fubfcriber in New York, fhall have the above reward, and all reafonable char-ges paid. BENJAMIN HALSTED.

155. *Pennsylvania Packet,* May 1, 1784. Courtesy of the Library of Congress.

156. Peter Hill, red walnut case clock, 7' 6" tall, dial, ca. 1812. National Museum of American History, Smithsonian Institution.

revolution and became "famous in his neighborhood as a musician."

All these are but shadows of the real and potential burgeonings of a black presence in art and craft, exhumed from old records. The black carpenters and blacksmiths who were designers and builders of fine houses from New Hampshire to Virginia, described in the thousands of advertisements for fugitive slaves in the press of the revolutionary era, bear testimony also to the waste of black gifts and powers in a slave society.

VI

Against the Odds

In white America of the independence time, it was hard for talented black men and women—slave or free—to rise tall out of the swamp of racism, to forge ahead fulfilling all their powers. Looking backward, it seems almost incredible that more than a few from Attucks and Banneker to Wheatley and Equiano managed to carve their names—and sometimes their faces—on the great shield of Afro-American history. The odds against them were great. Yet what of the others, the tens of thousands, north and south, who lived through that time, slaving in the fields and kitchens, working as farmhands and woodcutters, drovers and wagoners, as craftsmen in shops and forges, the men of the sea, the whalemen and the sealmen—the breathless runaways, the brave women doubly oppressed—must not the plain folk also be counted as part of the black presence in the time of the American Revolution?

Of late, diggers into the black American past have been exhuming hitherto forgotten figures who emerged as men and women of mark in their hour and place—individuals whose lives disclose a great deal about the voiceless masses from whom they arose. The historian assembles the image with more or less success from hints and scraps—an epitaph on a weathered gravestone, a paragraph hidden in a county history, a stained marriage record, a last will and testament, a strain of folklore that is nearly true. Here are some of these modest lives.

Lucy Terry Prince: Vermont Poet and Advocate

Lucy Terry Prince, who, like Phillis Wheatley, was stolen from Africa as a child, was one of the most remarkable women of her time. Like Wheatley she was a poet, but only a single poem of her making remains to delight us. What is known of her life would suggest a body of verse and eloquent talk that to our loss have not survived.

Lucy was born in 1724 and was baptized

in the summer of 1725 in Deerfield, Massachusetts, during the revival known as the Great Awakening. She was the infant slave of Ebenezer Wells. Nineteen years later, in 1744, she was admitted to the "fellowship of the church" [figs. 157–61]. When she was twenty-two years old, an Indian war party attacked the frontier town; the bloodshed, which she could not forget, stirred her later to write some rough-hewn verse on the tragedy:

> August 'twas the twenty-fifth,
> Seventeen hundred forty-six;
> The Indians did in ambush lay,
> Some very valient men to slay,
> The names of whom I'll not leave out.
> Samuel Allen like a hero fout,
> And though he was so brave and
>   bold,
> His face no more shall we behold.
> Eleazer Hawks was killed outright,
> Before he had time to fight,—
> Before he did the Indians see,
> Was shot and killed immediately.
> Oliver Amsden he was slain,
> Which caused his friends much grief
>   and pain.
> Simeon Amsden they found dead,
> Not many rods distant from his head.
> Adonijah Gillett we do hear
> Did lose his life which was so dear.
> John Sadler fled across the water,
> And thus escaped the dreadful
>   slaughter.
> Eunice Allen see the Indians coming,
> And hopes to save herself by running,
> And had not her petticoats stopped
>   her,
> The awful creatures had not catched
>   her,
> Nor tommy hawked her on her head,
> And left her on the ground for dead.
> Young Samuel Allen, Oh lack-a-day!
> Was taken and carried to Canada.

Her ballad titled "Bars Fight" ("Bars" was a colonial word for meadow), which got into print for the first time a century later, was handed down in the oral memory of Deerfield people. As late as 1893, an old woman of the town remembered another version of the ballad that began with the lines: " 'Twas nigh unto Sam Dickinson's mill, / The Indians there five men did kill."

On May 17, 1756, Lucy Terry married Abijah Prince, a free black twice her age who owned land and paid taxes in a nearby town. They lived in Deerfield in a house near a brook, still called Bijah's Brook, and began to raise a family. "One of the most noteworthy characters in the early history of Deerfield was a colored woman, known as 'Luce Bijah,' " wrote Josiah Gilbert Holland, Emily Dickinson's friend, who in 1855 printed Lucy's poem for the first time in his *History of Western Massachusetts:* "She was noted for her wit and shrewdness. Her house was the constant resort of the boys, to hear her talk."

Meanwhile Abijah Prince was looking elsewhere for a permanent home. When Deacon Samuel Field left him a one hundred acre lot in Guilford, Vermont, the Princes in the 1760s moved north.

Guilford, with its two thousand citizens, was an unusual village, a kind of Concord in Vermont. It was busy with its farms, brickyards, tanneries, quarries, and potasheries, but it kept its schools open all year and paid its teachers well. The villagers owned pianos, melodeons, and other musical instruments, and in 1790 the Guilford Social Library boasted a circulation of three hundred volumes. Townspeople were proud of writers like playwright Royall Tyler and poet Henry Denison, who lived among them. It was an ambiance that a woman like Lucy Prince, with her gift of pen and tongue, might find congenial.

Life was not all smooth sailing in

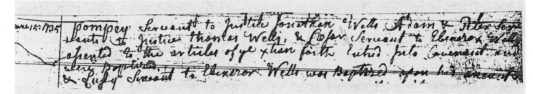

157. "June 15, 1725 . . . Lucy Servant to Ebenezer Wells was Baptized. . . ." Record, First Church of Deerfield, on deposit with PVMA Library, Deerfield, Massachusetts.

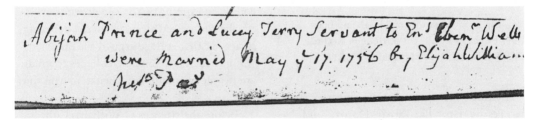

158. "August 19, 1744 . . . Lusey Servant to Ebenezer Wells was admitted to the fellowship of Chh," on deposit with PVMA Library, Deerfield, Massachusetts.

159. "Abijah Prince and Lucey Terry Servant . . . married," May 17, 1756. Book of Records, PVMA Library, Deerfield, Massachusetts.

Guilford. In 1785 Lucy Prince first showed her mettle in standing up for her rights in a public forum. When the Princes were threatened with violence by their white neighbors, the Noyses, she, her husband, "and others" appeared before governor Thomas Chittenden and his Council and asked for protection. The Council found in her favor and ordered the selectmen of Guilford to defend the black family.

160. Births in the family of Abijah and Lucy Terry Prince, 1757 to 1769. Book of Records, PVMA Library, Deerfield, Massachusetts.

By this time, there were six children: Cesar, Festus, Drucilla, Tatnai, Duroxa, and Abijah, Jr. Eager that at least one of her sons might have a good education, she applied for his admission to Williams College. "He was rejected on account of his race," wrote George Sheldon, the historian of Deerfield. "The indignant mother pressed her claim before the trustees in an earnest and eloquent speech of three hours, quoting an abundance of law and Gospel, chapter

At Sunderland, Vt. July 11th, Mrs. Lucy Prince, a woman of colour.— From the church and town records where she formerly resided, we learn that she was brought from Bristol, Rhode Island, to Deerfield, Mass. when she was four years old, by Mr. Ebenezer Wells: that she was 97 years of age—that she was early devoted to God in Baptism: that she united with the church in Deerfield in 1744—Was married to Abijah Prince, May 17th, 1756, by Elijah Williams, Esq. and that she has been the mother of seven children. In this remarkable woman there was an assemblage of qualities rarely to be found among her sex. Her volubility was exceeded by none, and in general the fluency of her speech captivated all around her, and was not destitute of instruction and edification. She was much respected among her acquaintance, who treated her with a degree of deference.

Vt Gaz.

161. Obituary, *Franklin Herald,* Greenfield, Massachusetts, August 21, 1821. PVMA Library, Deerfield, Massachusetts.

and verse, in support of it, but all in vain. The name of no son of Lucy Prince graces the catalogue of Williams College." What could she expect? In 1834, a dozen years after she had passed away, when the debating society of that college argued the question, "Ought the New England colleges to graduate people of colour?" the negative won the day.

Before the trustees of Williams College, Lucy Prince had lost her case, but somewhat later, before the Supreme Court of the United States, she triumphed with éclat. This time the issue was an attempt by one Colonel Eli Bronson to steal a lot that the Princes owned on the Batten Kill in Sunderland, not far from the house of Ethan Allen. Lawsuits followed. Sheldon is once again the source of the tradition:

The town at length took the matter up, and finally it reached the Supreme Court of the United States, where, we may suppose, Col. Bronson met a Waterloo defeat, and Luce Bijah gained a national reputation. The Court was presided over by Hon. Samuel Chase of Maryland. Col. Bronson employed two leading lawyers of Vermont, Stephen R. Bradley and Royall Tyler, the wit and poet, and afterwards chief justice of the state. Isaac Tichenor, later governor of Vermont, managed the case of Abijah and Lucy. He drew the pleadings, and our Lucy argued the case at length before the court. Justice Chase said that Lucy made a better argument than he had heard from any lawyer at the Vermont bar.

There is not much more to tell. When the War of Independence broke out, Cesar and Festus, the two oldest sons, went down to Massachusetts and enlisted in the army. Cesar perhaps fought with the Green Mountain Boys. Festus, a gifted musician who could play a number of instruments, after the peace married a white woman and farmed in Sunderland. Duroxa had a reputation as a poet, although some thought she was insane. Abijah died in 1794. In 1803, Lucy went to Sunderland to live, and in her extreme old age rode a horse back and forth to Bennington eighteen miles away. As long as she lived, she made an annual pilgrimage over the Green Mountains to visit her husband's grave. She died at Sunderland, ninety-seven years old. Her obituary appeared during the summer of 1821 in the *Franklin Herald* of Greenfield, Massachusetts.

Some ten years ago the black playwright Ed Bullins wrote a play for children called *I Am Lucy Terry,* in which she is presented as "an original American pioneer, freedom fighter and revolutionary."

Alice: Pioneer of Philadelphia

All that is known of Alice is on a few pages of a curious volume, a mélange of a hundred sketches of *Eccentric Biography; or, Memoirs of Remarkable Female Characters, Ancient and Modern,* printed by Isaiah Thomas, Jr., in 1804.* Arranged alphabetically, Alice and her portrait come first, followed by "Arc, Joan of" [fig. 162].

Alice was born a slave in Philadelphia in 1686, of parents shipped from Barbados, and she lived in that city until she was ten. Then her master moved to Dunk's Ferry, where she continued to the end of her days. Like du Sable in Chicago, she knew the site of a great city when it was primeval forest; like Yarrow Mamout she lived so long that she became a kind of oral historian, a repository of the memory of things. When Jefferson wrote the Declaration, she still had a quarter century to live. Here is her story, slightly abridged:

> She remembered the ground on which Philadelphia stands, when it was a wilderness, and when the Indians [its chief inhabitants] hunted wild game in the woods, while the panther, the wolf, and the beasts of the forest were prowling about the wigwams and cabins in which they lived. Being a sensible intelligent woman, and having a good memory, which she retained to the last, she would often

---

*"Many of the slaves in the better families became well-known characters—as Alice, who for forty years took the tolls at Dunk's Ferry; Virgil Warder, who once belonged to Thomas Penn, and Robert Venable, a man of some intelligence" (W. E. Burghardt Du Bois, *The Philadelphia Negro: A Social Study* [Philadelphia, 1899], 17).

162. *Alice,* engraving, frontispiece in *Eccentric Biography; or Memoirs of Remarkable Female Characters, Ancient and Modern* (Worcester, 1804). Yale University Library.

make judicious remarks on the population and improvements of the city and country; hence her conversation became peculiarly interesting, especially to the immediate descendants of the first settlers, of whose ancestors she often related acceptable anecdotes. She remembered William Penn, the proprietor of Pennsylvania, Thomas Story, James Logan, and several other distinguished characters of that day. During a short visit which she paid to Philadelphia last fall, many respectable persons called to see her, who were all pleased with her innocent cheerfulness, and that dignified deportment, for which (though a slave and uninstructed) she was ever remarkable. In observing the increase of the city, she pointed out the house

next to the episcopal church, to the southward, in Second street, as the first brick building that was erected in it. . . . The first church, she said, was a small frame that stood where the present building stands, the ceiling of which she could reach with her hands from the floor. She was a worthy member of the episcopal society, and attended their public worship as long as she lived . . . she has often been met on horseback, in a full gallop, to church, at the age of 95 years. The veneration she had for the bible induced her to lament that she was not able to read it; but the deficiency was in part supplied by the kindness of many of her friends, who, at her request, would read it to her, when she would listen with great attention, and often make pertinent remarks. She was temperate in her living, and so careful to keep to the truth, that her veracity was never questioned; her honesty also was unimpeached, for such was her master's confidence in it, that she was trusted at all times to receive the ferriage money, for upwards of forty years. This extraordinary woman retained her hearing to the end of her life, but her sight began to fail gradually in her ninety-sixth year, without any visible cause than from old age. At one hundred she became blind . . . she would frequently row herself out into the middle of the stream, from which she seldom returned without a handsome supply of fish for her master's table.—About the one hundred and second year of her age, her sight returned. . . . Before she died, her hair became perfectly white, and the last of her teeth dropt sound from her head at the age of 116 years. At this

age she died (1802) at Bristol in
Pennsylvania.

Belinda of Boston: "Marked with the Furrows of Time"

On February 14, 1783, "Belinda an affrican," at three score and ten, submitted to
the General Court a personal plea signed
with her mark full of pain and anger
[fig. 163]. It is possible that Phillis Wheatley or Prince Hall listened carefully as she
poured out her grief, and then edited her
words into the formal language of a petition. Even so, her own anguished voice,
speaking for many sisters and brothers forgotten by the revolution, pierces through
the rhetoric of the times, as she begins with
her childhood memories of Africa:

> seventy years have rolled away, since
> she, on the banks of the Rio de Volta,
> received her existence. The moun-
> tains, covered with spicy forests—the
> vallies, loaded with the richest fruits
> spontaneously produced—joined to
> that happy temperature of air, which
> excludes excess, would have yielded
> her the most complete felicity, had
> not her mind received early impres-
> sions of the cruelty of men, whose
> faces were like the moon, and whose
> bows and arrows were like the
> thunder and lightning of the clouds.
> The idea of these, the most dreadful
> of all enemies, filled her Infant slum-
> bers with horror . . . before she had
> twelve years enjoyed the fragrance of
> her native groves . . . even when she,
> in a sacred grove, with each hand in
> that of a tender parent, was paying
> her devotions to the great Orisa, who
> made all things, an armed band of
> white men, driving many of her
> countrymen in chains, rushed into

163. "The Petition of Belinda an affrican to the
General Court of Massachusetts, February 14,
1783," *American Museum or Universal Magazine*
1 (1787). Courtesy of the Library of Congress.

> the hallowed shades! Could the tears,
> the sighs, the supplication, bursting
> from tortured parental affection, have
> blunted the keen edge of avarice, she
> might have been rescued from agony,
> which many of her country's children
> have felt, but which none have ever
> yet described.

She could not forget the horror of the slave
ship: "three hundred Africans in chains, suffering the most excruciating torment; and
some of them rejoicing that the pangs of
death came like a balm to their wounds."
And then America!

alas! how unlike the land where she received her being! . . . She learned to catch the ideas, marked by the sounds of language, only to know that her doom was slavery, from which death alone was to emancipate her. What did it avail her, that the walls of her lord were hung with splendor. . . . Fifty years her faithful hands have been compelled to ignoble servitude for the benefit of an Isaac Royall, until as if nations must be agitated, and the world convulsed, for the preservation of that freedom, which the Almighty Father intended for *all* the human race, the present war commenced.

Isaac Royall had fled, and aged Belinda, who slaved her whole life to increase his estate, was free at last—to starve:

> The face of your petitioner is now marked with the furrows of time, and her frame feebly bending under the oppression of years, while she, by the laws of the land, is denied the enjoyment of one morsel of that immense wealth, a part whereof hath been accumulated by her own industry, and the whole augmented by her servitude.

She asks for minimal justice: "Wherefore, casting herself at the feet of your honours . . . she prays that such allowance may be made her, out of the estate of colonel Royall, as will prevent her, and her more infirm daughter, from misery in the greatest extreme, and scatter comfort over the short and downward path of their lives. . . ."

The General Court quickly responded to Belinda's plea, granting her an annual pension of some fifteen pounds out of the expropriated rents and profits of her former master. But this pension came to a halt after the first year. Time passed; despite her many requests for relief, she "never could obtain any more. . . ." During the spring of 1787, she again memorialized the legislature [fig. 164]. In June, the sympathetic editor of a Philadelphia journal printed her original petition. In November, the Court granted the old woman another year's pension.

How long "Belinda an affrican" and her "more infirm daughter" plodded along in Boston is not known.

Elizabeth Freeman and the Bill of Rights

"A woman once lived in Massachusetts," wrote Harriet Martineau in 1838, "whose name ought to be preserved in all histories of the State":

> Mum Bett, whose real name was Elizabeth Freeman, was born, it is supposed, about 1742. Her parents were native Africans. . . . At an early age she was purchased, with her sister . . . by Colonel Ashley, of Sheffield, Massachusetts.* The lady of the mansion, in a fit of passion, one day struck at Mum Bett's sister with a heated kitchen shovel. Mum Bett interposed her arm and received the blow, the scar of which she bore to the day of her death.

She "resented the insult and outrage," left the house of her master, and refused to return:

---

*"Elizabeth was born in Claverack, N.Y., and was purchased from Mr. Hogeboom of that town, by Colonel Ashley, at the age of six months. It was in the winter, and she was brought on the bottom of a sleigh, covered with straw to Sheffield" (Electa F. Jones, *Stockbridge, Past and Present* . . . [Springfield, 1854], 194).

164. "The Memorial of Belinda, an African, formerly a Servant to the late Isaac Royal Esq an Absentee." Massachusetts Archives, *Acts and Resolves,* October Session, 1787, chapter 142.

Colonel Ashley appealed to the law for the recovery of his slave. Mum Bett called on Mr. Sedgwick, and asked him if she could not claim her liberty under the law. He inquired what could put such an idea into her head. She replied that the "Bill o' Rights" said that all were born free and equal, and that, as she was not a dumb beast, she was certainly one of the nation.

When people later asked her how she learned the doctrine on which she based her case, she replied, "By keepin' still and mindin' things":

But what did she mean, she was asked, by keeping still and minding things? Why, for instance, [she replied] when she was waiting at table, she heard gentlemen talking over the Bill of Rights and the new constitution of Massachusetts; and in all they said she never heard but that all people were born free and equal, and she thought long about it, and resolved she would try whether she did not come in among them.

Theodore Sedgwick of nearby Stockbridge, a young lawyer and future senator with anti-slavery ideas who would later befriend Agrippa Hull, listened carefully to the angry black woman and took her case. Brom, another of Ashley's slaves, joined her in court. Thus did Elizabeth Freeman, an ancestor of W. E. B. Du Bois, inaugurate her historic suit against Colonel John Ashley, wealthy landowner and merchant. Sedgwick argued the case before the county court in the town of Great Barrington. When the jury set Freeman and Brom free—and ordered the colonel to pay them thirty shillings and costs—the legal fact was established that a Bill of Rights, in Massachusetts at least, had indeed abolished slavery {fig. 165}.

In 1781, toward the end of the war, when all this took place, Elizabeth Freeman was a widow nearing forty with a young daughter, "Little Bett"; her husband had

165. Court Order to pay
Elizabeth Freeman,
August 22, 1781. Stock-
bridge Public Library,
Stockbridge,
Massachusetts.

fallen on a battlefield of the revolution.
Colonel Ashley pleaded with her to return
to his home and work for wages. She refused. In gratitude to the lawyer who had
fought for her freedom, she stayed on with
the Sedgwicks as housekeeper for many
years. Her courage in defending their home
from foraging Shaysites was legendary in
the Berkshires. "She allowed them to search
the drawers," wrote Electa Jones, "knowing
that the valuable papers were on the hill,
and the silver all in her own chest, and to
run their bayonets under the beds . . . arming herself with the kitchen shovel . . . she
escorted them to the cellar, jeering them at
her pleasure, and assuring them that they
dared not strike a woman . . . entering
Betty's [room], one pointed to her chest,
and asked what that was. 'Oh, you had better search that,' she replied, 'an old nigger's
chest! you are such gentlemen; you had better search that—the old nigger's, as you call
me'; and thus she shamed them quite out of
it, and saved the silver."

Eventually she departed from the Sedgwicks and set up house with her daughter.
The Freeman property adjoined that of Ag-

rippa Hull. Two years after her death, in a
lecture delivered at the Stockbridge Lyceum
in which Theodore Sedgwick urged the abolition of slavery in the "Cause of Man," he
cited as his prime example, Elizabeth Freeman, well known to all in his audience:

> If there could be a practical refutation
> of the imagined superiority of our
> race to hers, the life and character of
> this woman would afford that refuta-
> tion . . . she had nothing of the sub-
> missive or subdued character, which
> succumbs to superior force. . . . On
> the contrary, without ever claiming
> superiority, she uniformly . . . ob-
> tained an ascendency over all those
> with whom she was associated in ser-
> vice. . . . Even in her humble sta-
> tion, she had, when occasion required
> it, an air of command which con-
> ferred a degree of dignity. . . . She
> claimed no distinction; but it was
> yielded to her from her superior expe-
> rience, energy, skill, and sagacity.

In later life, she was in great demand as
nurse and midwife: "Here she had no com-

166. Will of Elizabeth Freeman, October 18, 1829, excerpt. Stockbridge Public Library, Stockbridge, Massachusetts.

petitor. . . . When a child, wailing in the arms of its mother, heard her steps on the stairway, or approaching the door, it ceased to cry." Sedgwick had never known anyone of greater natural endowments:

> This woman, by her extreme industry and economy, supported a large family. . . . She could neither read nor write; yet her conversation was instructive, and her society was much sought. She received many visits at her own house, and very frequently received and accepted invitations to pass considerable intervals of time in the families of her friends.

Elizabeth Freeman lived to a ripe old age, through the revolution and the War of 1812, surrounded by her grandchildren and great-grandchildren. In her last will and testament she bequeathed to her daughter a black silk gown, gift of her African father, and a "short gown" that her African mother had worn [fig. 166]. In 1811, when she was almost seventy, young Susan Sedgwick lovingly painted her portrait in watercolors on a piece of ivory [fig. 167]. Another Sedg-

wick, Catherine, the famous novelist, for whom she had cared as a child, wrote a piece about her in 1853 recalling that the words that had inspired her to fight for her freedom came directly from the Declaration of Independence. In the Sedgwick family plot of the old burial ground in Stockbridge, she rests next to Catherine. A stone marks her grave [fig. 168]:

ELIZABETH FREEMAN.
known by the name of
MUMBET
died Dec. 28, 1829
Her supposed age was 85 Years.

—with the following inscription: "She was born a slave and remained a slave for nearly thirty years. She could neither read nor write yet in her own sphere she had no superior nor equal. She neither wasted time nor property. She never violated a trust nor failed to perform a duty. In every situation of domestic trial, she was the most efficient helper, and the tenderest friend. Good mother, farewell"—to which might be

167. Susan Sedgwick,
Elizabeth Freeman, water-
color on ivory, 1811.
Massachusetts Historical
Society.

added: "She struck the death blow of slavery
in Massachusetts."*

Felix Cuff: Massachusetts Maroon

Like Elizabeth Freeman in western Massachusetts, Felix Cuff of Waltham in the

---

*It is curious to note that the Massachusetts Con-
stitution of 1780 was never amended to abolish slavery. The historian George H. Moore rightly remarked
at the close of the Civil War that "slavery, having
never been formally prohibited by legislation in Massachusetts, continued to 'subsist in point of law' until
the year 1866, when the Grand Constitutional
Amendment terminated it forever in the United
States" (*Notes on the History of Slavery in Massachusetts*
[New York, 1866], 242).

east won his freedom in the same year but in
a different way.

Felix Cuff was a slave who during the
summer of 1780 served as a private for
twenty-four days in Captain Zaccheus
Wright's company of Colonel Cyrian Howe's
regiment, for which the town paid Cuff
£1,500 in paper money and sixty bushels of
corn. That same summer, after he returned
from service, Cuff and "other negro slaves"
ran away from their owners and hid out in a
deep cave (the Devil's Den) on Snake Hill,
so called because it was at one time infested
with rattlesnakes. Lieutenant Eliphalet
Hastings got up a posse of youngsters to
capture them, "but they met with a warm
reception and came back empty handed."

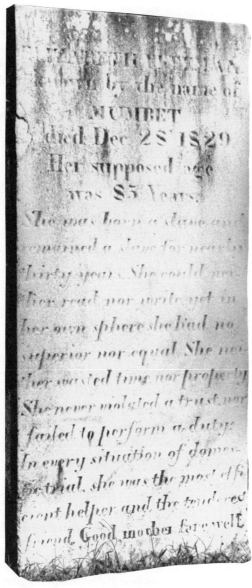

168. Tombstone of Elizabeth Freeman, Stockbridge, Massachusetts. [Photograph by Walter H. Scott] Stockbridge Public Library, Stockbridge, Massachusetts.

The maroons of Waltham had defended their self-won freedom bravely, and now they took the offensive. Filing a lawsuit against the lieutenant and his posse, they secured an indictment against them for riot. On September 10, 1781, when Hastings asked the town to defend him in court against Cuff's charges, the town turned down his request. Thus, the maroons had in effect abolished slavery, at least in Middlesex County.

Ten years later a Felix Cuffer is listed in the census of 1790 as head of a family of three.

Primus Hall: Soldier and Citizen

Primus Hall was the worthy son of the founder of African Freemasonry. In the year 1836, at the age of eighty-two, he wrote out part of his life story in his application for a veteran's pension:

I, Primus Hall of the City of Boston . . . was born in Beacon St. in this City on the 29th day of February of the year 1756. *my Fathers name was Prince Hall . . . my Mothers name was Delia Hall and she was a Servant* . . . at the age of one Month old I was given to a Mr. Ezra Trask of Danvers [who] was to bring me up and learne me the Trade of Shomaker—as soon as I was old enough, and that at the age of Twenty one years I was to be free—the same as any white person. . . . And accordingly at the age of ten years or thereabouts I began to work at said trade—and from then untill I was fifteen . . . the occupation of Shomaker did not suit me—and my health was much impared. . . . Trask gave me my freedom with full liberty. . . . I was thence afterwards in various ocupations some times as a Farmer at others as a Truckman in Salem. . . . At the age of Nineteen I enlisted. . . . Service Nineteen months and an half as a Soldier . . . in the Campaign against Genl Burgoyn . . . and in the Campaign on Rhode Island. . . .

On his return from the battlefield, Primus Hall continued to live with his father; in 1784, at the age of thirty, he married Phoebe Baker. The minutes of the African Lodge of Freemasons in Boston show him as an active member, and in 1790 the census lists him as a head of family with seven dependents. By this time, as a "master soap boiler," he had an estate worth six thousand dollars.

In 1798, a portion of the black community in Boston founded a school for the children of the neighborhood with two white Harvard students as instructors. The school-house was the home of Primus Hall. When the Baptist minister Thomas Paul, an active Mason, tried to raise money to set up a school for the children of his flock, Primus Hall and his friends appealed for help to black seamen in the port.

Primus Hall was pushing sixty when a call went out from the State House for citizens to go to Castle Island in order to build fortifications against the threatening British. The revolutionary veteran was one of the volunteers. He lived on for another thirty years and died when he was over ninety. By way of obituary in an article titled "Anecdotes of Washington," printed in *Godey's Magazine* in 1849, there is a story about Hall that delighted Nell, a fellow Bostonian:

There lately died, in the city of Boston, a very respectable negro, named Primus Hall. He lived to an advanced age, and was the possessor of considerable property. Throughout the Revolutionary war he was the body servant of the late Col. Pickering, of Massachusetts. He was free and communicative, and delighted to sit down with an interested listener and pour out those stores of absorbing and exciting anecdotes with which his memory was stored. . . .

On [one] occasion, the great general was engaged in earnest consultation with Col. Pickering in his tent until after the night had fairly set in . . . and Washington signified his preference to staying with the colonel over night, provided he had a spare blanket and straw.

"Oh, yes," said Primus, who was appealed to; "plenty of straw and blankets—plenty."

Upon this assurance, Washington continued his conference with the colonel until it was time to retire to rest. Two humble beds were spread, side by side, in the tent, and the officers laid themselves down, while Primus seemed to be busy with duties that required his attention before he himself could sleep. He worked, or appeared to work, until the breathing of the prostrate gentlemen satisfied him that they were sleeping; and then, seating himself on a box or stool, he leaned his head on his hands. . . . In the middle of the night, Washington awoke. . . .

"Primus!" said he, calling; "Primus!"

Primus stared up and rubbed his eyes. "What, general?" said he.

Washington rose up in his bed. "Primus," said he, "what did you mean by saying that you had straw and blankets enough? Here you have given up your blanket and straw to me, that I may sleep comfortably, while you are obliged to sit through the night."

"It's nothing, general," said Primus. "It's nothing. I'm well enough. Don't trouble yourself about me, general, but go to sleep again. No matter about me. I sleep very good."

"But it is matter—it is matter," said Washington, earnestly. "I cannot do it, Primus. If either is to sit up, I will. But I think there is no need of either sitting up. The blanket is wide enough for two. Come and lie down here with me."

"Oh, no, general!" said Primus, starting, and protesting . . . "No; let me sit here. I'll do very well on the stool."

"I say, come and lie down here!" said Washington, authoritatively.

"There is room for both, and I insist upon it!"

He threw open the blanket as he spoke, and moved to one side of the straw. Primus professes to have been exceedingly shocked at the idea of lying under the same covering with the commander-in-chief, but his tone was so resolute and determined that he could not hesitate. He prepared himself, therefore, and laid himself down by Washington; and on the same straw, and under the same blanket, the general and the negro servant slept until morning.

Lydia Maria Child wrote a shortened version of this tale of George Washington and Primus Hall for her *Freedmen's Book* of 1865.

Yarrow Mamout: Maryland Muslim

Just how many African Muslims sweated as slaves in Christian America is a question that scholars have not yet settled.* Ben-Ali, a young student in the western Sudan, had the misfortune to find himself on a slave ship bound for America in an early year of the nineteenth century; in the Georgia State Library there is a manuscript in his fine Arabic hand consisting of long excerpts from the *Risalah,* a well-known text of the Malikite school of Mohammedan law dealing with the ritual of ablutions and the call to prayer. Half a century later in the same

---

*The authority on this subject is Alan D. Austin's *African Muslims in Antebellum America,* a brilliant survey that covers the United States. Another survey of black Muslims in the New World is needed. The French artist Pierre Eugene Du Simitiere, visiting St. Domingue in January 1773, met an Islamic Mandingo priest, enslaved in Leoganne, who, in his presence, wrote out in Arabic a "gris-gris," a West African charm, which still exists.

state, another Muslim, dubbed London by his master, wrote out in Arabic a phonetic transcription of the four Gospels and several hymns. In the early 1730s, the celebrated Job Ben Solomon, prince of Boudou in the land of Futa—who knew the whole Koran by heart—spent two years in Maryland as a slave, until a letter that he wrote to his father in purest Arabic came to the attention of Sir Hans Sloane, the linguist of Oxford University, which led to his freedom and an African throne [fig. 169].

Still another black Muslim, who had been kidnapped in Africa and sold as a slave in Maryland long before Job Ben Solomon, bought his own freedom, lived through the revolution, acquired property, never gave up his religion, and lived to be over a hundred years old. His name was Yarrow Mamout. One winter day in the year 1819, the artist Charles Willson Peale (his son Raphaelle had painted Absalom Jones) who was visiting Washington to record the visages of American worthies for his Baltimore Museum, rode over to Georgetown to do the centenarian's portrait [fig. 170]. In his diary for that day, the only source for the life of Yarrow Mamout, he wrote at length:

> I spent the whole day and not only painted a good likeness of him, but also the drapery and background— However to finish it more completely I engaged him to set the next day— and early in the morning went to see some of the family who had knowledge of him for many years & whose Ancestors had purchased him from the ship that brought him from Africa. A Mr. Bell in a Bank directed me to an ancient widow who had set him free—on making inquiry of this Lady about his age, for he told me that he would be 134 years old in next March, I found that he counted

12 moons to the year, and that he was 35 years old when he was first brought to America by Cptn Dow— But the widow Bell told me that it was a practice in former times when slaves was brought into the Country, they were valued by a committee who estimated their age and she thought that he had been sold as 14 years or thereabout, yet he might be a little older—That at the decease of Mr Bell he became the property of her husband—that Yarrow was always an industrious hard working man and had served them faithfully for many years, and her Husband intending to build a large House in Georgetown, told Yarrow if he would be very industrious in Making the Bricks for that House and out houses, that when he had made all the Bricks, that he would set him free. Yarrow completed his task, but his master died before he began the House, and the widow knowing the design of her Husband, told Yarrow that as he had performed his duty, that she had made the necessary papers to set him free & now he was made free. Yarrow made a great many Bows thanking his mistress and said that [if] ever mistress wanted work done, Yarrow would work for her . . . after Yarrow obtained his freedom he worked hard and saved his money until he got 100$ which [he] put into an old gentlemans hands to keep for him—that person died and Yarrow lost his money—however it did not dispirit him, for he still worked as before and raised another 100$ which he put into the care of a young merchant in Georgetown, and Yarrow said young man no die—but this merchant became a Bankrupt and thus Yarrow met a 2d heavy loss—yet

169. *Job Ben Solomon,* engraving, *Gentleman's Magazine,* June 1750, p. 272. By permission, Rare Book Room, Library, Smith College.

JOB Ben Solomon was a person of great distinction in his own country. In the year 1731, as he was driving his herds of cattle a-cross the countries in Jagra, he was seized and carried to Joar; where he was sold to capt. Pyke, commander of the ship Arabella, who carried him to Maryland, and sold him to a planter. Here Job lived about a year without being once beat by his master; at the end of which he had the good fortune to have a letter of his own writing in the Arabic tongue conveyed to England. This letter coming to the hand of Mr Oglethorpe, he sent it to Oxford to be translated; the translation pleased him so much, and gave him so good an opinion of the man, that he directly ordered him to be bought from his master. But soon after setting out for Georgia, before he returned from thence, Job was brought to England; where waiting on the learned Sir Hans Sloane, he was found to be a perfect master of the Arabic tongue, by translating several manuscripts and inscriptions upon medals into English, of which he had acquired a competent knowledge

during his servitude and passage to England; this gentleman recommended him to his grace the duke of Montagu, who being pleased with the sweetness of humour and mildness of temper, as well as genius and capacity of the man, introduced him to court, where he was graciously received by the royal family, and most of the nobility, from whom he received distinguishing marks of favour. After he had continued in England about fourteen months, he wanted much to return to his native country and his father, to whom he sent letters from England. He received many valuable presents from Q. Caroline, the D. of Cumberland, the D. of Montagu, the E. of Pembroke, several ladies of quality, Mr Holden, and the royal African company, who ordered their agents to show him the greatest respects. He arrived safe in Africa; and Mr Moor in his travels met with, and gives some farther account of him.

not dispirited he worked & saved a 3d sum amounting to 200$, some friend to Yarrow advised him to Buy bank stock in the Columbia Bank—this advice Yarrow thought good for he said Bank no die—and he was amongst the first who contributed to that Bank about 26 years past. . . .

Yarrow owns a House and lotts & is known by most of the Inhabitants of Georgetown & particularly by the Boys who are often teazing him which he takes in good humour. It appears to me that the good temper of the man has contributed considerably to longevity. Yarrow has been noted for

170. Charles Willson Peale, *Yarrow Mamout,* oil, 1819. The Historical Society of Pennsylvania.

sobriety & a cheerfull conduct, he professes to be a Mahometan, and is often seen & heard in the Streets singing Praises to God—and conversing with him he said man is no good unless his religion come from the heart. he said never stole one penny in his life—yet he seems delighted to sport with those in company, pretending that he would steal something—The Butchers in the Market can always find a bit of meat to give to Yarrow—sometimes he will pretend to steal a piece of meat and put it into the Basket of some gentleman, and then say me no tell if you give me half—

The acquaintances of him often banter him about eating Bacon and drinking Whiskey—but Yarrow says it is no good to eat Hog—& drink whiskey is very bad.

I retouched his Portrait the morning after his first setting to mark what rinkles & lines to characterize better his Portrait. . . .

It is said that Peale was interested in Yarrow Mamout only because he was a specimen of healthy, cheerful old age, but something more is caught forever in the portrait. The face of the venerable black Muslim is shrewd, sad, witty, cynical. He had seen a lot in his long life.

Venture Smith: Colonial John Henry

"I was born at Dukandarra, in Guinea, about the year 1729," related old Venture Smith of Haddam Neck, Connecticut, to Elisha Niles, schoolteacher and revolutionary veteran: "My father's name was Saungm Furro, Prince of the tribe of Dukandarra. My father had three wives. Polygamy was not uncommon in that country, especially among the rich, as every man was allowed to keep as many wives as he could maintain. By his first wife he had three children. The eldest of them was myself, named by my father, Broteer. . . . I descended from a very large, tall and stout race of beings, much larger than the generality of people in other parts of the globe. . . ." Like Olaudah Equiano, Smith was an early victim of the African slave trade. At the age of eight, one of 260 blacks canoed from "the castle" to a Rhode Island slaver, he was purchased by a steward as a private speculation for four gallons of rum and a piece of calico, and re-

named "Venture." A quarter of the cargo perished in the Middle Passage to Barbados. His third owner gave him a surname—thus Broteer, son of a Guinea prince, became Venture Smith, New England slave.

A Narrative of the Life and Adventures of Venture, a Native of Africa: But Resident above Sixty Years in the United States of America, Related by Himself is an epic of heroic labor that became a myth. Venture Smith according to tradition was straight and tall, weighed over three hundred pounds, and measured six feet around the waist. He was a New England John Henry who swung his ax to break his chains.

But there is no humor in the tale of this black Bunyan. Venture Smith was no ringtailed roarer who told tall tales. At nine, he carded wool and pounded corn for the poultry, and for the next dozen years worked day and night for his master while he hungered for freedom and planned to win it one way or another. He was abused. One day his master's son ordered him "very arrogantly" to drop what he was doing and take on another task:

> I replied to him that my master had given me so much to perform that day, and that I must faithfully complete it in that time. He then broke out into a great rage, snatched a pitchfork and went to lay me over the head therewith, but I as soon got another and defended myself with it. . . . He immediately called some people . . . and ordered them to take his hair rope and come and bind me with it. They all tried to bind me, but in vain, though there were three assistants in number.

Later, when Venture felt it was useless further to resist, he was taken "to a gallows made for the purpose of hanging cattle on" and suspended therefrom for an hour.

At twenty-two he married Meg, another slave on the farm, and with three indentured whites stole his master's boat, stocked it with food, and at midnight, "mutually confederated not to betray or desert one another on pain of death," steered for Montauk Point and the Gulf of Mexico. But the conspirators fell out and the plan aborted. When Venture defended Meg from being beaten by her mistress, she turned her frenzy on him: "She took down her horse whip, and while she was glutting her fury with it, I reached out my great black hand, raised it up and received the blows of the whip on it which were designed for my head. Then I immediately committed the whip to the devouring fire." This was not the end. In revenge, his master clubbed him on the head from behind, and later, with a brother, ambushed him on horseback as he walked down a lonely road. "I became enraged at this and immediately turned them both under me, laid one of them across the other, and stamped them both with my feet. . . ." The two whites summoned help to manacle his hands and padlock his legs with a large oxchain: after a few days "my master asked me with contemptuous hard names whether I had not better be freed from my chains and go to work. I answered him 'No,' 'Well, then,' said he, 'I will send you to the West Indies, or banish you. . . .' I answered him, 'I crossed the waters to come here and I am willing to cross them to return.'"

This giant black man who would suffer no insult was a problem for his owners, although they profited by his sinews: "One time my master sent me two miles after a barrel of molasses, and ordered me to carry it on my shoulders. [He did.] When I lived with Capt. George Mumford, only to try my strength I took upon my knees a tierce of salt containing seven bushels, and carried it two or three rods. Of this fact there are several eye witnesses now living."

Meanwhile he toiled and scraped to hoard enough to buy his freedom. He managed to put away "two johannes, three old Spanish dollars, and two thousand of coppers . . . by cleaning gentlemen's shoes and drawing-boots, by catching muskrats and minks, raising potatoes and carrots . . . by fishing in the night," and Meg contributed five pounds. Through a free black friend, he acquired a piece of land and in two years farmed ten pounds out of it. A new master allowed him to hire himself out once in a while and let him keep part of his earnings. One fall and winter he worked on Long Island: "In that six months' time I cut and corded four hundred cords of wood, besides threshing out seventy-five bushels of grain. . . . At night I lay on the hearth, with one coverlet over and another under me." In 1765, his master finally liberated him for "seventy-one pounds two shillings." He was thirty-six years old: "I had already been sold three different times, made considerable money with seemingly nothing to derive it from, had been cheated out of a large sum of money, lost much by misfortunes and paid an enormous sum for my freedom."

ALTHOUGH he was now free, his wife and children were still slaves. He settled on Long Island where he performed prodigies of labor while he lived like a Spartan to pile up the dollars to free his family. His hired ax toppled grove after grove. He purchased Meg for forty pounds (and "thereby prevented having another child to buy, as she was pregnant") and his daughter Hannah for forty-four, paid four hundred dollars to liberate his sons, Solomon and Cuff, and redeemed from slavery three black friends. (Solomon died soon after of scurvy on a whale ship; Cuff enlisted in the East Haddam militia and fought in the army of the revolution.) Venture never stopped. Chartering a thirty-ton sloop, he took on a crew and plied the wood trade to Rhode Island, fished with set-nets and pots for eels and lobsters, shipped out on a seven-month whaling voyage, and raised cartloads of watermelons for market.

When he was forty-seven, he sold out and moved to Connecticut, bought land, built a house, and hired two black farm-hands. When one of them defaulted on a debt, he procured a warrant and carried him on his shoulders two miles to court. As time went on, he acquired "boats, canoes and vessels, not less than twenty." His enormous labor paid off, but being black he had to work three times as hard as white for the same returns. There was heartache. Fleeced by a Captain Elisha Hart of Saybrook, he found that justice was hard to come by:

> I applied to several gentlemen for counsel in this affair, and they advised me, as my adversary was rich, and threatened to carry the matter from court to court till it would cost me more than the first damages would be,—to pay the sum and submit to the injury, which I accordingly did, and he has often since insultingly taunted me with my unmerited misfortune. Such a proceeding as this committed on a defenceless stranger, almost worn out in the hard service of the world, without any foundation in reason or justice, whatever it may be called in a Christian land, would in my native country have been branded as a crime equal to highway robbery. But Captain Hart was a *white gentleman,* and I a *poor African,* therefore it was *all right, and good enough for the black dog.*

When his *Narrative* was printed in New London in 1798, he said in it [fig. 171]:

> I am sixty-nine years old. . . . My strength which was once equal if not superior to any man whom I have ever seen, is now enfeebled so that life is a burden, and it is with fatigue that I can walk a couple of miles, stooping over my staff. . . . But amidst all griefs and pains, I have many consolations; Meg the wife of my youth, whom I married for love and bought with my money, is still alive. My freedom is a privilege which nothing can equal.

A village historian, over a century later, repeated a pleasant story of his wedding day:

> It is related of Venture that on the occasion of his marriage he threw a rope over the house of his master, where they were living, and had his wife go to the opposite side of the house and pull on the rope hanging there while he remained and pulled on his end of it. After both had tugged at it awhile in vain, he called her to his side of the house and by their united effort the rope was drawn over to themselves with ease.

He then explained the object lesson: "If we pull in life against each other we shall fail, but if we pull together we shall succeed."

The strength and skill of Venture Smith were talked about in Connecticut and Long Island for a hundred years after his death. Stories about this folk work-hero passed into tradition with variations of all kinds. One old-timer remembered that when Venture lifted the great tierce of salt, his brogan shoes burst off his feet. Another recalled that a "noted wrestler tried his skill in wrestling with Venture, but found he might as

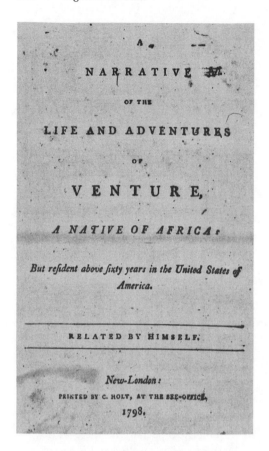

171. *Narrative of the Life and Adventures of Venture . . . Related by Himself* (New London, 1798). Courtesy of the Library of Congress.

well try to remove a tree." He was too heavy to ride on a horse's back, so used a two-wheeled cart. "Sometimes his horse did not behave well, and then, Venture would put one hand in front of his horse's forelegs and one hand behind them and jounce the fore parts of the horse up and down a few times and remark, 'There!' The horse would usually behave well after such a jouncing."

Venture's ax was almost always a part of the tale. It was reported that this ax weighed nine pounds and that he never raised it higher than his head—said he didn't believe in chopping air. He could cut up nine cords in a day and often paddled his canoe forty-five miles across Long Island

Sound and back to chop wood and bring back clams. Once, when he was old, blind, and had to be led by his grandchildren, he moved a loaded scow stuck high up on the beach. Venture said, "Lead me down. True, I am blind, but I can give you a lift." The timbers "fairly cracked as his great hands touched the scow. She swept into the water like a bird on the wing." Another tradition has it that after his sight failed, when he bought oxen he seized each ox by its hind legs and raised it up to estimate its weight.

Borne down by age and illness, Venture Smith died on September 19, 1805, in his seventy-seventh year. Like an epic warrior, his body was conveyed in a boat across the cove and carried three miles by four men, two white and two black, to the burial ground of the First Congregational Church. As they arrived at the cemetery, one of the black pallbearers, crushed by the weight of the bier, exclaimed: "Durned great Negro! Ought to have quartered him and gone four times. It makes the gravel stones crack under my feet." On the brownstone slab that marks his grave, next to his wife's, is the inscription: "Sacred to the Memory of Venture Smith, African. Though the son of a King, he was kidnapped and sold as a slave, but by his industry he acquired money to purchase his freedom."

Moses Sash: "A Captain & One of Shaises Councill"

When debt-ridden farmers led by the revolutionary veteran Captain Daniel Shays arose in western Massachusetts during the winter of 1786–87, Prince Hall in Boston pledged the support of his lodge of black Masons to the crushing of the rebellion. Whatever Hall's real reasons may have been, Governor Bowdoin rejected the offer. It is doubtful that more than a few black troops marched west to suppress this "little rebellion" that so alarmed the men of "wealth and talent" of the state. (In Berkshire County, Jack Burghardt, another ancestor of W.E.B. Du Bois, found himself on the anti-Shays side.) Were there Afro-Americans who stood openly with Shays? The names of black farmers Tobias Green of Plainfield and Aaron Carter of Colrain appear briefly as insurgents in the documents of the time, but there is record of at least one black veteran of the revolution who fought in the uprising and possibly served as an officer in a section of the guerrilla army.

AT the time of the uprising, Moses Sash of Worthington was twenty-eight years old. Six years earlier, like Shays, he had enlisted in the Continental Army and at the end of the war had trudged home from West Point to resume the old life. The documents describe him as farmer and laborer; five feet, eight inches high; complexion, black; hair, wool.

Among the records of the Supreme Judicial Court of Massachusetts there is a crumbling packet of grand jury indictments naming thirty-two traitorous rebels variously denominated yeoman, husbandman, tanner, tradesman, laborer. Moses Sash is the only black man of the group, the only laborer, and the only rebel to have two indictments leveled against him.

The first indictment reads as follows [fig. 172]:

> The jurors of the Commonwealth of Massachusetts upon their oath present that Moses Sash of Worthington . . . a negro man & Labourer being a disorderly, riotous & seditious person & minding & contriving as much as in him lay unlawfully by force of arms to stir up promote incite & maintain riots mobs tumults insurrections in this Commonwealth & to disturb impede & prevent the Gov-

> ernment of the same & the due administration of justice in the same, & to prevent the Courts of justice from sitting as by Law appointed for that purpose & to promote disquiets, uneasiness, jealousies, animosities & seditions in the minds of the Citizens of this Commonwealth on the twentieth day of January in the year of our Lord Seventeen hundred & eighty seven & on divers other days & times as well before as since that time at Worthington . . . unlawfully & seditiously with force & arms did advise persuade invite incourage & procure divers persons . . . of this Commonwealth by force of arms to oppose this Commonwealth & the Government thereof & riotously to join themselves to a great number of riotous seditious persons with force & arms thus opposing this commonwealth & the Government thereof as aforesaid & the due administration of justice in the same, and in pursuance of his wicked seditious purposes aforesaid unlawfully & seditiously, did procure guns, bayonets, pistols, swords, gunpowder, bullets, blankets & provisions & other warlike instruments offensive & defensive & other warlike supplies, & did cause & procure them to be carried & conveyed to the riotous & seditious persons as aforesaid in evil example to others to offend in like manner against the peace of the Commonwealth aforesaid & dignity of the same.

Thus, Moses Sash, on January 20, 1787, as a participant in an insurrectionary demonstration called by a rebel convention, had tried to stop the courts from foreclosing mortgages and jailing debtors in "the due administration of justice." Five days later,

172. Indictment of Moses Sash by the Supreme Judicial Court of Massachusetts, April 9, 1787, excerpt. Supreme Judicial Court for Suffolk County.

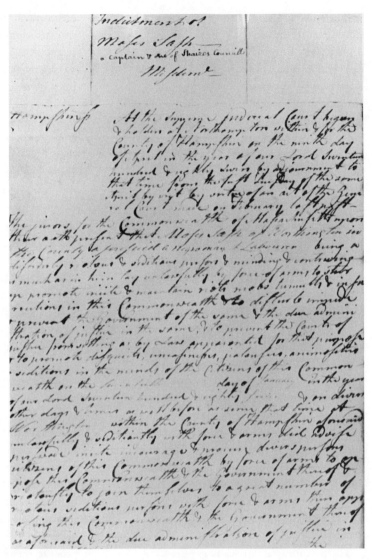

in fact, he would flee with Shays after government mortars had scattered the rebels from Arsenal Hill in Springfield. As Bowdoin's general pursued the insurgents through Chicopee and South Hadley, Shays rallied his band on two hills in Pelham, sending out parties to forage for food and guns. Thus, the second indictment against Sash, who on January 30 "fraudulently, unlawfully & feloniously two guns to the value of five pounds of certain persons to the jurors unknown with force and arms did steal away."

Eventually, the new governor, John Hancock, pardoned almost all the insurgents, leaders, and followers. On the back of the first indictment against Moses Sash are the words: "a Captain & one of Shaises Councill." It is the only indictment of the packet so endorsed. Thus far, the archives have not yielded any further data to account for the high place of this black private of the first revolution in the second revolution of Daniel Shays. No further record has turned up to reveal a personal relationship between Captain Sash and Captain Shays. In his

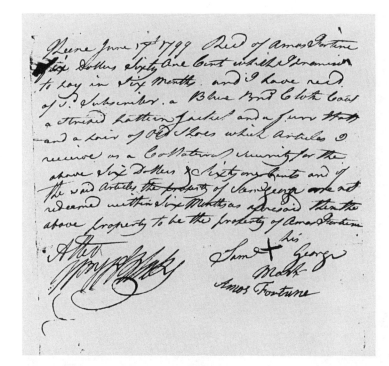

173. Freedom papers of
Amos Fortune, 1770.
Jaffrey [New Hampshire]
Public Library.

youth, Shays worked as a laborer on a large farm, the Brinkley estate in Hopkinton (where he was born), along with fifteen or twenty blacks, probably slaves.

After the rebellion was over, Moses Sash continued to live in Worthington, where he began to raise a family. In 1820, in his sixties and now living in Connecticut with his wife and her elderly mother, he wrote to Worthington in his own hand, asking for a pension: "I have no property, real or personal. I am by occupation a day laborer at farming [and] can labor but very little. . . . I have been partly supported by the town of Hartford for several years."

Amos and Violate Fortune: First Citizens of New Hampshire

On January 28, 1796, at the parsonage of a small town in New Hampshire, a meeting was held "for the purpose of forming a Collection of Usefull books to be called the So-cial Library in Jaffrey." Among the twenty-two charter members present that day was venerable Amos Fortune, a free black and one of the more literate citizens of the town, a man who as a boy had been purchased from a Yankee slave dealer and had served as a chattel for half a century.

Where he got the name of Fortune no one knows. It was in Boston, possibly during his youthful years, that he learned to read and write and bind books. As a slave in Woburn, Massachusetts, he learned the art of the tanner from his master, Ichabod Richardson. For nearly forty years Fortune slaved for Richardson until in the year 1770 he was permitted to buy himself free [fig. 173]. Sixty years old, he now began to live. He was a master tanner and business was good. He paid his church and town taxes regularly and in 1774 purchased a half-acre on the Wilmington Road. When he was sixty-eight, tired of being a bachelor, he bought and wedded Lydia Somerset in nearby Lexington, where the war had

174. Gravestones of Amos and Violate Fortune, Jaffrey, New Hampshire, fiberglass facsimiles. Smithsonian Institution, Office of Exhibits.

started a few years earlier. When Lydia died a few months after the marriage, he bought and wedded Violate Baldwin; she would outlive him by a year.

In 1781, for reasons unknown, the Fortunes moved to Jaffrey, New Hampshire. There he set up a tannery and again he prospered. After a time he took in apprentices, black and white—a white doctor sent him his son to learn tanning, as well as reading and writing. He joined the church and became one of the first citizens of Jaffrey.

There were a few other free black families in Jaffrey, but none had done as well as the Fortunes. Amos reached out to them. He knew enough law to act as an attorney for a brother in distress, and he took into his household two black girls who became part of the family.

In 1796, after he had paid in his three

dollars as a founding member of the Social Library—a dollar and a half was a good day's pay at the time—he began to rebind the books in the collection, using his own fine leather, which is still soft and warm.

Five years later, at the age of ninety-one, Fortune died. In his will he left everything to his wife except a few pieces of furniture and a foot-wheel loom that went "to Celyndia Fortune, my adopted daughter." The final item of the will reveals the public benefactor: if there is any money left after Violate's death, it is to be used "to give a handsome present . . . to the Church of Christ in this town, and the remaining part . . . a present for the Support of the School. . . ." The church acquired a silver communion service; the fund he bequeathed to the school is still used for annual prizes.

Another item in Amos Fortune's will reveals his pride in a long life well lived: "I order my executor after my decease and after the decease of . . . my beloved wife that handsome grave Stones be erected to each of us if there is any estate left for that purpose." The "handsome grave Stones" stand today in the churchyard behind the Meeting House in Jaffrey {fig. 174}. Carved on the gray slate, beneath the urn and willow, are two epitaphs that Amos himself perhaps composed.

Three Concord Blacks: John Jack, Brister Freeman, Casey Whitney

In Concord, Massachusetts, not far from Emerson's "rude bridge," John Jack, former slave of the shoemaker Benjamin Barron, built a cabin in 1761 after he had purchased his freedom. At the same time, he asked lawyer Daniel Bliss to draw up his will, leaving everything after burial expenses to his wife, Violet. John Jack died two years before the shot heard round the world, and Daniel Bliss, later a Tory expatriate, wrote the epitaph carved on his tombstone, which a London newspaper printed as an "ironic comment" on the claims of the Sons of Liberty. When the original stone wore away, the lawyers of Concord in 1830 replaced it with a replica {fig. 175}.

Colonel John Cuming of Concord, a wealthy physician, farmer, and land speculator, owned a slave named Brister whose service in the army included the campaign against Burgoyne, after which he seems to have changed his name to Brister Freeman. Two years later, in 1779, at the age of thirty-one, Freeman reenlisted. In 1790, the Concord census lists him as a freeman, head of a family of seven. His services in war and peace did not protect him from harassment by his white neighbors, who at one time tricked him into an encounter with an angry bull and laughed as he fought for his

175. Gravestone of John Jack, Concord, Massachusetts, fiberglass facsimile. Smithsonian Institution, Office of Exhibits.

life. No wonder he came to be known in the town as "a very passionate man" who would not suffer "boys who loved to insult and plague him."

The abolitionist Henry David Thoreau, curious about Concord's ancient history, records another black man of Concord who lived in the revolutionary time, an African slave named Casey Whitney, who also loved liberty. He was about twenty "when stolen from Africa; left a wife and one child there," wrote Thoreau in his journal in 1858. One day his master's son "threw snowballs at him . . . and finally C., who was chopping in the yard, threw his axe at him. . . ." Master "said he was an ugly nigger and he must put him in jail." Casey ran away, "pursued by his neighbors, and hid himself in the river up to his neck till nightfall" and then "cleared far away, enlisted, and was freed as a soldier after the war." It was toward the end of the war when he joined the ranks. "Case" Whitney ("age, 37 yrs.; stature, 5 ft. 5 in.; complexion black; occupation, farmer," on the muster roll) enlisted in the nearby town of Lancaster for a three-year term in the Continental Army. Casey "used to say that he went home to Africa in the night and came back again in the morning; i.e., he dreamed of home. . . ."

No doubt, before the war, John Jack knew Casey Whitney and Brister Freeman. Did they talk together about their dreams of Africa?

VII

The Incomplete Revolution

How black people, slave and free, as time went on, would come to view the Declaration of 1776 and its celebration is matter for another chronicle. As Benjamin Quarles has explained in a lucid bicentennial essay, for many blacks who half a century after the revolution still lived in a land of bondage and were sick of spread-eagle rhetoric in the "spirit of '76," the Fourth of July would go unobserved. Blacks shifted their day of celebration to the Fifth of July, and then to the First of August—the anniversary of emancipation in the British West Indies in 1834. Indeed, within the black communities of the nation before the Civil War, the meaning of Jefferson's Declaration for the political struggles of the day would be a subject of hot debate.

TOWARD the end of June 1852, newspapers and posters in the city of Rochester, New York, carried the news that Frederick Douglass would deliver a Fourth of July oration in Corinthian Hall [fig. 176]. The speech was one of the most profound utterances of his career. His great voice soared out of the hall to address the nation.

> Fellow citizens, why am I called upon to speak here today? What have I, or those I represent, to do with your national independence? Are the great principles of political freedom and of natural justice, embodied in that Declaration of Independence, extended to us? and am I, therefore, called upon to bring our humble offering to the national altar, and to confess the benefits and express devout gratitude for the blessings resulting from your independence to us?

ON February 12, 1793, George Washington signed "An Act respecting Fugitives from Justice, and Persons escaping from the Services of their Masters" [fig. 177]. This first Fugitive Slave Act—sixty-four years before Judge Taney sent Dred Scott back to

176. J. W. Hurn, Philadelphia, *Frederick Douglass,* photograph, not dated. Courtesy of the Library of Congress.

his master—reenforced the legality of slavery in the newly born United States of America.

Four years later, during the spring of 1797, one Louis-Philippe, a foreign visitor destined to be king of France, on his youthful travels abroad, visited the new federal capital (which Benjamin Banneker had helped to survey) and then sailed down the Potowmack to Mount Vernon to pay his respects to the recently retired president. On April 5, 1797, he recorded in his diary:

The general owns ten thousand acres of land around Mount Vernon. Hardly half of it is under cultivation. There are about 400 blacks scattered among the different farms. . . . Virginia law imposes the same punishment on a master who kills a slave as on any other murderer, but the law is very rarely applied; as slaves are denied by statute the right to bear witness, the charge is never proved. General Washington has forbidden the use of the whip on his blacks, but unfortunately his example has been little emulated. Here Negroes are not considered human beings. When they meet a white man, they greet him from a distance and with a low bow, and they often seem amazed when we return their greeting, for no one here does so. All agricultural labor in Virginia is performed by blacks, who on the various farms are housed in wretched wooden shacks here called quarters. . . .

The last census in Virginia showed 770,000 inhabitants. It is estimated that some three-fourths of them are blacks. This ratio is terrifying, and

177. "An Act respecting Fugitives from Justice, and Persons escaping from the Services of their Masters," Second Congress, broadside, approved by President George Washington, February 12, 1793. Courtesy of the Library of Congress.

will sooner or later prove deadly to the southern states. Ideas of freedom have already made headway among them; apparently Quakers, Anabaptists, and Methodists circulate the doctrine. The general's blacks told Beaudoin [Louis-Philippe's valet] that they had clubs in Alexandria and Georgetown, that Quakers came to visit, and they hoped they would no longer be slaves in ten years—not that they wanted to follow the example of the blacks in Santo-Domingo, they would do no harm to any man, etc. . . . The general's cook ran away,

being now in Philadelphia, and left a little daughter of six at Mount Vernon. Beaudoin ventured that the little girl must be deeply upset that she would never see her father again; she answered, *Oh! sir, I am very glad, because he is free now.*

A year after the Declaration, the General Assembly of the revolutionary government of North Carolina, alarmed by the headlong flight of slaves to the British lines and angered by the growing abolitionism of local Quakers, borrowed Jefferson's language to pass an act "to prevent domestic Insurrections." Sheriffs began to sell newly freed slaves at public auctions unless they could prove that they had served in the patriot army. Neither the victory at Yorktown nor the adoption of the federal constitution put an end to this practice. In North Carolina in 1790 a slaveholder was denied the right to free his slave unless he obtained the approval of a county court [fig. 178].

During the summer of 1797, four runaways from North Carolina—Jupiter and Jacob Nicholson, Joe Albert, and Thomas Pritchet—working and hiding out in Philadelphia, came with their anguish to the Reverend Absalom Jones. Now they feared that slave catchers would kidnap them to the south. What could they do, they asked Absalom Jones, to save themselves?

The abolitionist Jones listened, pondered—and picked up his pen. It was time—twenty-one years after the Declaration of Independence—for another indictment of the institution of slavery, now embedded in the Constitution of the United States. Days passed as he formulated the items of the indictment in their proper order. When he put down his pen, the runaways could submit to president and Congress their petition in defense of Afro-American rights—the first, probably, that the government of the new republic would be forced to consider [fig. 179].*

As Absalom Jones framed the document, it opened with a statement of their case:

> Being of African descent, late inhabitants and natives of North Carolina, to you only, under God, can we apply with any hope of effect, for redress of our grievances . . . reduced to the necessity of separating from some of our nearest and most tender connexions, and of seeking refuge in such parts of the Union where more regard is paid to the public declaration in favor of liberty and the common right of man, several hundred [have] been hunted day and night, like beasts of the forest, by armed men with dogs, and made a prey of as free and lawful plunder.

Then, with painstaking care, Jones wrote out their individual stories in exact detail:

> I, Jupiter Nicholson, of Perquimans County, N.C., after being set free by my master, Thomas Nicholson, and having been about two years employed as a seaman in the service of Zachary Nickson, on coming on shore, was pursued by men with dogs and arms; but was favored to escape by night to Virginia, with my

wife, who was manumitted by Gabriel Cosand, where I resided about four years in the town of Portsmouth, chiefly employed in sawing boards and scantling; from thence I removed with my wife to Philadelphia, where I have been employed, at times, by water, working along shore, or sawing wood. . . .

> I, Jacob Nicholson, also of North Carolina, being set free by my master, Joseph Nicholson, but continuing to live with him till, being pursued night and day, I was obliged to leave my abode, sleep in the woods, and stacks in the fields, &c, to escape the hands of violent men. . . .

> I, Joe Albert, manumitted by Benjamin Albertson . . . we were night and day hunted by men armed with guns, swords and pistols, accompanied with mastiff dogs. . . . After binding me with my hands behind me, and a rope around my arms and body, they took me about four miles to Hartford prison, where I lay four weeks . . . with the assistance of a fellow-prisoner (a white man) I made my escape and for three dollars was conveyed, with my wife, by a humane person, in a covered wagon by night, to Virginia. . . . On being advised to move northward, I came with my wife to Philadelphia, where I have labored for a livelihood upwards of two years, in Summer mostly, along shore in vessels and stores, and sawing wood in the Winter.

> I, Thomas Pritchet . . . built myself a house, cleared a sufficient spot of woodland to produce ten bushels of corn . . . this I was obliged to leave . . . being threatened by Holland Lockwood . . . that if I would not come and serve him, he would ap-

---

*There were also earlier black petitions (to state legislatures) even as the federal constitution was being written and ratified—for instance, the petitions of Prince Hall and his associates in October 1787 and February 1788, already noted. In Charleston, South Carolina, a memorial of 1791, signed with a flourish by three blacks—a bricklayer and two butchers "on behalf of themselves & other Free-Men of Colour"—pointed out that "at all times since the Independence of the United States" they had paid their taxes and supposedly enjoyed "the Rights and Immunities of Citizens," yet now were in fact subject to trial without benefit of jury. The senate of South Carolina rejected their memorial.

178. "An Account of the Sale of Sundry Negroes . . . to Prevent Domestick Insurrections . . . 1788." Perquimans County Slave Papers, North Carolina State Department of Archives and History, Raleigh.

prehend me, and send me to the West Indies; Enoch Ralph also threatening to send me to jail, and sell me for the good of the country; being thus in jeopardy, I left my little farm, with my small stock and utensils, and my corn standing, and escaped by night into Virginia, where shipping myself for Boston . . . but my mind being distressed on account of the situation of my wife and children, I returned to Norfolk in Virginia, with a hope of at least seeing them, if I could not obtain their freedom; but finding I was advertised in the newspaper, twenty dollars the reward for apprehending me, my dangerous situation obliged me to leave Virginia, disappointed of seeing my wife and children, coming to Philadelphia, where I resided in the employment of a waiter upward of two years.

Jones then broadened the plea:

We beseech your impartial attention to our hard condition, not only with respect to our personal sufferings, as freemen, but as a class of that people who, distinguished by color, are therefore with a degrading partiality, considered by many, even of those in eminent stations, as unentitled to that public justice and protection which is the great object of government. . . .

If, notwithstanding all that has been publicly avowed as essential principles respecting the extent of human right to freedom . . . we cannot claim the privilege of representation in your councils, yet we trust we may address you as fellow-men, who, under God, the sovereign Ruler of the Universe, are intrusted with the distribution of justice, for the terror of evil-doers, the encouragement and protection of the innocent, not doubting that you are men of liberal minds . . . who can admit that black people (servile as their condition generally is throughout this Continent) have natural affections, social and domestic attachments and sensibilities. . . .

He was now ready for his essential point, the final question, the meaning of the revolution:

179. The earliest black petition to Congress, January 30, 1797. *The Debates and Proceedings in the Congress of the United States; Fourth Congress, Second Session (December 5, 1796 to March 3, 1797)* (Washington, 1849). Courtesy of the Library of Congress.

2015   **HISTORY OF CONGRESS.**   **2016**

H. of R.]   *Manumitted Slaves.*   [JANUARY, 1797.

by his speech, give an idea to the public, that this would be a saving of so much money; but it would, in reality, make no difference.

After a few observations from other members, the question was put and negatived—37 to 30.

The Committee then rose, and had leave to sit again. And the House adjourned till Monday.

MONDAY, January 30.

GEORGE LEONARD, from Massachusetts, appeared and took his seat.

Mr. S. SMITH, from the committee appointed to bring in a bill to alter and amend the act for ascertaining and fixing the Military Establishment, reported a bill, which was twice read, and ordered to be committed to a Committee of the Whole on Wednesday next.

A report was made by Mr. NICHOLAS and read from the committee appointed to inquire into the progress made in the sale of lands Northwest of the river Ohio and above the mouth of Kentucky river. The report was twice read, and referred to a Committee of the Whole.

Mr. SWANWICK moved, that the Committee of the Whole should be discharged from the further consideration of the bill relative to certain officers, collectors of duties and tonnage, as to additional compensation. This was, that it might be referred back to the Committee of Commerce and Manufactures. This was done accordingly.

Mr. SWANWICK, from the Committee of Commerce and Manufactures, made a report on the memorial of Richard D'Cantillon and Daniel Lefferts, owners of a ship which had been sold under execution, through the want of a register, which had been lost, and a new one could not be obtained, without delivering the old one up; on account of this, they reported the following resolution:

" *Resolved,* That provision be made by law for granting certificates of registry, enrollment, and licenses, without surrender of the old ones, in certain cases on sales, by proof of law, of any ship or vessel."

Ordered, That a bill or bills be brought in accordingly by the Committee of Commerce and Manufactures.

MANUMITTED SLAVES.

Mr. SWANWICK presented the following petition:

To the President, Senate, and House of Representatives.

The Petition and Representation of the under-named Freemen, respectfully showeth:—

That, being of African descent, late inhabitants and natives of North Carolina, to you only, under God, can we apply with any hope of effect, for redress of our grievances, having been compelled to leave the State wherein we had a right of residence, as freemen liberated under the hand and seal of humane and conscientious masters, the validity of which act of justice, in restoring us to our native right of freedom, was confirmed by judgment of the Superior Court of North Carolina, wherein it was brought to trial; yet, not long after this decision, a law of that State was enacted, under which

men of cruel disposition, and void of just principle, received countenance and authority in violently seizing, imprisoning, and selling into slavery, such as had been so emancipated; whereby we were reduced to the necessity of separating from some of our nearest and most tender connexions, and of seeking refuge in such parts of the Union where more regard is paid to the public declaration in favor of liberty and the common right of men, several hundreds, under our circumstances, having, in consequence of the said law, been hunted day and night, like beasts of the forest, by armed men with dogs, and made a prey of as free and lawful plunder. Among others thus exposed, I, Jupiter Nicholson, of Perquimans county, North Carolina, after being set free by my master, Thomas Nicholson, and having been about two years employed as a seaman in the service of Zachary Nixson, on coming on shore, was pursued by men with dog and arms; but was favored to escape by night to Virginia, with my wife, who was manumitted by Gabriel Cosand, where I resided about four years in the town of Portsmouth, chiefly employed in sawing boards and scantling; from thence I removed with my wife to Philadelphia, where I have been employed, at times, by water, working along shore, or sawing wood. I left behind me a father and mother, who were manumitted by Thomas Nicholson and Zachary Dickson; they have been since taken up, with a beloved brother, and sold into cruel bondage.

I, Jacob Nicholson, also of North Carolina, being set free by my master, Joseph Nicholson, but continuing to live with him till, being pursued day and night, I was obliged to leave my abode, sleep in the woods, and stacks in the fields, &c., to escape the hands of violent men who, induced by the profit afforded them by law, followed this course as a business; at length, by night, I made my escape, leaving a mother, one child, and two brothers, to see whom I dare not return.

I, Job Albert, manumitted by Benjamin Albertson, who was my careful guardian to protect me from being afterwards taken and sold, providing me with a house to accommodate me and my wife, who was liberated by William Robertson; but we were night and day hunted by men armed with guns, swords, and pistols, accompanied with mastiff dogs; from whose violence, being one night apprehensive of immediate danger, I left my dwelling, locked and barred, and fastened with a chain, being at some distance from it, while my wife was by my kind master locked up under his roof. I heard them break into my house, where, not finding their prey, they got but a small booty, a handkerchief of about a dollar value, and some provisions; but, not long after, I was discovered and seized by Alexander Stafford, William Stafford, and Thomas Creesy, who were armed with guns and clubs. After binding me with my hands behind me, and a rope round my arms and body, they took me about four miles to Hartford prison, where I lay four weeks, suffering much for want of provision; from thence, with the assistance of a fellow-prisoner, (a white man,) I made my escape, and for three dollars was conveyed, with my wife, by a humane person, in a covered wagon by night, to Virginia, where, in the neighborhood of Portsmouth, I continued unmolested about four years, being chiefly engaged in sawing boards and plank. On being advised to move Northward, I came with my wife to Philadelphia, where I have labored for a livelihood upwards of two years, in Summer mostly, along shore in vessels and stores, and sawing wood in the Winter. My mother was set free by Phineas Nickson, my sister by John Trueblood, and

the unconstitutional bondage in which multitudes of our fellows in complexion are held, is to us a subject sorrowfully affecting; for we cannot conceive this condition (more especially those who have been emancipated and tasted the sweets of liberty, and again reduced to slavery by kidnappers and man-stealers) to be less afflicting or deplorable than the situation of citizens of the United States, captured and enslaved through the

unrighteous policy prevalent in Algiers. . . . May we not be allowed to consider this stretch of power, morally and politically, a Governmental defect, if not a direct violation of the declared fundamental principles of the Constitution; and finally, is not some remedy for an evil of such magnitude highly worthy of the deep inquiry and unfeigned zeal of the supreme Legislative body of a free and enlightened people?

both taken up and sold into slavery, myself deprived of the consolation of seeing them, without being exposed to the like grievous oppression.

I, Thomas Pritchet, was set free by my master Thomas Pritchet, who furnished me with land to raise provisions for my use, where I built myself a house, cleared a sufficient spot of woodland to produce ten bushels of corn; the second year about fifteen, and the third, had as much planted as I suppose would have produced thirty bushels; this I was obliged to leave about one month before it was fit for gathering, being threatened by Holland Lockwood, who married my said master's widow, that if I would not come and serve him, he would apprehend me, and send me to the West Indies; Enoch Ralph also threatening to send me to jail, and sell me for the good of the country: being thus in jeopardy, I left my little farm, with my small stock and utensils, and my corn standing, and escaped by night into Virginia, where shipping myself for Boston, I was, through stress of weather landed in New York, where I served as a waiter for seventeen months; but my mind being distressed on account of the situation of my wife and children, I returned to Norfolk in Virginia, with a hope of at least seeing them, if I could not obtain their freedom; but finding I was advertised in the newspaper, twenty dollars the reward for apprehending me, my dangerous situation obliged me to leave Virginia, disappointed of seeing my wife and children, coming to Philadelphia, where I resided in the employment of a waiter upward of two years.

In addition to the hardship of our own case, as above set forth, we believe ourselves warranted, on the present occasion, in offering to your consideration the singular case of a fellow-black now confined in the jail of this city, under sanction of the act of General Government, called the Fugitive Law, as it appears to us a flagrant proof how far human beings, merely on account of color and complexion, are, through prevailing prejudice, outlawed and excluded from common justice and common humanity, by the operation of such partial laws in support of habits and customs cruelly oppressive. This man, having been many years past manumitted by his master in North Carolina, was under the authority of the aforementioned law of that State, sold again into slavery, and, after having served his purchaser upwards of six years, made his escape to Philadelphia, where he has resided eleven years, having a wife and our children; and, by an agent of the Carolina claimer, has been lately apprehended and committed to prison, his said claimer, soon after the man's escaping from him, having advertised him, offering a reward of ten silver dollars to any person that would bring him back, or five times that sum to any person that would make due proof of his being killed, and no questions asked by whom.

We beseech your impartial attention to our hard condition, not only with respect to our personal sufferings, as freemen, but as a class of that people who, distinguished by color, are therefore with a degrading partiality, considered by many, even of those in eminent stations, as unentitled to that public justice and protection which is the great object of Government. We indulge not a hope, or presume to ask for the interposition of your honorable body, beyond the extent of your Constitutional power or influence, yet are willing to believe your serious, disinterested, and candid consideration of the premises, under the benign impressions of equity and mercy, producing upright exertion of what is in your power, may not be without some salutary

effect, both for our relief as a people, and towards the removal of obstructions to public order and well-being.

If, notwithstanding all that has been publicly avowed as essential principles respecting the extent of human right to freedom; notwithstanding we have had that right restored to us, so far as was in the power of those by whom we were held as slaves, we cannot claim the privilege of representation in your councils, yet we trust we may address you as fellow-men, who, under God, the sovereign Ruler of the Universe, are intrusted with the distribution of justice, for the terror of evil-doers, the encouragement and protection of the innocent, not doubting that you are men of liberal minds, susceptible of benevolent feelings and clear conception of rectitude to a catholic extent, who can admit that black people (servile as their condition generally is throughout this Continent) have natural affections, social and domestic attachments and sensibilities; and that, therefore, we may hope for a share in your sympathetic attention while we represent that the unconstitutional bondage in which multitudes of our fellows in complexion are held, is to us a subject sorrowfully affecting; for we cannot conceive their condition (more especially those who have been emancipated and tasted the sweets of liberty, and again reduced to slavery by kidnappers and man-stealers) to be less afflicting or deplorable than the situation of citizens of the United States, captured and enslaved through the unrighteous policy prevalent in Algiers. We are far from considering all those who retain slaves as wilful oppressors, being well assured that numbers in the State from whence we are exiles, hold their slaves in bondage, not of choice, but possessing them by inheritance, feel their minds burdened under the slavish restraint of legal impediments to doing that justice which they are convinced is due to fellow-rationals. May we not be allowed to consider this stretch of power, morally and politically, a Governmental defect, if not a direct violation of the declared fundamental principles of the Constitution; and finally, is not some remedy for an evil of such magnitude highly worthy of the deep inquiry and unfeigned zeal of the supreme Legislative body of a free and enlightened people? Submitting our cause to God, and humbly craving your best aid and influence, as you may be favored and directed by that wisdom which is from above, wherewith that you may be eminently dignified and rendered conspicuously, in the view of nations, a blessing to the people you represent, is the sincere prayer of your petitioners.

JACOB NICHOLSON,
JUPITER NICHOLSON, his mark,
JOB ALBERT, his mark,
THOMAS PRITCHET, his mark.

PHILADELPHIA, *January* 23, 1797.

The petition being read—

Mr. SWANWICK said, he hoped it would be referred to a select committee.

Mr. BLOUNT hoped it would not even be received by the House. Agreeably to a law of the State of North Carolina, he said they were slaves, and could, of course, be seized as such.

Mr. THATCHER thought the petition ought to be referred to the Committee on the Fugitive Law. He conceived the gentleman mistaken in asserting these petitioners to be absolute slaves. They state that they *were* slaves, but that their masters manumitted them, and that their manumissions were sanctioned by a law of that State,

---

Could black men get a hearing in "the supreme Legislative body of a free and enlightened people?" News of the debate drifted back to Absalom Jones as he waited for Congress to act. Representative John Swanwick of Pennsylvania had sponsored the petition, but Blount of North Carolina would have none of it. Swanwick was eloquent: he was "surprised at the gentleman from North Carolina desiring to reject this petition; he could not have thought . . .

that the gentleman was so far from acknowledging the rights of man, as to prevent any class of men from petitioning":

The subject of their petition had a claim to the attention of the House. They state they were freed from slavery, but they were much injured under a law of the United States . . . their case was very hard. He animadverted on the atrocity of that reward of ten dollars offered for one of them if taken alive, but that fifty should be given if found dead, and no questions asked. . . . Horrid reward! Could gentlemen hear it and not shudder?

Blount did not shudder, but merely remarked that Swanwick was "mistaken in calling the petitioners free men." Another congressman remarked that "to encourage slaves to petition the House . . . would tend to spread an alarm throughout the Southern States; it would act as an 'entering wedge,' whose consequences could not be foreseen." James Madison concurred: the petition had "no claim on their attention."

SUPPOSE, now, it is the Fourth of July 1800—the year Gabriel Prosser was hanged and Nat Turner was born. (Nat is supposed to have said: "It was intended by us to have begun this work of death on the 4th of July last.") Suppose, also, the city is Philadelphia, the hall Richard Allen's Bethel Church. Absalom Jones is addressing a black congregation on the meaning of the historic day.

As he climbs into the pulpit, built by his friend Richard Allen with his own hands, he recalls that Congress had given short shrift to that first black petition. On the lapel of his clerical broadcloth is pinned a handsome medallion of basalt and jasper that shows a slave in chains asking the question, "Am I Not a Man and a Brother?"— the work of Josiah Wedgwood, the English abolitionist, commissioned by the London Society for the Abolition of Slavery [fig. 180]. Wedgwood had sent over a package of medallions to Benjamin Franklin for distribution to champions of the antislavery cause. "I have seen in their countenances," Franklin wrote to Wedgwood during the spring of 1787, "such Mark of being affected by contemplating the Figure of the

Suppliant (which is admirably executed) that I am persuaded it may have an Effect equal to that of the best written Pamphlet in procuring favour to those oppressed People" [fig. 181].

Beginning his Fourth of July oration, it is possible that Absalom Jones pointed to the medallion on his lapel as he thanked God for all the benefits the revolution had conferred on the black people of the infant nation. It was heartening to note that among white folk of property and standing—Franklin was one of them—societies for the abolition of bondage, formed in a number of states, were working to do away with the slave trade and slavery, boycotting the products of slave labor, buying slaves free, founding schools for black children. Six years earlier, in 1794, ten of these state societies, including those in Maryland and Virginia, had held their first national convention not far from Bethel.

As for the institution of slavery itself, the struggle for liberty and equality had indeed raised sharply in many a patriot breast the question of whether the spirit of seventy-six was broad enough to encompass black as well as white. Progress had been made, at least in those states where slaves were fewest. Pennsylvania had led off, and the legislatures or courts of Connecticut, Rhode Island, Massachusetts, New Hampshire, Vermont, and New York were putting an end to the evil system. In New York, New Jersey, and Pennsylvania, of their fifty thousand blacks, more than a quarter no longer wore chains. And, on the frontier, Congress had banned slavery forever in the territory of the Northwest.

Then, too, the soil of independence had proved fertile for the planting of black churches, for the bringing forth of black genius—warriors, preachers, writers, organizers, scientists, captains, colonizers, educators, and others. Could it not be said,

180. Josiah Wedgwood, *Am I Not A Man And A Brother?* medallion, basalt on jasper, 1787. Private Collection.

with some justice, that it was only with the revolution that black men and women in America started to see themselves for the first time as a people?

ABSALOM Jones paused on the question while the congregation waited, and then he went on. Some progress had been made, but that was only half the story. Six months before, on Christmas Day, in a mood of anger and despair, he had been moved to write another plea to the president and Congress, this time signed by seventy black citizens, including Richard Allen and himself [fig. 182]. Would it be appropriate for him now, as the second half of his oration for the Fourth of July, to read that petition aloud? There was a murmur of approval, and he began:

The petition of the People of
Colour, Freemen within the City and

Suburbs of Philadelphia—Humbly Sheweth, That thankful to God our Creator and the Government under which we live, for the blessing and benefit extended to us in the enjoyment of our natural right to Liberty, and the protection of our Persons and property from the oppression and violence which so great a number of like colour and National Descent are subjected; We feel ourselves bound from a sense of these blessings to continue our respective allotments and to lead honest and peaceable lives, rendering due submission to the Laws, and exciting and encouraging each other thereto, agreeable to the uniform advice of our real friends of every denomination.—Yet, while we feel impressed with grateful sensations for the Providential favours we ourselves

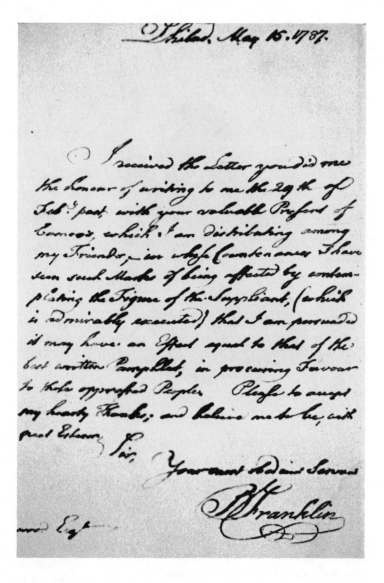

181. Benjamin Franklin to Josiah Wedgwood, May 15, 1787. Courtesy of the Library of Congress.

enjoy, We cannot be insensible of the conditions of our afflicted Brethren, suffering under curious circumstances in different parts of these States; but deeply sympathizing with them. We are incited by a sense of Social duty and humbly conceive ourselves authorized to address and petition you in their behalf, believing them to be objects of representations in your public Councils, in common with ourselves and every other class of Citizens within the Jurisdiction of the United States, according to the declared design of the present Constitution formed by the General Convention and ratified in the different States, as set forth in the preamble thereto in the following words—viz—"We the People of the United States in order to form a more perfect union, establish Justice, insure domestick tranquility, provide for the Common Defence, and to secure the blessings of Liberty

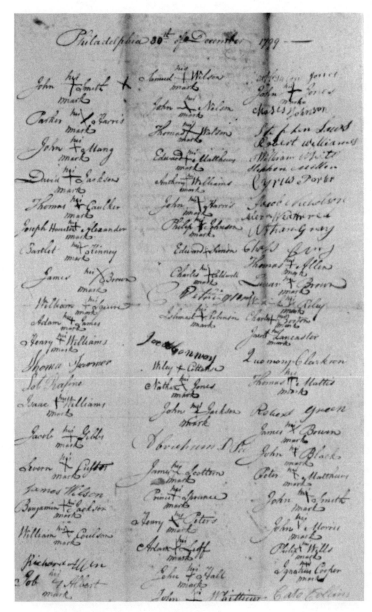

182. Signers, including
Absalom Jones and
Richard Allen, of the
Petition to Congress,
December 30, 1799.
National Archives,
Washington, D.C.

to ourselves and posterity, do ordain
&c."—We apprehend this solemn
Compact is violated by a trade carried
on in clandestine manner to the Coast
of Guinea, and another equally
wicked practised openly by Citizens
of some of the Southern States upon
the waters of Maryland and Delaware:
Men sufficiently callous as to qualify
for the brutal purpose, are employed

in kidnapping those of our Brethren
that are free, and purchasing others of
such as claim a property in them; thus
these poor helpless victims like droves
of Cattle are seized, fettered, and hurried into places provided for this most
horrid traffic, such as dark cellars and
garrets, as is notorious at Northurst,
Chester-town, Eastown, and divers
other places;—After a sufficient num-

ber is obtained, they are forced on board vessels, crouded under hatches, and without the least commiseration, left to deplore the sad separation of the dearest ties in nature, husband from wife, and Parents from children thus pocket'd together they are transported to Georgia and other places and there inhumanly exposed to sale: Can any Commerce, trade, or transaction, so detestably shock the feelings of Man, or degrade the dignity of his nature equal to this, and how increasingly is the evil aggravated when practised in a Land, high in profession of the benign doctrines of our blessed Lord who taught his followers to do unto others as they would they should do unto them!—Your petitioners desire not to enlarge the volumes [that] might be filled with the sufferings of this grossly abused class of the human species (700,000 of whom it is said are now in unconditional bondage in these United States.) but, conscious of the rectitude of our motives in a concern so nearly affecting us, and so essentially interesting to [the] welfare of this Country, we cannot but address you as Guardians of our Civil rights, and Patrons of equal and National Liberty, hoping you will view the subject in an impartial and unprejudiced Light.—We do not wish for the immediate emancipation of all, knowing that the degraded state of many and their want of education, would greatly disqualify for such a change; but humbly desire you may exert every means in your power to undo the heavy burdens, and prepare the way for the oppressed to go free, that every yoke may be broken.

The Law not long since enacted by Congress called the Fugitive Bill, is, in its execution found to be attended with circumstances peculiarly hard and distressing for many of our afflicted Brethren in order to avoid the barbarities wantonly exercised upon them, or thro fear of being carried off by those Men-stealers, have been forced to seek refuge by flight; they are then hunted by armed Men, and under colour of this law, cruelly treated, shot, or brought back in chains to those who have no just claim upon them.

In the Constitution, and the Fugitive bill, no mention is made of Black people or slaves—therefore if the Bill of Rights, or the declaration of Congress are of any validity, we beseech that as we are *men,* we may be admitted to partake of the Liberties and unalienable Rights therein held forth—firmly believing that the extending of Justice and equity to all Classes would be a means of drawing down the blessing of Heaven upon this Land, for the Peace and Prosperity of which, and the real happiness of every member of the Community, we fervently pray—

Absalom Jones had ended his oration. There was no applause, and the congregation filed out of the church. The suppliant slave on Franklin's medallion was still in chains, and to his imploring question, "Am I Not a Man and a Brother?" the revolution could hardly reply with a thundering yes.

THAT same summer, a tall, twenty-four-year-old slave by the name of Gabriel, born in the year of the Declaration, the property of one Prosser in Henrico County of Jefferson's Virginia, tried to organize a few thousand of his fellows to strike for their freedom. The plan failed. In the autumn, Gabriel and about thirty-five of his brothers were sent to the gallows. Gabriel would not talk. James Monroe, then governor of Virginia, questioned him, but he "seemed to have made up his mind to die, and to have resolved to say but little on the subject of the conspiracy." At the trial one of the conspirators testified that "he was present when Gabriel was appointed General. . . . That none were to be spared of the whites except Quakers, Methodists, and French people," and that he and a friend had intended "to purchase a piece of silk for a flag, on which they would have written 'death or Liberty.' " Another defendant declared that he "had nothing more to offer than what General Washington would have had to offer, had he been taken by the British and put to trial by them. I have adventured my life in endeavouring to obtain the liberty of my countrymen, and am a willing sacrifice to their cause. . . ."

"ARE the great principles of political freedom and of natural justice, embodied in that Declaration of Independence extended to us?"—a half-century has passed and Frederick Douglass, on the Fourth of July 1852, goes on to answer his question:

> Would to God, both for your sakes and ours, that an affirmative answer could be truthfully returned to these questions! Then would my task be light, and my burden easy and delightful. For *who* is there so cold, that a nation's sympathy could not warm him? . . . Who so stolid and selfish, that would not give his voice to swell the hallelujahs of a nation's jubilee, when the chains of servitude had been

torn from his limbs? I am not that man. In a case like that, the dumb might eloquently speak, and the "lame man leap as an hart."

> But such is not the state of the case. I say it with a sad sense of the disparity between us. I am not included within the pale of this glorious anniversary! Your high independence only reveals the immeasurable distance between us. The blessings in which you, this day, rejoice, are not enjoyed in common.—The rich inheritance of justice, liberty, prosperity and independence, bequeathed by your fathers, is shared by you, not by me. The sunlight that brought light and healing to you, has brought stripes and death to me. This Fourth of July is *yours,* not *mine. You* may rejoice, *I* must mourn. To drag a man in fetters into the grand illuminated temple of liberty, and call upon him to join you in joyous anthems, were inhuman mockery and sacrilegious irony. . . .

> What, to the American slave, is your 4th of July? I answer; a day that reveals to him, more than all other days in the year, the gross injustice and cruelty to which he is the constant victim. To him, your celebration is a sham; your boasted liberty, an unholy license; your national greatness, swelling vanity; your sounds of rejoicing are empty and heartless; your denunciation of tyrants, brass fronted impudence; your shouts of liberty and equality, hollow mockery; your prayers and hymns, your sermons and thanksgivings, with all your religious parade and solemnity, are, to Him, mere bombast, fraud, deception, impiety, and hypoc-

risy—a thin veil to cover up crimes which would disgrace a nation of savages. There is not a nation on the earth guilty of practices more shocking and bloody than are the people of the United States, at this very hour.

THREE years later, on the eve of the Civil War, at the close of his path-breaking volume, *The Colored Patriots of the American Revolution,* the black historian William C. Nell would view the historic event as incomplete and look forward to the future: "The Revolution of 1776, and the subsequent struggles in our nation's history, aided in honorable proportion, by colored Americans, have (sad, but true, confession) yet left the necessity for a second revolution, no less sublime than that of regenerating public sentiment in favor of Universal Brotherhood. To this glorious consummation, all, of every complexion, sect, sex and condition, can add their mite, and so nourish the tree of liberty, that all may be enabled to pluck fruit from its bending branches; and, in that degree to which colored Americans may labor to hasten the day, they will prove valid their claim to the title, 'Patriots of the Second Revolution.' "

Sources

Most sources described in the pages of the text and in the captions of illustrations are not repeated here. The material below is divided in each section and subsection into three categories: books, serials, and manuscripts, listed chronologically. The following abbreviations are used:

JNH	*Journal of Negro History*
MSSRW	*Massachusetts Soldiers and Sailors of the Revolutionary War* 17 vols. (Boston, 1904)
Nell	William C. Nell, *The Colored Patriots of the American Revolution* (Boston, 1855)
Quarles	Benjamin Quarles, *The Negro in the American Revolution* (Chapel Hill, 1961)
Windley	Lathan A. Windley, compiler, *Runaway Slave Advertisements; a Documentary History from the 1730s to 1790,* 4 vols. (Westport, Conn., 1983)

I: Homage to Liberty

Frederick Douglass, *Oration, Delivered in Corinthian Hall, Rochester . . . July 5, 1852* (Rochester, 1852); Harriet Beecher Stowe, *Uncle Tom's Cabin; or Life Among the Lowly* (Boston,

1852), chap. 11; Nell, 5, 13, 21–22; Quarles, vii; for Thomas Peters, see below, chap. 3, "In the Service of the King."

Robert C. Smith, "Liberty Displaying the Arts and Sciences: A Philadelphia Allegory by Samuel Jennings," *Winterthur Portfolio* 2 (1965): 85–105.

William C. Nell to Rev. R. C. Waterston, Boston, Aug. 22, 1862, The New-York Historical Society.

II: Preludes to the Declaration

Crispus Attucks and the Boston Massacre

The Trial of William Wemms . . . in his Majesty's 29th Regiment of Foot, for the Murder of Crispus Attucks, Samuel Gray, Samuel Maverick, James Caldwell, and Patrick Carr . . . Taken in Shorthand by John Hodgson (Boston, 1770), 114–76; Frederick Kidder, *History of the Boston Massacre . . .* (Albany, N.Y., 1870), 29 n.3; *A Memorial of Crispus Attucks, Samuel Maverick, James Caldwell, Samuel Gray and Patrick Carr from the City of Boston* (Boston, 1889); Wendell Phillips, *Speeches, Lectures and Letters,* 2d ser. (Boston, 1891), 75–76.

Massachusetts Gazette, March 12, 1770; *Liberator,* March 12, 1858; Dennis P. Ryan, "The Crispus Attucks Monument Controversy of

1887," *Negro History Bulletin* 40 (Jan.–Feb. 1977): 656–57.

Aftermath of Attucks

[John Allen], *An Oration Upon the Beauties of Liberty* . . . (Boston, 1773), 28–80; Charles F. Adams, ed., *Letters of Mrs. Adams, the Wife of John Adams* (Boston, 1841), 1:24.

The Shot Heard Round the World

General Gage's Instructions of 22d February 1775 . . . (Boston, 1779), 5, 6; Samuel Swett, *History of Bunker Hill Battle* . . . (Boston, 1826); *Journal Kept by Mr. John Howe, While He Was Employed as a British Spy, During the Revolutionary War* . . . (Concord, N.H., 1827), 5–9; Nell, 11, 20–21; Emory Washburn, *Historical Sketches of the Town of Leicester* . . . (Boston, 1860); Samuel Abbot Smith, *West Cambridge on the Nineteenth of April, 1775* . . . (Boston, 1864), 28–29; Benjamin Cutter and William R. Cutter, *History of the Town of Arlington* . . . (Boston, 1880), 57; Sherwin McRae, ed., *Calendar of Virginia State Papers* . . . (Richmond, 1886), 6:228; Josiah Howard Temple, *History of Framingham* . . . (Framingham, 1887), 281, 325, 327; *MSSRW* 2:110, 283; 5:157; 7:25; 9:452, 725; 12:520, 561, 576, 615–16; 13:743–44; 14:900; 17:153; Laura E. Wilkes, *Missing Pages in American History* (Washington, 1910), 27; Frank Warren Coburn, *The Battle of April 19, 1775* . . . (Lexington, 1916), 119; Herbert Aptheker, "The Negro in the American Revolution," in his *Essays in the History of the American Negro* (New York, 1945), 77; John Trumbull to Thomas Jefferson, London, Sept. 17, 1787, in *The Papers of Thomas Jefferson*, ed. Julian P. Boyd (Princeton, 1955), 12: 138–39; Jules David Prown, "John Trumbull as History Painter," in *John Trumbull, The Hand and Spirit of a Painter*, ed. Helen A. Cooper (New Haven, 1982), 50–94.

Salem Gazette, April 21, 1775; Richard Kidder Meade to Everard Meade, Dec. 19, 1775, *Southern Literary Messenger* 25 (1857): 24–25; "Description of the Battle of Lexington, by Lieutenant Mackenzie . . . ," *Massachusetts His-torical Society Proceedings*, 2d ser., 5 (1890): 394; "Lists and Returns of Connecticut Men of the Revolution, 1775–1783," *Collections of the Connecticut Historical Society* 12 (1909): 56; "The Narrative of General Gage's Spies," *Boston Society Publications* 9 (1912): 72–74; Colonel Woodford to the Virginia Convention, Dec. 1775, "The Woodford, Howe and Lee Letters," *Richmond College Historical Papers* 1 (1915): 119–20; L. P. Jackson, "Virginia Negro Soldiers and Sailors in the American Revolution," *JNH* 27 (July 1942): 183, 272–73, 276; J.J., ed., "The Battle of the Great Bridge," *Virginia Historical Register and Literary Companion* 6 (Jan. 1953): 1–6.

The Declaration of Independence

Connecticut Archives, Revolutionary War, 1st ser., 37, 235a, 246ab, 232ad; Charles Francis Adams, ed., *The Works of John Adams* . . . (Boston, 1850), 2:428; Moncure Daniel Conway, *The Life of Thomas Paine* . . . (New York, 1892), 1:80–81; Carl L. Becker, *The Declaration of Independence* (New York, 1948), 160; Herbert Aptheker, *A Documentary History of the Negro People in the United States* (New York, 1951), 1:10–13; Arthur Zilversmit, *The First Emancipation: The Abolition of Slavery in the North* (Chicago, 1967), 124–38.

New-Hampshire Gazette, July 15, 1780; George H. Moore, "A Note on Slavery in Massachusetts," *Historical Magazine* 5 (January 1869): 52–53; Isaac W. Hammond, "Slavery in New Hampshire," *Magazine of American History* 21 (1889): 62–65; Sidney Kaplan, "The 'Domestic Insurrections' of the Declaration of Independence," *JNH* 61 (July 1976): 243–55.

III: Bearers of Arms: Patriot and Tory

C. B. Wadstrom, *An Essay on Colonization* (London, 1794), pt. 2, 85–87; Samuel Hazard, ed., *Pennsylvania Archives* . . . (Philadelphia, 1853), 4:792; Francis Landon Humphreys, *Life and Times of David Humphreys* (New York, 1917), 1:191–92; *Letters from America 1776–1779: Being Letters of Brunswick, Hessian, and Waldeck Officers with the British Armies* . . . (Boston, 1924), 119; Elizabeth Donnan, ed., *Documents*

Illustrative of the Slave Trade to America (Washington, 1930–35), 3:82–83, 292–93, 311–12, 323–25, 331, 341, 353, 358–59, 374–75; Lorenzo J. Greene, *The Negro in Colonial New England 1620–1776* (New York, 1942); Herbert Aptheker, *American Negro Slave Revolts* (New York, 1943), chap. 8; Evelyn M. Acomb, ed., *The Revolutionary Journal of Baron Ludwig von Closen 1780–1783* (Chapel Hill, 1958), 89, 286–87; William H. Robinson, *Phillis Wheatley and Her Writings* (New York, 1984), 3–5.

Virginia Gazette (Rind), Jan. 25, 1770; John W. Jordan, "Bethlehem during the Revolution: Extracts from the Diaries in the Moravian Archives . . . ," *Pennsylvania Magazine of History and Biography* 13 (1889): 80; Clarence Winthrop Bowen, "A French Officer with Washington and Rochambeau," *Century Magazine* 73 (Feb. 1907): 531; Benjamin Quarles, "The Colonial Militia and Negro Manpower," *Mississippi Valley Historical Review* 45 (1959): 643–52.

A Trio with the Generals

WILLIAM LEE: Worthington Chauncey Ford, ed., *The Writings of George Washington* (New York, 1891), 10:397–98; John C. Fitzpatrick, ed., *The Writings of George Washington* (Washington, 1931–44), 27:451; 29:5; 37:276–77; Charles Coleman Sellers, *Charles Willson Peale* (Philadelphia, 1947), 186.

JAMES ARMISTEAD LAFAYETTE: *Acts passed at a General Assembly of . . . Virginia . . .* (Richmond, 1819), 188; W. W. Hening, ed., *The Statutes at Large . . . of Virginia* (Richmond, 1808–1823), 12:380–81; Louis Gottschalk, *Lafayette and the Close of the American Revolution* (Chicago, 1942), 401–2; Quarles, 94–95.

AGRIPPA HULL: Mason Wade, ed., *The Journals of Francis Parkman* (Boston, 1844), 1:251; Electa F. Jones, *Stockbridge, Past and Present . . .* (Springfield, 1854), 241–42; Thomas Egleston, *The Life of John Paterson, Major General in the Revolutionary Army* (New York, 1894), 142–44; *MSSRW* 8:477; Richardson Wright, *Grandfather Was Queer . . .* (Philadelphia, 1929), 108–11.

William Henry Lee, "An Address on the Life and Character of Major-General John Paterson,"

New York Genealogical and Biographical Record 21 (July 1890): 109; Louis Ottenberg, "A Testamentary Tragedy: Jefferson and the Wills of General Kosciuszko," *American Bar Association Journal* 44 (Jan. 1958): 22; Bernard Carman, "An Uncommon Man's Bicentennial," *Berkshire Eagle,* Aug. 15, 1959.

Agrippa Hull Collection, Stockbridge Public Library, Stockbridge, Massachusetts; National Archives, Service and Pension Records: Agrippa Hull.

A Muster of Brave Soldiers and Sailors

John Marshall, *The Life of George Washington . . .* (Philadelphia, 1850), 1:404; Ernest F. Rogers, *Connecticut's Naval Office at New London . . .* (New London, 1933), 59–61; John C. Fitzpatrick, ed., *The Writings of George Washington . . .* (Washington, 1936), 15:487–88; Page Smith, *A New Age Now Begins* (New York, 1976), 2:1457.

National Era (Washington), July 10, 1847; *Connecticut Archives, Revolutionary War,* 1st ser., 30, 37A.

Logbook of U.S. Ship of War Ranger, 235, Navy Dept., National Archives.

GARSHOM PRINCE: Oscar Jewell Harvey, *A History of Wilkes-Barre and Wyoming Valley* (Wilkes-Barre, 1909), 2:1006.

HARRY, CUPID, ABERDEEN: W. W. Hening, ed., *The Statutes at Large . . . of Virginia . . .* (Richmond, 1809–1823).

J. B., "The Schooner Liberty," *Virginia Historical Register* 1 (1848): 80.

JUPITER: William P. Palmer, ed., *Calendar of Virginia State Papers . . . 1652–1781 . . .* (Richmond, 1875), 1:604.

ANTIGUA: Thomas Cooper, ed., *The Statutes at Large of South Carolina . . .* (Columbia, 1838), 4:545.

PRINCE WHIPPLE: Nell, 198–99; *New Hampshire Provincial and State Papers . . .* (Concord, 1867), 2:580; Charles W. Brewster, *Rambles about Portsmouth,* 1st ser. (Portsmouth, 1873), 154–55.

Bill Belton, "Prince Whipple, Soldier of the American Revolution," *Negro History Bulletin* 35 (Oct. 1973): 126–27.

JAMES FORTEN: Nell, 166–81.

OLIVER CROMWELL: Nell, citing the *Burlington* [New Jersey] *Gazette,* 160–62.

GEORGE LATCHOM: Barton Haxall Wise, "Memoir of General John Cropper of Accomack County, Virginia," *Proceedings of the Virginia Historical Society* 11 (1892): 296–97.

BLACK SAMSON: Charles M. Skinner, *Myths & Legends of Our Own Land* (Philadelphia, 1896), 1:166–68; Pauline A. Young, "The Negro in Delaware . . . ," in *Delaware: A History of the First State,* ed. H. Clay Reed (New York, 1947), 2:598; *The Complete Poems of Paul Laurence Dunbar* (New York, 1950), 334–36.

EDWARD HECTOR: *Norristown* [Pennsylvania] *Free Press,* Jan. 15, 1834.

LAMBERT LATHAM AND JORDAN FREEMAN: Nell, 136–40; William W. Harris, ed., *The Battle of Groton Heights . . . ,* revised by Charles Allyn (New London, 1882), 89–93, 241–42; Frances Manwaring Caulkins, *The Stone Records of Groton* (Norwich, 1903), 58–60; Quarles, 76.

JACK SISSON: Mrs. [Catherine Head] Williams, *Biography of Revolutionary Heroes: Containing the Life of Brigadier Gen. William Barton, and also, of Captain Stephen Olney* (Providence, 1839), 48, 127; James Thacher, *Military Journal of the American Revolution . . .* (Hartford, 1862), 86; J. Lewis Diman, *The Capture of General Richard Prescott . . .* (Providence, 1877), 52–54; *MSSRW* 14:266; 16:714.

Pennsylvania Evening Post, Aug. 7, 1777; *Manufacturers' and Farmers' Journal* (Providence), June 25, 1835.

QUACO: John Russell Bartlett, ed., *Records of the State of Rhode Island . . .* (Providence, 1864), 9:493–94, 509–10.

POMPEY LAMB: Washington Irving, *Life of George Washington* (New York, 1859), 3:504; Benson J. Lossing, *The Pictorial Field-Book of the Revolution* (New York, 1859), 1:744; Henry B. Dawson, *The Assault on Stony Point . . .* (Morrisania, N.Y., 1863), 44–48; Quarles, xi.

SAUL MATTHEWS: W. W. Hening, ed., *The Statutes at Large . . . of Virginia* (Richmond, 1809–1823), 13: 619; Luther P. Jackson, *Virginia Negro Soldiers and Seamen in the Revolutionary War* (Norfolk, 1944), 40; Quarles, 95 n.3.

AUSTIN DABNEY: G. R. Gilmer, *Sketches of Some of the First Settlers of Upper Georgia . . .* (New York, 1855), 164–65, 212–13; Kenneth Coleman, *The American Revolution in Georgia 1763–1789* (Athens, 1958), 188; Quarles, 75.

Edward F. Sweat, "Social Status of the Free Negro in Antebellum Georgia," *Negro History Bulletin* 21 (1958):131.

CAESAR TARRANT: W. W. Hening, ed., *Statutes at Large . . . of Virginia* (Richmond, 1809–1823), 13:102–3; Robert Armistead Stewart, *The History of Virginia's Navy of the Revolution* (Richmond, 1933), 176, 255.

"The Virginia Navy of the Revolution," *Southern Literary Messenger,* n.s., 3, 24 (Feb. 1857): 137; Luther P. Jackson, "Virginia Negro Soldiers and Seamen in the American Revolution," *JNH* 27 (July 1942): 254, 263, 268, 274–77, 284.

Will of Caesar Tarrant, Feb. 19, 1797, Clerk's Office, 8th Judicial Circuit Court, Hampton, Virginia.

JUDE HALL: *New Hampshire, [Provincial and State Papers] Rolls of the Soldiers in the Revolutionary War May 1777 to 1780* (Concord, 1867), 15:440–44, 457.

TITUS: Nell, 214–15.

MINNY: *Proceedings of the Convention of Delegates . . . in the Colony of Virginia* (Richmond, 1816), 49, 72.

"CAPTAIN" MARK STARLINS: "The Schooner Liberty," *Virginia Historical Register* 1 (1848): 127–31.

JOHN PETERSON: Nell, 5–8.

JEHU GRANT: *Index of Revolutionary War Pension Applications in the National Archives* (Washington, 1976); John C. Dann, *The Revolution Remembered . . .* (Chicago, 1979), 26–28.

Three Black Units

BLACK REGIMENT OF RHODE ISLAND: Samuel Greene Arnold, *History of the State of Rhode Island . . .* (New York, 1860), 2:427–28; John Russell Bartlett, ed., *Records of . . . Rhode Island* (Providence, 1863), 8:358–61, 398–99, 640–41; *The Centennial Celebration of the Battle of Rhode Island . . . August 29, 1878,* Rhode Island Historical Tracts no. 6 (Providence, 1878);

Sidney S. Rider, *An Historical Inquiry concerning the Attempt to Raise a Regiment of Slaves by Rhode Island* . . . (Providence, 1880); Evelyn M. Acomb, ed., *The Revolutionary Journal of Baron von Closen 1780–1783* (Chapel Hill, 1958), 92–93; Quarles, 55–56, 60, 69, 73, 80–82, 153; François Jean, marquis de Chastellux, *Travels in North America in the Years 1780, 1781, 1782,* trans. Howard C. Rice, Jr. (Chapel Hill, 1963), 1:229; Howard C. Rice, Jr., and Anne S. K. Brown, *The American Campaign of Rochambeau's Army* . . . (Princeton, 1972), 2:xxi–xxii.

Sidney S. Rider, "The Experience of Rhode Island with Her Negro Troops," *Book Notes* 5 (March 3, 1888): 21–24; Lorenzo J. Greene, "Some Observations on the Black Regiment of Rhode Island in the American Revolution," *JNH* 37 (April 1952): 142–72; Duc de Castries, ed., "Dans L'Armée de La Fayette . . . ," *La Revue de Paris* 64 (July 1957): 107; Paul Barnett, "The Black Continentals," *Negro History Bulletin* 37 (Jan. 1970): 6–9; "Rhode Island Negroes in the Revolution: A Bibliography," *Rhode Island History* 29 (Feb. and May 1970).

BUCKS OF AMERICA: L. M. Child, cited by Nell, 24–27; Boston. Record Commissioners. *Report. Containing . . . the names of the inhabitants of Boston in 1790, as collected for the first census* (Boston, 1890), 309, 482; Boston. Record Commissioners. *Report. Boston marriages 1752–1809* (Boston, 1903), 2:260, 441, 479; Quarles, 54–55; Debra L. Newman, *List of Free Black Heads of Families in the First Census of the United States 1790.* Special List no. 34 (Washington, 1973), 18; Charles H. Wesley, *Prince Hall: Life and Legacy* (Washington, 1977), 50, 83, 131, 142.

Liberator, March 12, 1858; *Massachusetts Historical Society Proceedings* 6 (1862–63): 85, 404; 10 (March 1896):470; Arthur D. White, "The Black Leadership Class and Education in Antebellum Boston," *Journal of Negro Education* 42 (Fall 1973): 505–15.

HAITIAN BLACK BRIGADE: [J. B. Hough], *The Siege of Savannah . . . 1779* (Albany, N.Y., 1866); T. G. Steward, *How the Black St. Domingo Legion Saved the Patriot Army in the Siege of Savannah, 1779,* Occasional Paper no. 5, American Negro Academy (Washington,

1899); Kenneth Coleman, *The American Revolution in Georgia 1763–1789* (Athens, 1958), 145; Quarles, 144.

In the Service of the King

Jared Sparks, ed., *Writings of George Washington* (Boston, 1834), 1:167; Charles Francis Adams, ed., *The Works of John Adams* (Boston, 1850), 2:428; William Bacon Stevens, *A History of Georgia* . . . (Philadelphia, 1859), 2:276–77; Frank Moore, *Diary of the American Revolution* . . . (New York, 1860), 2:322–23; William L. Saunders, ed., *Colonial Records of North Carolina* (Raleigh, 1886), 10:94–95; Charles C. Jones, *The Life and Services of the Honorable Major Gen. Samuel Elbert of Georgia* (Cambridge, Mass., 1887), 36–37, 47; B. F. Stevens, ed., *Facsimiles of Manuscripts in European Archives Relating to America 1773–1783* (London, 1895), 101; Historical Manuscripts Commission, *The Manuscripts of the Earl of Dartmouth* (London, 1895), 2:354; Ralph H. Gabriel and Stanley T. Williams, eds., *Sketches of Eighteenth Century America by St. John Crèvecour* (New Haven, 1925), 310; F. W. Butts-Thompson, *Sierra Leone in History and Tradition* (London, 1926), 89–103; Percy G. Adams, ed., *A Cruising Voyage Round the World by Captain Woodes Rogers* (New York, 1928), 181; Clarence Edwin Carter, ed., *The Correspondence of General Thomas Gage* . . . (New Haven, 1933), 2:684–85; Herbert Aptheker, *American Negro Slave Revolts* (New York, 1943), 202; Julian P. Boyd, ed., *The Papers of Thomas Jefferson* (Princeton, 1952), 5:640–43; *The Journal of Henry Melchior Muhlenberg* (Philadelphia, 1958), 3:78; Quarles, 112, 149 n.49, 172–73; Christopher Fyfe, *Sierra Leone Inheritance* (London, 1964), 118–19; Robin W. Winks, *The Blacks in Canada* (New Haven, 1971), 31–42, 61–78; Mary Beth Norton, *The British-Americans: The Loyalist Exiles in England 1774–1789* (Boston, 1972); Gerald W. Mullin, *Flight and Rebellion: Slave Resistance in Eighteenth Century Virginia* (New York, 1972), 59, 131, 196; Page Smith, *A New Age Now Begins* (New York, 1976), 1:630, 632; Peter H. Wood, " 'Taking Care of Business' in Revolutionary South Carolina: Republicanism and the

Slave Society," in *The Southern Experience in the American Revolution,* ed. Jeffrey J. Crow and Larry E. Tiso (Chapel Hill, 1978), 284–86; Clyde R. Ferguson, "Functions of the Partisan Militia in the South during the American Revolution," in *The Revolutionary War in the South* . . . , ed. W. Robert Higgins (Durham, N.C., 1979), 24; Joseph P. Tustin, ed., *Diary of the American War / A Hessian Journal / Captain Johann Ewald / Field Jäger Corps* (New Haven, 1979), 186, 298, 304–6, 335–36; Robert L. Scribner and Brent Tarter, eds., *Revolutionary Virginia: The Road to Independence,* vol. 6, *The Time for Decision, 1776: A Documentary Record* (Charlottesville, 1981); Gary B. Nash, *Race, Class and Politics* . . . (Urbana, 1986), 269–81.

Virginia Gazette (Rind), Jan. 25, 1770; *The Connecticut Gazette and The Universal Intelligencer* (New London), April 21, 1775; *Virginia Gazette* (Purdie), Nov. 24, 1775; *American Archives* (Washington), 4th ser. (1774–1776), 4:811, 1639; 5th ser. (1776–1783), 1:7, 16, 518; 2:159–60; 3:1051; *Pennsylvania Packet,* Oct. 3, 1780; *New Jersey Gazette* (Trenton), June 5, 1782; *Massachusetts Gazette,* Nov. 17, 1786; "Memoirs of the Life of Boston King, a Black Preacher. Written by Himself . . . ," *Methodist Magazine, for the Year 1798* . . . (London), 105–10, 157–60, 209–13, 261–65; "The Brunswick Contingent in America, 1776–1783," *Pennsylvania Magazine of History and Biography* 15 (1891): 224; *Virginia Magazine of History and Biography* 15 (Jan. 1908): 295–96; *William and Mary College Quarterly Historical Magazine* 16 (1908): 43–46; William Renwick Riddell, "Observations on Slavery and Privateering," *JNH* 15 (1930): 362; "Diary of Grace Growden Galloway Kept at Philadelphia," *Pennsylvania Magazine of History and Biography* 55 (1931): 36; Christopher Fyfe, "Thomas Peters, History and Legend," *Sierra Leone Studies,* n.s. 1 (Dec. 1953): 4–13; Benjamin Quarles, "Lord Dunmore as Liberator," *William and Mary Quarterly* 15 (Oct. 1958): 494–507; Phyllis R. Blakely, "Boston King: A Negro Loyalist Who Sought Refuge in Nova Scotia," *Dalhousie Review* 48 (Autumn 1968): 347–56; Pauline Maier, "Charleston Mob . . . ," *Perspectives in American History* (Cambridge, Mass., 1970), 4:177;

John H. Grant, "Black Immigrants into Nova Scotia," *JNH* 58 (July 1973): 253, 270; Mary Beth Norton, "The Fate of Some Black Loyalists of the American Revolution," *JNH* 58 (Oct. 1973): 402–26.

Patrick Henry, Circular Letter, Nov. 20, 1775, Library of Congress; John André, Report of Intelligence before May 12, 1780, 26, Sir Henry Clinton Papers, Clements Library, Ann Arbor, Michigan; "The Memorial of Benjamin Whitecuff, a black . . . ," June 3, 1784, Public Record Office, London, A o 12119 / 1227061; Letterbook, Henry Laurens Collections, South Carolina Historical Society, microfilm, roll 5, South Carolina Department of Archives.

IV: The Black Clergy

Virginia Gazette (Purdie and Dixon), Feb. 27, 1772; Sept. 8, 1775, cited in Windley 1:109, 248. *Maryland Journal and Baltimore Advertiser,* June 14, 1793.

Founders of the African Baptist Church

Johann David Schöpf, *Reise . . . nach Ost-Florida . . . 1783 und 1784* (Erlangen, 1788), trans. Alfred J. Morrison, *Travels in the Confederation* (Philadelphia, 1911), 2:230; John Rippon, *The Baptist Annual Register for 1790, 1791, 1792, and Part of 1793* . . . (London, 1794), 332–44, 366–67, 540–45; James M. Simms, *The First Colored Baptist Church in North America* . . . (Philadelphia, 1888); Carter G. Woodson, *The History of the Negro Church* (Washington, 1921); Edgar Garfield Thomas, *The First African Baptist Church of North America* (Savannah, 1925).

Virginia Gazette (Purdie), May 1, 1778, cited in Windley 1:269–70; *Virginia Gazette and Weekly Advertiser* (Nicolson & Prentis), Oct. 25, 1783, cited in Windley 1:221; *Virginia Gazette or American Advertiser* (Hayes), May 17, 1786, cited in Windley 1:385; "Letters Showing the Rise and Progress of the Early Negro Churches of Georgia and the West Indies," *JNH* 1 (1916): 69–88; John W. Davis, "George Liele and Andrew Bryan, Pioneer Negro Baptist Teachers," *JNH* 3 (April 1918): 119–27; *Negro History Bulletin* 12 (1949): 110–11.

Founders of the African Methodist Church

RICHARD ALLEN: A. J. and R. A., *A Narrative of the Proceedings of the Black People During the Late Awful Calamity in Philadelphia, in the Year 1793* (Philadelphia, 1794); Thomas Condie and Richard Folwell, *History of the Pestilence, commonly called Yellow Fever* (Philadelphia, 1799); *Articles of Association of the African Methodist Episcopal Church of the City of Philadelphia . . .* (Philadelphia, 1799); Richard Allen and Jacob Tapisco, *The Doctrines and Disciplines of the African Methodist Episcopal Church* (Philadelphia, 1817); James A. Handy, *Scraps of African Methodist Episcopal History* (Philadelphia, n.d.); George Freeman Bragg, *Richard Allen and Absalom Jones* (Baltimore, 1915); Charles H. Wesley, *Richard Allen: Apostle of Freedom* (Washington, 1935); Hallie Q. Brown, ed., *Homespun Heroines . . .* (Freeport, N.Y., 1971), 11–12.

Address by Richard Allen, Dec. 29, 1799, *Philadelphia Gazette,* Dec. 31, 1799; "Public Notice" of AME meeting in Flushing, N.Y., Aug. 23, 1827, *Freedom's Journal* (New York), Aug. 13, 1827; "A Letter from Bishop Allen," *Freedom's Journal,* Nov. 2, 1827; "Richard Allen," *Freedom's Journal,* Feb. 22, 1828; Richard Allen's obituary, *The Genius of Universal Emancipation,* 3d ser., I (March 1831): 185; Anna Bustill Smith, "The Bustill Family," *JNH* 10 (1925): 638–44; Melvin H. Buxbaum, "Cyrus Bustill Addresses the Blacks of Philadelphia," *William and Mary Quarterly* 29 (Jan. 1972): 99–108.

An Addrass to the Blacks in Philadelphiea 9th month 18th 1787, Historical Society of Pennsylvania; Petition to the Select and Common Councils of the City of Philadelphia (ca. 1795), Historical Society of Pennsylvania.

ABSALOM JONES: Wm. Douglass, *Sermons Preached in the African Protestant Episcopal Church of St. Thomas* (Philadelphia, 1854); Wm. Douglass, *Annals of the First African Church in the United States of America, Now Styled The African Episcopal Church of St. Thomas, Philadelphia* (Philadelphia, 1862); George Freeman Bragg, *Heroes of the Eastern Shore: Absalom Jones, The First of the Blacks* (Baltimore, 1939); Margaret C. S. Christman, *Fifty American Faces* (Washington, 1978), 54–59.

Stephen Decatur, "A Collection of Masonic China," *American Collector* 9 (March 1940): 8–11.

C. W. Peale to Rembrandt Peale, Feb. 3, 1810, Charles Willson Peale Papers, National Portrait Gallery, Washington.

PETER WILLIAMS: Nell, 320–23; J. B. Wakely, *Lost Chapters Recovered from the Early History of American Methodism* (New York, 1858), 438–49; Samuel A. Seaman, *Annals of New York Methodism . . .* (New York, 1892), 36–39, 485–91.

Shelton H. Bishop, "A History of St. Philips Church in New York City," *Historical Magazine of the Protestant Episcopal Church* 15 (Dec. 1946): 298–317.

Three Black Ministers

JOHN MARRANT: *A Narrative of the Lord's Wonderful Dealings with John Marrant, A Black,* ed. Rev. William Aldridge (London, 1785); *A Journal of the Rev. John Marrant . . .* (London, 1790); *A Narrative of the Life of John Marrant . . .* (Halifax, 1813).

Monthly Review (London) 73 (Nov. 1785): 399.

JOHN CHAVIS: Henry Kollock, *A Sermon Preached before the General Assembly of the Presbyterian Church . . . May 27, 1803* (Philadelphia, 1803), 29; G. C. Shaw, *John Chavis, 1763–1838 . . .* (n.p., 1931); John Hope Franklin, *The Free Negro in North Carolina: 1790–1860* (New York, 1943), 107; Rayford W. Logan, *Howard University: The First Hundred Years, 1867–1967* (New York, 1969), 4; Carter G. Woodson, *The History of the Negro Church* (Washington, 1972), 67–69.

Stephen B. Weeks, "John Chavis: Ante-Bellum Negro Preacher and Teacher," *Southern Workman* 42 (Feb. 1914): 101–6; Edgar W. Knight, "Notes on John Chavis," *North Carolina Historical Review* 7 (1930):326–45; W. Sherman Savage, "The Influence of John Chavis and Lunsford Lane on the History of North Carolina," *JNH* 25 (Jan. 1940): 14–24; Gossie Harold Hudson, "John Chavis, 1763–1838: A Social Psychological Study," *JNH* 64 (Spring 1979): 142–56.

Trustees' Minutes of the College of New Jersey, Sept. 26, 1792, University Archives, Princeton University.

LEMUEL HAYNES: Lemuel Haynes, *The Sufferings, Support, and Reward of Faithful Ministers . . . the Substance of Two Valedictory Discourses Delivered at Rutland, West Parish, May 24th, A.D. 1818* (Bennington, 1820), 20–27; *MSSRW* 7:277; Wilbert H. Siebert, *Vermont's Anti-Slavery and Underground Railroad Record* (Columbus, Ohio, 1937), 6–12; Paul Douglass, *Black Apostle in Yankeeland* (Brandon, Vt., 1972); Helen M. MacLam, "Black Puritan on the Northern Frontier: The Vermont Ministry of Lemuel Haynes," in *Black Apostles at Home and Abroad . . . ,* ed. David W. Wills and Richard Newman (Boston, 1982), 3–20; Richard Newman, *Lemuel Haynes: A Bio-Bibliography* (New York, 1984).

"Memoir of Rev. Lemuel Haynes," *Colored American* (New York), March 11, 1837; "The Remarkable Life of a 'Poor, Hell-deserving Sinner'—Master of Arts, 1804," *Middlebury College Newsletter,* Spring 1973, 4–11; Ruth Bogin, " 'Liberty Further Extended': A 1776 Antislavery Manuscript by Lemuel Haynes," *William and Mary Quarterly,* 3d ser., 40 (Jan. 1983): 85–105.

Lemuel Haynes, "The Battle of Lexington" by "Lemuel, a Young Mollato," Wendell Family Papers, bMSAm 1907, no. 601, Houghton Library; Lemuel Haynes, "Liberty Further Extended . . . ," Wendell Family Papers, bMSAm 1907, no. 608, Houghton Library.

V: The Emergence of Gifts and Powers

Benjamin Banneker

Thomas Jefferson, *Notes on the State of Virginia* (Richmond, 1784); James McHenry to William Goddard and James Angell, August 20, 1791, in *Benjamin Banneker's Pennsylvania, Delaware, Maryland and Virginia Almanack and Ephemeris . . . 1792* (Baltimore, [1791]); Benjamin Banneker, *Copy of a Letter . . . to the Secretary of State* (Philadelphia, 1792); *Banneker's Almanack and Ephemeris for the Year . . . 1793* (Philadelphia, 1792; *Memoir of Susannah Mason, by her Daughter, R. Mason* (Philadelphia, 1836); Martha E. Tyson, *A Sketch of the Life of Benjamin Banneker . . .* (Baltimore, 1854); Will W. Allen and Daniel Murray, *Banneker, The Afric-American Astronomer* (Washington, 1921); Shirley Graham, *Your Most Humble Servant: The Story of Benjamin Banneker* (New York, 1949); Herbert Aptheker, ed., *A Documentary History of the Negro People in the United States* (New York, 1951), 1:23–26; Silvio A. Bedini, *The Life of Benjamin Banneker* (New York, 1972); Marion Barber Stowell, *Early American Almanacs . . .* (New York, 1977), 102–3.

Obituary, *Federal Gazette and Baltimore Daily Advertiser,* Oct. 28, 1806; Henry E. Baker, "Benjamin Banneker, the Negro Mathematician and Astronomer," *JNH* 3 (1918): 99–118; T. F. Mulcrone, "Benjamin Banneker, Pioneer Negro Mathematician," *Mathematics Teacher* 68 (Jan. 1961): 32; Sidney Kaplan, "Dr. Benjamin Rush's Plea for Universal Peace," *Massachusetts Review* 25 (Summer 1984): 270–84.

Benjamin Banneker to George Ellicott, Oct. 13, 1789, Maryland Historical Society; Benjamin Banneker to Thomas Jefferson, Aug. 19, 1791, and Thomas Jefferson to Benjamin Banneker, Aug. 30, 1791, Massachusetts Historical Society.

Captain Paul Cuffe

Memoir of Captain Paul Cuffee, A Man of Colour . . . (York, England, 1812); *A Brief Account of the Settlement and Present Situation of the Colony of Sierra Leone . . . as Communicated by Paul Cuffe* (New York, 1812); Peter Williams, Jr., *A Discourse, Delivered on the Death of Captain Paul Cuffe . . .* (New York, 1817); W. Alexander, ed., *Memoir of Captain Paul Cuffee, A Man of Color* (New York, 1819); *The History of Prince Lee Boo, to which is added, The Life of Paul Cuffee, a Man of Colour . . .* (Dublin, 1820); *Narrative of the Life and Adventures of Paul Cuffe, A Pequot Indian: during Thirty Years Spent at Sea . . .* (Vernon, N.Y., 1839), 3, 6–7; Wilson Armistead, *Memoir of Paul Cuffee, A Man of Color* (London, 1840); Daniel Ricketson, *The History of New Bedford . . .* (New Bedford, 1858), 252–65,

270; Edward Pease to Hadwen and Margaret Bragg, March 25, 1811, in *The Diaries of Edward Pease: The Father of English Railways*, ed. Alfred E. Pease (London, 1907), 54; Horatio P. Howard, *A Self-Made Man: Captain Paul Cuffee* (New Bedford, 1913); Sterling Stuckey, *The Ideological Origins of Black Nationalism* (Boston, 1972); Sheldon H. Harris, *Paul Cuffe: Black America and the African Return* (New York, 1972); Dorothy Sterling, *Speak Out in Thunder Tones* (Garden City, N.Y., 1973), x, 13–27, 47–51, 373–74; Floyd J. Miller, *The Search for a Black Nationality: Black Emigration and Colonization 1787–1863* (Urbana, 1975), chap. 2; Lamont D. Thomas, *Rise to Be a People: A Biography of Paul Cuffe* (Urbana, 1986).

Leigh Hunt, "Negro Civilization," *Examiner* (London), Aug. 4, 1811; "Memoir of Captain Paul Cuffee, Written for the Liverpool Mercury," *Liverpool Mercury*, Oct. 4 and 11, 1811; *Niles Weekly Register*, Jan. 22, 1814; "Memoirs of Capt. Paul Cuffee," *Freedom's Journal* (New York), March 30, 1827; *Anti-Slavery Reporter* (London) 1, Sept. 23, 1840; Henry Noble Sherwood, "Paul Cuffe and His Contribution to the American Colonization Society," *Proceedings of the Mississippi Valley Historical Association . . .* 6 (1918): 370–404; H. N. Sherwood, "The Formation of the American Colonization Society," *JNH* 2 (July 1917): 209–28; H. N. Sherwood, "Paul Cuffe," *JNH* 8 (April 1923): 153; "Negro Membership in the Society of Friends," *JNH* 21 (1936): 197–99; M. C. F. Easmon, "Paul Cuffee," *Sierra Leone Studies*, n.s., no. 9 (Dec. 1957): 196–99; Sheldon H. Harris, "Paul Cuffe's White Apprentice," *American Neptune* 23 (July 1963): 192–96; Sally Loomis, "The Evolution of Paul Cuffe's Black Nationalism," *Negro History Bulletin* 37 (1974): 298–302.

Petition to Massachusetts General Court, signed by Paul Cuffe et al., Feb. 10, 1780, Massachusetts Historical Society; Paul Cuffe, letter June 6, 1808, Paul Cuffe Papers, New Bedford Free Public Library; James Pemberton to Paul Cuffe, June 6, 1808, Paul Cuffe Papers, New Bedford Free Public Library; Capt. Paul Cuffe to John James and Alexander Wilson, Westport, June 10, 1809, National Archives, Legislative Records Area, 8E-3, RG233; Paul Cuffe, Jour-

nal, May 5, 1812, Paul Cuffe Papers, New Bedford Free Public Library; "Catalogue of the families on board the Brig Traveller going from America for Sierra Leone in Africa. Sailed 12 month 10, 1815 from Westport," Paul Cuffe Papers, New Bedford Free Public Library; Paul Cuffe to Jedediah Morse, Westport, Aug. 10, 1816, Historical Society of Pennsylvania; James Forten to Paul Cuffe, Jan. 25, 1817, Paul Cuffe Papers, New Bedford Free Public Library.

Jean Baptiste Point du Sable

Arent Schuyler de Peyster, *Miscellanies by an Officer* (Dumfries, Va., 1813), 3–15; A. T. Andrews, *History of Chicago . . .* (Chicago, 1884), 1:70–72, 92, 605; Moses Kirkland, *History of Chicago, Illinois* (Chicago, 1895), 1:27–31; Louise Phelps Kellogg, *Frontier Advance on the Upper Ohio 1778–1779* (Madison, 1916), 13–15, 30–33; Charles F. Lummis, *The Spanish Pioneers and the California Missions* (Chicago, 1929), 106 ff; Milo M. Quaife, *Chicagou: From Indian Village to Modern City, 1673–1835* (Chicago, 1933); National Desaible Society, *Some Historical Facts about Jean Baptiste Point Desaible* (Chicago, 1933); Jerémie, *Dessables* (Port-au-Prince, 1948); A. Odell Thomas, *The Negro in California before 1890* (San Francisco, 1973), 1–3.

"Augustin Grignon's Recollections," *Collections of the State Historical Society of Wisconsin . . . 1856*, 3 (1857): 195–97; "Early Visitors to Chicago," *New England Magazine* 6 (April 1892): 202–6; *Collections: Report of the Pioneer Society of . . . Michigan . . .* 9 (1908): 391–605, 661; Mercer Cook, "Chicago's Haitian Ancestor," *Américas* 4 (Feb. 1952): 24–27, 41; William E. Schmidt, "What's Wrong with City's Seal? Racism, to Some," *New York Times*, Sept. 14, 1987.

Dick Pointer

[Anne Newport Royall], *Sketches of History, Life and Manners in the United States by a Traveler* (New Haven, 1826), 66–69; Otis K. Rice, *The Alleghany Frontier: West Virginia Beginnings, 1730–1830* (Lexington, Ky., 1970), 103–4; Otis K. Rice, ed., *Memoir of Indian Wars . . . by*

the late Colonel Stuart, of Greenbrier. Presented to the
Virginia Historical and Philosophical Society, by
Charles A. Stuart . . . (Parsons, W. Va., 1971),
29–31.

Dr. James Derham and Thomas Fuller

American Museum 5 (Jan. 1789): 61–63; B. L.
Plummer, ed., "Letters of James Derham
(1789–1802) to Benjamin Rush," *JNH* 65
(Summer 1980): 261–69.

Phillis Wheatley

Rita Susswein Gottesman, *The Arts and
Crafts in New York 1777–1799* (New York,
1948), vol. 2, citing *Columbian Gazetteer,* Feb.
21, 1794; "The Prospects of America," in *The
Literary Remains of Joseph Brown Ladd, M.D. Collected by Mrs. Elizabeth Hoskins* (New York,
1832), 35; Margaret Matilda Odell, *Memoir and
Poems by Phillis Wheatley* (Boston, 1834); B. B.
Thatcher, *Memoir of Phillis Wheatley, a Native African and a Slave . . . ,* 3d ed. (Boston, 1838),
22; Evert A. Duyckinck and George L. Duyckinck, *Cyclopedia of American Literature* (New
York, 1855), 1:368; Benson Lossing, *Pictorial
Field Book of the Revolution* (New York, 1860),
1:556; N. F. Mosell, *The Work of the Afro-American Woman* (Philadelphia, 1894), 13, 54–58,
74; Augustus C. Buell, *John Paul Jones . . .*
(New York, 1900), 1: 135–36; Boston. Record
Commissioners. *Report. Boston marriages 1752–
1809* (Boston, 1903), 2:441; Thomas Jefferson
to Henri Grégoire, Feb. 25, 1809, in *The Writ-
ings of Thomas Jefferson,* ed. A. A. Lipscomb
(Washington, 1903–4), 12:255; Sarah Tytler,
The Countess of Huntingdon and Her Circle
(London, 1907); James H. Stark, *The Loyalists of
Massachusetts . . .* (Boston, 1910), 310–11;
Benjamin Brawley, *The Negro in Literature and
Art* (New York, 1934), 34; Quarles, 46;
Julian D. Mason, Jr., ed., *The Poems of Phillis
Wheatley* (Chapel Hill, 1966), 54 n.20;
William H. Robinson, ed., *Early Black Ameri-
can Poets* (Dubuque, 1969), 110 n.5, 111;
William H. Robinson, *Phillis Wheatley in the
Black American Beginning* (Detroit, 1977);
William H. Robinson, *Phillis Wheatley: A Bio-*

Bibliography (Boston, 1981); William H. Robin-
son, *Phillis Wheatley and Her Writings: Essays in
Criticism* (New York, 1984); Lisa Baskin, *Phillis
Wheatley: Exhibition Checklist . . .* (Amherst,
Mass., 1985).

Horatio, "Elegy on the Death of a Late Cele-
brated Poetess," *Boston Magazine,* Dec. 1784;
Massachusetts Gazette, Dec. 8, 1786 (Obituary of
Dr. Joseph Ladd); J.H.T., "Phillis Wheatley's
Poems," *Historical Magazine . . . Concerning the
Antiquities . . . of America* 2 (1858): 178–79;
"Letters of Phillis Wheatley . . . ," *Massachusetts Historical Society Proceedings* 7 (1864): 267–
79; Mel Gussow, "[Ed Bullins's] Mystery of
Phillis Wheatley," *New York Times,* Feb. 4,
1976; William H. Robinson, "Phillis Wheatley
in London," *CLA Journal* 21 (Dec. 1977): 187–
201.

Jupiter Hammon

*A Narrative of the Uncommon Sufferings and Sur-
prizing Deliverance of Briton Hammon, A Negro
Man, —Servant to . . .* (Boston, 1760); Stanley
Austin Ransom, Jr., ed., *America's First Negro
Poet: The Complete Works of Jupiter Hammon of Long
Island* (Port Washington, N.Y., 1970).

Francis S. Forster, "Briton Hammon's Narrative: Some Insights into Beginnings," *CLA Journal* 21 (Dec. 1977): 179–86.

Wentworth Cheswill

Ebenezer Baldwin, *Observations on the Physi-
cal, Intellectual, and Moral Qualities of the Colored
Population* (New Haven, 1834), 44; *The Debates
and Proceedings of the Congress of the United
States . . .* 16th Cong. 2d sess., Dec. 1820
(Washington, 1855), 37:107–10; C. E. Potter,
The Military History of the State of New Hampshire
(Concord, 1866), 333–34; *Documents and Records
Relating to Towns in New Hampshire* (Concord,
1875), 9:573; *New Hampshire: Roles of the Soldiers
in the Revolutionary War . . .* (Concord, 1886),
15:416–17, 742–43; *Heads of Families at the
First Census . . . 1790: New Hampshire* (Wash-
ington, 1907), 73; *Miscellaneous Revolutionary
Documents of New Hampshire* (Manchester, 1910),
30:100–102; Nellie Palmer George, *Old New-*

market, New Hampshire (Exeter, 1932), 38, 55, 123–24; Richard Francis Upton, *Revolutionary New Hampshire . . .* (Hanover, 1936), chap. 13; John Mead Howells, *The Architectural Heritage of the Piscataqua: Houses and Gardens of the Portsmouth District of Maine and New Hampshire* (New York, 1937), xiii; Nell, 120–23.

Nellie Palmer George, "Mansion House of Wentworth Cheswill," *Granite Monthly* 48 (July 1916); James L. Garvin, "Portsmouth and the Piscataqua: Social History and Material Culture," *Historical New Hampshire* 26 (Summer 1971): 51.

New Hampshire Town Records, Newmarket, 1729–1828, April 13 and May 14, 1778, 236–37; March 31, 1780, 255; 1806, 271; *New Hampshire: Provincial and State Papers, Documents and Records* (Concord, 1875), 9:833–34; Letter, Patricia S. Busselle, Legislative Reference Librarian, New Hampshire State Library, Concord, to Sidney Kaplan, March 13, 1980.

Prince Hall

James Swan, *A Dissuasion to Great-Britain and the Colonies from the Slave Trade to Africa* (Boston, 1772); Jedidiah Morse, *A Discourse Delivered at the African Meeting House in Grateful Celebration of the Abolition of the African Slave Trade* (Boston, 1808); Nell, 61–64; George H. Moore, *Notes on the History of Slavery in Massachusetts* (New York, 1866), 225–37; Jacob Norton, "Early History of Masonry in Massachusetts," in Lewis Hayden, *Masonry Among Colored Men in Massachusetts* (Boston, 1871); William H. Grimshaw, *Official History of Freemasonry Among the Colored People in North America* (New York, 1903); William Bentley, *The Diary of William Bentley . . . Salem, Massachusetts* (Salem, 1905–1914), 3:321; George W. Crawford, *Prince Hall and His Followers* (New York, 1914), 4–8; Harold Van Buren Voorhis, *Negro Masonry in the United States* (New York, 1940); Herbert Aptheker, ed., *A Documentary History of the Negro People in the United States* (New York, 1951), 1: 20–21; Donn A. Cass, *Negro Freemasonry and Segregation* (Chicago, 1957); Charles H. Wesley, *Prince Hall: Life and Legacy* (Washington, 1977); James D. Essig, *The Bonds of Wickedness: Ameri-*

can Evangelicals against Slavery 1770–1808 (Philadelphia, 1982), 159–61, 199; "Moses Sash: 'A Captain & one of Shaises Councill,' " see below.

New York Packet, Feb. 26 and Aug. 29, 1788; *Massachusetts Spy,* April 24, 1788; *American Herald,* Aug. 29, 1788; "Queries respecting Slavery and Emancipation in Massachusetts, proposed by the Hon. Judge Tucker of Virginia, and Answered by the Rev. Dr. Belknap," *Massachusetts Historical Society Collections,* 1st ser., 4 (1796): 209–10; *Boston Gazette,* Dec. 2, 1807; "Queries Relating to Slavery in Massachusetts," *Massachusetts Historical Society Collections,* 5th ser., 3 (Boston, 1877): 22, 390; Robert Rantoul, Sr., "Negro Slavery in Massachusetts," *Historical Collections of the Essex Institute* 24 (April–June 1887): 94–95; William H. Upton, "Prince Hall's Letter Book," in *Ars Quatuor Coronatorum . . . Transactions of the Quatuor Coronati Lodge No. 2076,* ed. G. W. Speth (London, 1900), 13:54–58; Gaillard Hunt, "William Thornton and Negro Colonization," *Proceedings, American Antiquarian Society,* n.s., pt. 1, 30 (1920): 33–61; Harry E. Davis, "Documents Relating to Negro Masonry in America," *JNH* 21 (1936): 411–14, 419–21; Howard C. Rice, "James Swan: Agent of the French Republic 1794–1796," *New England Quarterly* 10 (1937): 465; Lorenzo J. Greene, "Prince Hall, Massachusetts Leader in Crisis," *Freedomways* 1 (Fall 1961): 238–58; John M. Sherman, "More about Prince Hall: Notes and Documents," *Philalethes* 15 (June 1962): 42–45; John M. Sherman, "More Data on Prince Hall Brought to Light . . . ," *Philalethes* 16 (April 1963): 32; Robert M. Spector, "The Quock Walker Case 1781–83," *JNH* 53 (Jan. 1968): 30; Arthur O. White, "The Black Leadership Class and Education in Antebellum Boston," *Journal of Negro Education* 42 (Fall 1973): 504–15; James Oliver Horton, "Generations of Protest: Black Families and Social Reform in Ante-Bellum Boston," *New England Quarterly* 49 (June 1976): 242–45.

Prince Hall's Manumission Paper, April 9, 1770, Price Notarial Records 1769–1792, Boston Athenaeum; Massachusetts Archives, 157:376½ and 212:132; Acts of 1787, chap. 48, March 26, 1788; Boston Marriages, Record Commissioners Report, 30:299; "Deposition of

Prince Hall, August 31, 1807," Suffolk County Registry of Deeds, vol. 221.

Olaudah Equiano

The Interesting Narrative of the Life of Olaudah Equiano, or Gustavus Vassa, the African, Written by Himself, 2 vols. (London, 1789); Douglas Grant, The Fortunate Slave (London, 1968); Chinua Achebe, Morning Yet on Creation Day (London, 1975), 59; Peter Linebaugh, "What if C. L. R. James Had Met E. P. Thompson in 1792?" in C. L. R. James: His Life and Work, ed. Paul Buhle (New York, 1986), 212–20.

Lorin Lee Cary and Francine C. Cary, "Absalom F. Jones, His Family, and Nantucket's Black Community," Historic Nantucket 25 (Summer 1977): 14–23; Folarin Shyllon, "Olaudah Equiano: Nigerian Abolitionist and First National Leader of Africans in Britain," Journal of African Studies 4 (Winter 1977): 433–51.

The Burgeoning of Art and Craft

UNKNOWN ARTIST, WROUGHT-IRON MAN: C. Malcolm Watkins, "A Plantation of Difference—People from Everywhere," in A Nation of Nations, ed. Peter C. Marzio (New York, 1976), 55; John Michael Vlach, The Afro-American Tradition in Decorative Arts (Cleveland, 1978), 108–9.

Virginia Gazette (Dixon & Hunter), Nov. 1, 1786, cited in Windley 1:178.

JOHN BUSH: Vital Records of Shrewsbury, Massachusetts, To . . . 1849 (Worcester, 1904), 134, 246.

William H. Guthman, "Why the David Baldwin Powder Horn Is Important to Me," Maine Antique Digest, January 1988, 2-c.

POMPEY FLEET: Isaiah Thomas, The History of Printing in the U.S. (Worcester, Mass., 1810), 1:94; Sinclair Hamilton, Early American Book Illustrators and Wood Engravers 1670–1870 (Princeton, 1958), xxix; Marcus A. McCorison, The History of Printing in America with a Biography of Printers . . . by Isaiah Thomas (Barre, Mass., 1970), 94.

Virginia Independent Chronicle (Davis), Jan. 28, 1789, cited in Windley 1:402; James A. Porter,

"Four Problems in the History of Negro Art," JNH 27 (Jan. 1942): 12.

PHEBE CASH: Ethel Stanwood Bolton and Eva Johnston Coe, American Samplers (Princeton, 1973), 27.

NEPTUNE THURSTON: Edward Peterson, History of Rhode Island and Newport (New York, 1853), 153–54.

PETER HILL: Carl W. Drepperd, Clocks and Clockmakers (Boston, 1958), supp. 4, 23–24, 235.

Pennsylvania Magazine of History and Biography 24 (1900–1901): 155.

ZELAH: Lorenzo J. Greene, The Negro in Colonial New England (New York, 1942), 249, citing Samuel Abbott Green, Slavery in Groton, Massachusetts in Colonial Times (Cambridge, Mass., 1909), 6.

VI: Against the Odds

Lucy Terry Prince

Josiah Gilbert Holland, History of Western Massachusetts . . . (Springfield, 1855), 2, pt. 3, 359–60; Josiah H. Temple and George Sheldon, History of Northfield, Mass. (Albany, N.Y., 1875), 1:282; E. P. Walton, ed., Records of the Governor and Council of the State of Vermont (Montpelier, 1875), 3:66.

George Sheldon, "Negro Slavery in Old Deerfield," New England Magazine, n.s., 8 (March–Aug. 1893): 52–60; Martha R. Wright, "Bijah's Luce of Guilford, Vermont," Negro History Bulletin 28 (April 1965): 152 ff.; Bernard Katz, "A Second Version of Lucy Terry's Early Ballad?" Negro History Bulletin 29 (April 1966): 183–84; Mel Gussow, "Bullins Turns 'Lucy Terry' into History Lesson," New York Times, Feb. 12, 1976.

Alice

Eccentric Biography; or, Memoirs of Remarkable Female Characters, Ancient and Modern . . . (Worcester, 1804), 9–11; A. Mott, Biographical Sketches (New York, 1837), 22–24; John F. Watson, Annals of Philadelphia and Pennsylvania, the Olden Time . . . (Philadelphia, 1855), 1:378–80, 515–16, 601.

Belinda of Boston

"Resolve granting *fifteen pounds twelve shillings,* per annum, to *Belinda,* an African, arising from the rents and profits of the estate of *Isaac Royal's* estate," *Acts and Resolves . . .* Massachusetts (Boston, 1893), Jan. Session 1782 chap. 70, Feb. 22, 1783, 399; "Resolve on the Memorial of Belinda . . . ," Oct. Session 1787, chap. 142, 816; "Petition of Belinda an affrican" to the General Court of Massachusetts, Feb. 14, 1783, *Massachusetts Archives,* wrongly dated with minor changes, in *The American Museum . . .* (Philadelphia), June 1787, 538–40; Memorial of Belinda to the General Court and Resolve of the Court, Nov. 23, 1787, *Massachusetts Archives.*

Elizabeth Freeman and the Bill of Rights

Theodore Sedgwick, *The Practicability of the Abolition of Slavery: A Lecture, delivered at the Lyceum in Stockbridge, Massachusetts, February, 1831* (New York, 1831); Harriet Martineau, *Retrospect of Western Travel* (New York, 1838), 1:245–49; Electa F. Jones, *Stockbridge, Past and Present . . .* (Springfield, Mass., 1854), 193–95, 238–41; Dudley Atkins Tyng, *Reports of Cases . . . in the Supreme Judical Court of . . . Massachusetts: Vol 5 . . . 1809* (Boston, 1864), 358–81.

Miss Sedgwick, "Slavery in New England," *Bentley's Miscellany* 24 (1853): 412–24; *Massachusetts Historical Society Collections,* 5th ser., 3 (1877): 438–42; *Proceedings of the Massachusetts Historical Society,* 2d ser., 1 (1884–85): 3, 41–42; James M. Rosenthal, "Free Soil in Berkshire County: 1781," *New England Quarterly* 10 (Dec. 1937): 781–85; William O'Brien, "Did the Jennison Case Outlaw Slavery in Massachusetts?" *William and Mary Quarterly* 17 (April 1960): 219–41; John D. Cushing, "The Cushing Court and the Abolition of Slavery in Massachusetts: More Notes on the 'Quock Walker Case,' " *American Journal of Legal History* 5 (1961): 118–44; Richard E. Welch, Jr., "Mumbet and Judge Sedgwick (A Footnote to the Early History of Massachusetts Justice)," *Boston Bar Journal,* Jan. 1964, 13–19; Robert M. Spector, "The Quock Walker Cases

(1781–1783)—Slavery, Its Abolition, and Negro Citizenship in Early Massachusetts," *JNH* 53 (1968): 12–32; Arthur Zilversmit, "Quock Walker, Mumbet, and the Abolition of Slavery in Massachusetts," *William and Mary Quarterly* 25 (Oct. 1968): 614–24; Elaine MacEacheren, "Emancipation of Slavery in Massachusetts: A Re-examination 1770–1790," *JNH* 55 (Oct. 1970): 289–306.

Elizabeth Freeman Collection, Stockbridge Public Library, Stockbridge, Massachusetts.

Felix Cuff

Charles A. Nelson, *Waltham, Past and Present . . .* (Cambridge, Mass., 1882), 105–6; *MSSRW,* 4:292; *Heads of Families at the First Census . . . 1790: Massachusetts* (Washington, 1908), 159.

Kenneth W. Porter, "Three Fighters for Freedom," *JNH* 28 (Jan. 1943): 51–52.

Primus Hall

Nell, 29–32; Charles H. Wesley, *Prince Hall: Life and Legacy* (Washington, 1977), 77, 144, 148–53.

Obituary, Primus Hall, *Boston Daily Atlas,* March 25, 1842; Henry F. Harrington, "Anecdotes of Washington," *Godey's Magazine & Lady's Book,* June 1849, 427–28; Arthur O. White, "The Black Leadership Class and Education in Ante-Bellum Boston," *Journal of Negro Education* 42 (Fall 1973): 506–10.

Yarrow Mamout

William Brown Hodgson, *The Gospels, written in the Negro patois of English, with Arabic Characters by a Mandingo slave in Georgia* (New York, 1857); Alan D. Austin, *African Muslims in Antebellum America; a Sourcebook* (New York, 1984); *Pierre Eugene Du Simitiere: His American Museum 200 Years After* (Philadelphia, 1985), 5:21.

Joseph H. Greenberg, "The Decipherment of the 'Ben Ali Diary,' " *JNH* 25 (July 1940): 372–75; Richard R. Wright, "Negro Companions of the Spanish Explorers," *Phylon* 2, no. 4 (1941): 349 ff.

Moses Sash

MSSRW 13:826; James H. Stark, The Loyalists of Massachusetts and the Other Side of the American Revolution (Boston, 1910), 396; The Autobiography of W. E. B. Du Bois: A Soliloquy on Viewing My Life from the Last Decade of Its First Century (New York, 1968), 62.

Sidney Kaplan, "A Negro Veteran in the Shays' Rebellion," JNH 33 (April 1948): 123–29; Sidney Kaplan, "Blacks in Massachusetts and the Shays Rebellion," Contributions in Black Studies, no. 8 (1986–87): 5–14.

Indictment of Moses Sash, April 1787, Supreme Judicial Court for Suffolk County, Boston.

Amos and Violate Fortune

Elizabeth Yates, Amos Fortune, Free Man (New York, 1950); F. Alexander Magoun, Fortune's Choice: The Story of a Negro Slave's Struggle for Self-Fulfillment (Freeport, Me., 1964).

Dawud B. Ziyad and George R. Johnson, "Amos Fortune and the Early American Library Movement," Negro History Bulletin 42 (July–Sept. 1979): 77–78.

Three Concord Blacks

George Tolman, John Jack, the Slave, and Daniel Bliss, the Tory (Concord, 1902), 16–18; MSSRW 4:204; 6:32; 17:157; Heads of Families at the First Census of the United States . . . 1790, Massachusetts (Washington, 1908), 139; Brad-

ford Torrey and Francis H. Allen, eds., The Journals of Henry D. Thoreau (New York, 1962), 10:284–85; Robert A. Gross, The Minutemen and Their World (New York, 1976), 94–98, 151, 186–87.

VII: The Incomplete Revolution

Thomas R. Gray, The Confessions of Nat Turner . . . (Baltimore, 1831), in Herbert Aptheker, Nat Turner's Slave Rebellion (New York, 1966), 138; Annals of the Congress of the United States, 4th Cong., 2d sess. (Washington, 1849), 6:2015–24; Nell, 380; Herbert Aptheker, A Documentary History of the Negro People in the United States (New York, 1951), 1:38–44; Gerald W. Mullin, Flight and Rebellion: Slave Resistance in 18th Century Virginia (New York, 1972), 138–74 (Gabriel Prosser); Diary of My Travels in America / Louis-Philippe, King of France, 1830–1848, preface by Henry Steele Commager (New York, 1977), 2–3, 31–33; Jeffrey J. Crow, The Black Experience in Revolutionary North Carolina (Raleigh, 1977), 62–63, 82–84; Benjamin Quarles, Black Mosaic (Amherst, 1988).

Virginia Gazette, Jan. 25, 1770; Herbert Aptheker, "Eighteenth Century Petition of South Carolina Negroes," JNH 31 (1946): 98–99.

Memorial of Thomas Cole, bricklayer; P. B. Matthews and Mathew Webb, butchers, Jan. 1, 1790, South Carolina Archives, Senate Petitions 1789–92.

Index